The Exercise of the Spatial Imagination in Pre-Modern China

Welten Ostasiens –
Worlds of East Asia –
Mondes de l'Extrême-Orient

___

Im Auftrag der Schweizerischen Asiengesellschaft –
On behalf of the Swiss Asian Society –
Au nom de la Société Suisse-Asie

Volume 31

The Exercise of the Spatial Imagination in Pre-Modern China

Shaping the Expanse

Edited by
Garret Pagenstecher Olberding

DE GRUYTER

This publication was made possible due to the support of the Swiss Academy of Humanities and Social Sciences (SAGW).

Schweizerische Akademie der Geistes- und Sozialwissenschaften
Académie suisse des sciences humaines et sociales
Accademia svizzera di scienze umane e sociali
Academia svizra da scienzas umanas e socialas
Swiss Academy of Humanities and Social Sciences

ISBN 978-3-11-135846-8
e-ISBN (PDF) 978-3-11-074982-3
e-ISBN (EPUB) 978-3-11-074992-2
ISSN 1660-9131
DOI https://doi.org/10.1515/9783110749823

Library of Congress Control Number: 2021948050

Bibliographic information published by the Deutschen Nationalbibliothek
The Deutsche Nationalbibliothek lists this publication in the Deutschen Nationalbibliografie; detailled bibliografic data are available from the internet at http://dnb.dnb.de

Cover image: Nikada/E+/Getty Images
Typesetting: Integra Software Services Pvt. Ltd.
Pringting and binding: CPI books GmbH, Leck

www.degruyter.com

To my mother, a Pagenstecher in carriage and spirit, from whom my life has received its moral and intellectual compass

Acknowledgments

This volume arose out of a workshop, "Designing Space: The Exercise of the Spatial Imagination in Pre-Modern China," held at the University of Pittsburgh, May 26–27, 2017. Its publication would have been impossible without the assistance of numerous parties. First, sincere gratitude must go to the workshop participants, many of whom are contributors to this volume, for their provocative papers and lively discussions, as well as for their exceptional patience and kindness during my extended efforts to arrange the workshop and publish this volume. I thank most profoundly Vincent Leung, who found funds from several quarters at the University of Pittsburgh, both from the University's Asian Studies Center and the Chi-chung Yu Lectureship in Early China Studies, established in honor of Dr. Cho-yun Hsu by the China Times Cultural and Education Foundation. The Chiang Ching-Kuo Foundation for International Scholarly Exchange for the second time in my career provided exceptionally munificent support for the conference, without which the conference would not have come to pass. The publication of this volume was underwritten by the Swiss Asia Society, with additional support given by the Office of Vice President for Research and Partnerships and the Office of the Provost at the University of Oklahoma. My chair, Dr. Elyssa Faison, and my department's financial administrator, Christa Seedorf, were ever ready to provide the underwriting necessary to bring this project to completion. The staff at DeGruyter – Christina Lembrecht, Maxim Karagodin and Katja Lehming, among others – as well as the editor of their Worlds of East Asia series, Wolfgang Behr, have been very considerate regarding all the complications involved in the project. And last but not least, I owe a debt to David Prout for compiling the index, a complex task, given the interdisciplinary range of the essays. I am truly grateful for everyone's magnanimity.

An alternate version of Garret Pagenstecher Olberding's essay, "Diplomacy as Transgression in Early China," was published in *Designing Boundaries in Early China: The Composition of Sovereign Space* (New York: Cambridge University Press, 2022).

A previous version of Linda Rui Feng's essay, "Evolving Spatial Conceptions of the Yellow River's Source in Medieval China," has been published in Chinese: Feng, Linda Rui (冯令晏). "元前文献图籍所载黄河河源 [Sources of the Yellow River as Represented on Maps and Texts Prior to the Yuan Dynasty]." 云南大学学报 (社会科学版) [Academic Journal of the University of Yunnan] 19, no. 2 (2020): 71–79.

Contents

Acknowledgments —— VII

List of Contributors —— XI

Garret Pagenstecher Olberding
Introduction —— 1

Martin J. Powers
External and Internal: Absolute and Relative Space in Song Literati
Painting —— 11

FOONG Ping
Producing Shu Culture: Why Painters Needed Court Titles in Tenth-
Century Sichuan —— 29

Alexis Lycas
The Recollection of Place in Li Daoyuan's *Shuijing zhu* —— 55

Vincent S. Leung
Chuci and the Politics of Space under the Qin and Han Empires —— 77

H. M. Agnes Hsu-Tang
A Tomb with a View: Axonometry in Early Chinese Cartography —— 103

Linda Rui Feng
Spatial Conceptions of the Yellow River's Origin in Medieval Chinese
Texts —— 123

Daniel Patrick Morgan
Remarks on the Mathematics and Philosophy of Space-time in Early
Imperial China —— 149

Garret Pagenstecher Olberding
Diplomacy as Transgression in Early China —— 189

Index —— 217

List of Contributors

1. Linda Rui Feng, Associate Professor, Department of East Asian Studies, University of Toronto
2. FOONG Ping, Foster Foundation Curator of Chinese Art, Seattle Art Museum
3. H. M. Agnes Hsu-Tang, Distinguished Consulting Scholar, University of Pennsylvania Museum of Archaeology and Anthropology, and Senior Research Scholar (Adjunct), East Asian Languages and Cultures, Columbia University
4. Vincent S. Leung, Head and Associate Professor, Department of History, Lingnan University
5. Alexis Lycas, Assistant Professor, École pratique des hautes études (EPHE), PSL University
6. Daniel Patrick Morgan, Researcher, CRCAO, CNRS, EPHE-PSL, Collège de France, Université de Paris
7. Garret Pagenstecher Olberding, Associate Professor, Department of History, University of Oklahoma
8. Martin J. Powers, Professor Emeritus, Department of History of Art, University of Michigan

Garret Pagenstecher Olberding

Introduction

Having a "sense of place" is to understand oneself as belonging in, or at least occupying, a distinctive location. It is to be situated in an environment or locale – one is somewhere and that "somewhere" is not just anywhere. To have this sense is to be experientially grounded, to find experience framed or contoured to a landscape. But our "sense of place" is increasingly undermined by technological changes. Our technologies can simultaneously map with great precision where we presently are and have us communicating with or accessing the distant and faraway. These technologies "locate" and "place" us everywhere, and therefore nowhere. What does it mean to "find one's bearings" in such a world, much less to achieve a "sense of place" that would insistently remark where one physically stands? In some important way, while technology can always pinpoint where we are, we have worse bearings precisely because of our technological framing. Technology maps a world, but because the world so mapped lacks the symbolic and signifying ways place has most often mattered, it is a world in which we cannot as easily locate our ground and thus perhaps ourselves. We can know where we are and yet be utterly lost.

This volume will provide a clearer view of the importance of place through a contrastive temporal lens. In the premodern Chinese circumstance – which, in the essays for this volume, encompasses the Zhou to the Song dynastic periods – a sense of place, of situatedness lay at the root of how space was parcelled, represented, moved through and manipulated. And yet this deeper, more rooted emplacement did not stifle investigations into greater objective understandings and representations of space.

Abstractly conceived, lived space appears an untrammeled freedom, but in its possibilities it invites, as a blank canvas does, both control and opposition – whether artistic, mensurative, literary, political, or religious. When discussing space, our general focus is on its possibilities for control and resistance, with more specific attention given to its measurement and administration, as well as on human movement through space. Our volume will examine various operations of the spatial imagination and their impact on the construction of both physical and political space. It will speak not only to the function of and operating norms behind the pictorial depiction of space but to the connection between memory and place, religious and secular geography, the structuring effects of politics on the norms of landscape art, the possible spatial liberations in literature, and the importance of precise mensurative quantification for the use of space.

This topical complex reveals the understanding and representation of physical space in pre-modern China are not simply manifestations of a highly personal artistic preference or mathematic precision. Broad cultural definitions of a territory, the restrictions such definitions impose, and the expressive power of borders and boundaries, both in the secular and sacred worlds, have a deep and abiding impact on the ways in which physical space and its representations are formulated. Physical space was not treated merely as an area to be depicted precisely; borders were not just linear marks. Often in current scholarship physical space is discussed primarily as an area to be hegemonically controlled or occupied, with a ruling population supervising its domination and management. In order to truly probe the deeper import and effects of space, we must press for insight into its cultural facets. As experts in pre-modern Chinese geography, art, and science have demonstrated, the depiction and treatment of physical space in pre-modern China was developed in modes distinct from China's early European counterparts.[1] Here, we shall uncover structures underlying the mensurative and representational activities involved in forming terrestrial and celestial spatial relationships.

In both its sacred and mundane aspects, pre-modern Chinese viewings of space are often grounded in its panoptic representation, its visual segments based on the sense of a whole. Local areas of the empire, for instance, are grounded in a sense of empire as totality. Indeed, the understandings and representations of part and whole, of sacred and mundane, and even of terrestrial and celestial are to some extent mirrors of each other. Our volume will approach the exercise of the spatial imagination across five general areas: pictorial representation,

---

1 See, for instance, Vera Dorofeeva-Lichtmann, "Ritual Practices for Constructing Terrestrial Space (Warring States-Early Han)," in *Early Chinese Religion, Part One: Shang Through Han (1250 BC-220 AD)*, ed. John Lagerway and Marc Kalinowski (Leiden: Brill, 2009); D. Jonathan Felt, *Structures of the Earth: Metageographies of Early Medieval China* (Cambridge, Massachusetts: Harvard Asia Center Publications, 2021); Fan Lin, "The Local in the Imperial Vision: Landscape, Topography, and Geography in Southern Song Map Guides and Gazetteers." *Cross-Currents: East Asian History and Culture Review* 23 (2017): 10–39; Hsin-mei Agnes Hsu, "Structured Perceptions of Real and Imagined Landscapes in Early China," in *Geography and Ethnography: Perceptions of the World in Pre-Modern Societies*, edited by Kurt A. Raaflaub and Richard J. A. Talbert, 43–63. Malden, Massachusetts: Wiley-Blackwell, 2010; Vladimir Liščák. "'Wu-Yue' (Five Marchmounts) and Sacred Geography in China." *Archív Orientální* 62 (1994): 417–27; Gil Raz, "Daoist Sacred Geography," in *Early Chinese Religion, Part Two: The Period of Division (220–589 AD)*, 1399–422. Leiden: Brill, 2010; James Robson, "Buddhist Sacred Geography," in *Early Chinese Religion, Part Two: The Period of Division (220–589 AD)*, edited by John Lagerway and Pengzhi Lü, 1353–97. Leiden: Brill, 2010; Donald J. Wyatt and Nicola di Cosmo, eds. *Political frontiers, ethnic boundaries and human geographies in Chinese history*, New York: Routledge, 2003.

literary description, cartographic mappings, the mathematical quantification of space, and the ritual realm. Each of these areas offers a seminal, indispensable aspect. While acknowledging that the variety of our target sources permit multiple approaches, we aspire to address a shared body of questions that principally concern the conceptualization and depiction of space. How the representation of space is affected by artistic norms, how literature can reveal nuances in space's definition and use, how mathematical quantification of space was not merely for symbolic purposes,[2] how ritual aspects intimately affect secular divisions of space[3] – these investigations promise to expand our comprehension of the complexities of the spatial imagination.

The topics around which the volume is organized correspond to what we identify as significant characteristics informing an analysis of the spatial imagination. Topic one, "The Organization of Aesthetic Space," broached by Martin Powers and Foong Ping, will investigate the aesthetic norms behind the production of landscapes as well as spatially defined bureaucratic structures affecting the ranking of artists. Topic two, "Moving Through Imperial Space," covered by Alexis Lycas and Vincent Leung, will examine how landscapes were expressed in written form, whether in travel narratives or poetry. Topic three, "Geo-encoding of Sovereign Space," explored by Agnes Hsu-Tang and Linda Rui Feng, will appraise cartographic orderings of the Chinese world. Topic four, "The Calculus of Administrative Space-Time," investigated by Daniel Morgan, will consider the import of objective mensuration, even within political or metaphysical concerns. Our final topic, "The Abrogation of Ritual Space," as considered by Garret Pagenstecher Olberding, will assess ritual aspects of spatial organization.

Numerous questions are inspired by the essays that pertain to the spatial imagination, of which I enumerate only a few:
1. If facts are embedded in discursive structures, as they inevitably are, how does that alter our estimation of the structural shifts across time in representational art?
2. How are precise factual quotients in the measurement of space significantly valued for symbolic or representational purposes?
3. In what ways does the observing gaze influence the structure of space in a memorial circumstance?
4. How does memory guide the emplacement of space?

---

2 As Daniel Morgan explains in his essay, such symbolic purposes are underscored in the work of such esteemed sinologists as Marcel Granet.
3 The interplay between the ritual and the secular aspects of space are discussed in various essays, particularly those by Linda Feng and Garret Olberding.

5. How do religious organizations of space impact its secular organization and what does the transgression of religious boundaries effect?
6. By what means can we trace the effect of political power in the evaluation of what is good art, or true science, within the premodern circumstance, particularly as it relates to the evaluation or representation of space?
7. In what ways can the literary imagination liberate one from a totalitarian state geography?

The scholarly literature on the spatial imagination, when conceived broadly, would cover a dizzyingly vast range of topics, pertaining to geography, administration, ritual, diplomacy, the articulation of space in literary works, landscape art, and so forth. In English language scholarship, examples of relatively recent work touching more focusedly on the issues discussed in the volume are Mark E. Lewis' *The Construction of Space in Early China* (SUNY Press, 2006), which exhaustively catalogues various levels of spatial construction, from the micro-level of the body to the macro-level of the cosmos, and Francesca Bray, Vera Dorofeeva-Lichtmann, and Georges Métailié's edited volume, *Graphics and Texts in the Production of Technical Knowledge in China* (Brill, 2007), which speaks specifically to maps and mapping sensibilities pertaining to physical space. More philosophical work on space has been pursued in recent decades by scholars such as François Jullien, for example in his *The Great Image Has No Form: On the Nonobject Through Painting* (University of Chicago Press, 2003). Naturally, there are also innumerable art historical studies pertaining to the aesthetic representation of space.[4] To reiterate, this volume will narrow its focus on the spatial imagination as it pertains to the exercise of political power and the possibilities of liberation through space, in either knowledge structures or literary expression, as well as the memorialization of place in political systems. Below I offer a brief encapsulation of the argumentative thrust of each essay.

---

4 Following are several sample sinological studies: Foong Ping, *The Efficacious Landscape: On the Authorities of Painting at the Northern Song Court* (Cambridge, Massachusetts: Harvard University Asia Center, 2015); Martin Powers, "When Is a Landscape like a Body?," in *Landscape, Culture, and Power in Chinese Society*, ed. Wen-hsin Yeh (Berkeley: University of California Press, 1998); Dorothy C. Wong, "The Mapping of Sacred Space: Images of Buddhist Cosmographies in Medieval China," in *The Journey of Maps and Images on the Silk Road*, ed. Philippe Fôret and Andreas Kaplony (Leiden: Brill, 2008); Natasha Heller, "Visualizing Pilgrimage and Mapping Experience: Mount Wutai on the Silk Road," in *The Journey of Maps and Images on the Silk Road*, ed. Phillipe Forêt and Andreas Kaplony (Leiden: Brill, 2008); Hsin-mei Agnes Hsu and Anne Martin-Montgomery, "An Emic Perspective on the Mapmaker's Art in Western Han China," *Journal of the Royal Asiatic Society* 17, no. 4 (2007); and Michael Sullivan, *The Birth of Landscape Painting in China* (Berkeley: University of California Press, 1962).

Political power, even that which is spatially expressed, is most deeply en-sconced in the knowledge systems that underlie it. These knowledge systems express themselves in both text and graph, including in seemingly apolitical pictorial representations such as landscape art. Martin Powers' essay expounds on how in the ninth through eleventh centuries, a "factual" sensibility (*shi* 實) became more significant not only for the civil service examinations and govern-ment policy debates but also for pictorial art. In pictorial art, in the Northern Song, there arose a new way of displaying reality, through the employment of multiple interfering sightlines, and thus a new way of knowing the world. In pictorial art, Powers argues, "the treatment of space is contingent upon specific epistemological assumptions."[5] Within Northern Song literati painting, the facts displayed "were personal facts, such as the marks made by the artist's brush, the choice of style, literary citations or other personal interventions the artist might make."[6] This emphasis on the facts accords with debates over the importance of real merit when deciding bureaucratic appointments.

The connection between the bureaucratic and aesthetic worlds is pursued from the political perspective in Foong Ping's tracing of the awarding of official positions to Sichuan artists in the tenth century. The ranking of the bureaucratic appointment of court artists revealed how the art product – not just in itself but of itself – could exert a spatial force: The artist was ranked not simply for the intrinsic quality of the art but for how the art product of itself – through the fig-ure of the artist and his spatially defined position at court – expressed political influence. An artist's title could demonstrate his service "as a constituent ele-ment of a ruler's authority. By examining the titles that artists were permitted or prohibited, we better understand the roles art played in representing legitimate rule."[7] Furthermore, the ranking of artists and their works was bound to artistic space as a product of inter-state relations. According to Foong, "painting culture was a distinguishing product of the Shu region, playing a central role in inter-kingdom trade and diplomacy."[8] The titular awards "formalized Sichuan's paint-ing styles and family traditions as cultural products distinct to this geographic region", expressing the "the independence and regional power of Shu rulers just before Song reunification."[9]

---

5 See p. 12.
6 See p. 13.
7 See p. 30.
8 See p. 52.
9 See p. 30.

Though it investigates spatially organized memory rather than bureaucratic organization, Alexis Lycas' essay continues this theme, broadly described, of spatially demarcated assertion of political power in his exposition of Li Daoyuan's arrangement of imperial space in the *Shuijing zhu*. Therein Li "emplaces" imperial space through his travels. Li privileges memorialized sites, those with local or broader significance, and the memory that undergirds that privilege, his commentary serving as "a synthesis of geographical knowledge approached through a river study and a compendium of the cultural memory of the Empire."[10] According to Lycas, Li regarded spatial locations as the aggregate of human movement through time, localizing temporal significances and shaping spatially the connections between temporal events, within the location itself, but also across locations. Through such, the chronological and topographical interpenetrate. Although Li records the material characteristics of the places he visits, he also emphasizes their symbolic and literary value drawn from the narratives and signs of their historical import. Naturally, these sites are situated within the broader imperial frame, for these localized experiential perceptions are the connections that bind and form an imperial space.

Literary rebellion against the imperial frame is the subject of Vincent Leung's investigation into the *Chuci*. These elegiac poems, Leung argues, defiantly resisted homogenizing imperial spatial norms, offering a "poetics of displacement," acting as a "literary fallout of the spatial contention of the Qin-Han empires."[11] After introducing the rise of Chu lyric, a phenomenally popular form among the Han elite, Leung asks why these poems attracted such attention. Though they are not "landscape poetry" (*shanshui shi* 山水詩), do not take landscape, or nature, "as their primary object of poetic elaboration," a thematic thread running throughout the poems is a consistent interest in landscape: "In every *Chuci* poem, the narrative is always framed within a landscape or, at a minimum, situated within certain spatial relations."[12] Their spatial framing ties closely with the affective state of the poet, their traveling and gazing on their surroundings "to fulfill a lack,"[13] a literal spatial displacement borne of a frustration with an upside down, corrupt world. Rather than regarding the imperial world as being well-ordered – the crucial attribute of a properly governed state – with clear governmental orders circulating without obstruction, the *Chuci* poems saw the empire as a failed chaos. As outlined in his stele inscriptions, the Qin emperor envisioned a carefully demarcated,

---

10 See p. 56.
11 See p. 79.
12 See p. 85.
13 See p. 88.

perfectly functioning spatial organization, teeming with activity and reflecting moral propriety. But the landscapes described in the *Chuci* poems are desolate, "scattered with unwelcoming deities among things out of place."[14] The Chu spatial vision is thus the inversion of the Qin: "While the Qin stele inscriptions speak of a universal order with proper placement of all things, the *Chuci* imagines an inescapable chaos where everything is continually out of place and nothing can ever be at rest anywhere."[15]

How sovereign territory is cartographically represented is the subject of Agnes Hsu-Tang's and Linda Rui Feng's essays. Agnes Hsu-Tang's analyzes the hermeneutic implications of a second-century CE painted cartographic image's placement within its tomb, specifically its situation directly in line with the gaze of the tomb owner's painted image. Being installed in a tomb, the map is already something of a contradiction, for it is not necessarily meant to reflect any lived, perambulated space but a space useful for the dead. In this postmortem context, the mapped place is a mimicking of reality. What renders this particular mapped tomb image unique compared to other excavated cityscape images is that "artistic intention may have been ancillary to an imagined functionality."[16] This mental map is, Hsu-Tang emphasizes, a socio-political construct, a domain only partially represented to insinuate a great expanse, employing axonometric perspective, with all objects to size, giving the viewer a sense of their actual dimensions. Any spatial relation in the map is thus "situational," portraying pedestrian movement and not a consistent scale. What is truly striking about the image, Hsu-Tang points out, is that it is empty of any sign of life. In this lies a provocative juxtaposition: while its construction is lived, its finalized space absents any human form, functioning, Hsu-Tang hypothesizes, as a mental map for the tomb owner's "wayfinding" in the world of the dead.

The combination of secular and religiously inflected knowledge, applied to the comprehension and political use of terrestrial space, is the subject of Linda Rui Feng's essay, wherein she grapples with multifarious forms of knowledge from the Tang dynasty pertaining to the origin of the Yellow River. These diverse conceptions, Feng warns, should not be framed as contestations between the "inaccurate" and "accurate." New discoveries did not displace older conceptions; for instance, Mount Kunlun continued to be treated as an ultimate origin, this mythical name forcibly applied over non-Chinese geographic referents lying outside Chinese territory. Such demands we acknowledge that the "longue durée of

---

14 See p. 93.
15 See p. 93.
16 See p. 106.

knowledge formation was a contingent and disjunctive one, spanning an interface between myth and geography, between collective imagination and the assimilation of new evidence."[17] In her examination she focuses on descriptions of
the river's upper reaches found in *leishu* 類書, official geographical treatises and
a Buddhist geography relying on Xuanzang's 玄奘 travels, in addition to informal
narratives speaking to waterways, such as the *Youyang zazu*'s 酉陽雜俎 discussion of underground channels or the prose works in the *Taiping guangji* 太平廣
記 devoted to the category of "Water". Further complicating the study of the river's course are distinctions made between those portions that lie within and outside the barriers of Chinese territory, distinctions that affect the organization of
knowledge about the river. Those scholars who wished to avoid prioritizing the
area outside of Chinese territory would either follow "the river's source inside
China's borders" or "chart the river's flow in reverse."[18] In sum, the river becomes a site of intertwined, conjoined knowledge systems for which objective
mensuration does not in itself provide an acceptable resolution.

Yet as Daniel Morgan's evaluation of celestial calculations reveals, objective
mensuration should not be considered necessarily subsumed to political or religious forms of knowledge, though it can be and is frequently pressed into their
service. Indeed, Morgan demonstrates that scholars are incorrect when they insist
that religious or symbolic objectives invariably govern the appropriation and use
of calculations of celestial movements, of the binding of time to space. Morgan
challenges the insistence that Chinese calendrics deals exclusively with time. As
he underscores, measurements of time depend on the movement of space. *Li* 曆
are not calendars in the common definition; they are not tables of dates and
months. Previous modern scholarly arguments about *li*, and Chinese calendrics
and astronomy in general, assert their general lack of scientific or speculative interest. But *li*, Morgan detailedly illustrates, are more like algorithms, though the
involved calculations are certainly not rote. Through these *li*, measures of time
can be converted to spatial positions, and doing so, *li* are "transformational" and
thus can be connected to the transformations of the *Changes* 易經: "Round and
square, heaven and earth – space and time are *in communication* (*tong* 通), which
means that you can *pass freely* (*tong* 通) from one to the other and back."[19] However, this connection to the *Changes* does not render the mathematics behind *li*
simply symbolic numerology. The vocabulary of the *Changes* is connected to *li*

---

17 See p. 124–125.
18 See p. 131.
19 See p. 177.

calculations exegetically, "a heuristic framework . . . towards 'a mathematical research on the rationality of change.'"[20]

In the final essay, Garret Pagenstecher Olberding analyzes the abrogation of a ritualized definition of space in the pursuit of diplomatic missions. Intrinsic to the profession of the diplomat is the potential to upend political arrangements but also intrinsic are his rhetorical reframings, of either the mission or the current state of affairs. These destabilizing potentials underlie the administrative regulation of travel abroad, but they furthermore underly the ritual obligations imposed before departure and during the mission. The unsanctioned crossing of boundaries was a severe offense in one's ritualized duty to the state. Similarly, the prejudicial treatment of the diplomat as "guest" was also a danger to the state. Guests from within accepted cultural groups received treatment somewhat distinct from those who weren't. Yet it was within purview of the diplomat, as one who might, over the course of his mission, rhetorically or personally transgress ritualized norms, to ally himself with the foreign, "monstrous" other and contribute to the reshaping of his sovereign's hegemonic space.

---

20 See p. 181.

Martin J. Powers
External and Internal: Absolute and Relative Space in Song Literati Painting

In an essay on painting Bai Juyi (772–846) remarked "There is no constant standard in painting; painting takes resemblance as its standard; there is no constant teacher in learning; learning takes truth/facts as its teacher"[1] 畫無常工, 以似為工, 學無常師, 以真為師. Resemblance and facts both point to external reality as the standard, as opposed to medieval dogma or hereditary rank. From the ninth century through the eleventh, facts slowly became the normative standard in civil service examinations, in policy debate, and in pictorial art. Speaking of the New Policy reforms toward the end of the Northern Song (960–1127), Peter Bol observed:

> The policies themselves aimed to integrate the energies of a dynamic society and encourage economic growth. Rather than stabilizing the social order it expanded opportunities and through education enlarged the pool of talent that could serve in government. Moreover, it aimed to make use of the increase in wealth, the spread of education, and the development of the south to lessen inequalities, not to defend privilege . . . it was a government that believed that if people were properly educated, they too, like the ideologically-driven policy makers, would see that the policies were fundamentally correct and fully grounded in *reality*.[2]　　　　　　　　　　　　　　　　　　(emphasis added)

One manifestation of reality-based representation was a consistent horizon in landscape painting. Even in long handscrolls, the horizon doesn't waver, any more than it would in real life. It is this that creates in Northern Song landscape the illusion of spatial depth. In Northern Song literati painting however, the horizon disappears. In its place we find lines of sight, and sometimes multiple and contradictory lines of sight within a single scene. Such practices signal a complete rejection of spatial depth, for the horizon takes the external world as its reference, while line-of-sight privileges the artist's subjective point of view. This does not imply that literati artists rejected reality or facts; it is simply that they drew attention to a different, and equally real set of facts. Adopting a social and epistemological perspective, this paper examines the profound implications of the shift in pictorial space from horizon to line-of-sight, and by

---

1 Bai Juyi, *Ji hua* (*A Record of Painting*), Zhang Chunlin 张春林 ed., *Baijuyi quanji* (*Collected works of Bai Juyi*) (Beijing: Zhongguo wenshi chubanshe, 1996), 755–756.
2 Peter Bol, "Whither the Emperor: Emperor Huizong, the New Policies, and the Tang-Song Transition" *The Journal of Song-Yuan Studies* 31 (2001), 103–134, reference, 132–133.

extension, as explored in Ping Foong's and Daniel Morgan's essays, the effect of political power in the representation of the external world.

Style and epistemology

Heinrich Wölfflin (1864–1945), the "father" of modern art history, observed a hundred years ago that the range of information available to vision far outstrips what an artist can copy with pigments. Wölfflin understood that this limitation explained the origins and necessity of style, for there could never be a style that perfectly described nature. As a result, even if an artist's aim were to transcribe real appearances as faithfully as possible, s/he would be forced to adopt a style that privileged some kinds of information over others. Wölfflin's student Ludwig Bachhofer (1894–1976) pressed this insight further, observing that style is a filter that encodes a particular set of priorities. In other words, style is a function of epistemology: "No less ambiguous is the term 'stylization.' Those who use it are often apt to forget that a drawing by Rembrandt is as 'stylized' as one by an Egyptian painter . . . The reason is that different times have different ideas about what is accidental and what is basic."[3]

This consideration prompts the more general postulate that, in pictorial art, the treatment of space is contingent upon specific epistemological assumptions. It is not merely a matter of accuracy or skill. What information gets included depends upon what a particular visual community regards as significant knowledge. I make no claim to novelty here. Referring to the medieval windows in Canterbury Cathedral, Norman Bryson presumed that medieval styles were adapted to the conveyance of textual doctrine at the expense of descriptive detail: "By the 'discursive' aspect of an image, I mean those features which show the influence over the image of language - in the case of the window at Canterbury, the Biblical texts which precede it and on which it depends, the inscriptions it contains within itself to tell us how to perceive the different panels."[4] Bryson argued that medieval artists tended to suppress "irrelevant" visual details such as light, the time of day, the weight of cloth, or other accidents of the moment in favor of the textual message. What is most legible therefore are those "discursive" aspects of the image relating to Church dogma.

---

3 Ludwig Bachhofer, *A Short History of Chinese Art* (New York, 1946), 86.
4 Norman Bryson, *Word and Image: French Painting of the Ancien Regime* (Cambridge, 1980), 1–9.

On the other hand, in both China and Europe, early modern styles provide a rich range of information about the passage of time, whether it is the season, the time of day, or the effects of time on objects via wind, rain, and other forms of erosion. Artists in both China and Europe, moreover, adopted similar methods for representing deep space convincingly: the representation of objects according to scale; the diminution of size in accordance with distance from the picture plane; the use of atmospheric perspective; the use of a repoussoir to serve as a scale for distance, and so on. All of these techniques ensure that viewers of such paintings would become aware of the passage of time, as well as the relative height of objects, or the distances between them.[5]

One might be tempted to formulate a simple binary: less developed, premodern societies that prioritize social status or dogma over facts tend to favor simplified shapes, outlines, colors, and flattened space, while more modern, reality-based societies favor naturalistic representation. Unfortunately, matters are not so simple. Mao's China was certainly "modern" in the sense that it was industrialized and made use of modern administrative, military, and propaganda techniques, yet the favored style for poster art significantly reduced texture, simplified outlines, flattened color, and overall reduced descriptive detail so as to highlight textual doctrines that, often enough, were placed directly onto the poster. This description, moreover, could apply to a great many posters, from those of Toulouse-Lautrec to the iconic Obama posters of only a few years back. We must conclude then, that attention to time and space in pictorial art is not a matter of primitive versus advanced, or premodern versus modern. Whenever the discursive dimension is dominant, as in poster art, artists may reduce information about the changing conditions of real things so as to privilege a verbal message whose content is so important as to eclipse any incidental, factual, details.

Likewise, while literati painting abandoned the consistent use of horizon, atmospheric perspective, light, or the depiction of objects to scale, literati artists continued to place great value upon facts, and time. In literati painting the facts were personal facts, such as the marks made by the artist's brush, the choice of style, literary citations or other personal interventions the artist might make. As a result, Time remained a factor in literati painting, every bit as much as in naturalistic work.[6] The brushstroke, after all, was a direct record of the

---

5 Martin Powers, "Picturing Time in Song Painting and Poetry", in Joseph Lam et. al., eds., *The Senses of the City: Perceptions of Hangzhou and Southern Song China, 1127–1279* (Hong Kong: Hong Kong University Press, 2016), 55–72.
6 Martin Powers, "The Temporal Logic of Citation in Chinese Art," *Art History*, vol. 37, no. 4 (September, 2014), 745–763.

artist's movement over a specific period of time, whose speed and force could be inferred from the length and character of the brush mark. In the same way, references to historically defunct styles, when juxtaposed with contemporary styles, necessarily called to mind the passage of historical time. Unlike some political posters moreover, a literati painting made no timeless assertions. The main difference between literati landscapes and the naturalistic landscapes is that the latter convey publicly visible facts while the former convey personal, yet still sharable facts. These facts can be shared, however, only when the artist chooses to do so, whereas a mountain range can be assessed any time, so long as you are standing in the right place.

Facts and meritocracy

The literati decision to prioritize personal facts over publicly observable facts is understandable if we consider that the term for facts, *shí* 實, featured prominently in debates over meritocratic appointment. In a meritocratic system, men are chosen for public office according to the facts of their individual performance on examinations, or in office. During China's medieval period however, family lineage generally trumped facts in the assignment of office. True, Empress Wu Zetian (624–705) had revived and improved the examinations with a view to making room for talented men of ordinary birth, but in Tang times the examinations were not anonymous, so the aristocracy readily found ways to rig the system in their favor. As a result, the vast majority of appointments, especially for high office, went to men of noble lineage. This situation came under challenge in the first half of the eighth century when Li Ang was appointed as chief examiner. He objected to the fact that most of the appointments conferred previously, in his view, were merely decorative/*shì* 飾 and without substance/*shí* 實.[7] What did he mean by that?

The semantic range of *shí* at that time encompassed "real," "actual," "factual," and just plain facts. Li Ang contrasted this with *shì*, which implied useless ornament, empty display, or baseless claims. Li was determined to replace *shì* with *shí*, and so he issued orders that the grade assigned was to be based on the actual quality of the examination.[8] The source for this language was

---

7 以舉人皆飾名求稱, 搖蕩主司, 談毀失實, 竊病之而將革焉。Cited in Li Shu 李樹, *Zhongguo keju shihua* (中國科舉史話 A history of China's civil service examination) Jinan: Qilu shushe 2007, 14.
8 Li, *Zhongguo keju shihua*, 14.

classical bureaucratic theory. One branch of that theory, called *mingshi* theory, laid out procedures for appointing competent officials. Each office title, or *ming*, would be defined by a specific charge with powers limited to those required to fulfil its charge. If a man was thought suitable for an office, he would be assigned to it, and his actual/*shi* performance would be compared with his charge/*ming*. If the two matched, he would retain his title; if not, he would be dismissed.[9]

Li Ang in essence applied these classical principles to the grading of examinations so that the grade assigned would match the candidate's actual performance. Such reforms eventually made it possible for men of more ordinary lineage, such as Han Yu (768–824) or Bai Juyi, to acquire office via the examinations.[10] Not surprisingly Bai and his friends were highly conscious of the struggle between privilege and merit. In fact, they called explicitly for the overthrow of the aristocratic system and its replacement with a meritocratic administration.[11] This meant, in effect, rejecting the authority of the sage kings who, contemporaries avowed, had created the feudal system as a model for all time. Bai's friend Liu Zongyuan (773–819) deftly refuted that theory by arguing that historical change was a product of shizhilai 勢之來, the "force of circumstance," and had nothing to do with the sage kings.[12] One cannot easily overstate the radical nature of this claim. It would be as if Thomas Aquinas had argued that the normative social order had nothing to do with God's will.

In keeping with these sentiments, the *guwen* 古文, or "plain style" intellectuals took every opportunity to promote the core significance of *shi* in either personal or public policy decision-making. We have seen this already in Bai's remark that "In learning, there is no constant, meaning no "single" teacher; learning takes what is true (facts) as its teacher." This would have been a radical thing to propose in any premodern society, for it meant that you cannot decide the reliability of a statement on the basis of who said it, whether that be

---

9 Di, Yuzhong. *Zhengming: Chinese Logic* (Beijing: Central Compilation and Translation Press, 2013), 36–41. Some bureaucratic theorists used "performance and title" 形名, to convey much the same idea. See Martin Powers, *Pattern and Person: Ornament, Society, and Self in Classical China* (Cambridge: Harvard University Press East Asian Series, 2006), 194–206.
10 Li, *Zhongguo keju shihua*, 14–17.
11 Liu Zongyuan (773–819), 'Fengjian lun', in Lü Ch'ing-fei 呂晴飞, ed., *Liu Zongyuan sanwen*, 3 vols., Taipei, World publishing house, 1994), I:23–32; Bai Juyi, "Yi fengjian, lun junxian (against feudalism and for salaried administration)" in Zhang Chunlin 张春林 ed., *Baijuyi quanji* (白居易全集 Collected works of Bai Juyi), (Beijing: Zhongguo wenshi chubanshe, 1996), 1044–1045.
12 Martin Powers, *China and England: the Preindustrial Struggle for Justice in Word and Image* (London: Routledge, 2018), 52–53.

the sage kings, Jesus Christ, Confucius, or Mao. In the end, only the facts matter. Bai Juyi made this point more explicitly in the preface to his "New Folk Songs," a collection of his own poems castigating the abuse of the vulnerable by the nobility, the generals, the emperor, and even social convention:

> Their content is plain and factual/*shí*, so that those who recite them will earn the trust (of their listeners); their style is easy and straightforward, so that their message may spread widely in song . . . In a word, they were composed for the ruler, for the officials, for the people, for (real) things and for (real) affairs, not for the sake of literary language![13] 其事核而實, 使采之者傳信也。其體順而肆, 可以撥於樂章歌曲也 . . . 總而言之, 為君、為臣、為民、為物、為事而作, 不為文而作也。

The key concern in Bai's "New Folk Songs" was social reality, meaning injustice. This was primarily a question of public policy, but in matters of appointment to office, the reality at stake was the reality of an individual's learning, talent, experience, and dedication to the public good. Before the end of the Northern Song dynasty, these same criteria would be applied to literati painting.

Examinations were by nature about the individual, because the examinee's name, family background, religion, ethnicity, and personal preferences were all hidden from the examiners. This was accomplished by replacing the examinee's name with a number. Once the number was assigned, the examination text was to be copied by a scribe. The five examiners, whose grades were averaged, could not know who the author was.[14] A literati painting, however, while every bit as individual as an examination text, was not anonymous. How could an artist assert his or her (yes, there were women artists) personal views in such a way that the factual traces of individuality would not be missed?

Alfreda Murck has demonstrated in rich detail how poetic practice provided a natural model for literati painters. Not only did Du Fu 杜甫 (712–770) embody the ideal of a public-spirited intellectual, he was also a master of historical and poetic citation. Rather than simply ape famous poetic phrases, as Bai Juyi had characterized the work of earlier poets,[15] Du Fu "reworked arcane cliché's into fresh expressions, and incorporated the vernacular into classical forms."[16] In

---

13 Bai Juyi (772–846), *Bai juyi quanji* (the collected works of Bai Juyi), Liu Mingjie 刘明杰, annot. (Guangzhou, Zhuhai Press, 1996), 41.

14 Qu Chaoli, *Songdai difangzhengfu minshi shenpan zhineng yanjiu* (The function of civil courts in local government in Song times) (Chengdu: Bashu Shudian, 2003), 16.

15 Bai Juyi, "Yu yuanjiu shu" (A Letter for Yuan Zhen), in Zhou Shaoliang, ed., *Quan tangwen xinbian*, (Collected essays from the Tang dynasty), Vol. 3, No.3 (Changchun: Jilin wenshi Press, 2000), 7622.

16 Alfreda Murck, *Poetry and painting in Song China: the subtle art of dissent* (Cambridge: Cambridge University Press, 2000), 53.

other words, he "modernized" stylistically obsolete phrases by making them his own, and he mixed styles from different and incompatible genres in the same work. These qualities were especially appreciated by leading Northern Song literati: "He (Huang Tingjian) admired Du Fu's ingenuity at incorporating other poets' words and ideas into his verse and making appropriate allusions that paradoxically seemed fresh and natural."[17] For the literati, "natural" was understood in the fifth-century poet Tao Yuanming's 陶淵明 (317–420) sense, meaning according to one's own nature.[18] Du Fu's citations were natural precisely because he altered the reference sufficiently to mark it as originating with Du Fu, not with the source. Significantly, Murck demonstrates that the application of these ideals was not limited to poetry, but informed literati painting as well. Yet painting presumably presented greater challenges because of the historicity of pictorial space. In the history of painting, East and West, every pictorial style must adopt a particular set of procedures for dealing with pictorial space. Because these procedures change over time, they are specific to particular historical moments. Citing a phrase by Tao Yuanming does not require adopting his verse form, but citing a figure from the fourth-century artist Gu Kaizhi 顧愷之 (344–406) implies a spatial system completely different from that which was normative in Song times. How did Northern Song literati deal with this?

Here again, the late Tang *guwen* movement laid the foundations for Song literati practice. The key insight of the *guwen* movement was that human institutions are merely conventional, products of what Liu Zongyuan called "the force of circumstance" at a particular moment in history, and not the timeless inventions of the sage kings. Therefore institutions, individuals, and cultural practice all could be altered to improve social conditions in the present. Such insights into the contingency of historical institutions paved the way for heightened historical consciousness in Song times. Eventually this led to the understanding that pictorial style, too, was a product of historical circumstance and could be altered, adjusted, or cited at will.[19] Despite the widely recognized achievements of Song naturalism, there was no reason why an artist could not employ multiple styles from different periods in the same scene, just as s/he

---

17 Murck, *Poetry and Painting*, 55.

18 Martin Powers, "Recurrent dialogues in the history of Chinese and English garden design," in Malcolm Baker and Andrew Hemingway, eds., *Art as Worldmaking: Critical Essays on Realism and Naturalism* (Manchester: Manchester University Press, 2019), 115–127, reference 119–120.

19 Martin Powers, "Imitation and Reference in China's Pictorial Tradition," in Wu Hung, ed., *Reinventing the Past: Archaism and Antiquarianism in Chinese Art and Visual Culture* (Chicago: Art Media Resources, 2010), 103–126.

could cite, within the same poem, phrases from poets who worked in different styles and periods.

The literati infringement of the standard rules for depicting form, texture, light, or space and time, has been recognized for decades. Richard Barnhart was among the first to stress the radical overthrow of Song naturalism in the reappearance of formerly defunct, prenaturalistic pictorial styles: "The Gu Kaizhi tradition of secular figure painting, in contrast, was virtually moribund in the eleventh century . . . [The] relatively primitive landscape art [of Jing Hao] had been thoroughly overshadowed by the great masters of the tenth and eleventh centuries."[20] Yet, such moribund styles reappeared in the work of the literati artist Li Gonglin 李公麟 (1049–1106). Robert Harrist likewise noted the deliberate rejection of naturalistic standards by literati artists: "it appears that Li Gonglin willfully turned his back on the Chinese landscapist's hard-won mastery of naturalistic representation in favor of an eccentric pictorial language of his own devising."[21]

The key words here are "of his own devising." Nowhere in the world of the eleventh century, outside China, was an artist authorized to flaunt basic pictorial conventions, replacing accepted forms for completely eccentric forms "of his own devising." I do not refer here to the use of some novel flourish or ornament, or placing Abraham on the right side of the composition instead of the left, what historians of European art call "inventions". I am referring to the practice of breaking accepted conventions of spatial arrangement and replacing them with fundamentally different and personal modes of pictorial construction. How did this come about?

One can approach this question in two ways: 1) How did literati artists theorize these interventions into conventional style? 2) What enabled them to pursue such radical action? The first is easier to answer. Remember that Bachhofer saw every style as encoding a list of priorities. He presumed that these priorities would be those of the community for which the work had been made, for it would have been that community that gave rise, over time, to the style commonly employed by local artists or artisans. Literati painting also encoded a list of priorities, but to a significant extent these were the personal priorities of an individual master, not those of the general community. So, the question is, can

---

20 Richard Barnhart, "Li Kung-lin's Use of Past Styles," in *Artists and Traditions: Uses of the Past in Chinese Culture*, ed. Christian F. Murck (Princeton, NJ: Princeton University Press, 1976), 52.
21 Robert E. Harrist, *Painting and Private Life in Eleventh-Century China: Mountain Villa by Li Gonglin* (Princeton, NJ: Princeton University Press, 1998), 91.

we find in the art theory of the Northern Song some articulation of this principle? The answer is, yes.

There were two parts to this theory. The first was the redefinition of the word for natural/*ziran* 自然. In the art critical writings of Dong You 董卣 (1031–1095) it is evident that most professional artists of the time used *ziran* to mean something like "naturalistic," a pictorial image that closely matched the appearance of real objects. Dong You, however, like other literati, regarded this process as completely "unnatural." Dong interpreted *ziran* to mean "naturally." In the end, this meant to paint according to one's own, personal nature rather than following a fixed set of rules, as in the work of Tao Yuanming, or Du Fu.[22]

This view was reinforced in the art critical essays of Shen Kuo 沈括 (1031–1099). Like Dong You, Shen rejected the idea that the business of art consisted of following a set of mechanical rules to achieve a predetermined result. Instead, what was truly wonderful about the art of painting was its capacity for *shenhui* 神會, or imaginative encounter. He found a model for this in a passage describing Wang Wei's (699–759) painting style. Reportedly Wang completely ignored the unity of time and space, painting plants from different seasons together in the same scene. Shen deduced from this (erroneously one suspects) that Wang wilfully created his own, personal rules, in defiance of normal pictorial convention.[23] By peering at such a work, a viewer could enter into Wang Wei's alternative world in imagination: "Therefore the picture's logic enters into the imagination and returns as a natural thought."[24]

Such a theory would give an artist considerable license to alter conventional rules of representation. Seeing as both Dong and Shen placed high value on avoiding any appearance of mechanical obedience to rules, it would be incumbent on the artist to make evident to viewers his or her wilful interventions. Among the most effective ways to accomplish this would be to alter standard pictorial techniques for depicting space and time.

Elsewhere I have examined multiple examples of pictorial practices corresponding to these theoretical postulates.[25] Many are spatial in nature, including: eliminating the horizon; raising or lowering the plane of recession arbitrarily along the length of a handscroll; flattening the winding stream used to create a sense of deep space in naturalistic painting; using multiple and conflicting lines

---

22 Powers, "Recurrent Dialogues," 119.

23 Powers, "Recurrent Dialogues," 119.

24 Shen Kuo, *Mengxi bitan* 梦溪笔谈 (Notes from the stream of dreams), vol. 3 (Yangzhou: Guangling shushe, 2003), 152.

25 Martin Powers, "The Temporal Logic of Citation in Chinese Art," *Art History*, vol. 37, no. 4 (September, 2014), 745–763.

of sight within the same scene;[26] or juxtaposing incompatible historical styles from different periods within the same scene.[27] Among all these bold and unprecedented pictorial interventions, perhaps the use of multiple lines of sight is the most disorienting for the viewer. This device occurs in several works associated tangentially with Li Gonglin, but nowhere more startlingly than in the handscroll attributed to Qiao Zhongchang 喬仲常 (active 1120s) in the Nelson-Atkins Museum of Art. This artist employed the device twice in his scroll, in each case at a moment in the narrative where the protagonist, the poet and statesman Su Shi 蘇軾 (1037–1101), is unable to distinguish between illusion and reality.

Figure 1: Su Shi ascending the mountain. Qiao Zhongchang, Chinese (active late 11th–early 12th century). *Illustration to the Second Prose Poem on the Red Cliff*, Northern Song Dynasty (960–1127 C.E.). Handscroll, ink on paper. Image & colophon: 12 x 247 3/4 inches (30.48 x 629.29 cm). The Nelson-Atkins Museum of Art, Kansas City, Missouri. Purchase: Nelson Gallery Foundation, F80-5. Photography by the author.

In the first instance (Figure 1), Su Shi has left his companions behind; his surroundings grow increasingly strange as he climbs among eerily shaped rocks and trees to the top of a promontory. He is so high now that from that position he can peer into an eagle's nest while looking down to the rocks and waters below: "I suddenly let out a sharp cry. The plants and trees were startled and shook; mountains resounded, valleys echoed. Winds arose, and the water became agi-

---

26 Powers, "Temporal Logic," 748–751.
27 Powers, "Temporal Logic," 758–761.

Figure 2: A view from the mountain with three, contrasting lines of sight. Qiao Zhongchang, Chinese (active late 11th–early 12th century). *Illustration to the Second Prose Poem on the Red Cliff*, Northern Song Dynasty (960–1127 C.E). Handscroll, ink on paper. Image & colophon: 12 x 247 3/4 inches (30.48 x 629.29 cm). The Nelson-Atkins Museum of Art, Kansas City, Missouri. Purchase: Nelson Gallery Foundation, F80-5. Photography by the author.

tated."[28] At this stage of the poem the artist does not show us Su's image; instead he shows us what Su would have seen. This, the artist conveys by permitting us to look almost straight down into the roiling waters (Figure 2), yet at the same time, and from the same vantage point, we can look straight ahead at jagged rocks, with the two lines of sight crossing at almost ninety degrees. Should our gaze wander just a bit to the right, we can see other rocks in a normal three-quarter view, all within the same scene, a scene that lacks any hint of a horizon. To suggest that the visual confusion the artist introduced into this scene is unrelated to the mental confusion described in Su's poem would strain credulity, but should one need more evidence, a repetition of this device occurs again in the scroll the second time that Su Shi finds it difficult to distinguish fact from fantasy.

This moment occurs in the penultimate scene of the scroll (Figure 3). There we simultaneously see Su Shi asleep in his bed, and sitting beside himself in a dream where he converses with a couple Daoists (Figure 4). We view both the real Su Shi and the dream Su Shi head on, but just behind the building where he sleeps we can also see his courtyard. This should have been blocked from view

---

28 Translation by Richard Strassberg, trans. and annot., *Inscribed Landscapes: Travel Writing from Imperial China* (Berkeley: University of California Press, 1994), 188.

Figure 3: A view of Su Shi's cottage with the guest room courtyard behind at right angles to one another. Qiao Zhongchang, Chinese (active late 11th-early 12th century). *Illustration to the Second Prose Poem on the Red Cliff*, Northern Song Dynasty (960–1127 C.E). Handscroll, ink on paper. Image & colophon: 12 x 247 3/4 inches (30.48 x 629.29 cm). The Nelson-Atkins Museum of Art, Kansas City, Missouri. Purchase: Nelson Gallery Foundation, F80-5. Photography by the author.

by the structure in which he sleeps, but here it appears to the scroll viewer flipped up ninety degrees so that we can look down into the courtyard at the same time that we look straight ahead at Su Shi in his dream (Figure 3). Undoubtedly Su Shi is confused at this stage in the poem and, once again, in the painting, we gaze at the scene along two lines of sight meeting at ninety degrees. In short, the painting forces us to adopt highly personal lines of sight that lead us to experience confusion akin to that of the protagonists within the poem as well as within the scroll.

Clearly there is a kind of logic to what we find here, but it is a highly personal logic peculiar to an artist who has created pictorial effects of his own devising. In this instance, achieving these effects required him to violate multiple rules of deep space representation that were widely accepted as normative at the time. Ironically, it is precisely the personal and imaginative nature of the artist's interventions that lends them their facticity. Like the knowledge, insights, and arguments informing a civil service examination paper, these interventions were peculiar to the person who produced them and, in that sense, were perfectly factual.

So how should such developments have become possible? How did the late Northern Song literati find themselves so at odds with the mainstream norms of their time? At this stage we can hardly avoid considering the impact of the New Policies on the artistic practices of the Northern Song literati. Although the

Figure 4: Detail of Figure 3 showing Su Shi simultaneously asleep and conversing with Daoists in his dream. Qiao Zhongchang, Chinese (active late 11th-early 12th century). *Illustration to the Second Prose Poem on the Red Cliff*, Northern Song Dynasty (960–1127 C.E). Handscroll, ink on paper. Image & colophon: 12 x 247 3/4 inches (30.48 x 629.29 cm). The Nelson-Atkins Museum of Art, Kansas City, Missouri. Purchase: Nelson Gallery Foundation, F80-5. Photography by the author.

literature on the New Policies is voluminous,[29] Alfreda Murck's study of literati painting and poetry in that context is of special pertinence here. In one chapter, Murck provides a highly erudite reading of Du Fu's "Autumn Day in Kui Prefecture," a poem in which the master detailed the lives and sufferings of the rural folk under the yolk of oppressive policies.[30] But Su Shi and his circle had been criminalized precisely for exposing, and criticizing a remarkably similar set of injustices in their own time. Murck documents almost line by line how the injustices recorded in Du Fu's poem resonated for Northern Song literati with their own historical moment, and how creatively they could use Du Fu's work to amplify the political content of their poetry and painting.

    Su Shi for instance, in a poem that was reviewed as evidence during his trial, selected words from Du Fu's "Autumn Day" to end every line of his poem that ended in a rhyme. Note that this was not a *he* 和, a poem written to match

---

[29] Peter Bol's classic discussion of the problem is still the best starting point for this matter: Peter Bol, *This Culture of Ours* (Stanford: Stanford University Press, 1992), 33–75; see also Ronald Egan, *Word, Image and Deed in the Life of Su Shi* (Cambridge, 1994), 108–133. References to the New Policies' impact on period painting are scattered throughout Yu Hui, *Hidden Concerns and Indirect Dissent: Deciphering the 'Spring Festival on the River' Scroll* (Beijing: Peking University Press, 2015), [Chinese].

[30] Murck, *Poetry and Painting*, 52–99.

the rhymes of another poet's work. Rather, Su thoughtfully yet randomly selected particular terms so as to encode specific meanings. A similar strategy could be applied to painting: "The Luoyang exiles appear to have adopted the practice of encoding poetry and painting in ways recognizable only by the cognescenti."[31]

This strategy was a useful, perhaps necessary response to the unusually oppressive political climate of that moment in Chinese history. Su Shi, in his "Ten-thousand Word Policy Document," noted that the suppression of dissenting views, while common in pre-Song times, had not occurred since the beginning of the dynasty, yet had become standard policy under Wang Anshi 王安石 (1021–1086).[32] Nor was Su the last cultural icon to observe as much. Zhen Dexiu 真德秀 (1178–1235), an exemplary statesman and Confucian of the Southern Song, fulminated at the outrageous suppression of speech under Wang. Any decent person, he argued, could recognize immediately the rank tyranny of such practices.[33] Right through to the seventeenth century one can find comparable views. Wang Fuzhi 王夫之 (1619–1692) for one, did not mince words when speaking of Wang's disastrous impact on Emperor Shenzong's reign:

> Sometimes people talk big, but their words lack substance/*shí*; words lacking in substance are a bad sign. A wise monarch will recognize this; he will recognize that man's shortcomings and thus will become alarmed . . . I speak of those whose knowledge is limited but whose plans are big; whose ambition is base and who wish only to sugar coat/*shì* their incompetence, and who delight in exercising their meanness so as to lock up the mouths of the entire world, thereby flattering their own lies![34] 言有大而無實，無實者，不祥之言也。明主知之，知其拓落而以是相震 . . . 維知小而圖大，志陋而欲飾其短者，樂引取之，以鉗天下之口，而遂其非!

Notice that Wang Fuzhi, in describing Wang Anshi, contrasted *shí* with *shì* so as to expose the fact that the Chancellor was not worthy of his charge. For Wang, nothing revealed this more clearly than Wang's suppression of political speech. If the suppression of speech had been normative in late imperial China, as Cold War scholars encouraged us to imagine, its implementation would never have inspired such powerful rebukes from leading intellectuals across the centuries.

It makes more sense to view that moment from the literati perspective: Su Shi and his fellow exiles had grown up in an empire where public opinion had

31 Murck, *Poetry and Painting*, 99.
32 Egan, *Su Shi: Word, Image, and Deed*, 29–38.
33 *Wenyuange siku quanshu*, Vol. 1418, Shanghai guji chubanshe, 2003, P. 745.
34 Wang Fuzhi, *Essays on Song History*, In S. Y. Shu (ed.), *The Works of Wang Fuzhi* (Beijing: Zhonghua Publishing, 1964), 114.

an impact on policy and where open debate was normative,[35] yet in their prime they found themselves resisting an intolerant regime inclined to punish adversaries. Alienated and in many ways alone, they turned to culture, the one area where they could reject the court, the prime minister, and social convention, to assert their own, private vision.[36] Like Du Fu, they created highly personal works addressing issues of personal integrity and, like Du Fu, they made extensive use of citation to achieve that end. But to make an art historical citation, one would have to mark the historical moment to which the source was linked, and that required juxtaposing styles from different periods utilizing completely different spatial conventions.

Figure 5: Distant hills in the Dong Yuan style contrasting with Qiao's dry rocks in the foreground. Qiao Zhongchang, Chinese (active late 11th-early 12th century). *Illustration to the Second Prose Poem on the Red Cliff*, Northern Song Dynasty (960–1127 C.E). Handscroll, ink on paper. Image & colophon: 12 x 247 3/4 inches (30.48 x 629.29 cm). The Nelson-Atkins Museum of Art, Kansas City, Missouri. Purchase: Nelson Gallery Foundation, F80-5. Photography by the author.

A good example of this appears in the Qiao Zhongchang scroll (Figures 5 and 6), when the artist cites the rolling hills and "hemp fiber strokes" that were diagnostic of Dong Yuan's 董源 (934–962) style.[37] Dong Yuan was much admired by Su Shi's circle, Mi Fu 米芾 (1051–1107) having raised him to the status of a model. The reason was that his painting, in Mi's view, avoided all artifice and

---

35 Egan citing Su Shi, *Su Shi, Word, Image, and Deed*, 39.

36 This argument derives from an important insight first developed by Peter Bol, *This Culture of Ours* (Stanford: Stanford University Press, 1992), 59–66; 73–74.

37 Powers, "Temporal Logic," 759–761.

Figure 6: Distant hills in the Dong Yuan style beyond the gate to Su Shi's home. Qiao Zhongchang, Chinese (active late 11th–early 12th century). *Illustration to the Second Prose Poem on the Red Cliff*, Northern Song Dynasty (960–1127 C.E). Handscroll, ink on paper. Image & colophon: 12 x 247 3/4 inches (30.48 x 629.29 cm). The Nelson-Atkins Museum of Art, Kansas City, Missouri. Purchase: Nelson Gallery Foundation, F80-5. Photography by the author.

painterly skill. Rather than "naturalistic" *ziran*, he described Dong's work as "natural and authentic" *tianzhen* 天真.[38]

Recall that Du Fu's poetry had inspired similar epithets, for these were core literati values. Therefore, within the logic of poetic citation, Dong Yuan's style could serve as metonymy for those same qualities. In his handscroll, Qiao appears to be hinting that Su Shi, though exiled and a criminal, remained natural and authentic, for Dong Yuan hills appear outside Su's yard twice in the painting, and these are the only times Dong's style is referenced in the entire work. As with literati references to Du Fu's critical poetry, only the cognoscenti would recognize the meaning encoded within the style.

One might inquire, if the literati rejected the horizon and other technical tricks of naturalistic picturing, and moreover were using style to encode specific terms such as "natural" and "genuine," why did they not adopt a generalizing style like that of medieval art (East or West), or the poster art of modern times? The answer is that, unlike the conditions giving rise to those styles, facts and time remained key elements of the literati ethos. Their citations would make no sense except as tokens of specific moments in historical time. More critically still, the facts they employed to make their pictorial arguments were

---

38 Mi Fei (1051–1107), *Hua shi*, in *Meishu congshu*, series II, volume 9:11.

their own personal actions, sweeps of the brush or whimsical interventions that acquired meaning only in relation to the cultural conventions they flaunted. Ironically, it was those conditions that allowed these men so boldly to challenge pictorial and literary practice at a time when they could not do so in the political realm.

References

Bachhofer, Ludwig, *A Short History of Chinese Art* (New York, 1946).

Bai Juyi, *Ji hua* (*A Record of Painting*), Zhang Chunlin 张春林 ed., *Baijuyi quanji* (*Collected works of Bai Juyi*) (Beijing: Zhongguo wenshi chubanshe, 1996), 755–756.

Bai Juyi, "Yi fengjian, lun junxian (against feudalism and for salaried administration)" in Zhang Chunlin张春林 ed., *Baijuyi quanji* (Collected works of Bai Juyi) (Beijing: Zhongguo wenshi chubanshe, 1996), 1044–1045.

Bai Juyi, "Yu yuanjiu shu" (A Letter for Yuan Zhen), in Zhou Shaoliang, ed., *Quan tangwen xinbian*, (Collected essays from the Tang dynasty), Vol. 3, No.3 (Changchun: Jilin wenshi Press, 2000), 7622.

Barnhart, Richard, "Li Kung-lin's Use of Past Styles," in *Artists and Traditions: Uses of the Past in Chinese Culture*, ed. Christian F. Murck (Princeton, NJ: Princeton University Press, 1976), 51–72.

Bol, Peter, "Whither the Emperor: Emperor Huizong, the New Policies, and the Tang-Song Transition" *The Journal of Song-Yuan Studies* 31 (2001), 103–134.

Bol, Peter, *This Culture of Ours* (Stanford: Stanford University Press, 1992).

Bryson, Norman, *Word and Image: French Painting of the Ancien Regime* (Cambridge, 1980).

Egan, Ronald, *Word, Image and Deed in the Life of Su Shi* (Cambridge, 1994).

Harrist, Robert E., *Painting and Private Life in Eleventh-Century China: Mountain Villa by Li Gonglin* (Princeton, NJ: Princeton University Press, 1998).

Li Shu李樹, *Zhongguo keju shihua* (A history of China's civil service examination) (Jinan: Qilu shushe 2007).

Liu Zongyuan (773-819), 'Fengjian lun', in Lü Ch'ing-fei 吕晴飞, ed., *Liu Zongyuan sanwen*, 3 vols., (Taipei, World publishing house, 1994), I:23–32.

Mi Fu (1051–1107), *Hua shi* (A History of painting), in *Meishu congshu*, series II, volume 9: 11.

Murck, Alfreda, *Poetry and painting in Song China: the subtle art of dissent* (Cambridge: Cambridge University Press, 2000).

Powers, Martin, "Imitation and Reference in China's Pictorial Tradition," in Wu Hung, ed., *Reinventing the Past: Archaism and Antiquarianism in Chinese Art and Visual Culture* (Chicago: Art Media Resources, 2010), 103–126.

Powers, Martin, "Picturing Time in Song Painting and Poetry", in Joseph Lam et. al., eds., *The Senses of the City: Perceptions of Hangzhou and Southern Song China, 1127–1279* (Hong Kong: Hong Kong University Press, 2016), 55–72.

Powers, Martin, "Recurrent dialogues in the history of Chinese and English garden design," in Malcolm Baker and Andrew Hemingway, eds., *Art as Worldmaking: Critical Essays on Realism and Naturalism* (Manchester: Manchester University Press, 2019), 115–127.

Powers, Martin, *China and England: the Preindustrial Struggle for Justice in Word and Image* (London: Routledge, 2018).

Powers, Martin, "The Temporal Logic of Citation in Chinese Art," *Art History*, vol. 37, no. 4 (September, 2014), 745–763.

Qu Chaoli, *Songdai difangzhengfu minshi shenpan zhineng yanjiu* (The function of civil courts in local government in Song times) (Chengdu: Bashu Shudian, 2003), 16.

Shen Kuo, *Mengxi bitan* (Notes from the stream of dreams), vol. 3 (Yangzhou: Guangling shushe, 2003).

Strassberg, Richard, trans. and annot., *Inscribed Landscapes: Travel Writing from Imperial China* (Berkeley: University of California Press, 1994).

Wang Fuzhi, *Song lun* (Essays on Song History), In S. Y. Shu (ed.), *Wang Fuzhi zhi zhuzuo* (The Works of Wang Fuzhi) (Beijing: Zhonghua Publishing, 1964).

Yu Hui, *Yinyou yu qujian: qingmingshanghetu jiemalu* (Hidden Concerns and Indirect Dissent: Deciphering the 'Spring Festival on the River' Scroll) (Beijing: Peking University Press, 2015).

FOONG Ping

Producing Shu Culture: Why Painters Needed Court Titles in Tenth-Century Sichuan

Introduction

The government bureaucracy's system of official ranks and titles is a rich source for studying spatial imagination in middle period China. This is because titular hierarchy and its vocabulary intrinsically construct space, which in turn reflect power relations within the imperial city and beyond. As is well known, titles do not simply describe daily function. Nor does rank always precisely coincide with post. Instead, a dual-ranking system expressed personal rank status separately from one's actual job. Articulated in long and complicated sequences, titles provide information about salary levels and other aspects of official service – for example, education and mode of entry into service, and career ladders prescribed according to individual prestige that enabled routine promotions. Different types of titles, held in parallel with personal rank, indicated someone's work as a commission or duty assignment.[1]

Artists were interlopers within this highly competitive system and signs of their participation is therefore intriguing. The population of makers in an imperial city ranged from unskilled laborers to workshop craftsmen to technocrats who provided their skills as support staff. Of this last group, only calligraphers and painters concern us below. These two fields of artistic practice held differing amounts of prestige in middle period China. As the most literate of the technocrats, calligraphers were the most likely to crossover and be awarded titles usually held by the bureaucracy's regular officers. Professional painters generally came from families of lower social standing and could not qualify for careers as officials, but top painters occasionally held official titles too. These titles therefore contain rich information for evaluating their social and institutional status. From the Tang dynasty onwards, painters' titles were for the most part sinecures – nominal commissions having little to do with their painting ability. The titles may have provided a stipend above what they received in

---

1 For an introduction to the structure of the Song dynasty civil service, see Charles Hartman, "Sung Government and Politics." In Chaffee, John W. and Denis Twitchett, eds., *The Cambridge History of China, Volume 5, Part Two: Sung China, 960–1279* (Cambridge: Cambridge University Press, 2009), 19–138, see pages 49–80.

their regular position as artists. In any case, the extent to which the hierarchies of officialdom flexed to recognize certain artists is a little-studied phenomenon with broad implications for the roles that they played in political culture.

This paper considers title sequences held by Sichuanese painters from the kingdom of Shu in comparison with their Tang-dynasty predecessors. We first focus on key titles awarded to the 9th-century court painter Cheng Xiuji 程修己 (804–63), and those of Lü Yao 呂嶤 (9th century) and Zhu Qian 竹虔 (9th century) who served at the capital cities of both Tang and Shu. Parallels and departures between Tang and Shu practice emerge when we juxtapose these Tang painters against Shu painters active a century later. It becomes clear that Sichuan's rulers regularized stipendiary titles for their court painters to a greater extent, and likely had their own motivations for rewarding artists in this manner. The following analysis suggests that, by the 10th century, titular awards formalized Sichuan's painting styles and family traditions as cultural products distinct to this geographic region. This articulation of cultural distinction expressed the independence and regional power of Shu rulers just before Song reunification.

Painters' titles and their significances

When rulers use titles to acknowledge the value of court artists, these titles become a rich resource for examining conditions of court patronage. Painters' titles contain concrete data for quantifying one type of status: not personal social standing, but rather an individual's institutional status accorded through official channels of recruitment, education, rank, and promotion. Such processes recognize artists as bureaucratic functionaries, as elements in the machinery of government. A title offers not only economic recompense but can also show an artist's service as a constituent element of a ruler's authority. By examining the titles that artists were permitted or prohibited, we better understand the roles art played in representing legitimate rule. In short, titles provide an opportunity to study institutional patronage on its own terms rather than as an individual's patronage and collecting pathology – writ large.

One feature of institutional patronage is worthy of deep scrutiny. From the Tang dynasty onwards, top court calligraphers and painters were occasionally raised above their peers with titular privileges commonly awarded to regular officials of the bureaucracy. For government officers, a variety of titles denote different prize categories: some titles provide monetary stipends whereas others offer the recipient a higher rank status than their actual, official rank. For a professional painter, this form of superlative recognition was exceedingly rare since the two worlds could not be further apart. It almost goes without saying that painters rarely had the required education or family background to take advantage of such privileges – no matter if their access to the official rewards system was only temporary, provisional, or informal in nature.

If we take as a given that rulers regularly cultivated art and culture as a figure for dynastic stability, it is equally important to acknowledge that their purpose was not simply lavish expenditure. Titles are a principal means for a ruler (and his agents) to incorporate artists into a courtly establishment, and they therefore signify official endorsement of certain artistic styles or traditions that those artists represent. Titles define court-approved standards. They form the basis for building a tangible form of cultural power – a literal product that could then be deployed as a component of state diplomacy.

This was the case for Huang Quan 黃筌 (903?–965), by far our best recorded middle-period painter for the titles he received. According to written sources, he was a highly versatile professional painter who was excellent in multiple genres – bird-and-flower, landscape, and figural subjects – each being specializations that require very different skills. In Sichuan before the Song conquest, he provided distinguished service under the Meng regime of the Shu kingdom. While serving the second ruler of Later Shu 後蜀 (934–65), Meng Chang 孟昶 (b. 919, r. 934–65), Huang Quan's paintings cultivated interregional diplomacy and trade with neighboring kingdoms in the Yangzi region. As I have demonstrated elsewhere, he received four official titles during the 10th century and each title further enhanced the ability of his art to function as state gifts. He likely gained these entitlements due to some combination of his artistic and administrative talents, but especially because his art came to serve official purposes for Shu's rulers.[2]

Why do high titles with no substantive duties – in essence empty titles – merit our consideration? First of all, we must accept that designations without an attached job are valuable to study, that sinecures are meaningful. This recognition doesn't come easily because there are few more challenging problems than the complex workings of the bureaucracy's ranking system. A second factor that presents a challenge in this project is that our sample is inherently small: painters rarely received ranked official titles. They much more often held unranked titles related to their function, the most long-lived being the prestigious Hanlin *daizhao* 翰林待詔 (Expectant Official of the Hanlin) denoting

---

2 Huang Quan's titular recognition is discussed in Foong Ping, "On rulers and painters: Issues of institutional patronage and transmitted hierarchies," conference paper for the panel, "National Committee on the History of Art State of the Field: New Frontiers in Chinese Art." College Art Association, 102nd Annual Conference, Chicago, 2014.

various types of top servitors awaiting the emperor's summons at the Hanlin Academy (Hanlinyuan 翰林院).

Highly recognized painters were occasionally extended sumptuary benefits that belonged to the highest echelons of regular officers. The most notable and conspicuous of these benefits was official regalia known as "purple with gold fish-pouch" 紫金魚袋, which were honors normally designating high ministers Rank 3 and up. In Sichuan, Huang Quan received his purple robes after 926 CE from the founder of Later Shu, Meng Zhixiang 孟知祥 (879–934, r. 934). Huang's second son Huang Jubao 黃居寶 (dates unclear), also a noted calligrapher, and fifth son Huang Jucai 黃居寀 (933–ca. 993) were both conferred "purple with gold fish-pouch." Presumably, the sons were extended this honor based not only on their own successes but with regard to their father's achievement. In some respects, the rationale behind providing formal recognition to the Huang lineage with official robes is reminiscent of *yin* privilege 蔭補, the right of high officials to protect their families by directly appointing sons to office.

Huang Quan's fifth son Huang Jucai later served the first Song dynasty emperors and they awarded him a civil-service prestige title (*san guan* 散官) as Grand Master for Court Audiences (Chaoqing daifu 朝請大夫). To be sure this title denoted a relatively modest Rank 5b1 at level twelve of twenty-nine levels, but it was nevertheless a personal rank within the regular bureaucracy.[3] Given to all men who enter official service, a prestige title fixes one's rank status and assures a state emolument (grain allowance, money, provisions etc.) regardless of whether one is in active service with a commission or inactive. Huang Jucai's 5b1 rank gained him the associated state emolument but also a place during court audiences alongside others within the civil-service hierarchy – a rare and considerable honor for a professional painter. But why did Song emperors reward this Sichuan painter in this way? It does not suffice to describe the awards held by either Huang Quan or his sons as anomalous special treatment, merely a matter of royal largess.

---

3 The prestige title Grand Master for Court Audiences (Chaoqing daifu 朝請大夫) was held by civil-service officers, see Gong Yanming 龔延明, *Songdai guanzhi cidian* 宋代官制辭典 (Dictionary of Song dynasty official titles) (Beijing: Zhonghua shuju, 1997), 561. In the early Northern Song, the two types of prestige titles – civil and military – each had twenty-nine ranks. See Gong Yanming 30 and 31, Table 10 and Table 11, for lists of these civil prestige titles and military prestige titles, respectively.

Some nomenclature of official service for artists

A brief notice on the structural means for retaining artists at court is important to establish before going further. Men with different social backgrounds, specializations, and skill levels received different treatment. From Tang dynasty onwards, libraries and some other government agencies engaged scribes, copyists, illustrators, and other technical sub-officials as professional support staff. Posts at an agency were marked, for instance, with the suffix *zhi* 直, meaning to "take up duty." Men of learning 學士 charged with compiling imperially sponsored scholarly works in the Academy of Scholarly Worthies (Jixiandian shuyuan 集賢殿書院) had use of both *shuzhi* 書直 and *huazhi* 畫直, writers on clerical duty and illustrators on painting duty, respectively.[4]

Also during the Tang, men with calligraphic ability above that needed for clerical work were *shishu* 侍書 (Attendant Calligrapher). This title comprises the word *shi* 侍, "to serve," hence describes someone's function as calligrapher.[5] Some calligraphers also held a nominal title providing the appointee with a rank grade and the associated salary. Perhaps because calligraphers were regularly called to teach the art form to princes and other members of the royal family, this nominal title was often associated with the establishment of the Crown Prince (Donggong wangfu 東宮王府). Conceivably, another reason for providing calligraphers with official titles may have arisen out of a desire for visual symmetry in the carved inscriptions of public monuments. The texts of stone steles and epitaphs required collaboration, and so the names and titles of the

---

4 See Charles Hucker, *A Dictionary of Official Titles in Imperial China* (Stanford: Stanford University Press, 1998, first published 1985), 5420 and 2803, for *shuzhi* 書直 (Auxiliary Scribe) and *huazhi* 畫直 (Auxiliary Illustrator). From 731 CE to the end of Tang dynasty, both were retitled *zhiyuan* 直院 (Auxiliary). For more on *huazhi*, see Li Wankang 李万康, "Tang dai Hanlinyuan hua daizhao renyong zhidu kao shu" 唐代翰林院画待诏任用制度考述, *Gugong bouwyuan yuankan* 故宫博物院院刊 4 (2017): 46–57, see pages 49–50. Li Wankang argues through the case of celebrated painter Wu Daozi 吳道子 (ca. 689–after 755) that *huazhi* and Hanlin *daizhao* were separate systems with similar stipend rankings until around the 9th century of the middle-Tang period, when more systematic regulations instituted *daizhao* as a promotion for *huazhi*.
5 See Li Jiebing 李潔冰 and Li Zhenggeng 李正庚, "Lun Tang dai shishu ji qi zhidu hua" 論唐代侍書及其制度化, *Xueshu jiaoliu* 學術交流 4 (2008): 171–74. Wang Yuanjun 王元军, "Wan Tang yu nei gongfeng caoshu seng Bianguang shiji tantao" 晚唐御内供奉草书僧辩光事迹探讨, *Zhongguo shufa* 中国书法 2 (2005): 28–30, discusses titles held by Tang-dynasty monks in relation to known titles and combinations held by other calligraphers at court, including Hanlin *gongfeng* 翰林供奉, Hanlin *daizhao* 翰林待詔, *shishu* 侍書, *shishu daizhao* 侍書待詔, *shishu xueshi* 侍書學士, etc.

officer who authored the text and the calligrapher who provided the handwriting may appear acknowledged together.

For someone with creative talent during the Tang, the highest possible achievement was to become Hanlin *daizhao* as a member of the Hanlin Academy, an institution that comprised of all the emperor's most valued courtiers – including scholars, poets, Buddhist and Daoist priests, alchemists, diviners, calligraphers, chess players, and artisans. Or as one Tang-period source put it, "all those under Heaven called to serve for their artistic and artisanal skills" 天下以藝能伎術見召者.[6] Another important post was *nei gongfeng* 內供奉.[7] Under Emperor Tang Xuanzong 唐玄宗 (r. 712–56) in the 8th century, the title sometimes appears within a phrase referring to someone who is "called to serve in the inner palace" (*zhao runei gongfeng* 召入內供奉) or as a suffix to an official title. In either case, the title or suffix referred to people chosen on a rotational basis to be the emperor's close attendants, and the men on duty included those providing artistic services.[8]

By the mid-8th century, *gongfeng* became more distinct as a title and distinguishable from *daizhao*. Both titles were affiliated to the Hanlin Academy. This is known through the case of Liu Qin 劉秦 (8th century), a court calligrapher

---

6 Wei Zhiyi 韋執誼 (769–814), *Hanlinyuan gushi* 翰林院故事 (Stories of the Hanlin Institute), 786 CE, in Hong Zun 洪遵 (1120–74), comp. *Hanyuan qunshu* 翰苑群書 (Collected writings on the Hanlin Institute) (hereafter HYQS), 12 *juan* (Beijing: Zhonghua shuju, 1991), 11–16, see page 11. Also see Hong Zun, comp. *Hanyuan yishi* 翰苑遺事 (Incidents of past ages at the Hanlin Institute), in HYQS, 76–89, cited page 83. For surviving texts on the history of the Hanlin Academy and Hanlin Institute, see Friedrich Alexander Bischoff, *La forêt des pinceaux: Étude sur l'Académie du Han-lin sous la dynastie des T'ang et traduction du Han lin tche*, Bibliothèque de l'Institut des hautes études chinoises 17 (Paris: Presses Universitaires de France, 1963).

7 For an introduction to Hanlin *daizhao* and *gongfeng* titles held by Tang-dynasty calligraphers (monks included), see Wang Yuanjun 王元军, "Tang dai de Hanlin shu daizhao ji qi huodong kao shu" 唐代的翰林书待诏及其活动考述, *Meishu yanjiu* 美术研究 3 (2003): 100–104. Wang Yuanjun refutes other scholarship claiming Hanlin *daizhao* and Hanlin *gongfeng* to be synonymous. Also see Wang Haibin 王海宾, *Tang dai Hanlin shu daizhao zhidu zongkao* 唐代翰林书待诏制度综考 (M.A. Thesis, Jilin University, 2008), for epitaphs and surviving steles related to this subject in addition to the transmitted texts.

8 See Hucker, *Dictionary of Official Titles*, 3418–3423, for variations on *gongfeng* (literally, "those who wait upon" or "those who serve"). From the Tang, *gongfeng* and *nei gongfeng* appear as a suffix or appendix to titles, referring to men chosen on rotational basis to be the emperor's close attendants and to qualified officials on duty within the palace awaiting regular appointment. Hucker, *Dictionary of Official Titles*, 3422, from Song onwards, Palace Attendant (*gongfeng neiting* 供奉内庭) is "a collective reference to various kinds of eunuchs, palace women, officials, and specially talented outsiders in painting, etc." According to Gong Yanming, *Songdai guanzhi*, 598 and 591, Palace Servitor (*gongfeng guan* 供奉官) is established in 1112 CE as the highest of twelve rank titles granted to eunuchs.

whose title sequences are detailed in two surviving epitaphs where he is recorded as the calligrapher.[9] Liu served as Hanlin Academy *gongfeng* under Emperor Tang Xuanzong in 754 CE. He was promoted seven years later in 761 CE to Hanlin Academy *daizhao* under the next emperor, Tang Suzong 唐肅宗 (r. 756–62). His title sequences, before and after promotion, begin with a ranked prestige title followed by another ranked title for salary grade through an affiliation to a palace agency. Both sequences end with his function as calligrapher, with an unranked title indicating his level within the Hanlin Academy's hierarchy. Thus, we can examine the dynamics between Liu's personal rank and salary grade versus his actual job as calligrapher during this moment of career transition.

Before promotion, 754 CE:

Gentleman for Court Discussion (Rank 6a1),
Acting (*xing*) Director of Gatekeepers (Rank 6b2) in the Heir Apparent's Household, and Hanlin Academy *gongfeng*.[10]
朝議郎, 行太子宮門郎, 翰林院供奉

After promotion, 761 CE:

Gentleman for Court Discussion (Rank 6a1),
Acting (*xing*) Aide at the Court of Imperial Regalia (Rank 6b1),
and Hanlin Academy *daizhao*.[11]
朝議郎, 行衛尉寺承, 翰林院待詔

---

9 For Liu Qin's 劉秦 (8th century) epitaph dated 754 CE (Tianbao 天寶 13) that records his service as a calligrapher, see Zhou Shaoliang 周紹良 and Zhao Chaofu 趙超副 eds., *Tangdai muzhi huibian* 唐代墓誌彙編 (Compilation of Tang dynasty epitaphs), 2 vols. (Shanghai: Shanghai guji chubanshe, 1992), see vol. 2, 1711–12: Tianbao 258, "Da Tang Huang gu di wu sun muzhiming" 大唐皇故第五孫墓誌銘. For his epitaph dated 761 CE (Shangyuan 上元 2), see Lu Zengxiang 陸增祥, *Baqiong shi jinshi buzheng* 八瓊室金石补正, *juan* 59 (Beijing: Wenwu chubanshe, 1985), 407: "Liu Fengzhi muzhi" 劉奉芝墓誌.

10 For Gentleman for Court Discussion (Chaoyi lang 朝議郎), see *Tang liu dian* 唐六典, j. 2; Hucker, *Dictionary of Official Titles*, 325. For Director of Gatekeepers in the Heir Apparent's Household (Taizi gongmen lang 太子宮門郎), see *Tang liu dian*, j. 26; Hucker, *Dictionary of Official Titles*, 3451. Two Directors were responsible for gatekeeping duty in the Heir Apparent's household.

11 For Aide at the Court of Imperial Regalia (Weiwei si cheng 衛尉寺承), see *Tang liu dian*, j. 16. Hucker, *Dictionary of Official Titles*, 7683: the Court of Imperial Regalia was in charge of "manufacturing and storing weapons, tents, insignia, and other kinds of military regalia." See also Gong Yanming, *Songdai guanzhi*, 304: a salary rank (Rank 6b1) from Tang to early Song. Also Gong, 688, Table 12, #27: a salary rank in the Song dynasty that converted to Rank 8b2 during the Yuanfeng era 元豐 (1078–1085).

This is a good example of how the bureaucracy's dual-ranking system was applied in the case of an artist. Note that Liu kept the same prestige title as Gentleman for Court Discussion while changing his salary grade from Director of Gatekeepers in 754 CE to Aide at the Court of Imperial Regalia in 761 CE. However, even as Liu's salary was increased from Rank 6b2 to Rank 6b1, the prefix *xing* 行, "acting," is used to differentiate him from regular officers and to indicate that he was actually of lower status than was appropriate for the office (or that the office was temporary). Besides a pay increase, we further surmise a change in Liu's status per others at the Hanlin Academy because he was appointed *gongfeng* and *daizhao* in succession. Now holding the Hanlin Academy's top post, his standing was augmented even without a concurrent increase in his personal rank as Gentleman for Court Discussion.

The artist title Hanlin *daizhao* survives the fall of Tang, and aspects of both Tang and 10th-century legacies for rewarding painters survive Song unification. In the below, we examine how the 8th-century Tang practice of titling calligraphers Hanlin *daizhao* together with a sequence of seniority or stipendiary titles was extended to top painters more consistently by the 10th century in Sichuan. For painters' titles, the most distinctive pattern that I found relates to Hanlin *daizhao* plus honors (*ci* 賜, henceforth *ci*-honors) as the base qualification to be considered for extra income and lofty recognition through a prestige title and, above that, an additional sinecurial merit title (*xun* 勳). Another interesting pattern is the use of modifying prefixes such as "acting1" (*jianjiao* 檢校), "acting2" (*shou* 守), and "probationary" (*shi* 試), denoting painters' offices as temporary, rotational, or honorary. In Sichuan, such titles may indicate (temporary?) salary increases or perhaps they were extravagant ornaments to one's name. Yet the ornamentation was purposeful: high titles for painters not only raised the status of individual talents but also the overall prestige of Sichuan's painting traditions.

A spatial methodology

An imperial city's economy of power is expressed through an amalgam of physical and non-physical relationships, such as in locating government office buildings near the emperor and accommodating the bureaucracy of officers within palace walls and institutions. Take for example the expressions inner court (*neiting* 內庭) and outer court (*waichao* 外朝) describing those who served in the Song dynasty's imperial city. The former comprised the emperor's extended household, including empresses, eunuchs, and top artists, whereas the latter were civil-service officials entrusted with the power to discharge governance or to administer the central government's communications and records, from high ministers to library staff. Of course, each class of people had their own distinct, ranked hierarchies, but within the imperial city, the inner and outer courts combined their capacities.

For instance, the Institute of the Assembled Wise (Jixiandian 集賢殿) and the Hanlin Institute of Academicians (Hanlin xueshiyuan 翰林學士院) were populated by scholar-officials of the outer court but as non-administrative, advisory bodies, paralleled the inner court for their informal access to the emperor. Both Institutes were allowed to use calligraphers and painters attending the emperor in his palaces as their support staff. These elite artists-in-waiting generally held the top title of Hanlin *daizhao* as part of the inner court's Hanlin Academy, a eunuch-supervised organ. As expected, painters from the Tang to the Song dynasty were mainly members of the inner court but, surprisingly, they sometimes simultaneously held stipendiary outer-court titles. Great differences in social status between inner and outer court members notwithstanding, artists occasionally borrowed their bureaucratic location from the organizations which they served. Our attention to whether artist titles stem from the inner or outer court is therefore a study of spatial operations, but this analysis also has historical and geographic dimensions.

Inherently a spatial construct, titular rank in the official bureaucracy articulates one's hierarchic location relative to other officers. Expressed as inner or outer, civil or military, left or right, regular or honorary, permanent or temporary, an appointee's title sequence contains a precise calculation of rank and status negotiated in bureaucratic time and space. Sequences are combined from different categories to create different permutations, and they comprise of highly technical information to define a regular officer's personal rank and salary as opposed to his job. The prestige title noted above is one such category and the merit title is another. In the Tang dynasty, prestige titles were awarded based on nobility, meritorious service, performance assessment, morality, etc. They determined seniority for salary and allowances and (except for in the early Song dynasty) had no relation to an officer's actual function. Prestige titles are divided into two hierarchies. During the Tang, members of the civil service had twenty-nine levels from Rank 1b to 9b2, whereas the military service had forty-five levels for men with administrative responsibilities rather than those engaged in active military action (henceforth civil prestige title and military prestige title). Merit titles were originally non-hereditary awards for military achievement in the Tang, honorifics for both civil and military officers that were automatically earned along with personal rank and did not exceed it.[12]

Civil prestige titles were extended to elite artists and eventually merit titles too – first to calligraphers then painters. Artists were rarely given these kinds of titles and reports of the occasions usually survive only in fragments. Indeed, studying arcane nomenclature with such a small data set entails many complications, but some of the difficulties can be overcome by applying a spatial methodology. In fact, there are multiple ways to apply a spatial frame to artist titles and institutions and the results generated from different approaches have rich and related implications.

Since the Hanlin Academy took various forms as it evolved in different geographic regions during the 10th century, I noted versions of the institution for its political symbolism in a previous study. There were some similarities and variations in the Hanlin Academy organized by powers in different places: the Southern Tang court in Nanjing; the Former and Later Shu courts in Sichuan; and the Academy at the Song capital in Bianliang under the first Song dynasty emperors. As these powers each purported to revive a venerable Tang institution, thus the data takes on geospatial form.[13]

On the topic of artist titles, I have focused more specifically on the shape of the Song dynasty's Hanlin Painting Academy. This ongoing project takes hierarchy itself as the subject of analysis. The Song clearly built its Academy with more official tiers than ever before, but it is important to be aware of the many reasons for deepening hierarchy. One enduring factor was the technocratic need to classify artistic ability – to grade painters according to their skills and to define technical standards of painting practice. My research also elucidates how a taller hierarchy with more levels provided the means to combine painters recruited from different channels, such as by invitation, recommendation, and competition. During the founding of the Song dynasty, it was useful for integrating those

---

12 These definitions are based on Hucker, *Dictionary of Official Titles*, 4868 and 2711, and Xie Baocheng, trans. Chen Mirong, *A Brief History of the Official System in China* (London: Paths International Ltd., and Social Sciences Academic Press, China, 2013), "Ranks, titles, and salaries," 173–85. For further discussion of the changes enacted for prestige titles in the Song period, see Gong Yanming, *Songdai guanzhi*, 30–32. As did painters on occasion, the palace eunuch corps shared civil-service officer titles before they had their own scale of twelve levels by 1112 CE.

13 See Foong Ping, "The Structural Position of Court Artists in the Song Dynasty: Issues of Rank, Title and Legitimate Rule During the Founding Decades" 宋代宮廷畫家的官署機構, in Wu Hung, ed., *Tenth-Century China and Beyond: Art and Visual Culture in a Multi-centered Age* (Chicago: Center for the Art of East Asia, University of Chicago, and Art Media Resources, 2013), 350–63.

repatriated or captured from enemy territory, since artists too had to be suitably assimilated under Song rule.[14]

The present paper aims to further develop a spatial methodology for interpreting artist titles. Mentioned in the above survey of Tang nomenclature, upper-echelon artists mostly derived status from their positions as inner-court servitors. However, some rose above their technocratic function with the personal ranks and associated emoluments of outer-court officials. As for regular officers, it is important to distinguish rank and status from function for artists. But studying top artists also requires our close attention to two properties that underlie their title sequences, namely, hierarchy and classification. Hierarchy indicates somebody's relative standing higher or lower in a scale. Classification conceives of the appointee's status or function in relation to the inner court or outer court.

The case of Tang calligrapher Liu Qin discussed above well illustrates the need to examine each component of his title sequence for these two spatial properties. Recall now that Liu's title sequence establishes his structural location in three ways: through a personal title and rank; a salary title and rank; and a functional title. His civil prestige title establishes his place in a scale shared with outer-court civil officers. His salary originates from inner-court palace agencies, namely, the establishment of the Crown Prince before promotion, and Court Regalia after promotion. His artist title indicates his level at the Hanlin Academy as a member of the inner court. Unlike an officer's substantive, ranked duty assignment indicating work, titles at the academy are unranked. Instead, they judge the holder's skill level as an artist. At first graded Hanlin *gongfeng*, Liu Qin was re-evaluated worthy of rising to Hanlin *daizhao* and thus promoted.

We must note that the classification of Liu Qin's inner-court or outer-court status is neither static nor easily fixed. Indeed, complications in classification arise from the social standing and education of the appointee and from temporality, whether a position is ad hoc or permanent. Do we classify a calligrapher's *zhi* 直 duty at the Academy of Scholarly Worthies as outer court since it was a scholar's institution? How do we describe artists who served as supporting staff to central government officers as opposed to civil-service officers who

---

14 The evidence for how the Song Hanlin Painting Academy was impacted by its adoption of the Shu kingdom's system of painters' titles is discussed in Foong Ping, "Representing Nation at the Painting Academy of Song Taizong," on the panel, "Song Taizong's Culture Revolution: The Transformation of Imperial Art, Literature, and Statecraft during the Late Tenth Century," *Asia in Motion: Ideas, Institutions, Identities*. AAS-in-ASIA, Academia Sinica, Taipei, Taiwan, 2015.

also served as artists – are they inner or outer? Despite these hurdles it nevertheless remains important to evaluate how a title describes the value of an artist's service: whether closer to statecraft and hence to the outer court, or further away from statecraft and hence closer to the imperial court. An artist's standing is clearly not describable in black and white terms and indeed we discover the careers of calligraphers and painters expressed with ranks along an inner-outer continuum through a variety of accommodations in middle-period China.

In the below, we engage with the topic of Sichuan's painters as an inner-outer court spatial problem. For 9th- and 10th-century painters in the Shu kingdom, syntactical patterns come to light amidst bewildering detail from arranging their titles according to titular categories analogous to those discovered in Liu Qin's 8th-century case. Greater resolution is indeed gained by differentiating titles that denote artistic function and ability from those assumed from the outer court – that is, by paying attention to both hierarchy and classification.

Sichuan's painters according to Huang Xiufu

The most important source for middle-period painters' titles is undoubtedly Huang Xiufu's 黃休復 (b. ca. 954–59) *Yizhou minghua lu* 益州名畫錄 (Record of Famous Paintings in Yizhou). This book contains detailed descriptions of the careers of 10th-century Shu painters. Other early catalogs that modern scholars rely on for painters' biographies typically only include fragments of titular information, whereas Huang's contemporary account records full title sequences. Indeed, given his meticulous documentation, we can presume that the Sichuan native Huang Xiufu had access to original records not available to other authors.[15]

The table in Figure 1 contains all painters recorded in Huang Xiufu's book who received either Hanlin *daizhao* and/or official regalia from the late-9th to the 10th century. Eighteen distinct names are arranged roughly in chronological order. The list begins with late-Tang court painters Lü Yao, Zhu Qian, and

---

15 An important English-language study of Huang Xiufu's 黃休復 (b. ca. 954–59) *Yizhou minghua lu* 益州名畫錄 (Record of Famous Paintings in Yizhou) is Evelyne Mesnil, "Didactic Paintings between Power and Devotion: The Monastery Dashengcisi 大聖慈寺 in Chengdu (8th–10th c.)," in Christian Wittern and Shi Lishan eds., *Essays on East Asian Religion and Culture: Festschrift in honour of Nishiwaki Tsuneki on the occasion of his 65th birthday* (Kyoto: Editorial committee for the Festschrift in honor of Nishiwaki Tsuneki, 2007), 98–148. Mesnil has published extensively in French on the arts of the Shu kingdom.

Chang Zhongyin 常重胤 (9th century) who served Emperor Tang Xizong 唐僖宗 (r. 873–88). Lü and Zhu had already attained the level of Hanlin *daizhao* at the Tang court before arriving in Sichuan, whereas Chang received his title in Sichuan during Emperor Xizong's exile there. The author Huang Xiufu regarded the three men as Shu painters even though they were not Sichuan natives. The Sichuan natives recorded by Huang served as painters mostly under the Wang and Meng regimes of Shu. Note that Huang Quan and Huang Jucai each appear twice in the table. Huang Quan's second appearance near the end of the list refers to his final promotion in Shu, whereas the very last entry in the table records a set of titles that Huang Jucai received from the early Song-dynasty emperors after relocating from Sichuan to the Song capital of Bianliang.

Figure 1's titular categories are arranged in columns from left to right. Titles pertaining to the inner court are at left, outer court at right; unranked titles at left, ranked titles at right. The one exception is *ci*-honors. As earlier mentioned, official regalia comprising robes and the fish-pouch insignia visually displayed the ranks of regular officials, but high-ranked robe colors in purple and crimson were occasionally extended to calligraphers and painters. Title sequences invariable list *ci*-honors last, after someone's commission or merit title at the end of the sequence. And indeed this is the form for painters' titles in Huang Xiufu's book. But rather than follow this syntax, *ci*-honors is instead located adjacent to the Hanlin Academy column in our table because it sharpens the pattern. There is no detriment to the data's integrity in doing so because *ci*-honors are awarded to practically all the Hanlin *daizhao* listed and therefore can be treated as tied together reliably for our analysis.

By arranging Huang Xiufu's records according to their titular categories in Figure 1, we can now draw some initial conclusions. First, Sichuan's painters were rewarded the Hanlin *daizhao* title in much greater numbers than at the Tang court. Not including Lü Yao, Zhu Qian, and Chang Zhongyin, who received their titles under Emperor Tang Xizong, fifteen awards were made over a period of about sixty years during the Former Shu 前蜀 (907–25) and Later Shu under the Wang and Meng regimes. Nearly all received *ci*-honors as well – either purple robes plus gold fish-pouch, or crimson robes plus fish-pouch. In other words, Hanlin *daizhao* was practically synonymous with robes of office in 10th-century Sichuan. Second, this level of achievement was, in turn, the base qualification for additional outer-court titles. We discover from Figure 1 that a subset of five men received this consideration with prestige titles and other honorifics: Ruan Zhihui 阮知誨 (10th century), his son Ruan Weide 阮惟德 (10th century), Huang Quan, his son Huang Jucai, and Li Wencai 李文才 (10th century). However, the honorifics or commissions of these five men were prefixed "acting1" (*jianjiao*), "acting2" (*shou*), or "probationary" (*shi*). Just as Tang

Date	Served f/o Father of s/o Son of	Name	Inner court title and function										Outer court title and rank	
			Palace title	Hanlin Academy 翰林院	Ci-honors 賜	Other function	Prestige title 散官 (C) Civil prestige title 文散官 (M) Military prestige title 武散官	Rank 品級	Commission or duty assignment 差遣: zhi 直(署), wei 為 Acting 行 / Acting1 檢校 / Acting2 守 / Concurrent 兼 / Probationary 試	Rank 品級	Merit title 勳銜	Rank 品級	Salary rank 寄祿官	Rank 品級
880-885	Tang Xizong in Shu 唐僖宗	Lü Yao 呂嶤		(Previously) Hanlin daizhao 翰林待詔	Crimson robes, Fish-pouch 緋魚袋		(C) Court Gentleman for Ceremonial Service 將仕郎	9b2	Acting2 Assistant Magistrate of the Luo District of Han County 守漢州雒縣主簿	9a2-9b1				
880-885	Tang Xizong in Shu 唐僖宗	Zhu Qian 竹虔		(Previously) Hanlin daizhao 翰林待詔	Crimson robes, fish-pouch 緋魚袋		(C) Court Gentleman for Ceremonial Service 將仕郎	9b2	Acting2 Assistant Magistrate of the Luo District of Han County 守漢州雒縣主簿	9a2-9b1				
885	Tang Xizong in Shu 唐僖宗	Chang Zhongyin 常重胤 s/o Chang Can 常粲		Hanlin daizhao 翰林待詔	Crimson robes, fish-pouch 緋魚袋									
907-	Wang regime	Zhao Deqi 趙德齊 s/o Zhao Wenqi 趙溫奇		Hanlin daizhao 翰林待詔	Purple robes, gold fish-pouch 紫金魚袋									
907-	Wang regime	Gao Daoxing 高道興 f/o Gao Congyu 高従遇 and Gao Wenjin 高文進		Hanlin portraiture daizhao 翰林寫貌待詔	Purple robes, gold fish-pouch 紫金魚袋									
907-	Wang Jian 王建	Fang Chongzhen 房従真		Hanlin daizhao 翰林待詔	Purple robes, gold fish-pouch 紫金魚袋									
907-	Wang Jian 王建	Song Yi 宋藝		Hanlin daizhao 翰林待詔										
918-	Wang Yan 王衍	Du Nigui 杜齯龜		Hanlin daizhao 翰林待詔	Purple robes, gold fish-pouch 紫金魚袋									
919-	Wang Yan and Meng Zhixiang 孟知祥	Ruan Zhihui 阮知誨		Hanlin daizhao 翰林待詔			(C) Grand Master of Imperial Entertainments with Silver Seal and Blue Ribbon 銀青光祿大夫	3b	Acting1 Left Vice Director of the Department of State Affairs. Concurrently Censor-in-Chief 檢校尚書左僕射兼御史大夫	3b	Supreme Pillar of State 上柱國	2a		
925-	Meng Zhixiang	Zhang Mei 張玫		Hanlin daizhao 翰林待詔	Purple robes, gold fish-pouch 紫金魚袋									
925-	Meng Zhixiang	Huang Quan 黃筌		Hanlin daizhao 翰林待詔	Purple robes, gold fish-pouch 紫金魚袋	Overseer of Academy affairs 權院事								
925-	Meng regime	Huang Jubao 黃居寶 2nd s/o Huang Quan		Hanlin daizhao 翰林待詔	Purple robes, gold fish-pouch 紫金魚袋									
925-	Meng regime	Pu Shixun 蒲師訓		Hanlin daizhao 翰林待詔	Purple robes, gold fish-pouch 紫金魚袋									
925-	Meng regime	Ruan Weide 阮惟德 s/o Ruan Zhihui 阮知誨		Hanlin daizhao 翰林待詔	Crimson robes, fish-pouch 緋魚袋		(C) Court Gentleman for Ceremonial Service 將仕郎	9b2	Probationary Court Gentleman for Fasting in the Court of Imperial Sacrifices 試太常寺齋郎	n/a				
925-	Meng regime	Huang Jucai 黃居寀 5th s/o Huang Quan		Hanlin daizhao 翰林待詔	Purple robes, gold fish-pouch 紫金魚袋		(C) Court Gentleman for Ceremonial Service 將仕郎	9b2	Probationary Court Gentleman for Consultation for the Heir Apparent 試太子鎮郎	n/a				
934-	Meng Chang 孟昶	Li Wencai 李文才		Hanlin daizhao 翰林待詔	Crimson robes, fish-pouch 緋魚袋		(C) Court Gentleman for Ceremonial Service 將仕郎	9b2	Probationary Remonstrance Secretary for the Heir Apparent 試太子 [春坊] 司議郎	6a				
934-	Meng Chang	Du Jingan 杜敬安 s/o Du Zixiang 杜子瓌		Hanlin daizhao 翰林待詔	[Purple] robes, gold fish-pouch [紫]金魚袋									
934-	Meng Chang	Zhao Zhongyi 趙忠義 s/o Zhao Dexuan 趙德玄		Hanlin daizhao 翰林待詔	Purple robes, gold fish-pouch 紫金魚袋									
938-965	Meng Chang	Pu Yanchang 蒲延昌 s/o Pu Shixun 蒲師訓			Crimson robes, fish-pouch 緋魚袋									
After 944	Meng Chang	Huang Quan	Nei gongfeng 內供奉	Hanlin daizhao 翰林待詔			(C) Grand Master for Court Discussion 朝議大夫	5a2	Acting1 Vice Director of the Directorate for Imperial Manufactures 檢校少府少監	4b2	Supreme Pillar of State 上柱國	2a		
After 965	Song Taizu, Taizong 宋太祖 宋太宗	Huang Jucai		Hanlin daizhao 翰林待詔	Purple robes, gold fish-pouch 紫金魚袋		(C) Grand Master for Court Audiences 朝請大夫	5b1			Supreme Pillar of State 上柱國	2a	Aide of the Courts (?) 寺丞	?

Figure 1: Painters' titles in *Yizhou minghua lu* 益州名畫錄 (Record of Famous Paintings in Yizhou) by Huang Xiufu 黃休復 (b. ca. 954–59).

calligrapher Liu Qin's salary rank was modified by "acting" (*xing*), these other qualifiers defined the outer-court ranks held by the five top Shu painters as nominal, honorary, or temporary.

From Figure 1, we see that Ruan Zhihui and Huang Quan held the very highest ranks in 10th-century Shu. On top of their prestige title, they were additionally granted the highest available merit title of Supreme Pillar of State (Shangzhuguo 上柱國) (Rank 2a). According to Tang rules, a merit title conveys the privilege of official robes in a certain color and Supreme Pillar of State theoretically entitles an awardee the right to annex thirty *qing* of land by equitable-field (*juntian* 均田) land-ownership principles. We cannot assume that Tang principles were followed in Sichuan, but it is nevertheless interesting to see Supreme Pillar of State used to raise Ruan and Huang above their peers.[16]

Ruan Zhihui served as Hanlin *daizhao* under the reigns of Former Shu's second ruler, Wang Yan 王衍 (901–26, r. 918–25), and founder of Later Shu, Meng Zhixiang. He was the most prominent of all Shu painters, and if his titles are any measure, the penultimate painter of 10th-century Sichuan. This is because Ruan was simultaneously recognized with titles in three ranked, outer-court categories: a civil prestige title, commission, and merit title:

Grand Master of Imperial Entertainments with Silver Seal and Blue Ribbon (Rank 3b), Acting1 (*jianjiao*) Left Vice Director of the Department of State Affairs and concurrently Censor-in-Chief (Rank 3b), Supreme Pillar of State (Rank 2a).
銀青光祿大夫, 檢校尚書左僕射, 兼御史大夫上柱國

As we might expect, Ruan Zhihui's lofty title as "Left Vice Director of the Department of State Affairs and concurrently Censor-in-Chief" is modified by "acting1" 檢校 to indicate that his commission was not substantive. That is, Ruan probably didn't serve in capacities stated in the title but nevertheless was allowed to enjoy the high rank's prestige.

Serving about twenty-five years after Ruan Zhihui under Meng Chang, second ruler of Later Shu, Huang Quan held titles in the same three outer-court categories. However, Huang's civil prestige title as Grand Master for Court Discussion 朝議大夫 (Rank 5a2) was lower than Ruan's Grand Master of Imperial Entertainments

---

16 Supreme Pillar of State (Shangzhuguo 上柱國) was the highest of twelve merit title ranks in the Tang dynasty. Modern scholars Chen Zhongfu 陈仲夫 and Wang Su 王素 point out that even though the title is recorded in Dunhuang and Turfan manuscripts, not a single person received actual land rights. See Chen Zhongfu 陈仲夫 and Wang Su 王素 eds., *Han-Tang zhiguan zhidu yanjiu* 汉唐职官制度研究 (Study of the official system in Han and Tang dynasties) (Beijing: Zhonghua shuju, 1993), 98.

with Silver Seal and Blue Ribbon (Rank 3b). Huang's commission as Acting1 Vice Director of the Directorate for Imperial Manufactories 檢校少府少監 (Rank 4b2) was also below Ruan (Rank 3b).[17] Thus, we surmise that Huang's rank was below Ruan even though both discharged their painterly duties as Hanlin *daizhao*. Regardless, their outer-court titles may have enabled Ruan and Huang to join court audiences according to established protocol for regular officers of the outer court.

In summary, outer court means of recognition – appropriately discounted – were permitted to a few painters under the Wang and Meng regimes. These high designations may or may not have represented actual stipends or other emoluments. It is also unknown to what extent they rewarded artistic skill rather than administrative ability, or some combination. In any case, they undoubtedly demonstrate that Shu rulers held Sichuan's top artists in the highest esteem, and that Wang Yan, Meng Zhixiang, and Meng Chang found bureaucratic means to extend recognition to certain painters. However, these rulers' unusual use of the commission and merit title categories requires further scrutiny. In the following sections we consider the cases of Tang painters Lü Yao, Zhu Qian, and Cheng Xiuji, whose titles may have provided a model.

The precedent of Lü Yao and Zhu Qian

The titular sequences of Ruan Zhihui and Huang Quan appear to follow in the footsteps of Tang-dynasty painters Lü Yao and Zhu Qian, who received a prestige title plus a commission while in Sichuan during the late 9th century. Similarities between Lü and Zhu's title categories and those of Ruan and Huang suggest in the latter an effort to transmit canonical Tang titles in Sichuan. The only apparent difference is that the ranks offered to the two Sichuan painters were significantly more generous. However, even though we can identify continuities between painters' titles of the 9th and the 10th centuries, further analysis of Sichuan's application of Tang practice brings light to aspects that the Shu rulers innovated.

Keeping in mind Sichuan's system as exemplified by Ruan Zhihui and Huang Quan, let us consider the special situation that warranted Lü Yao and Zhu Qian's title sequence. From the little that survives in standard biographical

---

17 Huang Quan received Hanlin *daizhao* with purple robes plus gold fish-pouch *ci*-honors under Meng Zhixiang after 925 CE. Then he was (additionally?) titled *nei gongfeng* under Meng Chang after 944 CE. This evidence complicates our above analysis of Tang calligrapher Liu Qin proposing Hanlin *daizhao* as a promotion from *nei gongfeng*.

sources, we know Lü served as Hanlin *daizhao* between 873 and 888 CE. He was one of only three or four painters awarded this prestigious title at the Tang-dynasty capital of Chang'an. Lü left important Buddhist figural paintings at both Chang'an and Chengdu, the Shu capital, because he joined Emperor Tang Xizong's entourage during the emperor's exile in Sichuan from 880 to 885 CE. In other words, Lü was appointed Hanlin *daizhao* in Chang'an and kept this title after returning to Chang'an following the Tang emperor's Sichuan period.

Promotions offered to men with identical career tracks are often listed together in written sources, and Huang Xiufu lists Zhu Qian together with Lü Yao's name. Since Zhu also traveled to Sichuan with Emperor Tang Xizong, it seems likely that he received the same stipendiary titles as Lü even though Huang does not explicitly record them. Figure 1 therefore lists Zhu's name with Lü's titles. Zhu's identity is otherwise obscure today.

During the emperor's exile in Sichuan, Lü Yao and Zhu Qian were conferred crimson robes plus fish-pouch. They simultaneously received outer-court titles in two categories – a civil prestige title and a duty assignment:

Court Gentleman for Ceremonial Service (Rank 9a2),
Acting2 (*shou*) Assistant Magistrate of the Luo District of Han County (Rank 9a2–9b1).
將仕郎, 守漢州雒縣主簿

The second title is a nominal commission; these painters did not actually serve as Han County magistrates. As usual their quasi-official status is disclosed with a prefix, in this case "acting2" *shou* 守, which indicates that their rank was lower than appropriate for this title. Emperor Tang Xizong probably rewarded Lü Yao and Zhu Qian for their loyalty with a ranked, non-substantive duty assignment under the unexpected circumstances of the emperor's exile in Sichuan. During this extraordinary episode, a painter's allegiance was deemed deserving of recognition with an official rank and honors far beyond his existing inner-court Hanlin *daizhao* appointment.

From Lü Yao and Zhu Qian onwards, Hanlin *daizhao* became a title regularly held by painters. Just as significantly, their award served as a model for the Sichuanese practice of conferring nominal outer-court commissions and honorifics to the very top Hanlin *daizhao* painters. Going beyond this Tang model, the Shu kings then added the merit title as a painter's award category, and they apparently did this on account of two very special painters, namely Ruan Zhihui and Huang Quan.

Career advancement for Cheng Xiuji

If the Shu kingdom awarded outer-court titles to painters more regularly after Lü Yao and Zhu Qian's examples, then the case of Cheng Xiuji adds further nuance to our above characterization of Tang precedent. Cheng's example provides a good foil to Lü and Zhu because Cheng did not regard himself as a professional painter. Cheng had literary ability and came from an educated family, yet he was recognized for his painting talent instead.

Zhu Jingxuan's 朱景玄 (fl. ca. 806–40), *Tangchao minghualu* 唐朝名畫錄 (Record of famous painters of the Tang dynasty) describes Cheng Xiuji as a direct pupil of celebrated figure painter Zhou Fang 周昉 (ca. 730–800) (Figure 2). Zhu reports that Cheng studied for twenty years with Zhou. For our purpose, this lineage is not as important as the fact that, according to Zhu, Cheng was the only person at Chang'an whose official career advanced based on his painting ability:

> From the Zhenyuan era (785–805) on, he was the only individual in the capital who owed his advancement solely to his artistry as a painter and was continually graced by the imperial favor.[18]

> 貞元後, 以畫藝進身, 累承恩稱旨, 京都一人而已 。

From his perspective as an art critic, Zhu Jingxuan brings our attention to the important idea that painting talent could serve as the basis for imperial favor in the 9th century. Yet our understanding of Cheng Xiuji is much enhanced by other surviving sources. Because he was a government officer, Cheng's biography is recorded in an epitaph; most painters do not have any epitaphic record.[19] There is additionally an encomium mentioning Cheng composed by

---

18 Zhu Jingxuan 朱景玄, *Tangchao minghualu* 唐朝名畫錄 (Record of famous painters of the Tang dynasty), ca. 840s, in Lu Fusheng 盧輔聖 et al. *Zhongguo shuhua quanshu* 中國書畫全書 (Complete collected writings on Chinese calligraphy and painting), 10 vols. (Shanghai: Shanghai shuhua chubanshe, 1992–94), see vol. 1, page 167: "Miaopin zhong wu ren" 妙品中五人. Translation by Alexander C. Soper, "T'ang ch'ao ming hua lu. Celebrated Painters of the T'ang Dynasty by Chu Ching-hsüan of T'ang," *Artibus Asiae* 21, 3/4 (1958), 204–30, see 223.
19 Zhou and Zhao, *Tangdai muzhi huibian*, vol. 2, 2398, "Tang gu Jixian zhi yuan guan Rong wangfu zhang shi Cheng gong muzhiming bing xu" 唐故集賢直院官榮王府長史程公墓誌銘並敘. The epitaph notes that it was actually Cheng Xiuji's father, Cheng Yi 程儀, who studied with Zhou Fang. In any case, Cheng Xiuji eventually gained the favor of Emperor Tang Wenzong 文宗 (r. 826–40) for his well-researched illustrations of the *Mao shi* 毛詩 (Mao's edition of the Poetry Classic).

Figure 2: Traditionally attributed to Zhou Fang (傳)周昉 (ca. 730–ca. 800), Song dynasty. *Palace Ladies Playing Double Sixes*. Handscroll; ink and color on silk. Freer Gallery of Art, Smithsonian Institution, Washington, D.C., F1939.37 and F1960.4.

his contemporary, the famous poet Du Mu 杜牧 (803–52).[20] Together, these valuable descriptions provide us a much fuller picture than available for the careers of other mid-Tang painters.

Cheng Xiuji's family had enough history of office-holding for him to benefit from *yin* privilege. Cheng's epitaph confirms that he passed the imperial "Examination in Understanding the Classics" 應明經擢第 around 826 CE of the Baoli 寶曆 (825–27) era, after which he became eligible for appointment as an officer. Unusually, he then entered into the official hierarchy owing to his painting skills. The epitaph specifies that Cheng was appointed after the emperor's positive reaction to his illustrations of the Classics, specifically the images that he devised for the *Maoshi* 毛詩 (Mao's edition of the Poetry Classic).[21]

---

20 Du Mu 杜牧, *Fan Chuan wenji* 樊川文集, *juan* 19, "Zhang Youzhang, Cheng Xiuji chu zhu Wei jiangjun Hanlin daizhao deng zhi" 張幼彰程修已除諸衛將軍翰林待詔等製, in Wu Zaiqing 吳在慶, ed. *Du Mu ji xi nian jiao zhu* 杜牧集繫年校注 (Collected works of Du Mu with annotations and dates), *Zhongguo gudian wenxue jiben congshu* 中國古典文學基本叢, 4 vols. (Beijing: Zhonghua shuju, 2008), vol. 3, 1088–89 (*Sibu congkan* 四部叢刊, 14b–15a). For Wu Zaiqing's dating of Du Mu's encomium, see vol. 3, 1034–35, note 1. Cited by Li Wankang 李万康, ""Tang Cheng Xiuji muzhi" yu Cheng Xiuji shengping kaoshi" 唐程修已墓志与程修已生平考释, *Meishu yu sheji* 美术与设计 (Fine arts and design) 5 (2015): 40–46, esp. Part III, 42. I agree with Li Wankang's opinion that, "this is the only record of a Tang-dynasty court painter's official position and it has important historical value for understanding the Tang court's appointment and promotion system."

21 This epitaph received much attention in Chinese scholarship after its discovery in 1936. See Jin Weinuo 金维诺, "Wan Tang huajia Cheng Xiuji muzhi" 晚唐画家程修己墓志, *Wenwu* 文物

Cheng Xiuji's official epitaph is invaluable as a supplement to the art texts. It is also noteworthy for the information that it omits. For example, the epitaph never mentions Cheng as a Zhou Fang student, and so differs from Zhu Jingxuan's description. Another omission from the epitaph is Cheng's promotion to Hanlin *daizhao*. Luckily this information is recorded in Du Mu's encomium, which is datable to 851/12 CE or early 852 CE. The information in Figure 3 showing Cheng's career chronology is based on these extant sources.[22]

Dates	Career events	
825–27	Passed the Examination in Understanding the Classics	應明經擢第
ca. 831–40	Appointed Commandant of Fuliang (Rank 9b2),	授浮梁尉
	with crimson robes plus fish-pouch *ci*-honors,	賜緋魚袋
	and [painter] on duty (*zhi*) at the Academy of Scholarly Worthies.	直集賢殿
851	By decree, awarded the title Hanlin *daizhao*,	敕翰林待詔
	and Commandant for Glorifying the Martial (Rank 6a1).	昭武校尉
	Previously Acting2 (*shou*) Left General of the Courageous Guard (Rank 3b),	前守左驍衛將軍
	Supreme Pillar of State (Rank 2a),	上柱國
	with purple robe plus gold fish-pouch *ci*-honors.	賜紫金魚袋
After 851	Additional promotion to Secretariat of the Heir Apparent (Rank 5a1)	累遷至太子中舍
862	(In his 7th promotion) Administrator in a Princely Establishment (Rank 4b1)	凡七為王府長史

Figure 3: Titles awarded to Cheng Xiuji 程修己 (804–63), military service official and painter.

---

4 (1963): 39–43; Niu Zhiping 牛志平, "Cheng Xiuji muzhi kaoshi" 程修己墓志考釋, *Wenbo* 文博 1 (1986): 51–53; Cen Zhongmian 岑仲勉, "Jinshi zheng shi: Cheng Xiuji muzhi ming" 金石证史 · 程修己墓志铭, *Jinshi lun cong* 金石论丛 (Beijing: Zhonghua shuju, 2004), 72–75; Zhu Guantian 朱关田, "Tang huajia Cheng Xiuji muzhi kaoshi" 唐画家程修己墓志考释, *Chuguo ji: Zhu Guantian lun shu wenji* 初果集 · 朱关田论书文集 (Beijing: Rongbao zhai chubanshe, 2008), 220–24; Hu Kexian 胡可先, ""Tang Cheng Xiuji muzhi" de wenben shidu yu jiazhi lun heng" 唐程修己墓志的文本释读与价值论衡, *Zhongwen xueshu qian yan* 中文学术前沿 2 (2011): 85.

22 Modifying Li Wankang, "Tang Cheng Xiuji muzhi," Table 1, 43–44. See also pages 41–42 for discussion of Cheng Xiuji's duty as *huazhi* in the Academy of Scholarly Worthies. In contrast, Zhu Guantian, "Tang huajia Cheng Xiuji," 222, proposes that Cheng's first position was connected to the 834 CE promotion of his patron, Minister Chen Yixing 陳夷行 (d. 843).

Cheng Xiuji's official career began around 831 CE upon recommendation by Minister Chen Yixing 丞相陳夷行 (d. 843; chief minister 837–39, 841–42), about five years after passing the examinations. Cheng's first personal rank was as Commandant of Fuliang 浮梁尉 (Rank 9b2), with *ci*-honors of crimson robes plus fish-pouch. The title was one of several belonging to Officers of the Imperial Guards 環衛官.[23] Once referring to military units stationed at the capital as a defense force, they became largely decorative titles held by imperial family members and royal favorites, such as Cheng. He functioned as *huazhi*, serving as painter-on-duty at the Academy of Scholarly Worthies. These beginnings were followed by a major change in status when he gained access to the outer-court hierarchy with a nominal commission, the highest merit title, and higher *ci*-honors of purple robes plus gold fish-pouch. Presumably, this recognition resulted from the emperor's attention to Cheng's *Maoshi* illustrations.

Cheng Xiuji's new title sequence was as imperial bodyguard, prefixed "acting2," and thus followed the usual form to indicate that his advancement was fixed at a higher level than his actual rank:

Acting2 (*shou*) Left General of the Courageous Guard (Rank 3b),[24]
Supreme Pillar of State (Rank 2a),
with purple robes and gold fish-pouch honors.
守左驍衛將軍, 上柱國, 賜紫金魚袋

Cheng Xiuji remained at the above rank until 851 CE, when promoted again. Twenty years after first entering the service, Cheng now went up to Hanlin *daizhao* and also received the military prestige title of Commandant for Glorifying the Martial (Rank 6a1) 昭武校尉. In the subsequent decade, Chen continued to rise in rank through various palace affiliations. He was eventually appointed to the Heir Apparent's household and after that, from 862 CE, served one of the imperial sons (other than the Heir Apparent). The latter post offered Cheng his highest rank of 4b1 before he passed away the very next year in 863 CE. At his death, he had served under four Tang emperors: Wenzong 文宗 (r. 826–40), Wuzong 武宗 (r. 840–46), Xuanzong 宣宗 (r. 846–59), and (Xizong's father) Yizong 懿宗 (r. 859–73).

In sum, the epitaph paints a picture of an officer who was *also* a painter, downplaying his artistic talents. In contrast, Zhu Jingxuan's record – being primarily concerned with Cheng Xiuji's painting abilities – emphasized what Cheng's literary training brought to his images of classical and other subjects. While it is no surprise to find differing agendas between the two texts, putting them together provides a rare window into the dynamics between official rank and artistic

---

23 Hucker, *Dictionary of Official Titles*, 2830.
24 Gong Yanming, *Songdai guanzhi*, 433; Hucker, *Dictionary of Official Titles*, 2457.

function and illustrates how a painter's inner-court and outer-court standings were negotiated. Cheng's social status, scholarly background, and creative talent were all factors affecting his career path. His case illuminates how the imperial city's bureaucracy positioned an incumbent's hierarchic location in nuanced ways and illustrates my argument that artist titles were not static – that they sometimes moved along an inner-court, outer-court structural continuum.

Painting careers in a structural continuum

Side by side, the careers of Tang painters Cheng Xiuji, Lü Yao, and Zhu Qian offer us insight into the problem of an artist's official recognition. Clearly our evaluations must be based on a range of factors rather than on any single title or moment in time. Cheng Xiuji began at a lowly Rank 9b2 as an Officer of the Imperial Guard, serving entry-level duty as a painter at the Academy of Scholarly Worthies. After a twenty-year career, he eventually achieved Rank 6a1 in the outer-court hierarchy with a military prestige title and raised as a painter to Hanlin *daizhao*. In his final decade of life, Cheng gained proximity to inner-court household agencies of the imperial establishment, reaching Rank 4b1 before death. Therefore, this thirty-year career trajectory moved along a classification continuum from inner-to-outer court, and then closer again to the inner court. His educational background and his artistic ability allowed him a measure of both inner- and outer-court recognition.

In comparison to officer Cheng Xiuji, much less is known about the professional painter Lü Yao, and Zhu Qian even less still. However, we are now aware that Lü and Zhu's careers reached a peak with a Rank 9b2 civil prestige title and Rank 9a2-9b1 nominal commission. They received these outer-court honorary or stipendiary titles during Emperor Tang Xizong's exile in Sichuan. Let us therefore describe Lü and Zhu's careers as illustrating inner-to-outer court movement.

All three painters were Hanlin *daizhao* who also held "acting" commissions. Cheng Xiuji's outer-court commission came with the highest merit title of Supreme Pillar of State, and with purple robes plus gold fish-pouch *ci*-honors. The titles represent a pivot point in his career, but they do not necessarily signify exceptional treatment since Cheng placed into official service as a member of the educated class. Such titles were commonly granted to officers in the military service hierarchy, and not out of step with regular appointment and promotion practices. Perhaps Cheng's example then opened the door for loyal subjects Lü Yao and Zhu Qian's special treatment. In contrast to Cheng, Lü and

Zhu's titles were bestowed as ad hoc imperial favors rewarding their loyalty during dangerous times for their sovereign.

Top-tier Shu painters benefited from a process that originated in the 9th century with the three painters Cheng Xiuji, Lü Yao, and Zhu Qian – who in turned may have followed the titular example of 8th-century calligrapher Liu Qin. By the 10th century, Sichuan's painters received Hanlin *daizhao* and robes plus fish-pouch *ci*-honors with some regularity. A subset of five men received further outer-court recognition in their title sequences – the above discussed Ruan Zhihui, Huang Quan, their sons Ruan Weide and Huang Jucai, and Li Wencai. The five were awarded civil prestige titles and nominal commissions in the manner of Lü Yao and Zhu Qian. Ruan Zhihui and Huang Quan were the only two Sichuan natives given merit titles on top of their civil prestige titles and nominal commissions. Cheng Xiuji was perhaps the Tang-period model for this award, although in the Tang, painters were not offered merit titles; Cheng's merit title was based on his status as a military service official. It follows that the merit titles extended to Ruan Zhihui and Huang Quan was an innovation of the Shu kingdom on account of their two top painters. Indeed, the careers of Sichuan's elite painters exhibit various progressions in classification from inner-to-outer court, a feature that builds upon Tang precedent but exceeds it with a taller hierarchic structure.

Conclusion

Why did painters need court titles in Sichuan? To provide an answer, we must address why Shu rulers were motivated to combine inner and outer court awards to acknowledge their artistic ability and also offer them recognition in the official bureaucracy. It is not enough to describe such tactics as a ruler's prerogative to grant special treatment to certain individuals, or as a desire to exaggerate the ornamental effects of titles. While these factors are certainly at play, our reply must also take stock of the political dimensions of painters' collective memberships.

In the 10th century, the physically remote and historically independent southwestern Shu kingdom developed a unique system of titular awards that conceived of court painters in a hierarchy with several tiers. Some of these titles were similar to ones earlier held by 9th-century painters at the Tang dynasty's Hanlin Academy, and so they transmit Tang canonical court titles in Sichuan. The kings of Shu may have wished to preserve this aspect of Sichuan's Tang legacy – a legacy which arose after two Tang emperors took refuge in Sichuan while in exile. The Wangs and Mengs took up this powerful history and went further. By the mid-10th century, the Sichuanese had created several tiers of top painters based on Hanlin *daizhao* with and without stipendiary titles. They systematized rather uncommon Tang precedents to form the upper-level structure of a painter's institution. In fact, our attention to the spatial properties of titular categories not only clarified the career trajectories of 9th-century painters Cheng Xiuji, Lü Yao, and Zhu Qian, but also revealed this institutional innovation in 10th-century Sichuan.

The autonomous Shu kingdom certainly benefited from the prestige of copying Tang patterns of personnel administration, but clearly there existed circumstances in the 10th century that necessitated multiplying traditional offices. We discovered that Hanlin *daizhao* awards for painters increased in number, and the status of Sichuan's top painters was augmented with nominal commissions that embedded them into official hierarchies. While the artist titles examined above may be sinecures, they are far from meaningless. On the contrary, these titles defined court painters as inner court members with outer court recognition to display the authority of their art and activities. Indeed, painting culture was a distinguishing product of the Shu region, playing a central role in inter-kingdom trade and diplomacy. Painters received outer-court sinecures commensurate with the important role that their paintings played in functions of the state. Shu rulers were thus able to take advantage of the cultural capital that their patronage produced for cultivating relations with other southern kingdoms.

Besides political symbolism, diplomatic relations, and administrative expediency, one other reason to establish a formal system for recognizing painters was the value produced by hierarchy itself. Representing Shu painting families within an institutional structure added greatly to the value of Sichuan's family traditions, such as those represented by the talents of the Ruans and Huangs, and also the Changs 常, Zhaos 趙, Dus 杜, and Pus 蒲. In this way, the surnames of generations of Shu painters were established as part of Sichuan's cultural legacy, an inheritance materialized in the official record.

References

Bischoff, Friedrich Alexander, *La forêt des pinceaux: Étude sur l'Académie du Han-lin sous la dynastie des T'ang et traduction du Han lin tche*, Bibliothèque de l'Institut des hautes études chinoises 17 (Paris: Presses Universitaires de France, 1963).
Cen Zhongmian 岑仲勉, "Jinshi zheng shi: Cheng Xiuji muzhi ming" 金石证史·程修己墓志铭, *Jinshi lun cong* 金石论丛 (Beijing: Zhonghua shuju, 2004).

Chen Zhongfu 陈仲夫 and Wang Su 王素 eds., *Han-Tang zhiguan zhidu yanjiu* 汉唐职官制度研究 (Study of the official system in Han and Tang dynasties) (Beijing: Zhonghua shuju, 1993).

Du Mu 杜牧 (803–ca. 852), *Fan Chuan wenji* 樊川文集 (Collected writings of Du Mu), 21 *juan*, in Wu Zaiqing 吳在慶, ed. *Du Mu ji xi nian jiao zhu* 杜牧集繫年校注 (Collected works of Du Mu with annotations and dates), *Zhongguo gudian wenxue jiben congshu* 中國古典文學基本叢, 4 vols. (Beijing: Zhonghua shuju, 2008).

Foong Ping, "The Structural Position of Court Artists in the Song Dynasty: Issues of Rank, Title, and Legitimate Rule During the Founding Decades" 宋代宮廷畫家的官署機構, in Wu Hung, ed., *Tenth-Century China and Beyond: Art and Visual Culture in a Multi-centered Age* (Chicago: Center for the Art of East Asia, University of Chicago, and Art Media Resources, 2013), 350–63.

Foong Ping, "On rulers and painters: Issues of institutional patronage and transmitted hierarchies," conference paper for the panel, "National Committee on the History of Art State of the Field: New Frontiers in Chinese Art." College Art Association, 102nd Annual Conference, Chicago, 2014.

Foong Ping. "Representing Nation at the Painting Academy of Song Taizong," on the panel, "Song Taizong's Culture Revolution: The Transformation of Imperial Art, Literature, and Statecraft during the Late Tenth Century," *Asia in Motion: Ideas, Institutions, Identities*. AAS-in-ASIA, Academia Sinica, Taipei, Taiwan, 2015.

Gong Yanming 龔延明, *Songdai guanzhi cidian* 宋代官制辭典 (Dictionary of Song dynasty official titles) (Beijing: Zhonghua shuju, 1997).

Hartman, Charles, "Sung Government and Politics," in Chaffee, John W. and Denis Twitchett, eds., *The Cambridge History of China, Volume 5, Part Two: Sung China, 960–1279* (Cambridge: Cambridge University Press, 2009), 19–138.

Hong Zun 洪遵 (1120–74), comp. *Hanyuan qunshu* 翰苑群書 (Collected writings on the Hanlin Institute), 12 *juan* (Beijing: Zhonghua shuju, 1991). HYQS.

Hong Zun 洪遵 (1120–74), *Hanyuan yishi* 翰苑遺事 (Incidents of past ages at the Hanlin Institute), in HYQS, 76–89.

Hu Kexian 胡可先, ""Tang Cheng Xiuji muzhi" de wenben shidu yu jiazhi lun heng" 唐程修己墓志的文本釋讀與價值論衡, *Zhongwen xueshu qian yan* 中文学术前沿 2 (2011): 85.

Huang Xiufu 黃休復 (b. ca. 954–959), *Yizhou minghua lu* 益州名畫錄 (Record of Famous Paintings in Yizhou) (short title YZMHL), in *Huashi congshu* 畫史叢書 (Collectanea of painting histories), 4 vols. (Taiwan: Wenshizhe chubanshe, 1983), vol. 3, 1375–1432.

Hucker, Charles O. *A Dictionary of Official Titles in Imperial China* (Stanford: Stanford University Press, 1998, first published 1985).

HYQS, see Hong Zun, *Hanyuan qunshu*.

Jin Weinuo 金维诺, "Wan Tang huajia Cheng Xiuji muzhi" 晚唐画家程修己墓志, *Wenwu* 文物 4 (1963): 39–43.

Li Jiebing 李潔冰 and Li Zhenggeng 李正庚, "Lun Tang dai shishu ji qi zhidu hua" 論唐代侍書及其制度化, *Xueshu jiaoliu* 學術交流 4 (2008): 171–74.

Li Wankang 李万康, ""Tang Cheng Xiuji muzhi" yu Cheng Xiuji shengping kaoshi" 唐程修己墓志与程修己生平考释, *Meishu yu sheji* 美术与设计 5 (2015): 40–46.

Li Wankang 李万康, "Tang dai Hanlinyuan hua daizhao renyong zhidu kao shu" 唐代翰林院画待诏任用制度考述, *Gugong bowuyuan yuankan* 故宫博物院院刊 4 (2017): 46–57.

Lu Zengxiang 陆增祥, *Baqiong shi jinshi buzheng* 八琼室金石补正 (Beijing: Wenwu chubanshe, 1985).

Mesnil, Evelyne, "Didactic Paintings between Power and Devotion: The Monastery Dashengcisi 大聖慈寺 in Chengdu (8th–10th c.)," in Christian Wittern and Shi Lishan eds., *Essays on East Asian Religion and Culture: Festschrift in honour of Nishiwaki Tsuneki on the occasion of his 65th birthday* (Kyoto: Editorial committee for the Festschrift in honor of Nishiwaki Tsuneki, 2007), 98–148.

Niu Zhiping 牛志平, "Cheng Xiuji muzhi kao shi" 程修己墓志考释, *Wenbo* 文博 1 (1986): 51–53.

Soper, Alexander C. "T'ang ch'ao ming hua lu. Celebrated Painters of the T'ang Dynasty by Chu Ching-hsüan of T'ang," *Artibus Asiae* 21, 3/4 (1958), 204–230.

Wang Haibin 王海宾, *Tang dai Hanlin shu daizhao zhidu zongkao* 唐代翰林书待诏制度综考 (M.A. thesis, Jilin University, 2008).

Wang Yuanjun 王元军, "Tang dai de Hanlin shu daizhao ji qi huodong kao shu" 唐代的翰林书待诏及其活动考述, *Meishu yanjiu* 美术研究 3 (2003): 100–104.

Wang Yuanjun 王元军. "Wan Tang yu nei gongfeng caoshu seng Bianguang shiji tantao" 晚唐御内供奉草书僧辩光事迹探讨, *Zhongguo shufa* 中国书法 2 (2005): 28–30.

Wei Zhiyi 韋執誼 (769–814), *Hanlinyuan gushi* 翰林院故事 (Stories of the Hanlin Institute), 786 CE, in HYQS, *juan* 4, 11–16.

Xie Baocheng, trans. Chen Mirong, *A Brief History of the Official System in China* (London: Paths International Ltd., and Social Sciences Academic Press, China, 2013).

YZMHL, see Huang Xiufu, *Yizhou minghua lu.*

Zhou Shaoliang 周绍良 and Zhao Chaofu 趙超副 eds., *Tangdai muzhi huibian* 唐代墓誌彙編 (Compilation of Tang dynasty epitaphs), 2 vols. (Shanghai: Shanghai guji chubanshe, 1992).

Zhu Guantian 朱关田, "Tang huajia Cheng Xiuji muzhi kaoshi" 唐画家程修己墓志考释, *Chuguo ji: Zhu Guantian lun shu wenji* 初果集 · 朱关田论书文集 (Beijing: Rongbao zhai chubanshe, 2008).

Zhu Jingxuan 朱景玄 (act. mid-9th c.), *Tangchao minghua lu* 唐朝名畫錄 (Record of famous painters of the Tang dynasty), ca. 840s, in Lu Fusheng 盧輔聖 et al. *Zhongguo shuhua quanshu* 中國書畫全書 (Complete collected writings on Chinese calligraphy and painting), 10 vols. (Shanghai: Shanghai shuhua chubanshe, 1992–94), vol. 1, 161–69.

Alexis Lycas
The Recollection of Place in Li Daoyuan's *Shuijing zhu*

Introduction: Li Daoyuan and the *Shuijing zhu*

The aim of this chapter is to examine how an Early Medieval Chinese geographer perceived, imagined, and represented space. For this purpose, I will consider the geography of the Middle Yangzi basin through the places of memory as presented in the *Shuijing zhu* 水經注 (Annotated Itineraries of Waterways). It was written by Li Daoyuan 酈道元 (d. 527), a Chinese literatus who lived under the Northern Wei (386–534), a dynasty founded by a Tabgatch tribe.[1]

Li Daoyuan's work sketches an unprecedented synthesis between an empire-wide space and the human environment that shaped it, through man-made traces. Such traces can belong to the material realm (city walls, remnants of early civil engineering, monasteries, tombs), the immaterial world (literature, stories, myths), or blur the boundaries between the two (through inscribed writings for instance). As the author of a work that is both technical and literary, Li Daoyuan acted as a direct witness when he traveled to observe and record, and as an indirect witness when he used other narratives and documents.

---

1 The life of Li Daoyuan is essentially known through two official biographies taken from Wei Shou's 魏收 (506–572) *Wei shu* 魏書 (Book of Wei) and Li Yanshou's 李延壽 (618–676) *Bei shi* 北史 (History of the Northern Dynasties). He is classified in the *Wei shu* as a harsh official, and he is placed within the biography of his ancestor in the *Bei shi* (which bears a significantly higher number of information). Originally from Henan, Li Daoyuan was born between 465 and 472 into an official family. His father's professional assignments allowed him to travel across North China from an early age. After he entered the civil service, Li Daoyuan encountered as many promotions as demotions. His severity as well as his skills as an educator are highlighted in both biographies. In 527, he was murdered by the henchmen of defector Xiao Baoyin 蕭寶寅. He wrote his *Commentary* between 515 and 523. See *Wei shu* 魏書, Wei Shou 魏收 (Beijing: Zhonghua shuju, 1974), 89. 1925–1926, *Bei shi* 北史, Li Yanshou 李延壽 (Beijing: Zhonghua shuju, 1997), 27.994–996, and Jörg Henning Hüsemann, *Das Altertum vergegenwärtigen: Eine Studie zum* Shuijing zhu *des Li Daoyuan* (Leipzig: Leipziger Universitätsverlag, 2017), 27–47.

Note: For their comments on earlier versions of this text, I would like to thank Garret Olberding, Dagmar Schäfer, former colleagues from the Max-Planck-Institut für Wissenschaftsgeschichte, and two anonymous reviewers.

As a rule, the narrative of the *Shuijing zhu* follows the itinerary of a river course, for it is the river that presides over the hierarchy of the information that is given. As the spatial progression unfolds, the text stops at each important place, goes back in time, sometimes without reference to a logical or chronological sequence of events. Li Daoyuan presents the *Shuijing zhu* as the potamological commentary of a short anonymous text–the *Shuijing* 水經, or *Itineraries of Waterways*. Although the structure of the *Shuijing zhu* formally follows that of the *Shuijing* in terms of trajectory and spatial progression, the commentary turns out to be a sum of geographical and historical knowledge that leads to an episteme of space. It is both a synthesis of geographical knowledge approached through a river study and a compendium of the cultural memory of the Empire.[2]

Here, I will not so much focus on motion in space as I will examine movement in time. Li Daoyuan's relation to the past occurs through the constant evocation of places and environments of memory. He did not visit in person all the places he described in the *Shuijing zhu*: due to the partition of the Empire, he never had the opportunity to cross the Yangzi river and see the southern rivers and sites with his own eyes. When Li Daoyuan lacks the empirical knowledge to comment, or when he wants to complement written sources, he uses myths, legends, testimonies, as well as certain aspects of local lore, to portray as vividly as possible a place he is not familiar with. That being said, he could also decide not to describe a place in case of insufficient material or when in doubt about the reliability of a source. Whether textual or empirical, his investigation is extremely well documented, and provides an inventory of the known world in the beginning of the 6th century. This chapter therefore focuses on the recollection of the past within a specific region, that of the Middle Yangzi area.

---

2 The *Shuijing zhu* has been the subject of numerous exegetical studies in China over the last three centuries: see the early 20th century *Shuijing zhu tu* 水經注圖, by Yang Shoujing 楊守敬 (Beijing: Zhonghua shuju, 2009), and Chen Qiaoyi's 陳橋驛, four volume *Shuijing zhu yanjiu* 水經注研究 (1985–2003). Outside China, sinologists have shown a growing interest in this often-neglected work: besides Édouard Chavannes' "Les Pays d'occident d'après le *Wei Lio*," *T'oung Pao* 6 (1905): 519–71) and Rolf Stein's "Le Lin-yi, sa localisation, sa contribution à la formation du Champa et ses liens avec la Chine," *Han-hiue, Bulletin du centre d'études sinologiques de Pékin* 2 (1947): 1–335, more recent studies include contributions by Mori Shikazō 森鹿三 (*Tōyōgaku kenkyū: Rekishi chirihen* 東洋學研究: 歷史地理篇 (Kyoto: Dōhō, 1970)), Michael Nylan ("Wandering in the Ruins: the *Shuijing zhu* Reconsidered," in Alan K. Chan and Yuet-Keung C. Lo, eds., *Interpretation and Literature in Early Medieval China* (Albany: SUNY Press, 2010), 63–101), Jörg Henning Hüsemann (*Das Altertum vergegenwärtigen*), Alexis Lycas ("Le décentrement du regard géographique dans le *Shuijing zhu* de Li Daoyuan († 527)," *Bulletin de l'École française d'Extrême-Orient* 104 (2018): 241–66), and David Jonathan Felt (*Structures of the Earth: Metageographies of Early Medieval China* (Cambridge, Harvard University Center for Asia Center, 2021)).

1 Measuring the past

The usage of the past, including historical precedents for political legitimation, is a prominent feature of Chinese history and historiography. During Late Antiquity, exegesis became the privileged means for spreading one's own ideas. In that respect, the historical and exegetical significance of the *Shuijing zhu* is self-evident: even though the initial intention of the author was one of geography, Li Daoyuan gradually moves towards the search for historical traces.[3]

The places of the past are represented in geographical writings so that they can transmit its material, moral and symbolic characteristics to the future.[4] Li Daoyuan wishes to be exemplary and to pass on the lessons of the past by linking his own text to older works. To do so, he shapes the memory of the past and he legitimizes certain eras. As we shall see, this is expressed in the way the author names a state, a sovereign, a scholar, a general, and also through his use of historical precedents and edifying narratives, inscribed writings and dynastic names.[5] Li Daoyuan carries out a two-fold topographical study: in addition to recording all the sites of memory that recount the past, he collects and organizes various media of memory through transmitted literature.

Compiled before the 1st century BCE, the *Shanhai jing* 山海經 (Itineraries of Mountains and Seas) is generally considered the first attempt to mention places of worship as places of memory. However, the Early Medieval territorial fragmentation became a prominent subject of lament for many literati who regretted the end of imperial unity and had to migrate beyond the Yangzi. This type of nostalgia is clear in writings such as the 4th century *Huayang guo zhi* 華陽國志 (Monograph of the regions south of Mt. Hua) for the area of present-day Sichuan, the 6th century *Luoyang Qielan ji* 洛陽伽藍記 (Record of the Monasteries of Luoyang) for the capital Luoyang, and of course the *Shuijing zhu*. Remembrance

---

3 Hou Renzhi 侯仁之, *Zhongguo gudai dili mingzhu xuandu* 中國古代地理名著選讀 (Hong Kong: Zhonghua shuju, 1963), 96–97.
4 The historian Sima Qian 司馬遷 (145–86 BCE) expressed at the end of the famous letter he sent to his friend Ren An 任安 that "consequently, [they] narrated the past while thinking of future generations" (故述往事, 思來者). See *Han shu* 漢書, Ban Gu 班固 (Beijing: Zhonghua shuju, 1962), 62.2735, and translation in Stephen Durrant, Wai-yee Li, Michael Nylan, Hans van Ess, *The Letter to Ren An and Sima Qian's legacy* (Seattle: University of Washington Press, 2016), 28.
5 See Mark Edward Lewis, *The Early Chinese Empires: Qin and Han* (Cambridge: Belknap Press, 2010), 52, 65, and Martin Kern, "Announcements from the Mountains: The Stele Inscriptions of the Qin First Emperor," in Fritz-Heiner Mutschler and Achim Mittag, eds., *Conceiving the Empire. China and Rome Compared* (New York: Oxford University Press, 2008), 219–20.

bridges the (sometimes idealized) past and the (often uncertain) present.[6] The chronological structure of the *Shuijing zhu* is subordinated to the topographical landscape. As such, it reconstructs entire facets of Early Medieval local history. Moreover, it foreshadows many later works such as "local gazetteers" (*difangzhi* 地方志), with their rich repository of historical, social and cultural data.

The Northern and Southern dynasties (420–589) as well as the Sui (581–618) and the Tang (618–907) sought their model from the unified Han empire with its state rituals: sacrifices, worship of imperial ancestors, court ceremonies, and imperial rhetoric. Medieval emperors gained legitimacy by being associated with the emperors of the glorious Han and with the wise monarchs of ancient times.[7] Although it can be traced to earlier periods, this "experience of the past" emerges in the literary and especially in the poetic production of the period, which tends to recreate bygone events.[8]

The remembrance of sites operates on a symbolic level within literary and historical practices. Homer's catalogue of ships and catalogue of the Trojans (as well as his account of Troy as a whole) are written manifestations of an oral memory.[9] Similarly, the Roman "art [of memory] seeks to memorize through a technique of impressing 'places' [*loci*] and 'images' [*imagines*] on memory."[10] In the present case, we will encounter artefacts that are as much inscribed memories of the past as they are devices that transmit this very past.[11] However, I am more interested in examining how Li Daoyuan's recollection of the past can be understood as a source of empirical information.[12] Li Daoyuan frames his narrative through a thematic series (the rivers of the ecumene), within which other series are revealed: series of mountains, stelae, festivals, legends, etc. He uses or creates a framework – temporal, spatial, and ultimately literary – to record and transmit select past events. Such events are part of an individual mnemonic

---

6 Arthur Wright, "The Sui Dynasty (581–617)," in Denis Twitchett, ed., *The Cambridge History of China Volume III. Sui and T'ang China. Part I* (Cambridge: Cambridge University Press, 1979), 49, and Charles Holcombe, "Southern Integration: The Sui-Tang (581–907) Reach South," *The Historian* 66.4 (2004): 760.

7 Howard Wechsler, *Offerings of jade and silk: ritual and symbol in the legitimation of the T'ang Dynasty* (New Haven: Yale University Press, 1985), 135–141.

8 Stephen Owen, *Remembrances: The Experience of the Past in Classical China* (Cambridge: Harvard University Press, 1986), 8, 12.

9 Homer (trans. A. T. Murray, rev. William F. Wyatt), *Iliad, Volume I: Books 1–12* (Cambridge: Harvard University Press, 1924), 99–127.

10 Frances Yates, *The Art of Memory* (London: Pimlico, 1992 ed.), 11.

11 On material aspects of public memory in Early China, see Kenneth Brashier, *Public Memory in Early China* (Cambridge: Harvard University Asia Center, 2014).

12 Dagmar Schäfer, personal communication.

operation conducted by the author, insofar as it involves the choice of an object within the aforementioned series.

Technically, the *Shuijing zhu* transmits the characteristics of a place as a historical site in two sequences. First, Li Daoyuan records and catalogs the materiality of a site, its nature as *realia*: he historicizes a natural or supernatural event by localizing and spatializing it.[13] Second, the transmission of the symbolic and literary value of a place enables the author to recreate and/or preserve the environment of memory that shaped it, through the narratives and the signs that bring a site to life.[14] Thus, places are as much mental and literary (the environment of memory and the text itself) as they are physical (administrative units, natural sites, cultural relics). In any case, they are the basis upon which Li Daoyuan builds his argument.

How then does Li Daoyuan historicize his text? He can either describe an event with great precision (year, month, day), or remain rather vague ("originally", *ben* 本, "formerly", *xi* 昔). Hence, one may wonder why Li Daoyuan can be more or less specific depending on the case? The case of the Battle of Red Cliffs summarizes relatively well the *Shuijing zhu*'s scope on that matter:

> The [Yangzi] River passes by the southern slopes of Mount Bairen (hundred-men) on the left, then it passes by the northern slopes of Mount Chibi (red-cliffs) on the right. This is where Zhou Yu's and Huang Gai's deception of the great army of [emperor] Wu of Wei began.
>
> 江水左逕百人山南. 右逕赤壁山北, 昔周瑜與黃蓋詐魏武大軍所起也.[15]

Li Daoyuan only dedicates one line to this major historical event, which proves that he has little interest for a plain event-oriented history. There are several reasons for this. First, Li Daoyuan usually does not feel the need to repeat an episode known to all. Then, he prefers to focus on anecdotes that concern remarkable individuals, but only when their actions are directly linked to the political or religious efficacy of a place. Li Daoyuan often uses allusion and he does not necessarily explain the most important anecdotes, either because they are known or because quoting them would not bring significant elements to the understanding of the place that he wants to convey.

---

13 Andrew Chittick, "The Development of Local Writing in Early Medieval China," *Early Medieval China* 9 (2003): 54.

14 See Pierre Nora, "Entre mémoire et histoire," in Pierre Nora, ed., *Les Lieux de mémoire* (Paris: Gallimard, 1997), 37, and Paul Ricœur, *La Mémoire, l'histoire, l'oubli* (Paris: Seuil, 2000), 302–303, 528.

15 *Shuijing zhu shu* 水經注疏, Li Daoyuan 酈道元 (Yang Shoujing 楊守敬 and Xiong Huizhen 熊會貞, eds., Nanjing: Jiangsu guji chubanshe, 1999), 35.2889.

Humans take possession of geographic sites in two ways: physically, as they leave traces when they pass by or create artefacts; in language and in writing, when they name, describe, and compare places. Geographic sites are thus transformed into temporal moments and acts of memory when Li Daoyuan inscribes them on paper.[16] Li Daoyuan's journey among the topographical space of the empire is complemented by a historical journey through time. The descriptive and thorough work of a geographer becomes the work of a historian too. By combining his philological concerns with spatial representations of the ecumene, Li Daoyuan conveys an innovative historical reflection on the past, and builds a cultural memory of the Empire.[17]

A typological study of the places (rivers, lakes, mountains, human constructions) that are evoked in the *Shuijing zhu* reveals a catalog of sites of memory, while human constructions (tombs, stelae, altars, walls) inscribe cultural and moral axioms in the *Shuijing zhu*. Because of their recurrence, these toponymic and onomastic elements structure Li Daoyuan's discourse on space. Whether natural or anthropized, the site is a support for memory, but also an active agent of the transmission of memory. The memory of natural and anthropized sites will be discussed in the following two parts.

2 Remembering: mountains, monoliths, islands

Although Li Daoyuan officially comments a potamological text, he describes a fair list of mountains. Chinese geographical writings undeniably contain a wealth of references regarding mountains and rivers, especially the first.[18] The oldest dictionaries designate them as a natural link between men and heaven. Like humans, mountains are subjected to hierarchy, from the most important to the most negligible.[19] At the top, one can find the Five Sacred Peaks (*wu yue* 五嶽) whose designation dates back to the ancient mythological literature. Mount

---

16 For similar questions in Ancient Greece, see Claude Calame, *Poetic and Performative Memory in Ancient Greece: Heroic Reference and Ritual Gestures in Time and Space* (Cambridge: Harvard University Press, 2009), 25–26.

17 On such a "dialogue with the past" in the *Shuijing zhu*, see Hüsemann, *Das Altertum vergegenwärtigen*, 119–148.

18 Michel Soymié, "Le Lo-feou chan: étude de géographie religieuse," *Bulletin de l'École française d'Extrême-Orient* 48 (1956): 1.

19 James Robson, *Power of Place: The Religious Landscape of the Southern Sacred Peak* [*Nanyue* 南嶽] *in Medieval China* (Cambridge: Harvard University Asia Center, 2009), 25–31.

Heng 衡, or the "Southern sacred peak" (*Nanyue* 南嶽) is described in the following way in the *Shuijing zhu*:

> The Xiang river flows to the north and passes by Hengshan county on the east. The mountain is located to the southwest, and has three peaks: Zigai (purple-canopy),[20] Shiqun (circular-stone-granary) and Furong (lotus), the highest and most majestic of all; when observed from afar, its density conceals the sky. Hence Luo Han wrote: "From a distance, [the mountain peaks are] like heaped clouds. The peaks can only be observed on two occasions: after the rain when the sky clears, and at dawn." The Dan river flows to its left, while the Li cataract runs to its right. [Mount Heng] is called Mount Goulou in the *Itineraries of Mountains*; it is the Southern [sacred] peak. On the foothills of the mountain is the temple of Shun,[21] and to its south the mounded tomb of [the tutelary god of fire] Zhurong. In the days of king Ling of Chu, landslides from the mountain destroyed the mound and the "Chart of the Nine heads from Yingqiu"[22] was discovered. When Yu [the Great] regulated the floods, the blood of a horse was used as a sacrifice to the mountain, and the *Jade characters on metal slips* were obtained. East from peak Furong is the cavern of an immortal. It is not uncommon to hear the clear sound of the declamations of scholars when they pass by.

> 湘水又北逕衡山縣東, 山在西南, 有三峰, 一名紫蓋, 一名石囷, 一名芙蓉, 芙容峰最爲竦傑, 自遠望之, 蒼蒼隱天. 故羅含云: 望若陣雲. 非清霽素朝, 不見其峰. 丹水湧其左, 澧泉流其右.《山經》謂之岣嶁山, 爲南嶽也. 山下有舜廟, 南有祝融冢. 楚靈王之世, 山崩, 毀其墳, 得《營丘九頭圖》. 禹治洪水, 血馬祭山, 得《金簡玉字之書》. 芙蓉峰之東, 有仙人石室, 學者經過, 往往聞諷誦之音矣.[23]

The Southern sacred peak is located in the eponymous county, along the Xiang river. It symbolically marks the southern border of the Chinese ecumene: besides connecting man with heaven, it is a natural demarcation, serving as a watchtower for the security of the Empire.[24] What's more, the mountain is the place where the memory of the empire can be inscribed, as shown in the records of the First Emperor's inspection tours and in the cultural and religious centers that are built on them.[25] Mount Heng is remembered through the mention of its

---

20 The purple canopy is one of the emperor's emblems, and it designates the court or the imperial carriage.

21 According to the *Chuxue ji* 初學記 quoting Luo Han's *Xiangzhong ji* 湘中記, Mount Heng possesses a temple dedicated to Shun, just like Mount Jiuyi (*Shuijing zhu shu*, 38.3138).

22 This is taken from Sheng Hongzhi's 盛弘之 *Jingzhou ji* 荊州記, without Li Daoyuan mentioning it explicitly.

23 *Shuijing zhu shu*, 38.3137–3138.

24 See Terry Kleeman, "Mountain Deities in China: The Domestication of the Mountain God and the Subjugation of the Margins," *Journal of the American Oriental Society* 114 (1994): 228, and Garret Olberding, "Movement and Strategic Mapping in Early Imperial China," *Monumenta Serica* 64.1 (2016): 32–33.

25 See below the anecdote of Sun Quan's takeover, and also *Shuijing zhu shu*, 35.2914–2916.

majesty and beauty, its link with Yu the Great, and its caverns in which scholars like to withdraw temporarily.

In premodern China, the mountain had several functions. It could be the home of men who had become immortals. By assigning prodigious power to a natural site such as a mountain, texts like the *Shanhai jing* or the *Shuijing zhu* transformed it into a sacred entity. Furthermore, many people retired in mountains for political reasons or eremitic purposes, as mountains could be places for self-reflection or artistic production free from social contingencies.[26] The mountain was also a difficult place to access, and it could be a refuge for non-Chinese populations, but also for exiles.

In antiquity mountains were both feared and venerated. However, from the Eastern Han onward, and particularly during the Northern and Southern Dynasties period, men gradually overcame their fear and acquainted themselves with their orographic environment.[27] One way of taming a mountain consisted in connecting it to the memory of travel over it or to confer it attributes that would be taken as referents for anyone who would have to describe or travel over it.[28] Similar to the description of Mount Heng, the following two passages exemplify the grandeur of a mountain. They also underline its potentially overwhelming power, which is linked to the difficulties that arose for those who wished to access it. The first description introduces the story of the encirclement of the Jin forces by the troops of Qiao Daofu 譙道福, a Shu general. Li Daoyuan insists on the sinuosity of the roads to emphasize the impregnability of the mountain:

> To the southwest [the ditch] dominates the Grand [Yangzi] River, the view is stunning. Only Peak Ma (horse) presents a slightly sinuous topographic relief. Since a road is pierced through the mountain, one must go through tortuous sheep's gut paths to finally reach the heights [of the peak].

> 西南臨大江, 闚之眩目. 惟馬嶺小差委迤, 猶斬山為路, 羊腸數轉, 然後得上.[29]

---

26 Alan Berkowitz, *Patterns of Disengagement: The Practice and Portrayal of Reclusion in Early Medieval China* (Stanford: Stanford University Press, 2000). Many mountains were also places were various social or religious communities would gather, often around the figure of a learned man who would teach among disciples. See Valérie Lavoix, "À l'école des collines: l'enseignement des lettrés reclus sous les Dynasties du Sud," in Catherine Despeux and Christine Nguyen Tri, eds., *Éducation et instruction en Chine, vol. III: Aux marges de l'orthodoxie* (Leuven: Peeters, 2004), 43–65.
27 Paul Demiéville, "La Montagne dans l'art littéraire chinois," *France-Asie* 183 (1965): 17, and Robson, *Power of Place*, 17–20.
28 *Shuijing zhu shu*, 38.3132.
29 *Shuijing zhu shu*, 33.2817.

As Mount Wu 巫 rises against one of the Three Gorges, Li Daoyuan's literary description goes:

> About ten *li* downstream [the Yangzi river] stands the great Mount Wu. Not only does it have no matches in the Three Gorges, but it rivals in height with Mounts Min and E[mei] and it reaches the summits of Mounts Heng and [Jiu]yi. The uninterrupted chain of its peaks pierces the azure clouds, and when they reach the firmament, one can then distinguish those that protrude.
>
> 其下十餘里, 有大巫山, 非惟三峽所無, 乃當抗峯岷、峨, 偕嶺衡、疑. 其翼附群山, 並槩青雲, 更就霄漢, 辨其優劣耳.[30]

Over the centuries, mountains performed many functions: artistic (as an aesthetic object, the subject of landscape painting or *shanshui* poetry); military (as a strategic location for battles, as a site to be civilized); social (as community place, as a site of disengagement or even banishment for scholars). The most important function, or at least the most studied, seems to be the religious aspect, especially when a mountain was a site of divinization and sacrifice to heaven.[31] Whether illustrious or less known, all the mountains are the seat of one or more deities, and the most important ones can sometimes be worshipped and even become divine sites.[32] In early medieval times, mountains became the epicenters of new religious traditions (messianic Taoist movements, Chan Buddhism), new literary forms (landscape poetry, travel diaries), and their aura reached a climax under the Tang, when poets regularly glorified them.[33]

The anthropization of sites is revealed in several ways: by the stelae, which recount the deeds of men, or by naming a place as a tribute to an illustrious person. There is also an anthropomorphism of the elements: on the Middle Yangzi, one can find a "remarkable rock, which resembles two men facing each other" (奇石. 如二人像).[34] In the following passage, an anthropomorphic megalith gives its name to the Ren 人 (human) embankment, and this phenomenon is linked to the fact that human figures detach themselves from it, via an almost supernatural mechanism:

> Yuan Shansong wrote that "the two banks are separated by a distance of two *li*. The waters [of the Yangzi] are high and steep when they reach the Ren (human) embankment.

---

30 *Shuijing zhu shu*, 34.2832.
31 See for instance Marianne Bujard, *Le Sacrifice au Ciel dans la Chine ancienne. Théorie et pratique sous les Han occidentaux* (Paris: EFEO, 2000), 152–156.
32 It is the case with the cult to Heaven on Mount Tai 泰. See Édouard Chavannes, *Le T'ai chan: essai de monographie d'un culte chinois* (Paris: Ernest Leroux, 1910), 3.
33 Demiéville, "La Montagne dans l'art littéraire chinois," 25.
34 *Shuijing zhu shu*, 34.2841.

On the south bank a blue rock sticks out: it is immersed in summer, and it emerges from the waters in winter. It is high and steep too. By going tens of paces towards its center, [one sees that] they all are shaped as human faces, some large, others small. By examining further, one can even detect hair and beard [on some faces]. This is the reason why it is called the Ren embankment."

袁山松曰二灘相去二里. 人灘水至峻峭, 南岸有青石, 夏沒冬出, 其石嵌崟, 數十步中, 悉作人面形, 或大或小. 其分明者, 鬢髮皆具, 因名曰人灘也.[35]

Because of their visibility, the warning they pose to ships and their symbolic value, megaliths are spatial markers too. Other cases displaying examples of inscribed folk etymology abound in the *Shuijing zhu*, especially in modern-day Sichuan: Li Daoyuan describes the Shilong 石龍 (stone-dragon) hamlet, the Yinding 淫頂 (excessive-tip) rock which is emerged in winter and submerged in summer, or the Bing 丙 (fishtail) cave which shelters barb fish.[36] Dangerous rocks often commemorate and symbolize sites of drownings, such as Gou Yanguang's 苟延光:

The Po (broken) rock emerges on the Yangzi. That is the reason why the embankment was named Shipo (broken-stone). It is here that Gou Yanguang drowned.

江上有破石. 故亦通謂之破石灘. 苟延光沒處也.[37]

The *Shuijing zhu* also contains the oldest references to rock art: it records a total of nineteen sites displaying petroglyphs (*yanhua* 巖畫).[38] Li Daoyuan has either heard of them, or seen them with his own eyes. The petroglyphs represent animal forms, spirits, human/animal chimeras, human and animal footprints, weapons and indecipherable signs. Megaliths, inscribed or not, attracted Li Daoyuan's attention, for he diligently records and describes them. South of the Middle Yangzi, he mentions different cases of megaliths, in the area of Changsha:

In the [Lincheng 臨承] district there is a stonedrum. It is six feet high, and the Xiang river runs through it. The sound of the stonedrum resonates when a battle is announced. Luo Junzhang said that "when [the stonedrum is] struck, its resonances propagate to several tens of *li* in the surrounding area, but nowadays it no longer emits sound." To the east of Guanyang district stands peak Pei (long), below which one can find a stonedrum, the

---

35 *Shuijing zhu shu*, 34.2843.
36 *Shuijing zhu shu*, 33.2805, 2812, 2817.
37 *Shuijing zhu shu*, 33.2809.
38 Chen Zhaofu 陳兆复, *Zhongguo yanhua faxian shi* 中國岩畫發現史 (Shanghai: Shanghai renmmin, 2009), 23–32; Endymion Wilkinson, *Chinese History: A New Manual* (Cambridge: Harvard University Asia Center, 2012), 666.

shape of which resembles that of a flipped boat. When it is struck, the echo spreads in the distance, along the same pattern as the former one.

縣有石鼓, 高六赤, 湘水所逕, 鼓鳴則土有兵革之事. 羅君章云: 扣之, 聲聞數十里, 此鼓今無復聲. 觀陽縣東有裴巖, 其下有石鼓, 形如覆船, 扣之清響遠徹, 其類也.

To the north, the Xiang river flows along the Yin (seal) stones which lie south of Hengshan district, on the right bank of the Xiang river. Some of the stones are large and others small. The stones on the banks of the river all bear marks on their upper part, and they are square like a seal. They are not inscribed and are all aligned in rows along the river for about two *li*. That is why these stones are called Yin (seal).

湘水又北歷印石, 石在衡山縣南, 湘水右側. 盤石或大或小, 臨水, 石悉有跡, 其方如印, 纍然行列, 無文字, 如此可二里許, 因名爲印石也.[39]

In the first case, both stones are drum-shaped and they resonate to announce future battles. The second occurrence indicates a string of originally marked stones–they were named Yin 印 ("seal")–although their inscriptions were erased over time. As with the stelae (see below, part 3), these patterned stones mark (one could say *shape*) the memory of the sites, with their presence altering the topography, and their shapes or inscriptions modifying the stones themselves.

Perhaps because they were seen as immersed mountains, islands are often the epicenter of battles, and are generally considered to be auspicious places. The "five islands" are the symbolic starting point of one of the campaigns of the Liu Song (420–479) emperor Xiaowu 孝武 (r. 453–464):

In the middle of the [Yangzi] River, five islands are connected to each other, which is why this place was named Wuzhou (five-islands). When the [Liu] Song emperor Xiaowu raised his troops in Jiangzhou, he established his headquarters on a set of islets, under the (auspicious) shade of a purple cloud. These are the [five] islands.

江中有五洲相接, 故以五洲為名. 宋孝武帝舉兵江州, 建牙洲上, 有紫雲蔭之, 即是洲也.[40]

The hundred islands scattered along the Middle Yangzi were home to foundational accounts of monarchs trying to seize power (successfully or not), or to the unfolding of a battle. At the beginning of the 5th century, the battle between Liu Yi 劉毅 (d. 412) and Huan Xuan 桓玄 (369–404) took place on the Zhengrong 崢嶸 island. The episode forecasts the victory of Liu Yu 劉裕 (363–422)

39 *Shuijing zhu shu*, 38.3136–3137.
40 *Shuijing zhu shu*, 35.2918–2919.

who would eventually establish the Liu Song dynasty.[41] The following account presents the uplift of an island as an auspicious sign, and focuses mainly on the place and its power:

> Of the dozens of islands scattered over the [Yangzi] River on each side of the county, the Baili island is one of the largest. It grows mulberry trees and other trees with sweet fruits; those growing at the edge of the water are reflected in the River. From the west of the district to Shangming, from the east to Jiangjin, there are no less than ninety-nine islands. A proverb of Chu goes: "As long as the number of islands does not reach a hundred, this place can never provide a sovereign." Huan Xuan intended to interrogate the tripod [for he intended to seize the throne],[42] so he added an island, thus reaching the number of one hundred. A few weeks after he had usurped the throne, his whole clan was exterminated and he was slaughtered. When the case was over, the island was also destroyed. Now that the current sovereign is to the west, an island was suddenly born naturally. Alluvial sediments quickly caused its uplift. Soon after, [the area between] the [Yangzi] River and the [Han] River witnessed the flight of a dragon.

> 縣左右有數十洲, 槃布江中, 其百里洲最為大也. 中有桑田甘果, 映江依洲. 自縣西至上明, 東及江津, 其中有九十九洲. 楚諺云洲不百, 故不出王者. 桓玄有問鼎之志, 乃增一洲, 以充百數. 僭號數旬, 宗滅身屠. 及其傾敗, 洲亦消毀. 今上在西, 忽有一洲自生, 沙流回薄, 成不淹時, 其後未幾, 龍飛江漢矣.[43]

As the previous example shows, this very set of islands can also be the site of a tragic double death, that of Huan Xuan and his son.[44] Huan Xuan was a warlord who proclaimed himself emperor of an ephemeral kingdom of Chu 楚, which he established in 403. He was killed the following year, during an offensive led by Liu Yu. Retrospectively considered a usurper because the founder of the Liu Song dynasty defeated him, Huan Xuan made a second mistake by adding an extra island and thus upset the order of things. As the second example shows, the natural uplift of a hundredth island coupled with the flight of a dragon signaled the advent of a sovereign,[45] in that case Liu Yu. There again, the place influences history, and vice versa. In the following section, I will analyze the different ways of remembering human traces.

---

41 *Shuijing zhu shu*, 35.2904.

42 It is a reference to the Nine tripods (*jiuding* 九鼎) cast by Yu the Great with the metal that was given to him by the Nine provinces he established. It went on to designate an unsuccessful plot to seize power.

43 *Shuijing zhu shu*, 34.2855.

44 *Shuijing zhu shu*, 34.2859.

45 As recounted for the first time in the *Yijing* 易經. See *Zhou yi zhengyi* 周易正義, *Shisan jing zhushu* 十三經注疏, Ruan Yuan 阮元, ed. (Beijing: Zhonghua shuju, 1980), 1.10a.

3 Commemorating: temples, tombs, stelae

As early as the 6th century, literati like Li Daoyuan or Yan Zhitui 顏之推 (531–591), the author of the *Yan shi jiaxun* 顏氏家訓 (Family Instructions of the Yan Clan), would confront epigraphic documents with classical learning.[46] Temples, tombs and stelae are commemorative sites which record the memory of the dead. They reveal, like the mountains, a set of practices such as ancestral cults, political events, expression of filial piety. The topography of the dead emphasizes the importance that should be given to these sites, as well as to the place that commemorates them.[47] These sites tell the story of the eras favored by Li Daoyuan in his narrative, namely High Antiquity, Han times and the Three Kingdoms period. The deities or spirits to which a temple is dedicated may be past emperors, eminent individuals, cosmic forces, nature spirits, etc. Although temples were mostly devoted to emperors and/or deities, commoners could also enjoy this privilege as long as their conduct justified it.

An illustration of Li Daoyuan's commemorative method can be found in the next example. In addition to mentioning a temple devoted to Yu the Great and located on Mount Tu 塗,[48] it mentions the site of memory of Xiang 象, Shun's 舜 younger brother. As Xiang's life was unworthy of Shun's, Li Daoyuan pretends to wonder why a temple dedicated to Xiang could be an auspicious place:

> The Ying river flows southeasterly and passes by the southern side of Youbi's [funeral] mound.[49] Wang Yin[50] writes: "Yingyang county was originally the northern part of Quanling [county]. Five *li* to the east stands Youbi's mound, where it is said that Xiang was enfeoffed. On the foothills of the mountain is the temple of Xiang, whose spirit is said to have had virtues of efficacy, and was capable of arousing clouds and rain [of benefits]." I have heard that the spirit of the saints was the soul, and that the essence of the wise was the spectre. Xiang not having led an enlightened life, once dead, where could his soul have stayed? The Ying river continues its course to the southeast and flows into the Xiang river.

---

46 See Olivier Venture, "Nouvelles sources écrites pour l'histoire des Qin," *Journal Asiatique* 301.2 (2013): 503.

47 Kenneth Brashier, *Ancestral Memory in Early China* (Cambridge: Harvard University Asia Center, 2011), 160–164.

48 *Shuijing zhu shu*, 33.2795.

49 It is the name of a fiefdom given to Xiang by Shun.

50 He was an early 4th century defector who joined the South before the dynastic transition. He wrote a *Jin shu*. See his biography in *Jin shu* 晉書, Fang Xuanling 房玄齡 (Beijing: Zhonghua shuju, 1974), 82.2141.

應水又東南流, 逕有鼻墟南. 王隱曰: 應陽縣本泉陵之北部, 東五里有鼻墟, 言象所封也. 山下有象廟, 言甚有靈, 能興雲雨. 余所聞也, 聖人之神曰靈, 賢人之精氣爲鬼, 象生不慧, 死靈何寄乎? 應水又東南流而注于湘水. [51]

Upstream from the Yangzi, we find an example of a prodigious temple and the respect it inspires to powerful men and commoners alike:

> On the Qutang embankment there is the temple of a [local] god, where prodigies have already occurred. When officials with the rank of regional inspector or two thousand bushels officers[52] pass here, no one is allowed to play the trumpet or to strike a drum. When merchants go down or up [the Yangzi River], they dread making noise by touching the rocks. That is why they wrap the tip of their pole with a piece of cloth. Although [these prodigies] no longer occur, sacrifices remain in practice.

瞿塘灘上有神廟, 尤至靈驗. 刺史二千石徑過, 皆不得鳴角伐鼓. 商旅上下, 恐觸石有聲, 乃以布裹篙足. 今則不能爾, 猶饗薦不輟. [53]

Many temples were built in remembrance of emperors and sovereigns. Under the Han, a memorial temple for Emperor Wu 武 was erected at the Tao 桃 pass.[54] A very interesting conflict between the future Eastern Han emperor Guangwu 光武 (r. 25–57) and Wang Mang 王莽 (45 BCE–23 CE) took place during the early first century:

> At the time when Shizu (Guangwu emperor of the Eastern Han) was still of humble condition,[55] he passed through Jiangyang county. He had a son. A diviner specializing in the observation of emanations had said that an eminent boy would appear in Jiangyang. Wang Mang had him fetched, captured and killed. Shizu was seized with hatred. He had an ancestral temple dedicated to his son built in the district. He blamed the people of the county and requested them to pay fines for several generations.

昔世祖微時, 過江陽縣, 有一子. 望氣者言江陽有貴兒象, 王莽求之, 而獠殺之. 後世祖怨, 為子立祠於縣, 謫其民罰布數世. [56]

Although Guangwu ended up erecting a temple to expiate Wang Mang's wrongdoings, this anecdote brings together different levels of historical signification, from the very local causes and consequences (a regional quarrel at the margins of the realm, the implicit involvement of the local community and the fiscal

---

51 *Shuijing zhu shu*, 38.3131–3132.
52 "Two thousand bushels" is a way to designate the inspectors and governors according to their annual stipend.
53 *Shuijing zhu shu*, 33.2819–2820.
54 *Shuijing zhu shu*, 33.2743.
55 That is "before seizing power."
56 *Shuijing zhu shu*, 33.2786.

consequences of their actions), to an impact on the imperial level (via the power of divination and the suggested impetus given to Guangwu). The memory of this event is mediated through the construction of the temple.

Sixty *li* northeast of the village where the great poet Qu Yuan 屈原 (*fl.* 4th–3rd centuries BCE) lived, stands the temple of his sister Nüxu 女嬃.[57] Another temple was erected for Wang Zixiang 王子香, a virtuous and benevolent official of the Eastern Han, who died while he was inspector of Jing 荆 province. His kindness manifested itself posthumously through the symbolic appearance of three white tigers who carried his remains. Moreover, an ancestral temple and a commemorative stele were built for him, and he was given the title of "gentleman-prince of the white tigers of Zhijiang" (枝江白虎王君).[58]

Li Daoyuan also presents the erection of the Damu 大姥 (venerable-ancestress) temple, which is related to the episode of Sun Quan's 孫權 (182–252) seizure of power as recorded in the *Wuchang ji* 武昌記 (Record of Wuchang); he then quotes Ying Shao's 應劭 2nd century *Han guan* 漢官 (Han officials [serving non-Chinese rulers]). The narrative pattern is the following: the event takes place, it has an impact (the coronation) and as a result a temple is built to commemorate the event. Thereafter, Li Daoyuan mentions the following generation (Sun Hao 孫皓 [242–284], the last sovereign of Wu, and Wang Fan 王蕃 [228–266]), before going back to Sun Quan's times: the description of his sacrificial altar evokes the various spatial stages of his coronation and his good government, through graphic descriptions of his own libations and his court:

> To the south of the wall is Mount Yuan, which is another name for Mount Fan. The *Record of Wuchang* says: "the Damu temple (venerable-ancestress) is located south of the Fan mouth. Sun Quan used to hunt on [the foothills of] the mountain. One evening, at dusk, he met an old lady who asked him what he had caught during the day. [Sun Quan] replied: 'I only caught a panther.' The woman said: 'And why do not you set upright the panther's tail?'[59] Then she suddenly disappeared." Ying Shao wrote in the introduction to the *Han Officials [serving non-Chinese rulers]*: "After the passage of the panther tail [caravan], the lictors[60] stop the procession and disperse. When the Imperial guard procession takes the road, the last car of the procession sports a panther's tail. It means that this is where the sovereign is seated." Since [Sun] Quan acceded to the imperial dignity here, he had a temple built on this site. Sun Hao also climbed this mountain: he sent a general to

---

57 *Shuijing zhu shu*, 34.2837.

58 *Shuijing zhu shu*, 34.2857.

59 That is "why don't you take responsibility and declare yourself emperor?" A symbol of the imperial caravan, a panther's tail (or a painting representing it) is attached to one of the cars (usually the last) and it is understood as an imperial banner.

60 *Zhijinwu* 執金吾 is an alternative form of *jinwu* (a supernatural bird who can remove evil spells; here, the imperial herald, during the Han).

kill the official Wang Fan, and convinced [Wang Fan's followers] that his head had been torn off by a tiger. To the north [Mount Yuan] borders the Grand [Yangzi] River on which there is a fishing terrace where [Sun] Quan liked to drink heavily. He said: 'We will not stop drinking until we fall backwards!' It was here that Zhang Zhao[61] came to offer his honest and benevolent admonitions [to Sun Quan]. To the west of the wall is the Jiao (peripheral) altar where [Sun] Quan offered a sacrifice to Heaven and obtained the position of emperor. Looking around him, he addressed his ministers: 'What Lu Zijing (172–217)[62] said in the past [happened], we must recognize his clairvoyance regarding the outcome of things in the world.' To the east of the wall is an old enclosure, which is said to have been erected by the Han general Guan Ying (d. 176 BCE).

城南有袁山, 即樊山也. 武昌記曰樊口南有大姥廟, 孫權常獵於山下, 依夕, 見一姥, 問權獵何所得. 曰止得一豹. 母曰何不豎豹尾. 忽然不見. 應助漢官序曰豹尾過後, 執金吾羅屯, 解圍. 天子鹵簿中, 後屬車施豹尾. 于道路, 豹尾之內為省中. 蓋權事應在此, 故為立廟也. 又孫皓亦嘗登之, 使將害常侍王蕃, 而以其首虎爭之. 北背大江, 江上有釣臺, 權常極飲其上曰墮臺醉乃已. 張昭盡言處. 城西有郊壇, 權告天即位於此, 顧謂公卿曰魯子敬嘗言此, 可謂明于事勢矣. 城東故城, 言漢將灌嬰所築也.[63]

The memory of space is transmitted through references to the toponyms and anthroponyms that are associated to a particular site. Enumerating them enables both the author and the reader to situate themselves and locate these sequences in space, physically and mentally. To attest the past existence of a site, one must associate to the name of the site the name of a person or of an event that occurred there. Here, Li Daoyuan mentions several persons, and he insists on the conditions of Sun Quan's rise to power, while blending supernatural anecdotes together with the "reality" of the imperial cult and the friendly libations. The "presence" of these persons gives an undeniable value to the place by attesting to its importance and inscribing it permanently in the political memory of Sun Quan's seizure of power. A place can become a site of memory only if something has happened at the site. What actually happened is not so important, provided it can bear witness to the site's strength and secularity, and as long as it is the product of human factors, individual or collective.

In the 3rd century, when the founder of the Shu kingdom Liu Bei 劉備 (161–223) died, his great minister and advisor Zhuge Liang 諸葛亮 (181–234) inherited power at the Yong'an 永安 palace. Li Daoyuan employs this event to highlight the power of Nature and especially of the tumultuous waters that destroyed the wall surrounding the palace. He emphasizes the importance of

---

61 Zhang Zhao 張昭 (156–236) was a scholar, close advisor and honest critic of Sun Quan.
62 It refers to Lu Su's 魯肅 social name. He was a politician, general and diplomat who advised Sun Quan during his conquest to power. He died before Sun Quan was crowned.
63 *Shuijing zhu shu*, 35.2914–2916.

remembering Nature's ability to regain ground and the ephemeral nature of these constructions:

> The plain between the two measures about twenty *li*. The long distance that separates mountains and rivers disappears once one enters the canyon. Leaning on the mountain and bordered by the [Yangzi] River, the surrounding walls have a perimeter of a dozen *li*. The enclosure was destroyed from all sides and invaded by brambles and wild bushes coming from all sides. Many local inhabitants now reclaim land among these ruins.

> 其閒平地可二十許里, 江山迴闊, 入峽所無. 城周十餘里, 背山面江, 頹塘四毀, 荊棘成林, 左右民居多墾其中.[64]

Temples and stelae are also erected to commemorate individuals from the past who perished from unnatural or natural death. They are often places where prodigies manifest themselves.[65] Apart from referring to the main characters of the Three Kingdoms, the temples mentioned in the *Shuijing zhu* refer to two other periods that are considered to be golden ages: the High Antiquity, with particular reference to Yu the Great and his descendants, and both Han dynasties.

The remembrance of individuals is concretized by the fact that stelae and tombs commemorate them. Li Daoyuan mentions a total of two hundred and seventy-eight stelae dedicated to remarkable individuals, who are mostly emperors, civil servants and generals. These stelae, however, only date back as far as the Han period.[66] They play a significant part in the transmission of memory, insofar as cults and stelae are intimately linked. In early China, governing often meant performing sacrifices, and erecting these stelae represented as much a religious testimony as a political memory that aims at inscribing official practices in space.[67] In doing so, stelae and other visually inscribed artifacts blur and bridge the frontier between the material and immaterial realms.

The memory of Shun seems all the more monumentalized since three temples and a stele were erected to convey it: two temples were built on Mount Jiuyi 九疑, while another temple was located further north on the foothills of Mount Heng, the Southern sacred peak.[68] The magnitude of Shun's stele and

---

64 *Shuijing zhu shu*, 33.2813.
65 Alexis Lycas, "La mort par noyade dans la littérature géographique du haut Moyen Âge chinois," *Études chinoises* 36.1 (2017): 51–77.
66 Shi Zhicun 施執存. *Shuijing zhu beilu* 水經注碑錄 (Tianjin: Tianjin guji chubanshe, 1987); Miranda Brown, *The Politics of Mourning in Early China* (Albany: SUNY Press, 2008), 16–17, 141.
67 Jean Levi, "The Rite, the norm and the Dao: philosophy of sacrifice and transcendence of power in Ancient China," in John Lagerwey and Marc Kalinowski, eds., *Early Chinese Religion. Part One: Shang through Han (1250 BC–220 AD)* (Leiden: Brill, 2009), 645–648.
68 *Shuijing zhu shu*, 38.3138.

the fact that he is given precedence over his son can be experienced in the topography of the place:

> The great Shun is buried at the adret of Mount [Jiuyi], while [his son] Shang Jun is buried at the ubac. To the south of the mountain is Shun's temple, in front of which a stele was erected. Its characters are eroded and incomplete, which makes their identification impossible. When raising one's head from the temple toward the highest peaks, one's gaze can rise to a hundred *li*. According to the traditions of the elders, no man ever reached the summits of these peaks. To the northeast of Mount [Jiuyi], at the border of Lingdao county, there is another temple dedicated to Shun. To the south of the county stands Shun's stele, which was erected by Xu Jian, the governor of Lingling.

> 大舜窆其陽, 商均葬其陰. 山南有舜廟, 前有石碑, 文字缺落, 不可復識. 自廟仰山極高, 直上可百餘里. 古老相傳, 言未有登其峰者. 山之東北, 泠道縣界, 又有舜廟. 縣南有《舜碑》, 碑是零陵太守徐儉立.[69]

Li Daoyuan also mentions two more stelae with apparently illegible inscriptions. Since he is unable to decipher them, he prefers not to attribute them to anyone, although it seems that they refer to persons of importance, most probably Shun in the first case, and perhaps the Marquis of Jie 節 in the second case.[70]

Conclusion

Most of the monuments listed in the *Shuijing zhu* refer to a glorious past, usually dating back more than a century before Li Daoyuan's times.[71] Their names are at the heart of the operation of remembrance: they are essential and iterative markers that enable the memory of places to endure. Such a process manifests itself near a fortress erected by Zinang 子囊 (d. 559 BCE), son of king Zhuang 莊 of Chu, with the tomb of Zhao Qi 趙岐 (108–201), who was known for commenting the *Mengzi* 孟子. This tomb "was built by [Zhao] Qi during his lifetime. Portraits of the host and his guests were drawn to inscribe their friendship and also to show what they ordinarily attached importance to." (岐平生自所營也. 冢圖賓主之容, 用存情好, 敘其宿尚矣).[72]

---

69 *Shuijing zhu shu*, 38.3123–3125.
70 *Shuijing zhu shu*, 38.3127.
71 Michael Nylan, "Wandering in the Ruins: the *Shuijing zhu* Reconsidered," in Alan K. Chan and Yuet-Keung C. Lo, eds., *Interpretation and Literature in Early Medieval China* (Albany: SUNY Press, 2010), 64–66. For a list of the Middle Yangzi stelae, see Shi, *Shuijing zhu beilu*, 381–433.
72 *Shuijing zhu shu*, 34.2865.

Monuments are not only mentioned to honor illustrious figures (emperors, mythical sovereigns) at the imperial level, but also to remember generals or local lords at the regional level. Thus, several stelae were erected near the mouth of the Mian 沔 river, next to a fort built by Lu Huan 陸渙 (3rd century governor of Jiangxia). They commemorate the actions of three soldiers–Liu Qi 劉琦 (d. 209) at the very end of the Han, Hu Fen 胡奮 (d. 288) and Wang Yi 王廙 (276–322) during the Three Kingdoms and Jin periods–who distinguished themselves in combat between the 3rd and 4th centuries:

> [Situated on the mountain, Lu Huan's fort] was established in the sixth year of the reign of the Han emperor Gao (201 BCE), and it was moved here under the Wu. The stele of "Hu Fen, inspector of Jing province and general of the expedition to the South of Jin" was erected in the middle of the fort, and so was the stele engraved by Wang Shijiang, the general for pacifying the South, which recounts the events of the punitive expedition against Du Zeng. One can also find there the tomb of Liu Qi and his ancestral temple.

> 漢高帝六年置, 吳乃徙此. 城中有晉征南將軍荊州刺史胡奮碑. 又有平南將軍王世將刻石記征杜曾事. 有劉琦墓及廟也. [73]

Liu Qi was the eldest son of Liu Biao 劉表 (142–208), the powerful governor of Jing province at the end of the Han. After having assisted Liu Bei in the Battle of Changban and participated in the Battle of Red Cliffs, he was appointed inspector of Jing province; he died shortly after his appointment.[74] Hu Fen was a famous Jin general known for fighting the Xiongnu and launching the final expedition against the Wu kingdom. Wang Yi 王廙 (276–322) was an official, a painter, a calligrapher, a musician, and the first cousin of the powerful and rebelious stateman Wang Dun 王敦 (266–324); he was appointed inspector of Jing province during the Eastern Jin.[75] As for Du Zeng 杜曾 (d. 319), he was a Western Jin felon who suffered two successive defeats in 317 and 319; the latter was fatal: he was betrayed and delivered by his officers to Zhou Fang 周訪 (260–320), an important general and inspector of Eastern Jin, who helped the dynasty to reaffirm control of the Middle Yangzi area.[76] Through an iterative process that displays the memory of the illustrious military men who fought in this area, these stelae both recollect and celebrate past worthies in linkage with the imperial topography.

Similarly and in addition to stelae, altars (*tan* 壇), such as the Jie 界 altar which marks the western boundary of the Badong 巴東 region, and cairns (*lei* 壘),

---

73 *Shuijing zhu shu*, 35.2895–2896.
74 *Hou Han shu* 後漢書, Fan Ye 范曄 (Beijing: Zhonghua shuju, 1965), 74B.2423–2424.
75 *Jin shu*, 76.2002–2012.
76 *Jin shu*, 58.1581.

such as the one erected as a tribute to Zhuge Liang's strategic talents, are commemorative monuments that contribute to the remembrance of a place.[77]

In conferring memory to natural as well as anthropized sites, Li Daoyuan recollects the past. In addition to recording numerous books (that were lost between his time and the Song dynasty), he also wishes to pass on remnants of material culture. This is not surprising, as inscribed artifacts are indeed a durable support used to engrave important events or texts.[78] The values attributed to those inscriptions are that of exemplarity and authority, and they are further commemorated through their dating. Overall, if we focus on descriptions of topographical objects (mountains, monoliths, islands) and man-made monuments (temples, tombs, stelae), Li Daoyuan's strategies in representing sites of memory come to the fore. The spatial configurations of the material past together with the retrospective gaze of the author reveal a deeply original way of representing places in Early Medieval China.

References

Primary sources

Bei shi 北史, Li Yanshou 李延壽 (Beijing: Zhonghua shuju, 1997).
Han shu 漢書, Ban Gu 班固 (Beijing: Zhonghua shuju, 1962).
Hou Han shu 後漢書, Fan Ye 范曄 (Beijing: Zhonghua shuju, 1965).
Jin shu 晉書, Fang Xuanling 房玄齡 (Beijing: Zhonghua shuju, 1974).
Shuijing zhu shu 水經注疏, Li Daoyuan 酈道元 (Yang Shoujing 楊守敬 and Xiong Huizhen 熊會貞, eds. Nanjing: Jiangsu guji chubanshe, 1999).
Shuijing zhu tu 水經注圖, Yang Shoujing 楊守敬 (Beijing: Zhonghua shuju, 2009).
Wei shu 魏書, Wei Shou 魏收 (Beijing: Zhonghua shuju, 1974).
Zhou yi zhengyi 周易正義, *Shisan jing zhushu* 十三經注疏, Ruan Yuan 阮元, ed. (Beijing: Zhonghua shuju, 1980).

---

77 *Shuijing zhu shu*, 33.2802, 2813.
78 See Marianne Bujard's ongoing research project on the temples and stelae of Beijing: *Beijing neicheng simiao beikezhi* 北京內城寺廟碑刻志 (Beijing: Guojia tushuguan chubanshe, 2011–2020).

Secondary sources

Berkowitz, Alan J. *Patterns of Disengagement: The Practice and Portrayal of Reclusion in Early Medieval China* (Stanford: Stanford University Press, 2000).

Brashier, Kenneth. *Ancestral Memory in Early China* (Cambridge: Harvard University Asia Center, 2011).

Brashier, Kenneth. *Public Memory in Early China* (Cambridge: Harvard University Asia Center, 2014).

Brown, Miranda. *The Politics of Mourning in Early China* (Albany: SUNY Press, 2008).

Bujard, Marianne, ed. et al. *Beijing neicheng simiao beikezhi* 北京內城寺廟碑刻志 (Beijing: Guojia tushuguan chubanshe, 2011–2020).

Bujard, Marianne. *Le Sacrifice au Ciel dans la Chine ancienne. Théorie et pratique sous les Han occidentaux* (Paris: EFEO, 2000).

Calame, Claude. *Poetic and Performative Memory in Ancient Greece: Heroic Reference and Ritual Gestures in Time and Space* (Cambridge: Harvard University Press, 2009).

Chavannes, Édouard. *Le T'ai chan: essai de monographie d'un culte chinois* (Paris: Ernest Leroux, 1910).

Chavannes, Édouard, "Les Pays d'occident d'après le *Wei Lio*," *T'oung Pao* 6 (1905): 519–71.

Chen Qiaoyi 陳橋驛. *Shuijing zhu yanjiu* 水經注研究 (Tianjin: Tianjin guji chubanshe, 1985–2003).

Chen Zhaofu 陳兆复. *Zhongguo yanhua faxian shi* 中國岩畫發現史 (Shanghai: Shanghai renmmin, 2009).

Chittick, Andrew, "The Development of Local Writing in Early Medieval China," *Early Medieval China* 9 (2003): 35–70.

Demiéville, Paul, "La Montagne dans l'art littéraire chinois," *France-Asie* 183 (1965): 7–32.

Durrant, Stephen, Li, Wai-yee, Nylan, Michael, van Ess, Hans. *The Letter to Ren An and Sima Qian's legacy* (Seattle: University of Washington Press, 2016).

Felt, D. Jonathan. *Structures of the Earth: Metageographies of Early Medieval China* (Cambridge, Harvard University Asia Center, 2021).

Holcombe, Charles, "Southern Integration: The Sui-Tang (581–907) Reach South," *The Historian* 66.4 (2004): 749–71.

Homer (A. T. Murray trans., William F. Wyatt rev.). *Iliad, Volume I: Books 1–12* (Cambridge: Harvard University Press, 1924).

Hou Renzhi 侯仁之, *Zhongguo gudai dili mingzhu xuandu* 中國古代地理名著選讀 (Hong Kong: Zhonghua shuju, 1963).

Hüsemann, Jörg Henning. *Das Altertum vergegenwärtigen: Eine Studie zum* Shuijing zhu *des Li Daoyuan* (Leipzig: Leipziger Universitätsverlag, 2017).

Kern, Martin, "Announcements from the Mountains: The Stele Inscriptions of the Qin First Emperor," in Fritz-Heiner Mutschler and Achim Mittag, eds., *Conceiving the Empire. China and Rome Compared* (New York: Oxford University Press, 2008), 217–40.

Kleeman, Terry, "Mountain Deities in China: The Domestication of the Mountain God and the Subjugation of the Margins," *Journal of the American Oriental Society* 114 (1994): 226–38.

Lavoix, Valérie, "À l'école des collines: l'enseignement des lettrés reclus sous les Dynasties du Sud," in Catherine Despeux and Christine Nguyen Tri, eds., *Éducation et instruction en Chine, vol. III: Aux marges de l'orthodoxie* (Leuven: Peeters, 2004), 43–65.

Levi, Jean, "The Rite, the norm and the Dao: philosophy of sacrifice and transcendence of power in Ancient China," in John Lagerwey and Marc Kalinowski, eds., *Early Chinese Religion. Part One: Shang through Han (1250 BC–220 AD)* (Leiden: Brill, 2009), 645–92.

Lewis, Mark Edward. *The Early Chinese Empires: Qin and Han* (Cambridge: Belknap Press, 2010).

Lycas, Alexis, "La mort par noyade dans la littérature géographique du haut Moyen Âge chinois," *Études chinoises* 36.1 (2017): 51–77.

Lycas, Alexis, "Le décentrement du regard géographique dans le *Shuijing zhu* de Li Daoyuan († 527)," *Bulletin de l'École française d'Extrême-Orient* 104 (2018): 241–66.

Mori Shikazō 森鹿三. *Tōyōgaku kenkyū: Rekishi chirihen* 東洋學研究: 歷史地理篇 (Kyoto: Dōhō, 1970).

Nora, Pierre, "Entre mémoire et histoire," in Pierre Nora, ed., *Les Lieux de mémoire* (Paris: Gallimard, 1997), 23–48.

Nylan, Michael, "Wandering in the Ruins: the *Shuijing zhu* Reconsidered," in Alan K. Chan and Yuet-Keung C. Lo, eds., *Interpretation and Literature in Early Medieval China* (Albany: SUNY Press, 2010), 63–101.

Olberding, Garret, "Movement and Strategic Mapping in Early imperial China," *Monumenta Serica* 64.1 (2016): 23–46.

Owen, Stephen. *Remembrances: The Experience of the Past in Classical China* (Cambridge: Harvard University Press, 1986).

Ricœur, Paul. *La Mémoire, l'histoire, l'oubli* (Paris: Seuil, 2000).

Robson, James. *Power of Place: The Religious Landscape of the Southern Sacred Peak [Nanyue 南嶽] in Medieval China* (Cambridge: Harvard University Asia Center, 2009).

Shi Zhicun 施執存. *Shuijing zhu beilu* 水經注碑錄 (Tianjin: Tianjin guji chubanshe, 1987).

Soymié, Michel, "Le Lo-feou chan: étude de géographie religieuse," *Bulletin de l'École française d'Extrême-Orient* 48 (1956): 1–139.

Stein, Rolf, "Le Lin-yi, sa localisation, sa contribution à la formation du Champa et ses liens avec la Chine," *Han-hiue, Bulletin du centre d'études sinologiques de Pékin* 2 (1947): 1–335.

Venture, Olivier, "Nouvelles sources écrites pour l'histoire des Qin," *Journal Asiatique* 301.2 (2013): 501–514.

Wechsler, Howard. *Offerings of jade and silk: ritual and symbol in the legitimation of the T'ang Dynasty* (New Haven: Yale University Press, 1985).

Wilkinson, Endymion. *Chinese History: A New Manual* (Cambridge: Harvard University Asia Center, 2012).

Wright, Arthur, "The Sui Dynasty (581–617)," in Denis Twitchett, ed., *The Cambridge History of China Volume III. Sui and T'ang China. Part I* (Cambridge: Cambridge University Press, 1979), 48–149.

Yates, Frances. *The Art of Memory* (London: Pimlico, 1992 ed.).

Vincent S. Leung
Chuci and the Politics of Space under the Qin and Han Empires

To create a new state is to create a new space. It entails the construction of a new environment for all things under its dominion.[1] This is true for any type of state, but it is particularly germane when we consider the formation of an empire. Empires are a type of political structure that is defined, most importantly, by their drive towards territorial expansion. As Charles Maier, in his study of empires in world history, noted: "An empire in the classic sense is usually believed, first, to expand its control by conquest or coercion, and, second, to control the political loyalty of the territories it subjugates."[2] In other words, empires are constituted through relations of domination by one group over another in a territory that is not originally their own. To create an empire, therefore, is to create an expansive political space, one that extends itself without compromising its political integrity. In this sense, all empires implicate and subsist on a politics of space; it is a form of political authority that is realized and maintained through a reconfiguration of spatial relations.

In this paper, I will explore this politics of space under the rise of the Qin and the Han empires (221 BCE-220 CE) in early China. What spatial claims did these early empires make, and what historical responses were there from the political elite? The text that I will be using as a point of entry for this historical contention over spatial relations is the *Chuci* 楚辭 (*Chu Lyrics*). This ancient collection of poetry is a somewhat unlikely choice. The *Chuci* does contain a few

Note: The author would like to acknowledge and thank the financial support from Lingnan University for the research and writing of this chapter through its Direct Grant program (DR19A8) from 2019–2020.

1 On the "spatiality of political life," see Adam T. Smith, *The Political Landscape: Constellations of Authority in Early Complex Polities* (Berkeley: University of California Press, 2003), esp. 12.
2 Charles S. Maier, *Among Empires: American Ascendancy and Its Predecessors* (Cambridge, MA: Harvard University Press, 2006), 24–25. There are many competing definitions of empires, but they all invariably emphasize this spatial dimension. For instance, Michael Hardt and Antonio Negri wrote, "First and foremost, then, the concept of Empire posits a regime that effectively encompasses the spatial totality, or really that rules over the entire 'civilized' world. No territorial boundaries limit its reign." *Empire* (Cambridge, Mass.: Harvard University Press, 2000), xiv; and in Michael Doyle's *Empires* (Ithaca, N.Y.: Cornell University Press, 1986), 19: "Empires are relationships of political control imposed by some political societies over the effective sovereignty of other political societies."

Han-period pieces, but it is more typically read in the context of its association with the Chu 楚 kingdom of the preceding Warring States era (ca. 475–221 BCE). Once a powerful southern kingdom at the central Yangzi valley, the Chu finally fell to the Qin armies after decades of resistance in the year 223 BCE.[3] Memory of the kingdom, however, persisted. In the next few centuries, under the early empires, there would be an extraordinary amount of memorial investment in the bygone kingdom of Chu. Lore about this once-influential southern kingdom proliferated, and literary pieces associated with it enjoyed wide currency.[4] Towards the end of the Han empire in the second century CE, this very active afterlife of the Chu kingdom would culminate in the compilation of the *Chuci zhangju* 楚辭章句 (*Chapter and Verse Commentary to the Lyrics of Chu*) by Wang Yi 王逸 (fl. 130s), an anthology of poems attributed to poets from both the Chu kingdom and the Han dynasty. This compilation had a defining effect for the Chu lyrics tradition; its nearly sixty poems established its basic repertoire, and Wang Yi's commentaries laid the first stone of the exegetical tradition of Chu lyrics that would develop in the centuries to come.

There are therefore (at least) two historical contexts for a reading of the *Chuci* poems. One can read them against the history and culture of the Chu kingdom, the purported origin for this distinctive style of poetry, or one can read them in the context of the early imperial era, a time when they enjoyed great popularity among the political elite who took to ensuring their preservation. In this paper, I will opt to do the latter. Reading the *Chuci* pieces alongside other early imperial texts, especially the court literature of the Qin and Han empires, will tell us a great deal about the contentious politics of space of this period. The abiding interest in the *Chuci* poems and their lore was no historical accident but an artifact of the spatial politics of the early imperial period. They were purposefully mobilized, as a well-wrought language for articulating displacement, in response to the spatial claims of the Qin-Han empires. Through their analysis, we can question how the aesthetic composition of space may provide opportunities for contestation against the state's possessive representation of its landscape.

---

3 For a summary of the history of Chu, see Barry B. Blakeley, 'The Geography of Chu', in *Defining Chu: Image and Reality in Ancient China*, ed. by Constance A. Cook and John S. Major (Honolulu: University of Hawai'i Press, 1999), 9–20.

4 For a great survey of the literary representations of the Chu kingdom in Han dynasty texts, see Gopal Sukhu, "Monkeys, Shamans, Emperors, and Poets: The *Chuci* and Images of Chu during the Han Dynasty," in *Defining Chu: Image and Reality in Ancient China*, ed. Constance A. Cook and John S. Major (Honolulu: University of Hawaii Press, 2004), 145–166; and Lu Kanru 陸侃如, "Han ren lun *Chuci*" 漢人論楚辭, in *Lu Kanru gudian wenxue lunwen ji* 陸侃如古典文學論文集 (Shanghai: Shanghai guji, 1987), 371–401.

The argument will unfold over three sections. In the first section, I will elaborate on what I have just briefly discussed, namely the history of the Chu lyrics under the early empires, especially the *Chuci zhangju* from the late Han empire. In the second section, I will offer a reading of some of the *Chuci* poems and discuss what I consider to be one of their salient features, namely a poetics of displacement. Then, in the third and last section, I will situate these *Chuci* poems in the context of other early imperial court writings and discuss how their juxtaposition would point us towards a history of spatial politics under the rise of empires in early China. The *Chuci* poems did not just happen to exist – and flourish – under the early empires but were a literary fallout of the spatial contention of the Qin-Han empires.

I *Chuci zhangju* and Chu Lyrics under the early empires

The origin and early history of the Chu lyrics tradition is a minor puzzle in the study of early Chinese literature and history. None of the poems in the Chu lyrics repertoire can be confidently attested from the time of the Chu kingdom, and even the term "Chuci" 楚辭 – "Chu lyrics" or "songs of the Chu" – did not appear in the extant corpus until the first century BCE in the hands of early Han politicians.[5] Speculations abound about the pre-imperial history of this poetic tradition, and inevitably, the discussion always returns to the first compilation and the oldest commentaries of the "Chu lyrics" in the aforementioned *Chuci zhangju* by Wang Yi, a collator (*jiaoshu lang* 校書郎) at the imperial library during the reign of Emperor An of the Han dynasty (Han Andi 漢安帝, r. 94–125).[6] The *Chuci zhangju* is divided into seventeen books, each with a

---

5 One of its first appearances of this term is in the *Shiji* 史記 by Sima Qian 司馬遷 (d. 86 BCE) (Beijing: Zhonghua, 1959), 122.3143. See You Guo'en 游國恩, "*Chuci* gailun" 楚辭概論, in *You Guo'en Chuci lunzhu ji* 游國恩楚辭論著集, 4 vols (Beijing: Zhonghua shuju, 2008), iii, 7–9. For a discussion of the probable pre-imperial origins of the Chu lyrics tradition, see You Guo'en游國恩, "*Chuci* de qiuyuan" 楚辭的起源, in *You Guo'en Chuci lunzhu ji* 游國恩楚辭論著集, 4 vols (Beijing: Zhonghua shuju, 2008), iv, 114–26.
6 Wang Yi's official career as a collator at the imperial library, and subsequently as a palace attendant (*daizhong* 侍中), may have extended into the reign of Emperor Shun (Han Shundi 漢順帝, r. 115–144 BCE). See Fan Ye 范曄, *Hou Hanshu* 後漢書 (Beijing: Zhonghua, 1965), 80.2618, with the commentary by Jiang Tianshu 蔣天樞, "*Hou Han shu* 'Wang Yi zhuan' kaoshi" 後漢書 王逸傳考釋, in his *Chuci lunwen ji* 楚辭論文集 (Xi'an: Shaanxi renmin chubanshe, 1982),

single or a cycle of poems appended with Wang Yi's commentaries; the nearly sixty poems in this compilation, as noted above, would come to define the repertoire of the Chu lyrics tradition, and all later editions of the *Chuci* would be based on this earliest collection.[7] This is the urtext of the Chu lyrics tradition.

Between the prefaces and interlinear glosses, Wang Yi offers in the *Chuci zhangju* not just explications of the individual poems but also an interpretive framework for the history of the Chu lyrics tradition. Like all commentarial texts, Wang Yi's exegesis is descriptive in gesture and prescriptive in substance. His explanation for how a poem should be read is really an argument for how it ought to be read. His basic commentarial strategy in the *Chuci zhangju* is to situate each of the Chu lyrics in the circumstances of their compositions. Put differently, for Wang Yi, the key to understanding a Chu lyric lies, in large part, in knowing how its author came to compose it. Accordingly, each of the seventeen books in the *Chuci zhangju* has a clear attribution, beginning with Chu writers from the late Warring States to the Han dynasty poets of his own time. The *Chuci zhangju*, in this sense, is more than just an anthology but also an history of the tradition of Chu lyrics through a selective compilation and explication of the works of successive poets over almost four centuries.

In Wang Yi's history of the Chu lyrics tradition, this poetic language originated in the southern kingdom of Chu. It was exemplified in the works by Qu Yuan 屈原 (ca. 340–278 BCE), a wrongfully disgraced minister of the kingdom, and to a lesser degree his younger contemporary Song Yu 宋玉 (fl. early third century BCE). Of the seventeen books in the *Chuci zhangju*, eight were attributed to the authorship of Qu Yuan. Two were attributed to Song Yu. Wang Yi did express some doubts regarding the authorship of the poem "Da zhao" 大招 ("The Great Summons"); even though he attributed it to Qu Yuan, he noted that it may also have been written by another Chu poet named Jing Cuo 景瑳 about whom we know nothing else.[8] As for the remaining seven books, they were attributed to various Han dynasty writers, including the "Jiu si" 九思 ("Nine Longings") by Wang

---

195–212. See also Wang Qizhou 王齊洲, "Wang Yi he *Chuci zhangju*" 王逸和《楚辭章句》, *Wen-xue yichan* 文學遺產 2 (1995), 23–30.

7 For the textual history of the *Chuci*, including the history of the different editions, see Kominami Ichirō 小南一郎, *Soji to sono chūshakushatachi* 楚辭とその注釈者たち (Kyoto: Hōyū sho-ten, 2003); and David Hawkes, "Ch'u tz'u," in *Early Chinese Texts: A Bibliographical Guide*, ed. Michael Loewe (Berkeley: The Society for the Study of Early China and the Institute of East Asian Studies, University of California, 1993), 48–55.

8 Hong Xingzu 洪興祖, ed., *Chuci buzhu* 楚辭補注 (Bejing: Zhonghua, 1983), 216. All references to the *Chuci* are based on this edition of the *Chuci zhangju* with additional annotations by Hong Xingzu (1090–1155). Unless otherwise noted, all translations from the *Chuci* are adapted from Hawkes, *The Songs of the South*, with some minor modifications.

Yi himself. For each book, he also included a preface on the historical circumstances of their composition. Some of these prefaces are more elaborate than the others; the ones for the pieces attributed to Qu Yuan are generally more detailed. Together, they gave us a picture of a virtuous courtier who, confounded by the moral perversions of the world, decided to drown himself as the only possible means of escape with his integrity intact.[9] The tradition continued to flourish after the death of Qu Yuan in the works of the later Chu poets. Han writers from the beginning of the empire to his own time, including Wang Yi himself, continued to write "Chu lyrics," even though the Chu kingdom had perished for centuries.

This is the basic outline of the history of the Chu lyrics tradition that emerged from a reading of the *Chuci zhangju*. It is certainly a plausible account, but one interesting problem quickly emerges if we started to read through the Warring States corpus for confirmation. These Chu poets Qu Yuan and Song Yu, as well as their lyrics collected in the *Chuci zhangju*, did not leave behind a single trace in the writings from their own time, say, the long third century BCE. The absence of evidence does not necessarily disprove the veracity of Wang Yi's account, of course, but nevertheless, it stands in contrast to the historical importance that Wang Yi had accorded to these Chu poets and their works. For the first traces of this narrative about the history of the Chu lyrics tradition, one would have to wait until *after* the destruction of the kingdom in 223 BCE. It was in the first decades of the Han empire, in the early second century BCE, that we have certain references to the poet Qu Yuan. One of his earliest appearances was in the "Diao Qu Yuan fu" 弔屈原賦 ("A Lament for Qu Yuan") by the early Han politician Jia Yi 賈誼 (200–168 BCE). With a prosody nearly identical to that of the pieces in the *Chuci*, this rhapsody ("fu" 賦) also suggests a familiarity with the biography of Qu Yuan consistent with the one given in Wang Yi's *Chuci zhangju*.[10] And interestingly, from this point onwards, we would find regular references to the Chu lyrics tradition and the various historical personalities associated with it across a wide range of texts for the rest of the Han empire, in contrast to their stark absence in the late Warring States corpus.

---

9 Hong Xingzu, *Chuci buzhu*, 1–2, 55, 85, 120–121. For this notion of the "invulnerability of integrity" in the representations of Qu Yuan, see the excellent discussion in Michael D. K. Ing, *The Vulnerability of Integrity in Early Confucian Thought* (New York, NY: Oxford University Press, 2017).
10 Sima Qian, *Shiji*, 84:2492–2495. I borrow the translation of this song title from David R. Knechtges and Taiping Chang, eds., *Ancient and Early Medieval Chinese Literature: A Reference Guide, Part One* (Leiden: Brill, 2010), 126.

In particular, there seemed to have been a surge of interest during the reign of Emperor Wu (Han Wudi 漢武帝, r. 141–87 BCE). For instance, a certain Zhu Maichen 朱買臣 (fl. 120–110 BCE) gained favor with Emperor Wu for his expertise of "Chu lyrics," according to an anecdote in the *Shiji*, where we also have the earliest attested use of the term "Chuci."[11] Emperor Wu also commissioned the Prince of Huainan Liu An 劉安 (179–122 BCE) to write a commentary on the "Li sao" 離騷 ("Li sao zhuan" 離騷傳 ["On Encountering Trouble"]), a poem attributed to Qu Yuan that will come to be the very centerpiece of the Chu lyrics tradition.[12] Around the same time, Sima Qian, the Senior Archivist at Emperor Wu's court, compiled a biography of Qu Yuan as part of his *Shiji*. In addition to the details of Qu Yuan's career, this earliest biography of his also cites one poem (i.e. "Huai sha" ["Embracing Sand"] 懷沙) in full and mentions a few others by name (i.e. "Li sao" 離騷, "Tian wen" 天問 ["Heavenly Questions"], "Zhao hun" 招魂 ["Summons of the Soul"], and "Ai Ying" 哀郢 ["A Lament for Ying"]), all of which will be collected in the *Chuci zhangju* two centuries later.[13]

References to the Chu lyrics tradition continued to appear after the time of Emperor Wu's reign. Liu Xiang 劉向 (79–8 BCE) and his son Liu Xin 劉歆 (46 BCE–23 CE) included the poetic corpus of Qu Yuan and Song Yu in their bibliography of the imperial library.[14] By this time, anecdotes about Song Yu also started to appear for the first time in texts such as the *Hanshi waizhuan* 韓詩外傳 and *Xinxu* 新序 by the same Liu Xiang.[15] Later on, Yang Xiong 楊雄 (53 BCE–18 CE) wrote the poem "Fan Li sao" 反離騷 ("Anti-'On Encountering Trouble'") which ruefully reflects on Qu Yuan's decision to commit suicide.[16] The same poem "Li sao" also attracted the attention of the great historian Ban Gu 班固 (32–92) a few decades later. He wrote a preface for it, the "Li sao zan xu" 離騷贊序 ("A Preface to 'On Encountering Trouble'"), that recounts the tragic

11 Sima Qian, *Shiji*, 122:3142.
12 Ban Gu, *Hanshu* 漢書 (Beijing: Zhonghua, 1962), 44.2145.
13 Sima Qian, *Shiji*, 84.2481–2491.
14 Yao Zhenzong 姚振宗, *Qi lüe bie lu yi wen*; *Qi lüe yi wen*七略別錄佚文; 七略佚文 (Shanghai: Shanghai guji chubanshe, 2008). Wang Yi also noted that Liu Xiang compiled an anthology of Chu poems, on the basis of which he compiled the *Chuci zhangju*. See Hong Xingzhu, *Chuci buzhu*, 1. I also found useful the recent discussion of the imperial bibliographical efforts in Michael Hunter, "The 'Yiwen Zhi' 藝文志 (Treatise on Arts and Letters) Bibliography in Its Own Context," *Journal of the American Oriental Society*, 138.4 (2018), 763–780.
15 See Li Longxian 李隆獻, "*Wenxuan* Song Yu 'Dui Chu wang wen' jianzheng ji xiangguan de liangge wenti" 《文選》宋玉「對楚王問」箋證及相關的兩個問題, *Taida zhongwen xuebao* 臺大中文學報, 6 (June 1994): 171–208.
16 Ban Gu, *Hanshu*, 87A:3515–3521.

circumstances of Qu Yuan's life.[17] And of course, in the last century of the Han empire, we have the first compilation and exegesis of Chu lyrics, namely Wang Yi's *Chuci zhangju*. It includes all the pieces that were already noted by these earlier Han writers as well as pieces that have never been mentioned before in our extant corpus. It also expands on the biography of Qu Yuan and draws a closer connection between the tragic circumstances of his life and the Chu lyric pieces attributed to him. One may say that the *Chuci zhangju* represents a culmination of the historical fabulation and intellectual investment in the Chu lyrics tradition, much of which centered on the figure Qu Yuan, over more than three centuries of the Han dynasty to Wang Yi's own time.

This is a rather curious history of a poetic tradition. All that we know about the Chu lyrics tradition came from sources that postdate the time of its eponymous kingdom. The absence of references to this purported tradition, and all its associated personalities and key pieces, in their own time stand in sharp contrast to the lavish attention that they received over the course of the Han empire. Accordingly, much of the modern scholarship on the *Chuci* has focused on the question of its origins. What were these songs from the southern region?[18] How were they performed and what functions did they serve? One popular answer is that these poems are remnants of a once flourishing shamanistic culture of the Chu kingdom, that they were "complete libretti" of certain shamanistic rituals.[19] It is one of the few rare and widespread consensuses in the scholarship on the *Chuci*.[20]

---

17 Hong Xingzu, *Chuci buzhu*, 51.

18 The question of origins is a veritable obsession of the scholarship on the *Chuci*. To name just a few example: Zhou Weifeng 周葦風, *Chuci xue fasheng yanjiu* 楚辭學發生研究 (Guilin: Guangxi shifan daxue chubanshe, 2008); Huang Bilian 黃碧璉, *Qu Yuan yu Chu wenhua yanjiu* 屈原與楚文化研究 (Taipei: Wenjin chubanshe, 1998); Zhao Kuifu 趙逵夫, *Qu Yuan yu tade shidai* 屈原與他的時代 (Beijing: Renmin wenxue chubanshe, 1996); and Zhao Hui 趙輝, *Chuci wenhua Beijing yanjiu* 楚辭文化背景研究 (Wuhan: Hubei jiaoyu chubanshe, 1995). There are, however, dissenting voices that suggested that the *Chuci* poems were all composed during the Han period: see He Tianxing 何天行, *Chuci zuo yu Han dai kao* 楚辭作於漢代考 (Shanghai: Zhonghua, 1948); and Hu Shi 胡適, "Du *Chuci*" 讀楚辭, in *Hu Shi wencun* 胡適文存 (Shanghai: Shanghai shudian, 1989), 2.139–148.

19 Arthur Waley, *The Nine Songs: A Study of Shamanism in Ancient China* (London: George Allen and Unwin, 1955), 5.

20 This reading of the *Chuci* poems as a shamanistic artifact has a long history and is widespread. See Fujino Iwatomo 藤野岩友, *Fukei bungakuron* 巫系文学論 (Tokyo: Daigaku Shobō, 1951); Hawkes, *The Songs of the South*, 42–51; and Ping-Leung Chan, "The Sacred and the Profane: A Study of the 'Chiu ko'," *Tamkang Review* XV, no. 1, 2, 3, 4 (1984–1985), 451–465; Burton Watson, *Early Chinese Literature* (New York: Columbia U.P., 1962), 242; K. C. Chang, *Art, Myth, and Ritual: The Path to Political Authority in Ancient China* (Cambridge: Harvard U.P., 1983), 47;

Whatever the origins of the Chu lyrics tradition may be, what interests me here the most is its immense popularity during the Han empire. It was a veritable phenomenon among a very visible segment of the political elite. Among the thousands of things that the Han disinherited from the Warring States and earlier periods, the Chu lyrics were definitely not one of them. They became an object of appreciation, reflection and debates soon after founding of the empire. Scholars in the past decades have written about this surprising career of the Chu lyrics tradition during the Han empire, especially the political controversy and debates over the "Li sao" and the legend of Qu Yuan.[21] However, these works are largely interested in *what* the history of the *Chuci* was during the Han empire but less the question of *why* there should be a history at all. What might have prompted this attention to the poetic form of a defunct kingdom? Why was it not simply forgotten and consigned to the dustbin of history?[22] Let us now turn to the text of the *Chuci* poems themselves for an answer.

Martin Kern, "The Verses of Chu," in *The Cambridge History of Chinese Literature*, ed. Kang-I Sun Chang and Stephen Owen (Cambridge: Cambridge U.P., 2010), 82, 84. And of course, this is a much elaborated theme in the recent series of works by Gopal Sukhu: "Monkeys, Shamans, Emperors, and Poets," 164–165; *The Shaman and the Heresiarch: A New Interpretation of the Li Sao*, SUNY Series in Chinese Philosophy and Culture (Albany: State University of New York Press, 2012); and *The Songs of Chu: An Ancient Anthology of Works by Qu Yuan and Others*, Translations from the Asian Classics (New York: Columbia University Press, 2017).

21 The pioneer work by Lu Kanru 陸侃如 called attention to the controversial history of the *Chuci* during the Han. See Lu Kanru, "Han ren lun *Chuci*," 371–401. For more recent work, see Michael Schimmelpfenning, "The Quest for a Classic: Wang Yi and the Exegetical Prehistory of His Commentary to the *Songs of Chu*," *Early China* 29 (2004), 111–162; Shi Wenying 石文英, "Liang Han de 'Li sao' lunzeng ji qi yanxu" 兩漢的《離騷》論爭及其延續, *Wen shi zhe*, 2 (1988), 68–73; and Laurence Schneider, *Madman of Ch'u: The Chinese Myth of Loyal and Dissent* (Berkeley: University of California Press, 1980).

22 Scholars have suggested that the Chu origin of many members of the early Han political elite, including the ruling house of Liu 劉, may have accounted for this unusual popularity of the southern lyrics. It may very well have been a factor. See *The Oxford Handbook of Classical Chinese Literature (1000 BCE-900 CE)*, ed. by Wiebke Denecke, Wai-Yee Li, and Xiaofei Tian (New York: Oxford University Press, 2017), 251; and You Guo'en 游國恩, "Qu Yuan" 屈原, in *You Guo'en Chuci lunzhu ji* 游國恩楚辭論著集, 4 vols (Beijing: Zhonghua shuju, 2008), iii, 539–548, which gives an exhaustive inventory of the Chu natives from amongst the first generation of the ruling elite of the Han empire.

II Poetics of displacement in the *Chuci*

Not surprising at all for an anthology of poetic pieces written over a few centuries, the *Chuci* is a diverse collection that is hardly susceptible to any simple generalization. There are, for instances, descriptions of cosmic journeys in the "Li sao" and "Yuan you" 遠遊 ("Far-off Journey"), failed encounters with deities in the "Jiu ge" ("Nine Songs") cycle, affectation of ignorance in the "Tian wen" ("Heavenly Questions"), expression of a scholar's frustration in the "Jiu zhang" 九章 ("Nine Pieces"), "Jiu bian" 九辯 ("Nine Changes"), and "Da zhao," summoning of souls in the "Zhao hun" ("Summons of the Soul"), and the anecdotal narratives in "Yufu" 漁夫 ("The Fisherman") and "Bu ju" 卜居 ("Divination"). And these are just the pieces that are attributed to the Chu poets. As for the other pieces attributed to the Han writers, they are mostly imitative, with permutations of the major themes and key vocabularies that resemble those in these supposedly earlier pieces.

Reading across the *Chuci* corpus, however, a few predominant themes do gradually emerge.[23] One that is particularly pertinent to the argument of this chapter is their consistent interest in the depiction of landscape. In every *Chuci* poem, the narrative is always framed within a landscape or, at a minimum, situated within certain spatial relations. That is not to say that Chu lyrics are "landscape poetry" (*shanshui shi* 山水詩) like the ones by the later medieval poets such as Xie Lingyun 謝靈運 (385–443) that take landscape – or nature at large – as their primary object of poetic elaboration.[24] Rather, in these Chu lyrics, there is always a construction of a landscape, or at the very least a reference to spatial markers, that serve as the narrative context for whatever subject matters the piece deals with. Sometimes, this landscape can be very minimal, as it is in the case of "Shan gui" 山鬼 ("Mountain Spirit") from the "Jiu ge" cycle:

> There seems to be someone in the fold of the mountain
> In a coat of fig-leaves with a rabbit-floss girdle,
> With eyes that hold laughter and a smile of pearly brightness:
> 'Lady, your allurements show that you desire me.'

若有人兮山之阿, 被薜荔兮帶女羅。既含睇兮又宜笑, 子慕予兮善窈窕。[25]

---

23 When referring to the "Chuci" or "Chu lyrics" in general, I am referring to the set of poems collected in the Wang Yi's *Chuci zhangju*.
24 See Wendy Swartz, "Naturalness in Xie Lingyun's Poetic Works," *Harvard Journal of Asiatic Studies*, 70.2 (2010), 355–86; and Francis A. Westbrook, "Landscape Transformation in the Poetry of Hsieh Ling-yün," *Journal of American Oriental Society*, 100, no. 3 (July-August, 1980), 237–254.
25 Hong Xingzu, *Chuci buzhu*, 79. Once again, unless otherwise noted, all translations from the *Chuci* are adapted from David Hawkes, *The Songs of the South*. See note 8 above.

Here, in the opening lines of the poem, we are immediately introduced to a landscape, however minimalistic it may be, i.e. "the fold of the mountain" (*shan zhi e* 山之阿). The narrative is very clearly situated at a particular point in space. The rest of the poem details the failed encounter between the poet and the titular "mountain spirit" on this unnamed hill. It concludes with the forlorn poet standing alone in an unwelcoming, desolate landscape:

> The thunder rumbles; rain darkens the sky:
> The monkeys chatter; apes scream in the night:
> The wind soughs sadly and the trees rustle.
> I think of my lady and stand alone in sadness.
>
> 靁填填兮雨冥冥, 猨啾啾兮又 夜鳴。風颯颯兮木蕭蕭, 思公子兮徒離憂。[26]

In "Xiang jun" 湘君 ("The Goddess of the Xiang"), another poem from the "Jiu ge" cycle, we are introduced to a similarly minimalistic landscape, centered around an island. It begins with the following stanza that immediately situates the narrative in space:

> The goddess comes not, she holds back shyly.
> Who keeps her delaying within the island in the center,
> Lady of the lovely eyes and the winning smile?
> Skimming the water in my cassia boat,
> I bid the Yuan and Xiang still their waves
> And the Great River make its stream flow softly.
>
> 君不行兮夷猶, 蹇誰留兮中洲? 美要眇兮宜修, 沛吾乘兮桂舟。 令沅湘兮無波,
> 使江水兮安流![27]

The rest of the poem details the poet's treacherous attempt to navigate the waters to meet the goddess. And like the narratives in all the other "Jiu ge" poems, it ends in failure:

> The stream runs fast through the stony shallows,
> And my flying dragon wings swiftly above it.
> The pain is more lasting if loving is faithless:
> She broke her tryst; she told me she had not time.
>
> 石瀨兮淺淺, 飛龍兮翩翩。交不忠兮怨長, 期不信兮告余以不閒。[28]

Minimally delineated landscape such as an unnamed mountain or a lone island in these "Jiu ge" poems provide the spatial backdrop for their narratives of

---

26 Ibid., 81.
27 Ibid., 59–60.
28 Ibid., 63–64.

failed encounters with deities. For a more expansive landscape, one can hardly find a better example than the "Li sao." Attributed to Qu Yuan, it begins with the poet's lamentation on the rampant corruptions in the world. In this world so thoroughly perverted, the poet can no longer find a place where his virtue is appreciated. And at that realization, he decided to take flight:

> Suddenly I turned back and let my eyes wander.
> I resolved to go and visit all the world's quarters.
>
> 忽反顧以遊目兮, 將往觀乎四荒。 [29]

Then, the poem recounts his journey through the cosmos, encountering different deities and fantastic creatures one after another at ever more elevated celestial sites, seeking the solace that he so desperately needs. In contrast to the stark landscape in the "Jiu ge" poems, focusing on just one single spot, the "Li sao" gives its readers the whole world. The very idea of a celestial journey itself already presupposes a spatial framework in the poem. Moreover, spatial markers structure its entire narrative throughout, and in the few moments when the poet in flight is not consorting with various deities at different corners of the cosmos, he would pause and look over the vast expanse of space in which he has found himself:

> I looked all around over the earth's four quarters,
> Circling the heavens till at last I alighted.
> I gazed on a jade tower's glittering splendor
> And spied the lovely daughter of the Lord of Song.
>
> 覽相觀於四極兮, 周流乎天余乃下。望瑤臺之偃蹇兮, 見有娀之佚女。[30]

The examples of "Li sao" and poems in the "Jiu ge" cycle we have just discussed here are typical of the *Chuci* repertoire as a whole. Representations of space, and the movement of things within it, are structural to all the poems in the *Chuci*. The narratives of each and every poem always take place ostensibly *at* a certain place and *in* space.[31]

But with that said, they are not just disinterested literary cartographies or topographical surveys. The spatial ventures that we see everywhere in the *Chuci* are

---

29 Ibid., 18.
30 Ibid., 32.
31 I follow Kümin and Usborne's suggestion in understanding "point" as a "physical grid-reference," "place" as "points where specific constellations of objects and agents constitute socially recognized sites of interaction," and finally, "space" as "fields of perception and maneuver experienced by humans at any point or place." See Beat Kümin and Cornelie Usborne, 'At Home and in the Workplace: A Historical Introduction to the "Spatial Turn",' *History & Theory*, 52.3 (2013), 317–318.

always, without exception, prompted and informed by the affective state of the poet. To illustrate this, let us turn to the opening lines of the poem "Yuan you":

> Grieved by the parlous state of this world's ways,
> I wanted to float up and roam far away.
> But my powers were too weak to give me support:
> What could I ride on to bear me upwards?
>
> 悲時俗之迫阸兮, 願輕舉而遠遊。質菲薄而無因兮, 焉託乘而上浮。[32]

The desire to "roam far away" (*yuan you* 遠遊) was provoked by the poet's unhappiness with the state of the world. His discontent was what prompted this sudden awareness of the space above him. There is a continuity and correlation between his affective interiority and the awareness of an open space beyond his immediate surrounding. It is on the foundation of his unhappiness that space became relevant and meaningful as a possible means of resolution. In these Chu lyrics, the poets do not travel and gaze upon the world for their own pleasure; they do so always to fulfill a lack. In the case of the "Yuan you," after these opening lines, the poet did indeed begin his journey through the cosmos, seeking relief for this unhappiness somehow. Towards the end of the poem, after a fantastic, exhilarating journey through the cosmos, it seems as if he has at last attained happiness:

> I wanted to leave for good, to forget about returning:
> My mind was exalted with a reckless sense of freedom;
> A boundless satisfaction suffused my being:
> I wanted to yield to this voluptuous contentment.
>
> 欲度世以忘歸兮, 意恣睢 担撟。內欣欣而自美兮, 聊媮娛 自樂。[33]

No longer feeling aggrieved, he was ready to "leave for good" (or more literally, "to transcend the world" [*du shi* 度世]). But then, he was suddenly plunged back into a great sadness:

> Traversing the blue sky, I was wandering freely,
> When suddenly I glimpsed my old home below me.
> My groom was homesick and my own heart downcast;
> The trace-horses looked back and would not go forward.
> I pictured my dear ones in imagination,
> And, with a heavy sigh, I brushed the tears away.
>
> 涉青雲 汎濫游兮, 忽臨睨夫舊鄉。僕夫懷余心悲兮, 邊馬顧而不行。思舊故 想像兮, 長太息而掩涕。[34]

---

32 Hong Xingzu, *Chuci buzhu*, 163.
33 Ibid., 171–172.
34 Ibid., 172.

The poet is caught in an impossible situation here. At the start of the poem, he was unhappy at home, and so he decided to take flight through the cosmos to find relief. When it seemed like he had at last succeeded, he nevertheless felt miserable for remembering that this newfound happiness was attained away from home where he belonged. There is no place in the world where he can be truly happy. Home is where his original unhappiness lies, and by removing himself away from it, whatever momentary sense of relief or even joy that he experiences is bound to be eclipsed by the sadness of being an exile. So, what final resolution might there be for the poet? The conclusion of the poem is ambiguous:

> I toured the Four Outlands,
> Traversed the Six Regions,
> Up to the lightning's fissure,
> And down to the Great Abyss.
> In the sheer depths below, the earth was invisible;
> In the vastness above, the sky could not be seen.
> When I looked, my startled eyes saw nothing;
> When I listened, no sound met my amazed ear.
> Transcending Inaction, I came to Purity,
> And entered the neighborhood of the Great Beginning.

經營四荒兮, 周流六漠。上至列缺兮, 降望大壑。下崢嶸而無地 兮, 上寥廓而無天。視儵忽而無見兮, 聽惝怳而無聞。超無為 至清兮, 與泰初而為鄰。[35]

Having journeyed through the entire cosmos – the "Four Outlands" (*si huang* 四荒) and the "Six Regions" (*liu mo* 六漠) – he finally attains some measure of peace, a state of "Purity" (*zhi qing* 至清) away from the foulness in the world that prompted his celestial journey in the first place, by being literally nowhere, a place with no sight and sound that is reminiscent of the primordial state of the world (i.e. the "Great Beginning"). The idea that he can only be at ease by being nowhere means that he is condemned to be terminally displaced in this world; there is literally not a single place for him in the entire cosmos. Agitated by his discontent with the ways of the world where he was, the poet escapes into the vast expanse of the cosmos, only to discover that the only place he truly belongs is nowhere. In the "Yuan you," the literary construction of this most expansive cosmic landscape, in the end, serves to articulate a most radical spatial displacement of an individual.

This idea of displacement, related through an affective landscape, so powerfully and elegantly set forth in the "Yuan you," is in fact quite typical throughout the *Chuci* corpus. Frustrated by the corrupt state of the world or anxious to

---

[35] Ibid., 174–175.

acquire something that he does not already have, the poet sets out on a journey in quest of whatever it is that he desperately desires, be it an encounter with a deity, the attainment of immortality, or just an appreciative audience. And in the end, he always fails. This is not a new observation about the *Chuci*; for instance, long ago, David Hawkes has noted the invariable failures of these quests of the poets, especially in the "Jiu ge" cycle.[36] What I would add here is that this discontent of the poets always implicates an engagement with space in the *Chuci*. It is an unhappiness founded on a sense of the displacement of things. In the "Li sao" and "Yuan you," it is the poet himself who is displaced, traversing the whole cosmos in search of a welcoming abode; in some other poems, such as "Huai sha" 懷沙 ("Embracing Sand"), the whole world is in utter disarray:

> White is changed to black;
> The high cast down and the low made high;
> The phoenix languishes in a cage,
> While hens and ducks can gambol free.

> 變白以為黑兮, 倒上以為下。鳳皇在笯兮, 雞鶩翔舞。[37]

Not only are things out of place, they are precisely where they are not supposed to be. It is a world turned upside down. We can find this motif elsewhere in the literature of the late Warring States and the early empires, but in the *Chuci* corpus, the focus on this idea of things being out of place is just absolutely relentless.[38] In one Chu lyric after another, we bear witness to a world where all things have become ruefully unmoored. And for its unhappy denizens, the only possible redemption is to be nowhere, figuratively as it was in "Yuan you" or literally as in the "Yufu" where Qu Yuan saw suicide as the only possible escape.[39] This poetics of displacement saturates the Chu lyrics. The *Chuci* is a world of unhappiness in space.

---

36 Hawkes, *The Songs of the South*, 49.

37 Hong Xingzu, *Chuci buzhu*, 143.

38 The poems at the end of the "Fupian" 賦篇 of the *Xunzi* 荀子(ca. third century BCE) are a great early example; it is also a common motif in the some of the Han dynasty *fu* 賦 pieces, such as the "Funiao fu" 鵬鳥賦by Jia Yi 賈誼 (200–168 BCE). See David Knechtges, "Riddles as Poetry: The *Fu* Chapter of the *Hsün-tzu*," in *Wen-lin*, ed. Chow Tse Tsung (Madison: University of Wisconsin; Hong Kong: The Chinese University of Hong Kong, 1989), 2.1–32.

39 Hong Xingzu, *Chuci buzhu*, 143.

III *Chuci* and the politics of space

All utterances are inherently dialogic.[40] What or who then did the Chu lyrics address? Given that the *Chuci* poems and their lore were the object of much attention under the Han empire, as we discussed earlier, who were their interlocutors and what concerns might have animated this persistent interest in them? With this reading of the *Chuci* corpus as a poetic language for articulating the idea of displacement, I would suggest that the poems were mobilized as a response to the spatial claims of the early empires. More specifically, it was a reaction to the politicization of space under the Qin and Han empires with their proclamation that they had created a perfectly ordered space. The presumption that a good state is one that creates a well-ordered space, with everything in its right place, has a long history that pre-dates the Qin and the Han, as Mark E. Lewis has demonstrated.[41] One can find an eloquent expression of this idea, for instance, in the "Yu gong" 禹貢 ("Tributes of Yu") chapter of the *Shangshu* 尚書 from the fourth or third century BCE.[42] In it, the legendary Great Yu 禹 was said to have fixed the great floods and remade the world into a well-demarcated, coherent space where all things circulated properly. In the court literature of both the Qin and Han empires, we can find very comparable arguments by the ruling elite about their work in ordering the space of their empires. They stand in sharp contrast to the language and content of the *Chuci* corpus that we have just discussed and provide, I would argue, an important context for understanding the history – especially the sudden interest – in Chu lyrics at the time.

The rise and the founding of the Qin empire had always been a project in and through spatial expansion and organization. The military conquest of one kingdom after another in the long third century BCE, and subsequently, the remaking of the territories of the old kingdoms (*guo* 國) into the thirty-six commanderies (*jun* 郡)

---

40 M. M. Bakhtin, *The Dialogic Imagination: Four Essays*, ed. by Michael Holquist, trans. by Michael Holquist and Caryl Emerson, University of Texas Press Slavic Series; No. 1 (Austin: University of Texas Press, 2004), esp. 259–422.

41 Mark Edward Lewis, *The Construction of Space in Early China* (Albany: State University of New York Press, 2006).

42 Qu Wanli 屈萬里, *Shangshu ji shi* 尚書集釋 (Taipei: Jinglian chuban shiye gongsi, 1983), 42–72. See the discussion in Robin McNeal, 'Spatial Models of the State in Early Chinese Texts: Tribute Networks and the Articulation of Power and Authority in *Shangshu* "Yu Gong" and *Yizhoushu* "Wang Hui"', in *Origins of Chinese Political Philosophy: Studies in the Composition and Thought of the Shangshu (Classic of Documents)*, ed. by Martin Kern and Dirk Meyer, Studies in the History of Chinese Texts (Leiden; Boston: Brill, 2017), 475–95.

were some of the key measures that it took to refashion the empire's landscape for political ends. After the founding of the empire, its initiatives to unify the writing script, measurement units, and axle lengths also point towards its desire for a homogeneous, coherent space that would allow for an unobstructed dissemination of its imperial commands.[43] Qin's political authority was, at least in part, constituted by a deliberate "making and remaking of landscapes."[44]

For evidence of how the Qin imagined this new space of the empire, let us turn to its court literature.[45] Specifically, let us look at the series of stele inscriptions commissioned by the First Emperor of the Qin (Qin shi huangdi 秦始皇帝, r. 221–210 BCE).[46] For example, the one erected on Mount Zhifu 之罘, from the year 218 BCE, begins as follows:

> In the twenty-ninth year the August Emperor set forth in spring, inspecting and visiting the distant regions. Advancing to the brink of the sea, he ascended Mt. Zhifu, gazing down at the morning sun.

> 維二十九年, 皇帝春游, 覽省遠方。逮于海隅, 遂登之罘, 昭臨朝陽。[47]

Here, the Qin emperor ascends to an elevated spot, overlooking the vast landscape that opens up before his eyes, not unlike the *Chuci* poets in "Li sao" and "Yuan you" who surveyed the cosmos from high above, as we have seen earlier. And what does he see? The inscription continues with the following marvelous description:

---

43 Sima Qian, *Shiji*, 6.239–240. See also Charles Sanft, *Communication and Cooperation in Early Imperial China: Publicizing the Qin Dynasty* (Albany: State University of New York Press, 2014), esp. 57–76.

44 Adam T. Smith, *The Political Landscape*, 5.

45 I refer to Jack Chen's definition of the "court" as a "spatial figuration of the various relationships among the sovereign (emperor, king, or prince), ministers, officials, and other court personnel," and therefore, physically, it can be "wherever the ruler and his officials were, whether in the capital, en route from one palace to another, or on the frontiers." Jack Chen, 'Sites I', in *The Oxford Handbook of Classical Chinese Literature (1000 BCE-900 CE)*, ed. by Wiebke Denecke, Wai-Yee Li, and Xiaofei Tian (New York: Oxford University Press, 2017), 426. See also Luke Habberstad, *Forming the Early Chinese Court: Rituals, Spaces, Roles*, The Modern Language Initiative (Seattle: University of Washington Press, 2017).

46 On the reliability of the stele inscriptions as historical sources for the Qin empire, see Martin Kern, *The Stele Inscriptions of Ch'in Shih-huang: Text and Ritual in Early Chinese Imperial Representation* (New Haven: American Oriental Society, 2000).

47 Sima Qian, *Shiji*, 6.250. Unless otherwise noted, translations from Sima Qian's *Shiji* are taken from Burton Watson, *Records of the Grand Historian: Qin Dynasty* (Hong Kong and New York: Columbia U.P., 1993) and *Records of the Grand Historian: Han Dynasty II* (Hong Kong and New York: Columbia U.P., 1993), with minor modifications.

The vista was vast and beautiful, and the ministers in his retinue all pondered, searching out the source of his supreme enlightenment. When the sage's laws were first promulgated, they brought purity and order within the borders and punished the unruly and powerful beyond them. His warlike might was brandished on wide, shaking the four corners of the land; he took captive the kings of the Six States. . . . Office holders have the honor due them, each understands his duties, so all proceeds without ill-feeling or doubt. The commoners have undergone transformation, near and far share a single rule, an achievement far surpassing antiquity.

觀望廣麗, 從臣咸念, 原道至明。聖法初興, 清理疆內, 外誅暴彊。武威旁暢, 振動四極, 禽滅六王。。。。職臣遵分, 各知所行, 事無嫌疑。黔首改化, 遠邇同度, 臨古絕尤。[48]

In contrast to the desolate landscape depicted in the *Chuci* poems, scattered with unwelcoming deities among things out of place, what the Qin emperor saw was the exact opposite: a perfectly ordered world, where all his ministers know exactly where they stand and have none of the sort of "ill-feeling" and "doubt" (*xianyi* 嫌疑) that are a constant source of anxiety for the forlorn, troubled poets in the *Chuci*.[49]

This vision of a grand, perfect order is ubiquitous throughout the Qin stele inscriptions. Here is another example from the Mount Langya inscription:

Within the six directions, the domain of the August Emperor, west to the flowing sands, south all the way to Beihu, east to the eastern sea, north beyond Daxia, wherever human tracks may reach, there are none who are not his subjects. In merit he tops the Five Emperors, his bounty reaching oxen and horses, none untouched by the ruler's virtue, each at rest in his home.

六合之內, 皇帝之土。西涉流沙, 南盡北戶。東有東海, 北過大夏。人迹所至, 無不臣者。功蓋五帝, 澤及牛馬。莫不受德, 各安其宇。[50]

This perfectly ordered cosmos are all the emperor's domain; everything is exactly where they belong and all can be "at rest in his home" (*ge an qi yu* 各安其宇). Once again, we see a world that is diametrically opposite to the world depicted in the *Chuci*, where all things are displaced, and home is where one wants to be but cannot remain. The spatial visions in these two bodies of texts – the *Chuci* and the Qin stele inscriptions – are the inversions of one another. While the Qin stele inscriptions speak of a universal order with proper placements of all things, the *Chuci* imagines an inescapable chaos where everything is continually out of place and nothing can ever be at rest anywhere.

---

48 Sima Qian, *Shiji*, 6.250.
49 Hong Xingzu, *Chuci buzhu*, 149.
50 Sima Qian, *Shiji*, 6.245.

These imperial claims about state spatial organization did not perish with the short-lived Qin empire; they were soon to be inherited by its successor the Han, especially under the reign of Emperor Wu, a period that saw the reconstitution of much of the centralized bureaucratic order first introduced by the Qin as well as a notable surge of interest in the Chu lyrics tradition, as we have noted earlier. In the "Hequ shu" 河渠書 ("Treatise on the Yellow River and Canals") of the *Shiji*, for instance, Sima Qian details the many efforts by Emperor Wu to position the waterways within the empire, at times even overtly following Great Yu's legendary plan as described in the "Yu gong," to achieve a spatial layout that will lead to a good order.[51] In the "Fengshan shu" 封禪書 ("The Treatise on the Feng and Shan Sacrifices"), also from the *Shiji*, we see Emperor Wu, following the example of the First Emperor of Qin, imagining his dominion as having extended to all things in the cosmos.[52] In the "Tian guan shu" 天官書 ("The Treatise on Celestial Offices"), likewise from the *Shiji*, we see reiterations of the idea that the creation of an imperial order necessarily involves an ordering of the cosmic space and an alignment of all the heavenly entities within it.[53] Together, these texts suggest a degree of continuity between the Qin of the First Emperor and the Han of Emperor Wu in their contention about the spatial order of the empires.

For a more dramatic illustration of the Han imperial spatial imagination under Emperor Wu's reign, we can hardly do better than to have a look at the "Da ren fu" 大人賦 ("Rhapsody on the Great One") by Sima Xiangru 司馬相如 (179–117 BCE). Written for Emperor Wu's audience, it recounts the cosmic journey of the "Great One," presumably a stand-in for the emperor himself given the context of the composition.[54] On first reading, it is reminiscent of the poems of cosmic journey in the *Chuci*; it even shares a few identical passages with the "Yuan you" in addition to their already very similar vocabulary and prosody. Both poems begin with this identical passage: "Grieved by the parlous state of this world's ways, I wanted to float up and away with it" (悲時俗之迫阨兮, 願輕舉而遠遊).[55] In the "Yuan you," as we have discussed earlier, this initial unhappiness was never fully expelled as the poet journeys through the cosmos. In contrast, whatever grief that

---

51 Ibid, 29.1413.
52 Ibid, 28.1355–1404, 6.235–263. See also the discussion in Michael Puett, *To Become a God: Cosmology, Sacrifice, and Self-Divinization in Early China* (Cambridge: Harvard U.P., 2002), 287–316.
53 Sima Qian, *Shiji*, 27.1346–1347.
54 Ibid, 117.3062.
55 Ibid, 117.3056; and Hong Xingzu, *Chuci buzhu*, 163.

the Great One might have experienced at the start of the "Da ren fu," it soon dissipates as he takes a triumphant and exhilarating journey across the universe. Traveling confidently from one celestial spot to another, he snatches stars and rainbows for his own adornments, and he commands divine figures and fantastic creatures throughout the cosmic realm to help him "survey the eight directions and the four outer wastes, ford the Nine Rivers and pass over the Five Streams" (徧覽八紘而觀四荒兮, 朅渡九江而越五河).[56] It is an orderly cosmos under the dominion of the emperor, with all things are exactly where they are supposed to be. Towards the end, after the climactic encounter with the Queen Mother of the West (*Xiwangmu* 西王母), the poem concludes as follows:

> Beneath him in the vastness, the earth has disappeared;
> Above his head the heavens vanish in endless space.
> Gazing about, his eyes swim and grow sightless;
> His ears are deafened and discern no sound.
> Riding upon the Void, he mounts on high
> Above the world of men, companionless, to dwell alone.

> 下崢嶸而無地兮, 上寥廓而無天。視眩眠而無見兮, 聽惝恍而無聞。乘虛無而上假兮, 超無友而獨存。[57]

This is nearly identical to the ending of "Yuan you," but nevertheless, the contexts of the two are vastly different. In the "Yuan you," the dejected poet ended up being nowhere in a world where he felt perpetually displaced. In the "Da ren fu," however, after a jubilant, commanding tour of the cosmos, the detached state of the Great One at the end connotes not a withdrawal from the world but its subjugation and transcendence. His solitude further correlates with the singularity of this attainment. No wonder that Emperor Wu, upon hearing the performance of the "Da ren fu," was "overcome with delight, declaring that it made him feel as though he were already whirling away over the clouds and filled him with a longing to wander about the earth and the heavens" (天子大說, 飄飄有凌雲之氣, 似游天地之閒意).[58] The "Da ren fu" celebrates a world

---

56 Ibid, 117.3060.
57 Ibid, 117.3062.
58 Ibid, 117.3063. Sima Xiangru's *fu* poems, of course, are not just simple celebration of the accomplishments of Emperor Wu, but they can also be read as subtle critique and remonstrance. See Wai-yee Li, 'Riddles, Concealment, and Rhetoric in Early China', in *Facing the Monarch: Modes of Advice in the Early Chinese Court*, ed. by Garret P. S. Olberding (Cambridge, Mass.; London: Harvard University Asia Center, distributed by Harvard University Press, 2013), 100–132; Fusheng Wu, "Han Epideictic Rhapsody: A Product and Critique of Imperial Patronage," *Monumenta Serica*, 55 (2007), 23–59.

properly ordered, and thus brought under control by its singular ruler, while the "Yuan you" bemoans the never-ending, all-encompassing chaos where the only hope for salvation is oblivion.

So, what are we to make of this dissonance between the spatial representations in the Han court literature and the *Chuci*? Recall that in our overview of the *Chuci* under the early empires, we noted that there was this consistent and persistent interest in the Chu lyrics tradition and its lore throughout the period of the Han empire. Over the four centuries of the Han dynasty, we saw the compositions of new imitative pieces, elaboration of its founding legends (i.e., the story of Qu Yuan), and the compilation of its canonical pieces (i.e. Wang Yi's *Chuci zhangju*). On one hand, we have a confident rhetoric of good spatial order in the court literature of the Qin and Han empires; on the other hand, there is also this attentiveness to a poetic language of displacement among the political elite of the empires at the same time. With this dissonance in mind, I would argue that this surge of interest in Chu lyrics under the Han was largely prompted by these radical spatial claims of the early empires, first made by the Qin and then the Han. The Chu lyrics tradition invited attention from Han politicians who recognized it as an intellectual and literary resource for reflecting upon or even critiquing the empire's claim of having fashioned a perfectly well-ordered space. In a world where everything is said to be already in its right place, Chu lyrics provides a refined, eloquent language that allows one to imagine otherwise. As a poetic language designed for articulating displacement, it became all the more resonant in a world that preemptively banished such spatial disorder as a thing of the past, an impossibility in the present.

The Chu lyrics afforded not just mere literary pleasure for its Han readers, but a critical resource for contemplating and interrogating the grandiose spatial claims of the new empires. Not surprisingly, therefore, Jia Yi turned to elaborating on the legend of Qu Yuan in his "Diao Qu Yuan fu" precisely at the moment when he was exiled from the Han capital to the periphery of this supposedly perfect order of the empire, or Sima Qian invoked Qu Yuan in his "Bao Ren An shu" 報任安書 ("Letter in Reply to Ren An") as an authorial model in his justification for the compilation of the *Shiji* after he was disgraced at the court of Emperor Wu.[59] Having been displaced from what they thought were their rightful positions in a supposedly perfectly ordered world, these Han politicians turned to the past and seized upon the tradition of Chu lyrics to imagine and articulate a

---

[59] Ban Gu, *Hanshu*, 62.2725–2736, esp. 2735. See Wai-yee Li, "The Letter to Ren An and Authorship in the Chinese Tradition," in *The Letter to Ren An & Sima Qian's Legacy*, ed. by Stephen W. Durrant and others (Seattle: University of Washington Press, 2016), 96–123.

world gone awry. In these moments of danger, to borrow a phrase from Walter Benjamin, these Han politicians seized hold of the memory of Chu kingdom and its lyrical tradition to try to make sense of it all.[60]

Put differently, the *Chuci* phenomenon in the early imperial period can be understood as a consequence of the radical politicization of space under the rise of empires in early China. The Qin and Han empires were founded, in part, on their work in re-ordering the spatial relations between all things in their ex-pansive dominions. The ideological fantasy, as we have seen in the example of the Qin stele inscriptions, is that the new spatial order that they have fashioned was perfect or even natural, in the sense that all things are now restored to where they rightfully belong in this new world that they have created. The good order that the empires have so painstakingly achieved has conferred upon the world a second nature to which all should happily submit.[61] In such a political landscape, one can imagine the great pleasure afforded by the Chu lyrics for its fabulation of a world displaced. Its elegant yet melancholic language allows for the articulation of dystopia in a purportedly utopian realm. In a more radical context, we can also see how the Chu lyrics tradition offered the political elite a language of political subversion. It was a well-wrought language that can be used to articulate an alternative description of this new space of the empires – one filled with things that were displaced, unmoored, or perverted. And of course, like all politically subversive languages, it was susceptible to appropri-ation by the state. The "Da ren fu" by Sima Xiangru was perhaps such a case; superficially, at least, it seemed to have proclaimed rather than interrogated this supposedly well-ordered space of the Han empire.

To create a new state is to create a new space, as I said at the very begin-ning. Not only did the Qin and the Han empires make and remake the spaces of their dominion, but they also proclaimed a lasting perfection for the new land-scape that they had fashioned.[62] The Qin empire fell in relatively short order,

---

60 Walter Benjamin, "On the Concept of History," in *Selected Writings*, ed. by Howard Eiland and Michael William Jennings, trans. by E. F. N. Jephcott, 4 vols (Cambridge, Mass.: Belknap Press, 1996), iv, 391.

61 This argument for the possibility of political innovations to align humanity with the natural order has a long genealogy that can be traced back to the ideas preserves in the *Xunzi*. See the discussion in Michael J. Puett, *The Ambivalence of Creation: Debates Concerning Innovation and Artifice in Early China* (Stanford: Stanford U.P., 2002), 64–73.

62 One may also relate this self-image of the Qin empire to its conceit that it had brought about the "end of history," a perfect form of government that will last indefinitely into the fu-ture. See Yuri Pines, 'From Historical Evolution to the End of History: Past, Present and Future from Shang Yang to the First Emperor', in *Dao Companion to the Philosophy of Han Fei*, ed. by Paul R. Goldin (Dordrecht: Springer Netherlands, 2013), 25–46.

but the Han did manage to sustain its imperial rule for centuries. The rise of the Qin and Han empires was, as this study of the *Chuci* would suggest, attended by the emergence of a contentious imagination of the spaces of empires, within which we find a whole range of positions between seeing the new imperial regimes as a sublime utopia of order or a ruinous dystopia of displacement, all of which could and were effectively articulated by way of the language of the Chu lyrics. It was for this reason, in part, that the *Chuci* was elaborated as a discursive site over the course of the Han empire.

The political transition from the old aristocratic kingdoms of the late Warring States to the new bureaucratic empires of the Qin and the Han was achieved, in part, through a remaking of landscape. In the process, space was inevitably politicized. Political ideals were articulated through specific spatial orders, and political authority rested on the creation and perpetuation of proper spatial relations. In this context, the tradition of Chu lyrics, with its refined poetics of displacement, emerged as an eloquent resource for articulating and reflecting on this new contentious imagination of the spaces of empires. The persistence and deepening of this interest in the lyrics of Chu, which extends to other legends and personalities such as Qu Yuan and Song Yu, from the first decades of the Han to the time of Wang Yi's *Chuci zhangju* in the last century of the empire, is perhaps indicative of the endurance of this contentious question of space throughout the early imperial period. Juxtaposing the *Chuci* and the Qin-Han court literature gave us a glimpse into this politics of space under the early empires at perhaps the most rarefied, abstract level. Much work remains to be done to flesh out the history of the production of space under the rise of empires in early China.

References

Bakhtin, M. M., *The Dialogic Imagination: Four Essays*, ed. by Michael Holquist, trans. by Michael Holquist and Caryl Emerson, University of Texas Press Slavic Series; No. 1 (Austin: University of Texas Press, 2004)

Ban, Gu 班固, *Hanshu* 漢書, 12 vols (Beijing: Zhonghua shuju, 1975)

Benjamin, Walter, 'On the Concept of History', in *Selected Writings*, ed. by Howard Eiland and Michael William Jennings, trans. by E. F. N. Jephcott, 4 vols (Cambridge, Mass.: Belknap Press, 1996), iv, 389–400

Blakeley, Barry B., 'The Geography of Chu', in *Defining Chu: Image and Reality in Ancient China*, ed. by Constance A. Cook and John S. Major (Honolulu: University of Hawai'i Press, 1999), 9–20

Chan, Ping-Leung, 'The Sacred and the Profane: A Study of "Chiu Ko"', *Tamkang Review*, 15 (1984), 451.

Chang, K. C., *Art, Myth, and Ritual: The Path to Political Authority in Ancient China* (Cambridge, Mass.; London: Harvard University Press, 1983)

Denecke, Wiebke, Wai-Yee Li, and Xiaofei Tian, eds., *The Oxford Handbook of Classical Chinese Literature (1000 BCE-900 CE)* (New York: Oxford University Press, 2017)

Doyle, Michael W., *Empires* (Ithaca, N.Y.: Cornell University Press, 1986)

Fan, Ye 范曄, *Hou Hanshu* 後漢書 (Beijing: Zhonghua shuju, 1965)

Fujino, Iwatomo 藤野岩友, *Fukei bungakuron* 巫系文学論 (Tōkyō: Daigaku Shobō, 26)

Habberstad, Luke, *Forming the Early Chinese Court: Rituals, Spaces, Roles*, The Modern Language Initiative (Seattle: University of Washington Press, 2017)

Hardt, Michael, and Antonio Negri, *Empire* (Cambridge, Mass.: Harvard University Press, 2000)

Hawkes, David, 'Ch'u Tz'u', in *Early Chinese Texts: A Bibliographical Guide*, ed. by Michael Loewe, Early China Special Monograph Series, no. 2 (Berkeley, Calif.: Society for the Study of Early China, Institute of East Asian Studies, University of California, Berkeley, 1993), 48–55

Hawkes, David, trans., *The Songs of the South: An Ancient Chinese Anthology of Poems by Qu Yuan and Other Poets*, Penguin Classics (Harmondsworth, Middlesex, England; New York, N.Y., U.S.A: Penguin Books, 1985)

He, Tianxing 何天行, *Chuci zuo yu Han dai kao* 楚辭作於漢代考, Jin dai ming jia san yi xue shu zhu zuo cong kan. Wen xue (Taiyuan: Shanxi renmin chubanshe, 2014)

Hong, Xingzu 洪興祖, *Chuci bu zhu* 楚辭補注 (Beijing: Zhonghua shuju, 1983)

Hu, Shi 胡適, 'Du *Chuci* 讀楚辭', in *Hu Shi Wencun* 胡適文存 (1989: Shanghai, Shanghai shudian), ii, 139–48

Huang, Bilian 黃碧璉, *Qu Yuan yu Chu wenhua yanjiu* 屈原與楚文化研究 (Taipei: Wenjin chubanshe, 87)

Hunter, Michael, 'The "Yiwen Zhi" 藝文志 (Treatise on Arts and Letters) Bibliography in Its Own Context', *Journal of the American Oriental Society*, 138.4 (2018), 763–780.

Ing, Michael D. K., *The Vulnerability of Integrity in Early Confucian Thought* (New York, NY: Oxford University Press, 2017)

Jiang, Tianshu 蔣天樞, '*Hou Hanshu* Wang Yi zhuan kaoshi 後漢書王逸傳考釋', in *Chuci lunwen ji* 楚辭論文集 (Xi'an: Shanxi renmin chubanshe, 1982), 195–212

Kern, Martin, *The Stele Inscriptions of Ch'in Shih-Huang: Text and Ritual in Early Chinese Imperial Representation*, American Oriental Series; v. 85 (New Haven, Conn.: American Oriental Society, 2000)

Kern, Martin, 'The *Verses of Chu*', in *The Cambridge History of Chinese Literature*, ed. by Kang-i Sun Chang and Stephen Owen, 2 vols (Cambridge, UK; New York: Cambridge University Press, 2010), i, 76–85

Knechtges, David, 'Riddles as Poetry: The "Fu" Chapter of the Hsun-Tzu', in *Wen-Lin: Studies in the Chinese Humanities*, ed. by Tsê-Tsung Chow (Madison: University of Wisconsin Press, 1989), ii, 1–31

Knechtges, David R., and Taiping Chang, eds., *Ancient and Early Medieval Chinese Literature: A Reference Guide Part One* (Leiden: Brill, 2010)

Kominami, Ichirō 小南一郎, *Soji to sono chūshakushatachi* 楚辭とその注釈者たち (Kyōto: Hōyū Shoten, 2003)

Kümin, Beat, and Cornelie Usborne, 'At Home and in the Workplace: A Historical Introduction to the "Spatial Turn"', *History & Theory*, 52 (2013), 305–318

Li, Wai-yee, 'Riddles, Concealment, and Rhetoric in Early China', in *Facing the Monarch: Modes of Advice in the Early Chinese Court*, ed. by Garret P. S. Olberding (Cambridge, Mass.; London: Harvard University Asia Center, distributed by Harvard University Press, 2013), 100–132

Li, Wai-yee, 'The Letter to Ren An and Authorship in the Chinese Tradition', in *The Letter to Ren An & Sima Qian's Legacy*, ed. by Stephen W. Durrant, Li, Wai-yee, Michael Nylan, and Hans van Ess (Seattle: University of Washington Press, 2016), 96–123

Li, Longxian 李隆獻, '*Wenxuan* Song Yu "Dui Chu Wang Wen" Jianzheng Ji Xianggauan de Liangge Wenti" 《文選》宋玉「對楚王問」箋證及相關的兩個問題', *Taida Zhongwen Xuebao* 臺大中文學報, 6 (1994), 171–208

Lu, Kanru 陸侃如, 'Han ren lun *Chuci* 漢人論楚辭', in *Lu Kanru gudian wenxue lunwen* 陸侃如古典文學論文集 (Shanghai: Shanghai guji chubanshe, 1987), 371–401

Maier, Charles S., *Among Empires: American Ascendancy and Its Predecessors* (Cambridge, MA: Harvard University Press, 2006)

Pines, Yuri, 'From Historical Evolution to the End of History: Past, Present and Future from Shang Yang to the First Emperor', in *Dao Companion to the Philosophy of Han Fei*, ed. by Paul R. Goldin (Dordrecht: Springer Netherlands, 2013), 25–46

Puett, Michael J., *The Ambivalence of Creation: Debates Concerning Innovation and Artifice in Early China* (Stanford, Calif: Stanford University Press, 2001)

Puett, Michael J., *To Become a God: Cosmology, Sacrifice, and Self-Divinization in Early China*, Harvard-Yenching Institute Monographs Series, 57 (Cambridge, Mass.: Harvard University Press, 2004)

Qu, Wanli 屈萬里, *Shang shu ji shi* 尚書集釋, Qu, Wanli. Works. 1983; 4. Y (Taipei: Lianjing chuban shiye gongsi, 72)

Sanft, Charles, *Communication and Cooperation in Early Imperial China: Publicizing the Qin Dynasty*, SUNY Series in Chinese Philosophy and Culture (Albany: State University of New York Press, 2014)

Schimmelpfennig, Michael, 'The Quest for a Classic: Wang Yi and the Exegetical Prehistory of His Commentary to the Songs of Chu', *Early China*, 29 (2004), 111–162

Schneider, Laurence A., *A Madman of Ch'u: The Chinese Myth of Loyalty and Dissent* (Berkeley: University of California Press, 1980)

Shi, Wenying 石文英, 'Liang Han de *Li Sao* Zenglun Ji Qi Yanxu 兩漢的《離騷》爭論及其延續', *Wen Shi Zhe* 文史哲, 2 (1988), 70–75

Sima, Qian 司馬遷, *Shiji* 史記, 10 vols. (Beijing: Zhonghua shuju, 1959)

Smith, Adam T., *The Political Landscape: Constellations of Authority in Early Complex Polities* (Berkeley: University of California Press, 2003)

Sukhu, Gopal, 'Monkeys, Shamans, Emperors, and Poets: The Chuci and Images of Chu during the Han Dynasty', in *Defining Chu: Image and Reality in Ancient China*, ed. by Constance A. Cook and John S. Major (Honolulu: University of Hawai'i Press, 1999), 145–65

Sukhu, Gopal, *The Shaman and the Heresiarch: A New Interpretation of the Li Sao*, SUNY Series in Chinese Philosophy and Culture (Albany: State University of New York Press, 2012)

Sukhu, Gopal, *The Songs of Chu: An Ancient Anthology of Works by Qu Yuan and Others*, Translations from the Asian Classics (New York: Columbia University Press, 2017)

Swartz, Wendy, 'Naturalness in Xie Lingyun's Poetic Works', *Harvard Journal of Asiatic Studies*, 70 (2010), 355–86

Waley, Arthur, *The Nine Songs; a Study of Shamanism in Ancient China* (London: Allen and Unwin, 1955)

Wang, Qizhou 王齊洲, 'Wang Yi He *Chuci Zhangju* 王逸和《楚辞章句》', *Wenxue Yichan* 文學遺產, 1995, 23–30

Watson, Burton, *Early Chinese Literature* (New York: Columbia University Press, 1962)

Watson, Burton, *Records of the Grand Historian: Han Dynasty II*, Records of Civilization, Sources and Studies, no. 65, Rev. ed (Hong Kong; New York: Columbia University Press, 1993)

Watson, Burton, *Records of the Grand Historian: Qin Dynasty* (Hong Kong; New York: Research Centre for Translation, Chinese University of Hong Kong; Columbia University Press, 1993)

Westbrook, Francis A., 'Landscape Transformation in the Poetry of Hsieh Ling-Yün', *Journal of the American Oriental Society*, 100 (1980), 237–254

Wu, Fusheng, 'Han Epideictic Rhapsody: A Product and Critique of Imperial Patronage', *Monumenta Serica*, 55 (2007), 23–59

Yao, Zhenzong 姚振宗, *Qi lüe bie lu yi wen; Qi lüe yi wen* 七略別錄佚文; 七略佚文 (Shanghai: Shanghai guji chubanshe, 2008).

You, Guo'en 游國恩, '*Chuci* de qiuyuan 楚辭的起源', in *You Guo'en Chuci lunzhu ji* 游國恩楚辭論著集, 4 vols (Beijing: Zhonghua shuju, 2008), iv, 114–26

You, Guo'en 游國恩, '*Chuci* gailun 楚辭概論', in *You Guo'en Chuci lunzhu ji* 游國恩楚辭論著集, 4 vols (Beijing: Zhonghua shuju, 2008), iii, 1–212

You, Guo'en 游國恩, 'Qu Yuan 屈原', in *You Guo'en Chuci lunzhu ji* 游國恩楚辭論著集, 4 vols (Beijing: Zhonghua shuju, 2008), iii, 406–548

Zhao, Hui 趙輝, *Chuci wenhua beijing yanjiu* 楚辭文化背景研究, Chu xue wen ku (Wuhan: Hubei jiaoyu chubanshe, 1995)

Zhao, Kuifu 趙逵夫, *Qu Yuan yu ta di shidai* 屈原與他的時代 (Beijing: Renmin wenxue chubanshe, 1996)

Zhou, Weifeng 周葦風, *Chuci fashengxue yanjiu* 楚辭發生學研究 (Guilin: Guangxi shifan daxue chubanshe, 2008)

H.M. Agnes Hsu-Tang

A Tomb with a View: Axonometry in Early Chinese Cartography

In a series of lectures on the revolution of modern science that he gave at the University of St. Andrews in 1955, Werner Heisenberg, the German Nobel Prize quantum physicist, lucidly explained the Copenhagen Interpretation of Quantum Physics[1] and emphasized that "we have to remember that what we observe is not nature herself, but nature exposed to our method of questioning."[2] Heisenberg's lectures were subsequently published in *Physics and Philosophy: The Revolution in Modern Science*, which has since become a seminal text of modern thought for his applications of quantum physics theory to social sciences and humanities. In 2016, at a conference on art and visuality in the global age, contemporary art historian and critic Celeste Ianniciello invoked Heisenberg and further suggested that, sixty years later, *Physics and Philosophy* continues to have a profound impact on our perceptions of the modern world.

> Quantum physics conceives reality as an unlocatable energy made of particles and waves which acquire form through a performative act of measurement. Matter is generated by this differential act, where the observer and the observed are inseparable and part of the world in its differential becoming. Matter then emerges through an act of contamination, migration, border-crossing. Difference is the process of mattering in which the world articulates itself differently.[3]

---

1 Jan Faye, "Copenhagen Interpretation of Quantum Mechanics", in Edward N. Zalta, ed., *The Stanford Encyclopedia of Philosophy* (Stanford: Stanford University Press, 2014). https://plato. stanford.edu/archives/fall2014/entries/qm-copenhagen/. "The Copenhagen interpretation was the first general attempt to understand the world of atoms as this is represented by quantum mechanics. The founding father was mainly the Danish physicist Niels Bohr, but also Werner Heisenberg, Max Born and other physicists made important contributions to the overall understanding of the atomic world that is associated with the name of the capital of Denmark." Also see Hermann Wimmel, *Quantum Physics & Observed Reality: A Critical Interpretation of Quantum Mechanics* (Singapore: World Scientific Publishing Pte. Ltd., 1992), 2–3.

2 Werner Heisenberg, *Physics and Philosophy: The Revolution in Modern Science* (New York: Harper and Brothers, 1958), 38. "This again emphasizes a subjective element in the description of atomic events, since the measuring device has been constructed by the observer, and we have to remember that what we observe is not nature in itself but nature exposed to our method of questioning."

3 Celeste Ianniciello, "Postcolonial Art: A Living Archive of Border-Crossings and Migrant Matters," in Anna Maria Guasch Ferrer, Nasheli Jimenez Del Val, eds., *Critical Cartography of Art*

Figure 1: Main section of the "townscape" mural found inside the Anping tomb; architectural features shown include a multi-story drum tower, *siheyuan* 四合院 quadrangles, and a defensive wall. Photo by author of a purported replica, 2001.

In this study of a second-century CE polychromatic monumental wall painting of a town found in an Eastern Han dynasty (25–220 CE) tomb (Figure 1), I begin with Heisenberg's principle to present a disaggregate approach based on post-processual archaeology, semantics, behavioral geography, modern architectural criticism, and Foucauldian discourse analysis. This unorthodox method of inquiry builds on a corpus of textual and visual studies on extant Early Chinese representations of geography. Earlier analyses were groundbreaking in their times; however, it has become necessary to propose a new paradigm to study ancient Chinese cartography as newly excavated evidence has come to light.

I have presented earlier iterations of this study to specialists in cartography, art history, and archaeology; the current inquiry is my response to the

and Visuality in the Global Age (Newcastle upon Tyne: Cambridge Scholars Publishing, 2014), 19–34, 31.

valuable and considered feedbacks offered by many generous colleagues. In 2008, I proposed that the significance of this ancient depiction of a place can only be fully understood in an emic context, i.e., a conscious viewing of the image from the eyes of the actors that produced and used the image within the culture to which they belonged, as opposed to from a cross-cultural, cross-temporal etic perspective.[4] In the emic context, however, this image found on the wall of an ancient tomb does not fit neatly into the rubrics that cartographic historians would apply to a traditional map, which Christian Jacob has defined as a concrete or monumental map, "deriving from a particular mimetic process in which the landscape is miniaturized, as a metonymic double of reality. In their primitive form, as in their technical avatars, they attest to a particular vocation of the map, in which are mixed a Gulliverian dream and belief in the effectiveness of sympathetic magic."[5] When I first proposed to treat this image as a "map", I knew what type of map this was *not*, but I did not know what it *was*. That was the impetus to continue to look for a different theoretical approach beyond Sinology, art history, and archaeology.

According to Ptolemy's classification that draws a distinction between geography, which are maps of the known world, and chorography, which are depictions of *khoros* χῶρος (place), this ancient Chinese pictorial representation is characteristically chorographic. Chorography is further defined in a 2013 study on medieval mapmaking in the Western world, in which Jesse Simon traces the etymological origins of chorography in the Ptolemaic tradition and explains:

> The first part of the word, however, presents us with something of a grey area: χώρα often refers to land or country in an indefinite, non-political sense, while χῶρος is neither as specific as a local place (τόπος) nor as all-encompassing as γῆ or κόδμος. It has been recent suggested that χῶρος may be understood in a similar way to the modern concept of 'landscape', that is, an area of land that can be apprehended and experienced by an observer. The defin-

---

4 An early version of this study was published in Hsin-Mei Agnes Hsu, "Structured Perceptions of Real and Imagined Landscapes in Early China," in Kurt A. Raaflaub and Richard J. A. Talbert, eds., *Geography and Ethnography: Perceptions of the World in Pre-Modern Societies* (Oxford: Wiley-Blackwell, 2010), 43–63. A revised version was presented on a panel on cartography at the European Association of Chinese Studies Annual Conference organized by Vera Lichtman and Hilde De Weerdt in 2012.

5 Christian Jacob, *The Sovereign Map: Theoretical Approaches in Cartography throughout History*, Tom Conley, ed. and Edward E. Dahl, trans. (Chicago: University of Chicago Press, 2006), 39.

ing characteristic of χῶρος, however, seems to be its limits. The word appears most often in classical sources to describe a space which is finite and bounded, land which need not necessarily be perceived in a single glance, but whose extent is nonetheless known.[6]

This classification is not unique to early Chinese maps, as many transmitted and excavated maps from other early cultures were also localized depictions of the mapmakers' perceived world.[7]

Formal analysis of this ancient chorograph shows a bird's-eye view of a town consisted of public structures, private spaces, pathways, and fortifications; for this reason I refer to this image as a "townscape" in the present study. I will demonstrate that while the place depicted was modeled after contemporary urban centers, it was most likely located in a rural region in the Northern frontiers of Han territories. At least six other examples of townscapes dating to Early China have been excavated and published,[8] but I will show that this particular representation is unique when studied against the other examples and in the context of this tomb's pictorial program. In this case, artistic intention may have been ancillary to an imagined functionality, aptly described by modern architectural critics and contemporary urban designers as "imageability."

Graphic representations of geography in the form of maps reflect a set of structured human perceptions specific to a culture and a time in history. A landscape as a natural phenomenon is devoid of preconceptions associated with artificial definitions; however, when a landscape is perceived and demarcated by its human possessor, it becomes ideologically significant. It can be said that the meanings of a map are processed as symbols and embedded intrinsically in a representational format. The relationship between symbol and object – in particular, the ideological purposes of landscape as represented in maps – has been explored by scholars across disciplines. Alfred Korzybski, widely recognized as the father of general semantics, offered an observation on this philosophical quandary in the 1930s: "A map is not the territory it represents, but, if correct, it has a similar structure to the territory, which accounts for its usefulness."[9] In other words, maps as a mode of

---

6 Jesse Simon, "Chorography reconsidered: An alternative approach to the Ptolemaic definition," in Keith D. Lilley, ed., *Mapping Medieval Geographies: Geographical Encounters in the Latin West and Beyond, 300–1600* (Cambridge: Cambridge University Press, 2013), 23–44.

7 Lloyd Brown, *The Story of Maps* (Boston: Little, Brown, and Co., 1949), 33.

8 Anneliese Bulling, "The Eastern Han Tomb at Ho-lin-ko-erh (Holingol)," *Archives of Asian Art* 31 (1977–8), 79–103.

9 Alfred Korzybski, *Science and Sanity: An Introduction to Non-Aristotelian Systems and General Semantics* (New York: International Non-Aristotelian Library Publishing Company, 1933), 747–61.

communication manifest meanings only when the observed (i.e., "nature herself exposed") is interpreted by the observer (i.e., "our method of questioning"). Heisenberg's principle helps us recognize that the etic method of interpretation is intrinsically biased because it presumes a common worldview between the ancient mapmaker in second-century China and the modern interpreter of the map in twenty-first century America. It is also important to remember that the "place" depicted in this image, sealed inside a tomb for almost two millennia, remains unchanged because it was "frozen in time" until its modern discovery, even though the actual structures and landscapes no longer exist. This image therefore ceased to be a practical illustration of the physical world at the time of the tomb owner's death. In the postmortem context, the "place" is a cognitive mimesis of a lost reality that is unique to the deceased, not to the modern researcher. This image became a mental map.

Mental maps were first known as "cognitive maps" in the early works of behavioral geographers whose approach to geography focused on the cognitive processes underlying spatial reasoning, decision-making, and behavior. A seminal work on mental maps is *The Image of the City*, published in 1960 by the noted American urban planner Kevin Lynch, a former student of Frank Lloyd Wright. Lynch went on to a distinguished 30-year academic career at the Massachusetts Institute of Technology. In *The Image of the City*, Lynch invented two concepts that have become standard semantic tools in modern architectural criticism, "imageability" and "wayfinding," both of which are applicable and valuable to our understanding of this early Chinese chorograph. Imageability is defined as a "character or quality held by a physical object" that triggers lucid images in the observer. Wayfinding is the employment of mechanisms that literally "guide the way." Lynch further posited that "we have the opportunity of forming our new city world into an imaginable landscape: visible, coherent, and clear. It will require a new attitude on the part of the city dweller, and a physical reshaping of his domain into forms which entrance the eye, which organize themselves from level to level in time and space, which can stand as symbols for urban life."[10] In the subsequent decade, writings by historian of geography David Stea were influential in the developing field of study of "mental mapping."[11] Fellow geography historian Elspeth Graham summarizes Stea's view as "an image resulting from the filtering and coding of sensory data and is somewhat subjective, private, unique."[12]

---

10 Kevin Lynch, *The Image of the City* (Cambridge: The MIT Press, 1960), 91.

11 Roger Downs and Dr. David Stea, *Maps in Minds: Reflections on Cognitive Mapping*, Harper & Row series in geography (New York: Joanna Cotler Books, 1977).

12 Elspeth Graham, "What is a Mental Map?" *The Royal Geographical Society (with the Institute of British Geographers)* v. 8, n. 4 (1976), 259–262, referring to D. C. D. Pocock, "City of

An intrinsic element in the study of mental mapping is the concept of domain, which was explored in depth by the French philosopher Michel Foucault. Foucault was not a historian of geography or a mapmaker, but he challenged the traditional academic study of cartography to demonstrate the power-knowledge concept inherent in the process of making and using maps in a 1976 interview with the French geography journal *Hérodote*.

> *Territory* is no doubt a geographical notion, but it's first of all a juridico-political one: the area controlled by a certain kind of power. *Field* is an economico-juridical notion. *Displacement:* what displaces itself is an army, a squadron, a population. *Domain* is a juridico-political notion. *Soil* is a historico-geological notion. *Region* is a fiscal, administrative, military notion. *Horizon* is a pictorial, but also a strategic notion.[13]

Foucault's discourse analysis was particularly influential in the scholarship of the renowned British historical geographer J. B. Harley, who with David Woodward co-edited the first three volumes of the important *History of Cartography Project* until his untimely passing in 1991. In his 1989 article in *Cartographica*, Harley summarized the paradigm shift from the historical study of maps as devices of communication of geography to the poststructuralist approach of treating maps as socio-political constructs. "From Foucault's writings, the key revelation has been the omnipresence of power in all knowledge, even though that power is invisible or implied, including the particular knowledge encoded in maps and atlases."[14]

The issue of domain has not been fully explored in Early Chinese cartography, even though numerous references to maps and mapmaking are found in extant texts from this period. Two notable examples in Sima Qian's 司馬遷 *Shiji* (Records of the Historian 史記) associated with the Progenitor Emperor of China are especially enlightening. One is the story of Jing Ke's 荊軻 failed attempt to assassinate the King of Qin. This legend has become an indelible part of the Chinese psyche that even primary school children today can recite the story. In 2008, an ahistorical version of the story was made into an international blockbuster film aptly titled "Hero." A gist of the story is as follows: in order to obtain an audience with the King of Qin, an assassin named Jing Ke pretends to be an aristocrat-envoy from a rival kingdom offering two precious

---

the Mind: A Review of Mental maps of Urban Areas," *Scottish Geographic Magazine* 88 (1972), 2, 115.

13 Michel Foucault, "Questions on Geography?" in Colin Gordon, ed. and trans., *Power/Knowledge: Selected Interviews and Other Writings, 1972–1977* (New York: Pantheon, 1980), 63–77, 68.

14 J. B. Harley, "Deconstructing the Map," *Cartographica*, v. 26, n. 2 (Spring 1989), 1–20.

gifts – a map of the territories that his lord would surrender and the head of a former Qin general, who had lost favor with the King of Qin (the general had virtuously sacrificed himself for this regicidal-suicidal mission). During his audience with the king, Jing Ke slowly unrolls the map until, suddenly, a (poisoned) dagger is revealed. Jing Ke deftly grabs the dagger and lunges at the king, but he misses. A madcap chase around a column ensues, and the royal physician valiantly throws his medicine bag at Jing Ke, allowing the king time to react. The king then draws his ceremonial sword and injuries Jing Ke, who in a desperate final attempt throws his dagger at the king, but misses again. The king stabs Jing Ke multiple times before the royal guards arrive and kill Jing Ke and his assistant. Shortly after Jing Ke's failed assassination attempt, the King of Qin completes his conquest and unifies all under heaven to become the self-styled Progenitor Emperor of China.

In another anecdote from the Progenitor Emperor's biography in *Shiji*, Sima Qian describes the emperor's purposeful creation of a three-dimensional map of the cosmic and terrestrial worlds inside his imperial tomb:

穿三泉，下銅而致槨，宮觀百官奇器珍怪徙臧滿之。令匠作機弩矢，有所穿近者輒射之。以水銀為百川江河大海，機相灌輸，上具天文，下具地理。(史记. 卷六. 秦始皇本纪)

They dug through three subterranean streams and poured molten copper for the outer coffin, and the tomb was fitted with models of palaces, pavilions and offices, as well as fine vessels, precious stones and rarities. Artisans were ordered to fix up crossbows so that any thief breaking in would be shot. All the country's streams, the Yellow River and the Yangtze were reproduced in quicksilver and by some mechanical means made to flow into a miniature ocean. The heavenly constellations were shown above and the regions of the earth below.[15]

These stories illustrate that maps were more than practical tools for administration in Early China; they were symbols of conquest and sovereignty. In life, and before the completion of his conquest of the warring kingdoms, there was no gift more enticing to the King of Qin than a pretty picture of the lands and peoples that he is about subdue. In eternity and as the Progenitor Emperor of a unified China, he believed that he would continue to command "all under heaven" by being entombed inside a simulated microcosm of his domain.

It is only in the last forty years that pictorial depictions of domain from Early China have come to light through archaeological discoveries. These excavated materials predate the accepted formal origin of the Chinese landscape painting tradition in the Northern and Southern dynasties (220–589 CE); for

---

15 Edmund Capon, *Qin Shihuang: Terracotta Warriors and Horses* (Clayton, Victoria, Australia: Wilke and Company Limited, 1983), 24.

this reason, previous attempts to study them from an anachronistic perspective have proven unsatisfactory – for while every domain is a landscape, not every landscape is a domain. Etymologically, the common Classical Latin verb *domare* denotes "to subdue."[16] Domain, therefore, connotes a conquered and controlled landscape by a human possessor. Archaeological evidence indicates that the practice of including maps as funerary accoutrements in Early China can be traced back to the Warring States period (c. 475–221 BCE). A set of seven fragmented maps on wooden planks – comparable to the ancient Greek concept of *pinax*[17] πίναξ – discovered in a tomb at Fangmatan in modern Gansu province are some of the earliest known examples of cartography in Chinese history; they have been dated to 239 BCE and depict the hydrology of the Wei River valley and its tributaries.[18] A set of topographic and garrison maps, dated to 168 BCE and recovered from Mawangdui tomb number three in Hunan province, further illustrates that the practice of making concrete maps was highly developed by the time of the early Western Han (202 BCE-9 CE).[19]

The townscape in our current inquiry postdates the concrete maps found at Fangmatan and Mawangdui. This image was discovered to have been painted on a wall inside a grand tomb in Anping 安平 county in modern southern Hebei province. The tomb is an impressive subterranean structure built to replicate a contemporary grand estate of multiple chambers. The interior walls were decorated with an extensive collection of polychromatic murals painted in mineral-based colors over dry plaster using an organic binding mixture. An inscription found in situ, 惟熹平五年 (fifth year of the Xiping Era), gives the terminus ante quem of 176 CE during the Eastern Han dynasty (25–220 CE).

This image was found on the western part of the northern wall in an ancillary chamber. All painted fragments and artifacts salvaged from the tomb were removed from the tomb after initial excavations in the early 1970s; it is believed

---

16 Domare is common in Classical Latin, which also offers with similar meaning domari. Also see George D. Chase, "The Form of Nominal Compound in Latin," *Harvard Studies in Classical Philology*, v. 11 (1900), 61–72.

17 Jacob, "The Sovereign Maps," 18. "In Ancient Greek, the term map is generally known as *pinax*, indicating the tablet (of wood, metal, or stone), then the 'plate' (in the bibliographical sense, meaning thus a 'plate' of papyrus or of parchment) on which forms are drawn, painted, or engraved. A *pinax* can present to the eye an alphabetical inscription (a text or list), geometrical figures, or figurative drawings or paintings."

18 Cordell Yee, "Reinterpreting Chinese Geographical Maps," in J.B. Harley and David Woodward, eds., *The History of Cartography Project, Volume 2, Book 2* (Chicago: University of Chicago Press, 1994), 35–70.

19 Hsin-Mei Agnes Hsu and Ann Martin-Montgomery, "An Emic Perspective of the Mapmaker's Art in Han China," *Journal of the Royal Asiatic Society*, ser. 3, v.17, n. 4 (October, 2007), 443–457.

that they were then transported to and have since remained in a storage facility at the Hebei Provincial Museum. My repeated requests to study the original fragments were never fulfilled; my understanding has been that only replicas are available for study and exhibitions. I have visited the site where the tomb was discovered, but only a modern landmark stands *in situ*.

According to the excavation report, the baseline of the townscape is set at 20 cm above ground; the painting itself is 230 cm long and 135 cm wide, and occupies two-thirds of the entire northern wall. Chinese scholars had proposed that the architectural plan is shown to have a southern exposure "in light of China's architectural tradition of 'sitting in the north and facing the south,' the upper part of the painting should be the north."[20] If we accept this interpretation, then the mural shows the southern, northern, and eastern parts of the town; the western part is only partially depicted. As for the method of representation, it has been suggested that the artist intentionally used the partial-view technique to demonstrate the town's expanse.[21] This presentation adheres to Jacob's theory that "the ephemeral (mental) map can be selective and partial, for it is focused on its illustrative function or on its functions as a point of reference determined by the immediate context of its drawing."[22] We will return to this point later.

Formal analysis indicates that rulers and T-squares were used to form clean outlines of the architectural elements in the painting. Illusion of depth and volume is created by the varying use of thick and thin lines. Doors, windows, and roofs are all painted in black. Corridors and some ridgepoles are painted in green. Other elements are painted in brown and almost invisible to the naked eye after two millennia of natural deterioration. Vermillion paint is used only to depict the drum and the pennant. This visual aide effectively articulates the prominence of these two features and their iconographic significance.

Buildings of various sizes, all arranged in the enclosure style (*siheyuan* 四合院), form the perimeter of the compound. There is an outer layer of walls; for this reason the layout resembles the Chinese graph *hui* 回, which is best described as a small square enclosed in a large square. The interior is further divided into smaller units of enclosed quadrangles, which seem to comprise a series of common spaces and residential areas connected by meandering pathways and covered corridors. The only entrance to this town is a set of double gates situated in the center of the southern perimeter. The outer gate is covered

---

20 Hebeisheng Wenwu Yanjiusuo, *Anping Dong Han bihua mu* (Beijing: Wenwu chuban she, 1990), 28.
21 Ibid.
22 Jacob, "The Sovereign Maps," 33.

with a roof of overhanging eaves. The inner gate is structurally similar to the outer one. The roofs of both gates are taller than the roofs of all other buildings. The inner gate opens into a large courtyard. At the northern end is a spacious hall situated on the east-west axis; this hall seems to be the nucleus of the town in the context of the overall layout. Two covered parallel corridors flank the courtyard and the audience hall to provide sheltered passage between the entrance in the southernmost part of the compound and its inner sanctum.

In his study on Chinese vernacular architecture Ronald Knapp observes that the origin of the enclosure style can be traced back to Early China and that it was already a common architectural element by the Eastern Han times.

> The overall composition of the *siheyuan*, a residential quadrangle, involves an orientation toward the south, clear axiality and balanced side-to-side symmetry. In both figures, the central courtyard and associated open spaces are generous portions of the overall dwelling, representing as much as 40 percent of the total area. Indeed, the principal courtyard is often larger than any of the structure which together makes up the house. These structures surrounding the courtyard are single-story units with narrow verandas, providing a covered circuit for movement about the complex. Symmetrical placement of trees, walkways, and gateways complements the balanced proportions of the *siheyuan* itself. Seclusion is ensured by the surrounding walls and gates. Yet from any position in the courtyard of these northern dwelling complexes, the sky appears to reach to distant horizons unobstructed either by the dwelling itself or by neighboring buildings. Larger *siheyuan* complexes, created by the addition of more rooms and courtyards, maintain the overall links between the encompassed earth and expanding sky.[23]

The Anping townscape is made up of enclosures of various sizes. The main courtyard is larger than all the buildings, including the central audience hall. Movement on foot, or wayfinding, within the compound would have been easy along the undulating but well-organized covered pathways. The layout is complex but conveys a sense of symmetry.

A tower on the northern perimeter and a freestanding structure inside a courtyard in the western part of the town are two structures that stand out. The latter is a small building with a southern exposure that sits on a platform with steps providing access to an elevated area. The structure is covered with a roof and its ridgepole has stylized owl-tail tips. Some have suggested that this structure is a pavilion.[24]

The tower consists of a tall platform and an open-air building; it is an impressive, but likely exaggerated or imagined, five-story structure. Rising above

23 Ronald G. Knapp, *China's Vernacular Architecture: House Form and Culture* (Honolulu, University of Hawaii Press, 1989), 38.
24 Hebeisheng Wenwu Yanjiusuo, "Anping Dong Han bihua mu," 28.

the roof of the tower is a short black pole, to which a pennant in the shape of a long bird-tail, painted in vermillion, is affixed. There are railings all around the open-air building, inside of which is a large red drum; traces of vermilion are still visible. Some scholars have called this edifice a watchtower (*wanglou*),[25] although it would not be inaccurate to call it a drum tower (*gulou*). Nancy Steinhardt's study on these towers and their functions confirm the possible dual purpose of this architectural form in the Anping townscape:

> Another feature of Chinese imperial city outer walls was the defensive projection, which took the form of a lookout tower or a protective battlement. Lookout towers were built at the four corners of a city and atop city gates, where troops could be quartered.[26]

> The last structure planned inside the walls of the Chinese imperial city was the freestanding tower. One and often two types of the multistoried structures stood on the main north-south axis of imperial Beijing and certain earlier Chinese capitals. The towers housed either a bell or a drum, and their functions were those of urban timekeeping devices. The bell or drum was sounded at regular intervals during the day and night.[27]

In the Anping townscape, the combination of the tower's strategic location on the northern perimeter, height, and crenellations indicate that its primary functions were observation and defense. The large drum in the watchtower could be used for marking time and sounding alarm – for internal emergencies and for when the town was threatened by an invasion. A logical explanation of the tower's dual function is that the Anping painting does not portray a typical Eastern Han city, but a frontier town built to resemble a contemporary city. In other words, the Anping mural depicts rural architecture infused with contemporary urban features.

The distinction between urban and rural Chinese architecture has been a topic of much scholarly debate, most notably between Frederick Mote and William Skinner. Skinner contested Mote's proposition that "Chinese urban structures were indistinguishable from rural structures,"[28] and argued that Chinese urban structures were noticeably different from rural structures in pre-modern times. "On the more prosaic level of architectural forms, Chinese cities did have their distinctive edifices: the drum tower and bell tower, the great examination hall, and the elaborate towers at the corners and gates of the city wall."[29] In a

---

25 Ibid.
26 Nancy S. Steinhardt, *Chinese Imperial City Planning* (Honolulu: University of Hawaii Press, 1990), 7.
27 Steinhardt, "Chinese Imperial City Planning," 16–18.
28 Frederic W. Mote, "The Transformation of Nanking, 1350–1400," in G. William Skinner, ed., *The City in Late Imperial China* (Stanford: Stanford University Press, 1977), 115–6.
29 G. William Skinner, "Introduction: Urban Development in Imperial China," in G. William Skinner, ed., *The City in Late Imperial China* (Stanford: Stanford University Press, 1977), 16–7.

later study on urban-planning in pre-modern China, Xu Yinong re-examined Skinner's theory and approached the study of urban architecture from the perspective that city walls had always been the fundamental feature of pre-modern city planning.[30]

> I have insisted that, in terms of architectural form and style, buildings in a traditional Chinese city can hardly be differentiated from buildings in its surrounding countryside. Structures that appear to be distinctively "urban," such as the city gate towers, the corner towers, the drum tower, and bell tower, were in fact a combination of one or two-story halls with the city walls or high raised, wall-like platforms on which the halls stood. The architectural form and style of these halls were not at all distinguishable from those on the ground; it was the city wall and wall-like platforms that rendered these particular "urban structures," in many cases (but not always), distinct from rural buildings.[31]

It is my analysis that the Anping mural depicts a place far away from the capital on the northern border of the Han empire. The absence of any form of vegetation, wells, and a moat indicates that the town is situated in a barren region of Chinese-controlled territories. The most convincing piece of evidence, however, is the town's layout. Zhou Changshan, a prominent Chinese urban historian whose groundbreaking scholarship includes the most credible calculation of the size of wards in Chang'an in the Western Han period, has asserted that Han cities in the northern border region were almost always built in the *hui* configuration with only one entrance in the center of the southern perimeter. Excavations at the ruins of an ancient frontier city at Huhehaotetatu in Inner Mongolia confirm this observation.[32] Zhou explains that this architectural configuration reflects the terrain of the northern region and the defensive nature of these frontier towns. The absence of a moat, which was a common defensive feature of cities in the Central Plain region, is indicative of the aridity of the northern border region. Further, because towns in the border regions were built as defensive fortresses against nomadic invaders from the north, any openings along the northern perimeter would have been strategically vulnerable.[33]

A key feature of the Anping townscape is the artist's use of axonometric perspective, more commonly known as the parallel perspective. In computer graphic terminology, this method of projection is in fact called the "Chinese perspective" because of the widespread belief that the practice had developed

30 Xu Yinong, *The Chinese City in Space and Time: The Development of Urban Form in Suzhou* (Honolulu: University of Hawaii Press, 2000), 175.
31 Xu, "The Chinese City in Space and Time," 43.
32 Zhou Changshan, *Handai chenshi yanjiu* (Beijing: Renmin chubanshe, 2001), 61.
33 Zhou, "Handai chenshi yanjiu," 43.

from the Chinese scroll painting tradition.[34] Axonometric perspective differs from the linear perspective, which is based on Euclidian optics, in that it has no explicit vanishing points, and in many cases, no explicit source of light. In a painting drawn from the axonometric perspective, objects farther away from the viewer are not smaller than those that are closer to the viewer. Thus, if information of the scale and properties of the projection in an axonometric drawing are provided, one can determine the size of any object in the drawing; this is also the reason that architects use axonometry in their concept renderings. In the words of architectural historian Bernard Schneider, "perspective shows what we see of an object, whilst axonometry shows what we know about it."[35] The horizon in an axonometric drawing is set above the painting, thus giving "many Chinese pictures the character of bird's-eye views."[36]

Joseph Needham clearly believed that the use of axonometric perspective could be traced back to as early as the Han times.[37] "Parallel perspective can be found already in the drawing of the scenes carved in relief in the stone tomb shrines of the Han period (Chu Wei, Wu Liang, etc.). Diagonal lines strike off from the front line of the picture, with figures or buildings along them."[38] Architectural plans shown in bas-relief and intaglio from the Han period, particularly those found in the Shandong province, such as the Wu Liang shrine and the Yinan tomb, have been examined in detailed studies by Wu Hung and Lydia Thompson. In a 2001 study, James Coswell further proposed an alternative term to describe the pre-modern Chinese way of viewing, which he called "situational perspective." He described a second-century CE depiction of a market scene on an impressed tile found in a tomb in Sichuan as follows:

> The disparate angles do at least two things. First they capture the hurly-burly of the market itself with lines leaning this way and that. Second, in a subtle but sophisticated way I believe they convey the sense of actually moving through the market where the visitor's vantage point changes with every step. In other words, there is no attempt in this tile to describe a unitary space or a single movement. In this regard it is important to note that all of the figures are of the same size, so even the mechanism of recession in size the farther an object is from the viewer is not used. The end result is of on-going activities, perhaps

---

34 J. Krikke, "Axonometry: A Matter of Perspective," *IEEE Computer Graphics and Applications* (2000), 7–11.

35 Anna, Norbert Miller, Werner Oechslin and Bernhard Schneider, eds., "Zeichnung als Medium der Abstraktion/Drawing as a Medium of Abstraction," *DAIDALOS* (1981), 81.

36 Joseph Needham, *Science and Civilization in China, IV* (Cambridge: Cambridge University Press, 1971), 112.

37 Ibid., fig. 776.

38 Needham, *Science and Civilization in China*, 114.

even in an eternal sense, which would be appropriate, for this picture was meant to accompany the deceased of the tomb where this tile was found into the hereafter where neither space nor time mattered."[39]

Painted directly across from the townscape in the Anping tomb is a rotund man shown seated on a dais under a canopy, attended by servants. He is literally "larger than life" as he is depicted three times larger than all other human figures in this tomb; he is also the only one shown in a frontal view. There is little doubt that this is a representation of the owner of this chthonic mansion. His bulbous eyes are wide open. His right hand is depicted as if he is beckoning the mourner. His dignified seated pose, ensemble, and accoutrements, are all manifestations of his moral character and his status as the tomb owner.[40] There are earlier images of deceased persons in Chinese art, but this painting is the earliest known example of a frontal, seated portraiture – a style that would become the standard form of portraiture in Chinese art for the next two millennia. In this painting, the tomb owner's gesture and pose are particularly significant when interpreted in the context of the pictorial program. The fact that the city is drawn from an axonometric perspective gives a sense that the tomb owner is looking down at it from a vantage point far above. The tomb's pictorial program was designed to illustrate the power dynamic between the man and the townscape, and that the townscape was, and remains in the post-mortem perpetuity, his domain.

Architectural murals have also been excavated from other tombs with evident Eastern Han characteristics, but the Anping townscape is unique among them. Six murals were found in a tomb at Helinge'er in modern Inner Mongolia; three were studied in depth by Anneliese Bulling in her meticulous account published in the late 1970s, in which she observed: "Houses are drawn in different perspectives, some showing only the roofs as if seen from above, others showing a building as seen from the front." Further studies of two of the murals, the so-called Ningcheng and Fanyangcheng townscapes, confirm that they, too, were drawn from an axonometric perspective.

In the Helinge'er tomb, the so-called Ningcheng architectural mural would have been the first of the six that a mourner encountered as it is positioned on the northern wall of the corridor connecting the antechamber and the central

---

39 James O. Caswell, "Some 'Secrets of the Trade' in Chinese Painters' Use of 'Perspectives'," *RES: Anthropology and Aesthetics*, n. 40 (Autumn, 2001), 188–210.
40 Audrey G. Spiro, *Contemplating the Ancients: Aesthetic and Social Issues in Early Chinese Portraiture* (Berkeley: University of California Press, 1990), 14.

chamber.[41] Bulling speculated that this mural was the most important among the six because "this was the place where the Master of the Tomb was stationed at the time when he had reached his highest position as a Hu Wu-huan hsiao-wei, Colonel Protector of the Wu-huan."[42] Wen Fong also examined this painting and commented that:

> A series of courtyard scenes created by parallelograms presents a bird's-eye view of enclosed spaces filled with rows of figures and buildings. Parallelograms also form the edges of a floor mat and the sides of a building to position the figures in space. As with the diagonal lines of the gabled-roof motif of the Helingol wall painting, overlapping triangular mountain motifs are used to form parallelograms to suggest spatial recession in landscape representation.[43]

While the Helinge'er murals are important to our formal analysis of the Anping painting, they differ in one critical aspect in that the Anping townscape is completely devoid of human presence. In contrast, all six Helinge'er murals show robust human activities and the hustling and bustling of town life, leading Steinhardt to comment that "indeed, one observes more varied activity on the painted wall than in the main intersection of Ningcheng today!"[44]

In Western art, the parallel perspective was the historically preferred method of representing space. It was an "alternative to the optical 'deceptions' of pictorial perspective" for achieving "precision in technical illustration."[45] The most notable works in this field of study were produced by Johann Heinrich Lambert, a Prussian military scientist, and Reverend William Farish, an English mathematician and engineer. Lambert was initially known for his work on military cartography that led him to become a pioneer in the study of non-Euclidian concepts.[46] His study on parallel projection resulted in the insight that it "became increasingly used to convey information," so that it was called the "military perspective."[47] Farish also championed the value of descriptive geometry in precision drawings; he called it "isometrical perspective." Development of the axonometric perspective in Western art suggests that this method of projection was not widely used for artistic enhancement but, because it shows descriptive geometry in precise terms, was most

---

41 Neimenggu Wenwu Gongzuodui and Neimenggu Bowuguan, "Helinge'er faxian yizuo zhongyao de Dong Han bihua mu," *Kaogu* 1 (1974), 11.

42 Bulling, "The Eastern Han Tomb at Ho-lin-ko-erh", 83.

43 Wen Fong, "Why Chinese Painting is History," *Art Bulletin* 85.2 (2003), 273.

44 Steinhardt, "Representations of Chinese Walled Cities in the Pictorial and Graphic Arts", 428.

45 Martin Kemp, *The Science of Art: Optical Themes in Western Art from Brunelleschi to Seurat* (New Haven: Yale University Press, 1990), 233.

46 Kemp, "The Science of Art," 222.

47 Kemp, "The Science of Art," 233.

suited to military cartography and for making engineering and architectural blue-prints. This may have been the case in Early China as well. Extant texts indicate that the concept of military cartography predated the Han dynasty, and the discovery of the Mawangdui topographic and garrison maps has proven that the concept was put to practice before 168 BCE.[48] In the Anping townscape, the painstakingly measured and meticulously executed lines reflect a high level of technical drafts-manship, leading a team of distinguished Chinese historical geographers to include the Anping townscape in their comprehensive survey on ancient Chinese cartography.[49] This categorization is significant because the concept of a *tu* (map) in Early China was ambiguous and widely inclusive.[50]

Although the Anping townscape is unique among known excavated examples from Early China, the concept of a mental map may not have been unique in the ancient world. Archaeological excavations have led to the discovery of a fresco in a buried gallery under Trajan's Bath.[51] The fresco was found on the transverse wall of a subterranean gallery below an exedra and has been described as remarkable for its subject and size. The subject is unique in the tradition of Classical wall painting in that rural landscapes predominate, and the mural occupies almost 10 square meters, roughly similar in size to the Anping townscape. The creation of this fresco predated the reign of Trajan and was likely made during the Flavian era.[52] Classical archaeologists have dubbed this fresco *città dipinta* (the painted city) because it shows a bird's-eye view of a walled city (Figures 2 and 3).

Buildings are represented in an axonometric perspective, among them, a theater, near which stands a statue of Apollo on a plinth; there is also a courtyard surrounded by porticoes with more statues inside. A temple is seen at the summit of a hill. In the middle of the town, there is a colossal statue painted in yellow (likely simulating bronze) at the crossing of two streets that divides the town into regular units. Scholars have debated about the identification of this "place" and, because of the complete absence of human figures in this image, many have questioned whether this town is real or imagined. I should also note that this townscape is shown in a partial view similarly to that of the Anping townscape.

---

48 Mei-Ling Hsu, "The Han Maps and Early Chinese Cartography," *Annals of the Association of American Geographers* 68.1 (1978), 45–60.
49 Wanru Cao, et al., eds., *Zhongguo gudai ditu ji: Zhanguo-Yuan* (Beijing: Wenwu chubanshe, 1990).
50 Hsu, "The Han Maps and Early Chinese Cartography," 45–60.
51 Eugenio la Rocca, "The Newly Discovered City Fresco from Trajan's Baths, Rome," *Imago Mundi* 53 (2001), 121–4. The only other English language publication on the painting is found in Caroline Vout, *The Hills of Rome: Signature of an Eternal City* (Cambridge: Cambridge University Press, 2012).
52 la Rocca, "The Newly Discovered City Fresco from Trajan's Baths, Rome," 123.

Figure 2: A detail of the *Città Dipinta* fresco found on the wall of a Vespasian-era structure beneath the Baths of Trajan, showing city walls, towers, a gate, houses, and public sculptures. Photo by Candace Livingston, 2005.

Figure 3: Another detail of the *Città Dipinta* fresco, showing a partial view of a port with docks and a theater. Photo by Candace Livingston, 2005.

Italian archaeologist Eugenio la Rocca wrote these words that were nearly identical to my own description of the Anping tomb around the same time. He stated: "We must be content with appreciating the fresco on the Oppian Hill as, in my view, an example of the 'chorographical genre' of painting, a style that would have been executed by a *topographos*, a landscape painter specializing in topographical maps. The purpose of the representation should thus be seen not as purely artistic and decorative, but as cartographical, descriptive and symbolic."[53]

My unorthodox approach to this ancient Chinese painting of a town as a chorograph from an emic perspective, based on the tomb's pictorial programming and relevant material evidence, was galvanized by previous unsatisfactory attempts to treat early depictions of space from traditional single-disciplinary perspectives. Having spent the last decade on exploring different methodologies of studying ancient cartography – first using Geographic Information System (GIS) technology to "read" the Mawangdui topographic and garrison maps, and subsequently, applying Foucauldian discourse analysis to "deconstruct" the Anping townscape – I have come to understand Heisenberg's observation on the limits of knowledge and the inherent paradox of cartography fittingly described by Christian Jacob: the map as a rational construction of an intellectual space guided by science, and "the map's power of seduction; its status as an image, its oneiric and mythic implications, the reverie it suggests to the gaze whenever the viewer's eyes slip freely over its surface. This type of representation would seem to constitute a privileged space of projection for the viewer's desires, aspirations, and affective and cultural memories."[54]

References

Anna, Norbert Miller, Werner Oechslin and Bernhard Schneider, eds., "Zeichnung als Medium der Abstraktion/Drawing as a Medium of Abstraction," *DAIDALOS* (1981)

Brown, Lloyd. *The Story of Maps* (Boston: Little, Brown, and Co., 1949)

Bulling, Anneliese. "The Eastern Han Tomb at Ho-lin-ko-erh (Holingol)," *Archives of Asian Art* 31 (1977–8), 79–103

Cao Wanru, et al., eds. *Zhongguo gudai ditu ji: Zhanguo-Yuan* (Beijing: Wenwu chubanshe, 1990)

Capon, Edmund. *Qin Shihuang: Terracotta Warriors and Horses* (Clayton, Victoria, Australia: Wilke and Company Limited, 1983)

Caswell, James O. "Some 'Secrets of the Trade' in Chinese Painters' Use of 'Perspectives'," *RES: Anthropology and Aesthetics*, n. 40 (Autumn, 2001), 188–210

Downs, Roger, and Dr. David Stea, *Maps in Minds: Reflections on Cognitive Mapping*, Harper & Row series in geography (New York: Joanna Cotler Books, 1977)

Faye, Jan. "Copenhagen Interpretation of Quantum Mechanics," in Edward N. Zalta, ed., *The Stanford Encyclopedia of Philosophy* (Stanford: Stanford University Press, 2014). https://plato.stanford.edu/archives/fall2014/entries/qm-copenhagen/.

---

53 Ibid.
54 Jacob, "The Sovereign Map," 2.

Foucault, Michel. "Questions on Geography?" in Colin Gordon, ed. and trans., *Power/Knowledge: Selected Interviews and Other Writings, 1972–1977* (New York: Pantheon, 1980), 63–77

Graham, Elspeth. "What is a Mental Map?" *The Royal Geographical Society (with the Institute of British Geographers)* v. 8, n. 4 (1976), 259–262

Harley, J. B. "Deconstructing the Map," *Cartographica*, v. 26, n. 2 (Spring 1989), 1–20

Harley, J. B. "Maps, Knowledge, and Power," in Denis Cosgrove and Stephen Daniels, eds., *The Iconography of Landscape: Essays on the Symbolic Representation, Design, and Use of Past Environment* (Cambridge: Cambridge University Press, 1988), 277–311

Hebeisheng Wenwu Yanjiusuo, *Anping Dong Han bihua mu* (Beijing: Wenwu chuban she, 1990)

Heisenberg, Werner. *Physics and Philosophy: The Revolution in Modern Science* (New York: Harper and Brothers, 1958)

Hsu, Hsin-Mei Agnes and Ann Martin-Montgomery. "An Emic Perspective of the Mapmaker's Art in Han China," *Journal of the Royal Asiatic Society*, ser. 3, v.17, n. 4 (October, 2007), 443–457

Hsu, Hsin-Mei Agnes. "Structured Perceptions of Real and Imagined Landscapes in Early China," in Kurt A. Raaflaub and Richard J. A. Talbert, eds., *Geography and Ethnography: Perceptions of the World in Pre-Modern Societies* (Oxford: Wiley-Blackwell, 2010), 43–63

Hsu, Mei-Ling. "The Han Maps and Early Chinese Cartography," *Annals of the Association of American Geographers* 68.1 (1978), 45–60

Ianniciello, Celeste. "Postcolonial Art: A Living Archive of Border-Crossings and Migrant Matters," in Anna Maria Guasch Ferrer, Nasheli Jimenez Del Val, eds., *Critical Cartography of Art and Visuality in the Global Age* (Newcastle upon Tyne: Cambridge Scholars Publishing, 2014), 19–34

Jacob, Christian. *The Sovereign Map: Theoretical Approaches in Cartography throughout History*, Tom Conley, ed. and Edward E. Dahl, trans. (Chicago: University of Chicago Press, 2006)

Kemp, Martin. *The Science of Art: Optical Themes in Western Art from Brunelleschi to Seurat* (New Haven: Yale University Press, 1990)

Knapp, Ronald G. *China's Vernacular Architecture: House Form and Culture* (Honolulu, University of Hawaii Press, 1989)

Korzybski, Alfred. *Science and Sanity: An Introduction to Non-Aristotelian Systems and General Semantics* (New York: International Non-Aristotelian Library Publishing Company, 1933)

Krikke, J. "Axonometry: A Matter of Perspective," *IEEE Computer Graphics and Applications* (2000), 7–11

la Rocca, Eugenio. "The Newly Discovered City Fresco from Trajan's Baths, Rome," *Imago Mundi* 53 (2001), 121–124

Lynch, Kevin. *The Image of the City* (Cambridge: The MIT Press, 1960)

Mote, Frederic W. "The Transformation of Nanking, 1350–1400," in G. William Skinner, ed., *The City in Late Imperial China* (Stanford: Stanford University Press, 1977), 101–153

Needham, Joseph. *Science and Civilization in China, IV* (Cambridge: Cambridge University Press, 1971)

Neimenggu Wenwu Gongzuodui and Neimenggu Bowuguan, "Helinge'er faxian yizuo zhongyao de Dong Han bihua mu," *Kaogu* 1 (1974): 8–23.

Simon, Jesse. "Chorography reconsidered: An alternative approach to the Ptolemaic definition," in Keith D. Lilley, ed., Mapping Medieval Geographies: Geographical Encounters in the Latin West and Beyond, 300–1600 (Cambridge: Cambridge University Press, 2013), 23–44.

Skinner, G. William. "Introduction: Urban Development in Imperial China," in G. William Skinner, ed., The City in Late Imperial China (Stanford: Stanford University Press, 1977), 3–31

Spiro, Audrey G. Contemplating the Ancients: Aesthetic and Social Issues in Early Chinese Portraiture (Berkeley: University of California Press, 1990)

Steinhardt, Nancy S. Chinese Imperial City Planning (Honolulu: University of Hawaii Press, 1990)

Steinhardt, Nancy S. "Representations of Chinese Walled Cities in the Pictorial and Graphic Arts," in J.D. Tracy, ed., City Walls: The Urban Enciente in Global Perspective (Cambridge: Cambridge University Press, 2000), 419–460

Wen Fong, "Why Chinese Painting is History," Art Bulletin 85.2 (2003), 258–280

Wimmel, Hermann. Quantum Physics & Observed Reality: A Critical Interpretation of Quantum Mechanics (Singapore: World Scientific Publishing Pte. Ltd., 1992)

Xu Yinong. The Chinese City in Space and Time: The Development of Urban Form in Suzhou (Honolulu: University of Hawaii Press, 2000)

Yee, Cordell. "Reinterpreting Chinese Geographical Maps," in J.B. Harley and David Woodward, eds., The History of Cartography Project, Volume 2, Book 2 (Chicago: University of Chicago Press, 1994), 35–70

Zhou Changshan, Handai chenshi yanjiu (Beijing: Renmin chubanshe, 2001)

Linda Rui Feng
Spatial Conceptions of the Yellow River's Origin in Medieval Chinese Texts

Introduction

The sediment-laden Yellow River, which traverses China's north central plains, has been pivotal in shaping China's physical domain as well as its cultural-political identities. While today it has been established that it originates from the Bayan Har Mountains in the Tibetan Plateau, details about its precise location were still being debated by a group of experts even as late as 1978.[1] This debate lies on the surface of a millennia-long history of evolving understanding regarding the river's genesis through cosmography, geography, and accounts of surveys and explorations. This long history is captured first in early written texts, and, later, on extant maps with images depicting the course of the Yellow River.[2] As conceptions of the headwaters evolved over the centuries, it presents us with a case for analysing shaping forces toward spatial imaginaries for a key geographical feature.

This paper aims to understand how conceptions of the river's origin have been transmitted, synthesized and accrued in the medieval era, by unpacking forms of cosmographic, hydrographical, and geographical knowledge that informed the representations of the Yellow River fountainhead in writings from the Tang dynasty (618–907 CE). The Tang constitutes a particularly evocative portion of this long history of grappling with the river's source, because it was a time when the empire's extensive territory called forth new forms of awareness in geographical thinking among the cultural elite, and when an increasing

---

1 See, for example, the proceedings of such a conference with ongoing discussion over the precise origin and the names of geomorphic features, in Qi Mingrong 祁明榮, ed, *Huanghe yuantou kaocha wenji* 黃河源頭考察文集 [Collected Essays on Surveys on the Yellow River's Origin]. (Xining: Qinghai Renmin, 1982), 4–5, 6–11; see also Tian Shang 田尚. "Huanghe heyuan tantao 黃河河源探討 [Discussion on the Source of the Yellow River]." 地理學報 *[Acta Geographica Sinica]* 36, no. 3 (1981): 338–44.
2 Because almost no maps survive from between the end of the Han dynasty and the Song dynasty, this gap in the cartographic record in the medieval period means that we know very little about how the Yellow River was depicted on maps during the Tang.

number of literary authors travelled across the empire to frontiers and engaged with geographical works such as the map-guide (*tujing* 圖經).[3]

The Yellow River is, of course, not a uniform entity in terms of its hydrography and ecological impact and by extension, environmental and cultural significance. The river's upper reaches are remote and relatively uninhabited while the middle and lower reaches pass through denser human settlements and have weightier ecological and economic implications. Historically, the middle and lower reaches of the river had the capacity to both build and destroy agriculture, habitat, and human livelihoods, and have been the focus of flood control and engineering as well as the site of waterworks and other forms of intervention and planning by the state.[4] In contrast, the river's headwaters lie beyond human habitat and – for the most part – outside of state control. As a consequence, its significance is more cosmological and epistemological than hydrological. Although less utilitarian, knowledge of the river's source nonetheless interested writers and geographers because it raised questions about the river's place in the known world, as well as how it fits with China's key geography and spatial boundaries.

By the end of the Tang dynasty, although accounts of the river's source varied considerably, three major features associated with the river's origins have been mentioned or described among the geographical texts: Mount Kunlun 崑崙, Mount Jishi 積石, Puchang Lake (蒲昌海) (Lop Nor Lake), as well a set of small lakes variously called *xingxiu hai* 星宿海 (Constellation Lake) or *xingxiu chuan* 星宿川 (Constellation River). These features of the headwaters would appear in various combinations and were given different degrees of emphasis in the accounts of how the river begins. Changes in the understanding of the river's source throughout history, however, is by no means a teleological trajectory of geographical knowledge moving from the "incorrect" to the "accurate." This longue durée of knowledge formation was a contingent and disjunctive one, spanning an interface between myth and geography, between collective imagination

---

[3] For a recent study of the new geographical consciousness among Tang writers, see Wang, Ao. *Spatial Imaginaries in mid-Tang China: Geography, Cartography, and Literature.* (Amherst, New York: Cambria Press, 2018), 19.

[4] For a case study of a Song-dynasty change in the river's course that had powerful consequences, see Zhang, Ling. *The River, the Plain, and the State: An Environmental Drama in Northern Song China, 1048–1128.* (Cambridge, UK: Cambridge University Press, 2016). As Ruth Mostern points out, "the river's medieval and early modern instability resulted from silt being borne downstream, a condition that followed from high rates of erosion precipitated by war and settlement on the Chinese-steppe frontier." "Mapping the Tracks of Yu: Yellow River Statecraft as Science and Technology, 1200–1600." In *Knowledge in Translation: Global Patterns of Scientific Exchange, 1000–1800 CE,* edited by Patrick Manning and Abigail Owen, 134–46. (Pittsburgh: University of Pittsburgh Press, 2018).

and the assimilation of new evidence. For example, observations from imperial surveys undertaken in the Yuan dynasty (1279–1368) and Qing dynasty (1644–1911) contended with but also coexisted alongside earlier, inherited notions about the river's origins. Even as late as the nineteenth century, the idea that the river originated with the *axis mundi* of Mount Kunlun persisted both in writing as well as on maps.[5]

Prior to the Tang, there was already a long tradition of accounts and debates on the source of the Yellow River. The *Shanhai jing* 山海經 (Mountain and Water Classic) from the first-century BCE, in its various sections, describes the river as issuing from Mount Kunlun;[6] the "Yugong" 禹貢 (Tribute of Yu) in *Shangshu* 尚書 (Book of Documents) identifies Mount Jishi 積石 as the river's source.[7] Other texts that discuss the river's origins include *Huainan zi* 淮南子 (Master of Huainan) by Liu An 劉安 (179–122 BCE), and lexicons such as Erya 爾雅 and *Shuowen jiezi* 說文解字. As an example of how earlier texts have been assimilated in the Tang, when the ninth-century miscellany *Youyang zazu* 酉陽雜俎 (Mixed Morsels of Youyang) by Duan Chengshi 段成式 (ca. 803–863) described the Yellow River Spirit (河伯) as having "a man's face, and rides two dragons,"[8] it cites as authority textual precedents such as the Warring-States text *Mu tianzi zhuan* 穆天子傳 (Biography of the Son of Heaven Mu), *Huainan*

---

5 Cen Zhongmian 岑仲勉 cites the case of Tao Baolian 陶葆廉 (1862–1938) who, even late in the 19th century, still advocated Mt. Kunlun as the river's source. Cen Zhongmian. *Huanghe bianqian shi* 黃河變遷史 [A History of Changes for the Yellow River] (Beijing: Renmin, 1957), 46. For a discussion about some of the reasons for this persistence across a longer span of history and including nineteenth century Korean "wheel" maps, see Vera Dorofeeva-Lichtmann, "A History of a Spatial Relationship: Kunlun Mountain and the Yellow River Source from Chinese Cosmography through to Western Cartography," *Circumscribere [International Journal for the History of Science]* 11 (2012): 1–31.

6 The relevant passage reads: "Four hundred *li* southwest [of Sophora River Mountain] is Mount Kunlun. It is actually the earthly capital of the Supreme God Di. [. . .] The Yellow River [河水] emanates from here and flows south, then east to Never-Reach River [無達]. The Red River [赤水] emanates from here and flows southeast into the River That Floods Heaven [氾天之水]. The Oceanic River [洋水] emanates from here and flows southwest into the Ugly Mire River [醜塗之水]. The Black River [黑水] emanates from here and flows west into the Dayu [大杅] River. Here, there are many strange birds and animals." English translation from Strassberg, Richard E. *A Chinese Bestiary: Strange Creatures from the Guideways through Mountains and Seas.* (Berkeley: University of California Press, 2002), 39.

7 For a recap of these early sources, see Dorofeeva-Lichtmann, Vera. "Where is the Yellow River Source? A Controversial Question in Early Chinese Historiography." *Oriens Extremus* 45 (2005): 88.

8 English translation in Carrie Reed, *Chinese Chronicles of the Strange: The "Nuogao ji."* (New York: Peter Lang, 2001), 34.

zi 淮南子, *Shenxian ji* 神仙記 (Records of Divine Transcendants), and *Bao pu zi* 抱朴子 (The Master Embracing the Unhewn), showing that all of these texts have had an influence in shaping a shared perception of the river's source during the Tang.

Early imperial histories such as the *Shiji* 史記 (Historical Records) and *Hanshu* 漢書 (History of the Han) take up the issue of the river source in multiple sections, in some cases evaluating and debating the relative merits of contradictory evidence. In the *Historical Records*, Sima Qian 司馬遷 discusses the river's source in the following passages:[9]

> West of Yutian [Khotan], all waters flow west to the Western Sea. On the east side of it the waters flow east into the salt lake. At the salt lake [water] moves underground, and on its south side emerges [as] the source of the [Yellow] River. [Yutian] has plenty of jade; the [Yellow] River flows into the Central Kingdom.

> 于寘之西, 則水皆西流, 注西海; 其東水東流, 注鹽澤。鹽澤潛行地下, 其南則河源出焉。多玉石, 河注中國。[10]

> As for the emissaries of the Han, they sought out the source of the River, where its mountains have plenty of jade. They brought the jade back. The Son of Heaven consulted ancient charts and books, and named the mountain where the River originated "Kunlun."

> 而漢使窮河源, 其山多玉石, 采來, 天子案古圖書, 名河所出山曰昆侖云。[11]

As Dorofeeva-Lichtmann points out in her in-depth study, in debates in early Chinese historiography, historians had begun to take into account observations from imperial expeditions such as that of Zhang Qian 張騫 (d. 114 BCE) who was sent by Emperor Wudi 武帝 (r. 141–87 BCE), and have begun to reconcile them into a system in which the upper reaches of the Yellow River consists of an "outside" part beyond China's borders, as well as an "inside" part within them.[12] Closer to the Tang, one of the most important hydrographic treatises is the sixth-century *Shuijing zhu* 水經注 (Annotated Itineraries of Waterways),

---

9 In addition, Sima Qian challenges the reliability of the Kunlun attribution as found in *Yu benji* 禹本紀 (Basic Annals of Yu). He notes that Zhang Qian did not verify the presence of Kunlun, and therefore concludes the appraisal with a sharp note of incredulity, that the "strange things" in the *Shanhai jing* are such that he "does not dare to speak of them." For a discussion and translation of this appraisal in the Biography of Dayuan (大宛列傳) by Sima Qian and also a similar opinion articulated by Ban Gu in the *Hanshu* 漢書, see Dorofeeva-Lichtmann, "Where is the Yellow River Source?" 72–3.
10 Sima Qian 司馬遷, *Shiji* 史記 [Historian's Records] (Beijing: Zhonghua shuju, 1975), 123.3160.
11 Ibid., 123.3173.
12 Dorofeeva-Lichtmann, "Where is the Yellow River Source?" 86–7.

which contains descriptive itineraries of 1252 rivers and waterways – the focus of Alexis Lycas's essay in this volume, which also examines how different forms of knowledge intertwine to inform a sense of geographic space. These pre-Tang works provide a framework of knowledge from which to examine medieval conceptions of the Yellow River's source.

Although there was no single, unified narrative of the river's source in the Tang, close scrutiny of the varying accounts below shows an amalgam of knowledge that drew from and incorporated conceptions of Buddhist sacred geography, ideas about administrative boundary-marking, correlative cosmography, as well as accounts of expeditions to the river's source in what was then the Tibetan empire.

1 Encyclopedic and geographical texts describing the Yellow River headwater

The geographical work *Kuo di zhi* 括地志 (Comprehensive Treatise of the Land), compiled in 642 by the royal prince Li Tai 李泰 (618–652), survives only as fragments quoted in other sources, but among these extant fragments includes one that describes the Yellow River, and it shows the ways in which it drew from Buddhist traditions as well as from classical texts:

> Mount Anavatapta is also named Mount Jianmoda, and also named Mount Kunlun. On its south side, the Ganges emerges from the lion's mouth, and passes through India and enters Mount Da. The Yan River is today called Lake Hu, and it emerges from the horse's mouth on the northwest corner of [Mount] Kunlun, and travels past the kingdoms of Anxi and Daxia toward the western sea. The Yellow River emerges from the ox's mouth in the northeast corner, flows eastward past the Youze [Marsh], submerges and re-emerges from the Greater Jishi Mountain, then reaches the north of Mount Hua, and flows further east into the sea. Each of these three rivers is thirty thousand *li* from the point where they enter the sea. This is the Greater Kunlun. Suzhou is called the Lesser Kunlun. The *Yu benji* [Yu's Basic Annals] says that the [Yellow] River emerges from Kunlun for over two thousand five hundred *li*, [this is where] the sun and moon hide away from each other in order to shine.

> 阿耨達山亦名建末達山, 亦名崑崙山。恒河出其南吐獅子口, 經天竺入達山。媽水今名為潛海, 出於昆侖西北隅吐馬口, 經安息、大夏國入西海。黃河出東北隅吐牛口, 東經[沕]澤, 潛出大積石山, 至華山北, 東入海。其三河去入海各三萬里。此謂大崑崙, 肅州謂小崑崙也。《禹本紀》云河出崑崙二千五百餘里, 日月所相隱避為光明也。[13]

---

[13] Li Tai 李泰. *Kuo di zhi jijiao* 括地志輯校 [Comprehensive Treatise of the Land]. Edited by He Cijun 賀次君. (Beijing: Zhonghua shuju, 1980), 4.228.

Using the phrase "also named" (亦名), this entry connects three names to the mountain that generates the Yellow River, and in doing so, moves among three systems of nomenclature. Its attribution of each of the three river's source to a zoomorphic portal – a horse, an ox, and a lion respectively – shows influence from Buddhist geography; the citation of *Yu benji* at the end provides an alternative account of the Yellow River as emerging from Mount Kunlun.

This juxtaposition of Buddhist geography with pre-Buddhist canonical texts is not new to *Comprehensive Treatise of the Land*, nor is it new. In early medieval texts such as *Annotated Itineraries of Waterways*, in the first two chapters, Li Daoyuan's commentary on the Yellow River cites a total of twenty-seven times the Buddhist travelogue *Foguo ji* 佛國記 (Records of the Buddhist Kingdoms) by Faxian 法顯 (ca. 340–421) who set out on his westward pilgrimage in 399.[14] A similar negotiation between secular and sacred space takes place in the *Da Tang xiyu ji* 大唐西域記 (Record of the Western Regions) by Xuanzang 玄奘 (602–664), a travelogue to India written in 646, just a few years later than *Comprehensive Treatise of the Land*. Laying out the geography of the continent of Jambudvīpa inhabited by humans, Xuanzang describes a lake from which four rivers flow out of the mouths of an ox, an elephant, a horse, and a lion respectively. Just as important, Xuanzang's depiction connects one of the effluent rivers from Lake Anavatapta to the Yellow River itself, which eventually flows into the borders of China.

> In the center of the Jambudvīpa is Lake Anavatapta, which is south of the Fragrant Mountain and north of the Great Snow Mountains, with a circuit of eight hundred *li*. Its banks are adorned with gold, silver, lapis lazuli, and crystal. It is full of golden sand, and its water is as pure and clean as a mirror. A bodhisattva of the eighth stage, having transformed himself into a Nāga king by the power of his resolute will, lives at the bottom of the lake and supplies water for Jambudvīpa. Thus from the mouth of the silver ox at the east side of the lake flows the Ganges, which after encircling the lake once enters the southeast sea; from the mouth of a golden elephant at the south side of the lake flows the Indus, which after winding around the lake once enters the southwest sea; from the mouth of a lapis lazuli horse at the west side of the lake flows the Oxus which after winding around the lake once enters the northwest sea; and from the mouth of a crystal lion at the north side of the lake flows the Sītā, which after encircling the lake once enters the northeast sea.[15] Some say it emerges from underground at Mount Jishi, and is the course of the Sītā River. It is said to be the source of the Yellow River in China.

---

14 Ray, Haraprasad, ed. *Chinese Sources of South Asian History in Translation: Data for Study of India-China Relations Through History*. Vol. 2. (Kolkata: Asiatic Society, 2004), 32.
15 Translation from Max Moerman, "Pilgrimage and the Visual Imagination: Text, Image, and the Map of the Buddhist World," in *The Japanese Buddhist World Map: Religious Vision and the Cartographic Imagination* (University of Hawai'i Press, forthcoming).

則贍部洲之中地者，阿那婆答多池也_{唐言無熱惱。舊曰阿耨達池，訛也。}在香山之南，大雪山之北。周八百里矣。金、銀、琉璃、頗胝飾其岸焉。金沙彌漫。清波皎鏡。八地菩薩以願力故，化為龍王。於中潛宅。出清泠水。給贍部洲。是以池東面銀牛口，流出殑_{舊曰勝反伽河，舊曰恒河又曰殑伽訛也}河，繞池一匝，入東南海；池南面金象口，流出信度河_{舊曰辛頭河訛也。}繞池一匝，入西南海；池西面琉璃馬口，流出縛芻河_{舊曰博又河，訛也。}繞池一匝，入西北海。池北面頗胝師子口，流出徙多河，_{舊曰私陀河，訛也。}繞池一匝，入東北海。或曰潛流地下出積石山。即徙多河之流。為中國之河源云。[16]

Here in Xuanzang's travelogue, it is a body of water, not a mountain, that gives rise to each of the rivers, and the sacred lake generates not three but four rivers on the Indian continent. Within this framework, the source region of the Yellow River stands out as a kind of an epistemological fulcrum upon which two distinct conceptions of space negotiated with each other but did not eclipse each other. In the last sentence, through the qualifier "some say" (或曰), India-centered Buddhist cosmography is brought into contiguity with the Yellow River and the Central States (中國). This turn of phrase signals an epistemological turn, which then transitions to the secular conception of Mount Jishi as the location within China's borders where the Yellow River is seen to emerge. In Xuanzang's description, Mount Kunlun (aka Mount Anavatapta in the previous description) is entirely absent.

Another type of text that gives us glimpses into the highly contingent process of knowledge-making concerning the river's source is the *leishu* 類書, categorical books of an encyclopedic nature. One example of *leishu* from the early Tang is the *Chuxue ji* 初學記 (Fundamentals of Learning), completed between the years 719–728 in the Kaiyuan 開元 era. It was compiled as a condensed and manageable how-to guide and primer for composition for the royal princes, and features a similar number of topical categories as other contemporary *leishu*.[17] Within the category of *di* 地 (terrain), a total of seven rivers are listed, and the Yellow River (*he* 河) is the first among them. As with all entries, this entry begins with a broad definition (*xushi* 敘事) based on the classics, and lays out its etymology:

The [book] *Shuowen* says: River means "low," or [that which] flows below the terrain through and through. The *Yuan shen qi* [Documents Adducing Spirits] says: the [Yellow] River is the lord of all waters; it corresponds above to the Celestial River. The *Biography of Son of Heaven Mu* says: "The [Yellow] River, along with the Jiang [Yangzi River], Huai

---

16 Ji Xianlin 季羨林, ed. *Da Tang xiyu ji jiaozhu* 大唐西域記校注 (Beijing: Zhonghua shuju, 1985), 39.

17 Albert Dien. "Chuxue ji," in Dien, Albert E., et al., eds. *Early Medieval Chinese Texts: A Bibliographical Guide* (Berkeley, CA: Institute of East Asian Studies, 2015), 53.

River, and Ji River, constitute the four major rivers." The [Yellow] River is called the ancestor of all rivers, the ancestor of the four major rivers.

說文云: 河者下也, 隨地下流而通也。援神契曰: 河者水之伯, 上應天漢。穆天子傳曰: 河與江淮濟三水為四瀆。河曰河宗, 四瀆之所宗也。[18]

This passage situates the position of Yellow River at the top of a hierarchy for rivers, and giving it a correspondence to the celestial river. When Li Bai 李白 (701–762) famously began his ballad with "Don't you see that the Yellow River's waters come from the sky above" (君不知黃河之水天上來), he was tapping into a perception of this correspondence as it prevailed in the collective imagination.

In the rest of this entry in the *Fundamentals of Learning,* there is a detailed description of the river's upper course, and involves underground flow, divergence and re-convergence of the river channel, as well as changes in flow direction:

The source of the [Yellow] River emerges from the hilltop of [Mount] Kunlun. It flows eastward underground until it arrives at Mount Guiqi [規期]. Going north, it splits into two sources [兩源]: one emerges in the Pamirs [蔥嶺], another in Khotan [于闐]. The [courses of the] river now come together again, and it flows eastwards into Puchang Lake [蒲昌海], and again flows underground until it emerges in the south from Mount Jishi 積石. It then flows southwest, then turns back east to enters the frontiers [of China]. It passes the prefectures of Dunhuang 敦煌, Jiuquan 酒泉, and Zhangye 張掖.

河源出昆侖之墟, 東流潛行地下, 至規期山; 北流分為兩源: 一出蔥嶺, 一出于闐。其河復合, 東注蒲昌海, 復潛行地下, 南出積石山, 西南流, 又東回入塞, 過敦煌酒泉張掖郡。[19]

This description represents a conception of the Yellow River as having multiple sources (重源).[20] This conception was present in the *Shanhai jing,* which identifies both Mount Kunlun and Mount Jishi as sources. In the *Annotated Itineraries of Waterways,* Li Daoyuan 酈道元 (d. 527) notes that the Yellow River has not two but three simultaneous sources (河水重源有三, 非惟二也).[21] In the context of an evolving spatial imagination, this multiplicity in a river's origin has a profound epistemological consequence, as it begets an intellectual pluralism

---

18 Dong Zhi'an 董治安, ed. *Tangdai si da leishu* 唐代四大類書 (Beijing: Qinghua Daxue, 2003), 3.1521a.
19 Ibid., 3.1521b.
20 The scholar Cen Zhongmian attributes this idea to observations of desert water behavior by early migrants from western China who came to settle in what is now central China. Cen Zhongmian, *Huanghe bianqian shi,* 35–42.
21 Li Daoyuan 酈道元. *Shuijing zhu jiaozheng* 水經注校證 [Annotated Edition of the Annotated Itineraries of Waterways], edited by Chen Qiaoyi 陳橋驛 (Beijing: Zhonghua shuju, 2007), 34.

that allows new interpretations and spatial imaginaries to be superimposed on existing ones.

The headwater's flow is described here as undergoing both a bifurcation (分) as well as a convergence (合). Two sections of the river's upper reaches – connecting Mount Kunlun and Mount Guiqi, and then between Puchang Lake and Mount Jishi – are described as subterranean (and hence invisible). As I will show in the next section, informal literature from the Tang has many other testaments to the mobility of water underground, thereby lending plausibility to the complexity of sources of rivers.

In *Fundamentals of Learning*, the description also highlights the point of transition when the river enters Chinese territory (入塞 in the text), and enumerates three prefectures it passes through (過敦煌酒泉張掖郡). In this way, the passing of this frontier transforms the river into an inner, domestic portion which is associated, for the first time in the text, with administrative place names. This transformation of the river as it crosses the border was also elaborated upon in earlier texts such as the *Annotated Itineraries of Waterways*, which enumerates the same three prefectures, and in which Li Daoyuan comments:

> From Puchang [Lake] and beyond, the River is proven to be submerged and hidden, and begins its entry into the frontiers through the passes. From this point on, the Classic ought to seek the solidity of evidence. The River water has multiple sources; its inception is beyond the western frontiers, and issues forth from the mountains of Jishi.

> 河自蒲昌, 有隱淪之證, 並間關入塞之始。自此, 《經》當求實致也。河水重源, 又發于西塞之外, 出于積石之山。[22]

In this context, a narrative following the river's genesis becomes, by necessity, a geography that proceeds from periphery to center, the opposite of the usual center-to-periphery logic in imperial geographies and dynastic histories, which always begin with the capital cities and enumerate administrative regions in the order of increasing distance from the capital.[23] The description of the course of the Yellow River, in contrast, inevitably moves from the hinterlands toward the heartland of China. Scholar-geographers of other eras who wished to avoid the outside-to-inside order of flow had two options: either to adhere to the river's source inside China's borders, or to chart the river's flow in reverse, from the sea to the source,

---

22 Li Daoyuan, *Shuijing zhu jiaozheng*, 41.
23 For example, the *Yuanhe junxian tuzhi* 元和郡縣圖志 [Records and Illustrations of the Prefectures and Counties of the Yuanhe Era], completed in 813, begins with the capital of Chang'an.

as in the case of the *Shuijing zhu tu* 水經注圖 (Maps for the Annotated Itineraries of Waterways) by the Qing scholar Wang Shiduo 汪士鐸 (1802–1889).[24]

How might the headwaters of the Yellow River been depicted in images during the Tang? Although no Tang maps survive to offer examples of how the Yellow River's upper reaches might have been represented cartographically, extant maps from the Song dynasty (960–1279) allow us a related glimpse. The treatise *Fozu tongji* 佛祖統紀 (General Records of the Founders of Buddhism), dated 1265–1270, includes three woodblock printed maps in fascicle thirty-three, which constitute the earliest surviving cartographic depictions of the geography as described by Xuanzang in the eighth century.[25] Although created centuries after Xuanzang's travels, these maps attempt to contextualize a Buddhist cosmography in relation to the more sinocentric geography routinely mapped in the empire's administrative units.[26]

The first map is a geographical map of China and Korea, titled *Dong Zhendan dilitu* 東震旦地理圖 (Geography of Eastern Cinisthana) using the Buddhist nomenclature for China.[27] The third map is titled *Xitu wuyin zhi tu* 西土五印之圖 (Map of the Five Indian States in the West) and depicts a Buddhist world view, and refers to Xuanzang's travelogue explicitly.[28] The second map, titled

---

24 See his illustrations of the Yellow River in Wang Shiduo 汪士鐸. *Shuijing zhu tu* 水經注圖 [Maps for the Shuijing zhu]. Edited by Chen Qiaoyi 陳橋驛. (Jinan: Shandong Huabao, 2003), vol. 2, 3–18.

25 Zheng Xihuang 鄭錫煌. "Guanyu Fozu tongji zhong sanfu ditu zouyi 關於《佛祖統記》中三幅地圖芻議." In Cao Wanru et al, eds., *Zhongguo gudai ditu ji (Zhanguo–Yuan)* 中國古代地圖集 (戰國 – 元) (Beijing: Wenwu, 1990), 81–84. See also discussion of these maps in Hyunhee Park, "Information Synthesis and Space Creation: The Earliest Chinese Maps of Central Asia and the Silk Road, 1265–1270," *Journal of Asian History* 49, no. 1–2 (2015): 119–40.

26 Park, "Information Synthesis and Space Creation," 121.

27 On this map, the Yellow River (黃河) is depicted as issuing forth from Jishi 積石, labeled above triangular icons of mountains at the western edge of the map. As the river continues eastward across China, it eventually terminates at a coastal point labeled "river enters the sea" (河入海). On the northwestern edge of the map and disconnected from the course of the Yellow River, Lop Nor Lake (蒲昌海) connects with a channel outlet that runs westward beyond the scope of the map, and is labeled *Conghe* 蔥河. The text describes the 36 states of the western regions, and details two river sources that merge and flow into Lop Nor Lake, also called Salt Lake, and from which the underground current emerges in the south at Mount Jishi. Zhipan 志磐. *Fozu tongji jiaozhu* 佛祖統紀校注 (Shanghai: Shanghai guji, 2012), 726. From its use of place names, scholars believe it is based on an administrative map from the Northern Song. The map's accompanying text chronicles the four major rivers of China (*si du* 四瀆), and succinctly states that the [Yellow] River emerges from Mount Jishi (河出積石). Zheng, "Guanyu Fozu tongji zhong sanfu ditu zouyi," 84.

28 The most pictorial elements of the map are mountain icons for the Pamirs. A minimally-depicted Lake Anavatapta is bounded by Fragrant Mountain and Great Snow Mountain to the

Han xiyu zhuguo tu 漢西域諸國圖 (Han-dynasty States in the Western Regions), is of the most interest here, because it offers a rare and detailed view of the Yellow River's source region in the form of a historical map of the Han dynasty's frontier region. Near the map's center, Puchang Lake (蒲昌海) is rendered prominently as an oval filled with waves, and the flow of *Chonghe* 蔥河 (Onion River) connects Puchang Lake with the Pamirs (蔥嶺) near the left (western) edge, depicted as a tall mountain with multi-tiered peaks. At the right (eastern) edge of the map, Mount Jishi is shown as smaller than the mountains to the west, and an annotation below it identifies it as the "Source of the [Yellow] River" which "flows for 9400 *li* eastward and enters the sea." A thinner river channel is shown to begin at Jishi and flows toward the northeast, continuing to beyond the edge of the map. In the same area are shown parapets representing the Great Wall, suggesting the borders of China proper.[29] (Figure 1) This depiction, in which the apparent lack of river channel between Lop Nor Lake and the mountains of Jishi can be interpreted as an underground – and hence unseen – flow, is consistent with the textual description of the riverhead in the Tang categorical book *Fundamentals of Learning*.

Viewed in the context of Xuanzang's seventh-century travel account and the thirteenth-century Buddhist treatise, representations of the Yellow River source region drew from both Buddhist geography as well as early texts that predated the transmission of Buddhism. This potential for connection – and negotiation among textual and imagistic forms – speaks to the immense malleability of the discourse about the river's source during the medieval era.

Another important illustrated geographical treatise from the second half of the Tang is the *Yuanhe junxian tuzhi* 元和郡縣圖志 (Records and Illustrations of the Prefectures and Counties of the Yuanhe Era), compiled in 813, which surveys all the administrative regions of the Chinese empire. While the text from this treatise has survived more or less intact, the accompanying maps have been lost.

---

north and south, consistent with Buddhist cosmography. Lop Nor Lake is depicted in this map on the eastern edge, with a waves-within-oval pictorial style similar to the first two maps, but Mount Jishi and any reference to the Yellow River have been pushed off the limit of the map. However, the spatial relationships of the various regions of India are more of an accretion of place-names in written form rather than in pictorial form. It includes annotations that describe the chronology of Xuanzang's westward pilgrimage, enumerates the three routes to India, and cites a passage from his *Record of the Western Regions*. A third annotative text block explains that the map shows the approximate locations of each of the kingdoms Xuanzang had encountered. Cao et al., eds. *Zhongguo gudai ditu ji*, Vol. 1, plate 154. The place names shown adhere faithfully to Xuanzang's travelogue, with only a few exceptions. For these minor exceptions, see Zheng, "Guanyu Fozu tongji zhong sanfu ditu zouyi," 84.

29 Zhipan, *Fozu tongji*, 729. See also Cao et al., eds. *Zhongguo gudai ditu ji*, Vol. 1, plate 153.

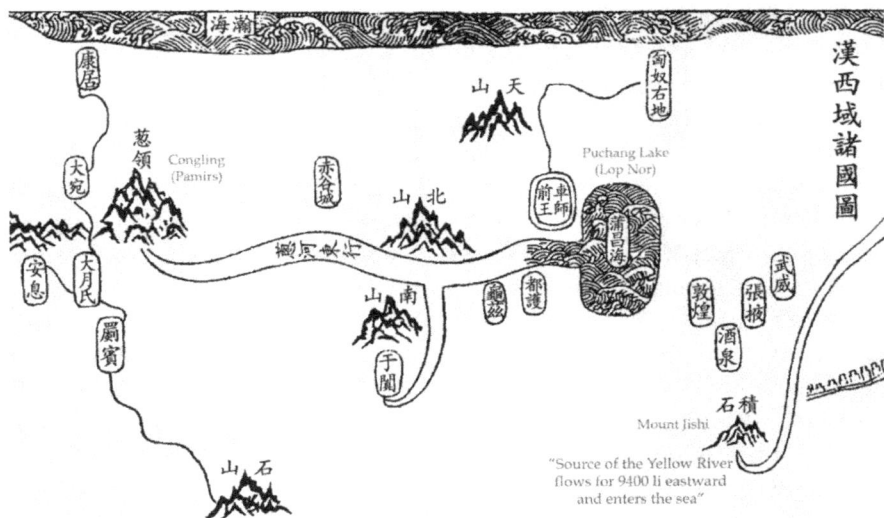

Figure 1: Illustration showing major hydrographical features on the map titled "Han-dynasty States in the Western Regions" (漢西域諸國圖), based on *Fozu tongji* 佛祖統紀 (General Records of the Founders of Buddhism), 1265–1270. Digital illustration by Tif Fan.

The Yuanhe treatise mentions Mount Kunlun, but not in relation to the Yellow River.[30] Instead, in describing the Yellow River's origin, it focuses on two versions of Mount Jishi, a "greater" and "lesser," both serving as landmarks in the river's genesis:

> Mount Jishi, also named Mount Tangshu, is today called Lesser Jishi Mountain. It is seventy *li* northwest from the county. The Yellow River emanates from Mount Jishi, which is situated among the barbarians of the southwest. [The Yellow River] flows into Puchang Lake, flows underground, and emerges from Jishi, where it becomes a river of the Central Kingdom. This is why nowadays people consider the former Greater Jishi, and this mountain [within the borders] Lesser Jishi.

> 積石山, 一名唐述山, 今名小積石山, 在縣西北七十里。按河出積石山, 在西南羌中, 注於蒲昌海, 潛行地下, 出於積石, 為中國河。故今人目彼山為大積石, 此山為小積石。[31]

---

30 The passage notes simply that Mount Kunlun is where the "Son of heaven, Mu, took so much delight in seeing Queen Mother of the West that he lost all thoughts of returning (周穆王見西王母樂而忘歸即此山)." Li Jifu 李吉甫. *Yuanhe jun xian tu zhi* 元和郡縣圖志 [Records and Illustrations of the Prefectures and Counties of the Yuanhe Era]. Edited by He Cijun 賀次君. (Beijing: Zhonghua shuju, 1983), 40.1023.
31 Ibid., 39.989.

In this geographical treatise with an emphasis on imperial administration, Mount Jishi, as a landmark, has itself bifurcated into two entities – Greater and Lesser – which share the name. This bifurcation disguises an epistemological shift and a geographical concession; it allows the description to simultaneously "concede" Jishi to the foreign territory beyond the Tang empire's western frontier, while still retaining its name (as "Lesser Jishi") as the gateway marker for the Yellow River as it flows into Chinese territory, as a form of continuity with numerous earlier texts. In this description we glimpse a fascinating process of geographical renaming without renaming as such.[32]

2 The River's source in literary allusions and the collective imagination

For the Tang, spatial imagination manifests not only in geographical treatises, but also in other written genres in which there is extensive world-building through literary language. As Ao Wang points out, for Tang writers, "geographical information meant not only knowledge and perspectives, but also words and letters to be matched with rhymes and woven in parallelism, or rhetorical devices that would empower the authorial voice in their literature."[33] Literary language built around spatial imaginaries was not merely ornamental flourish; it was an important mechanism for circulating knowledge, because literary interactions – the exchange of poetry, the recording of unusual phenomena and personal recollections – pervaded almost all aspects of Tang literati's official and private lives. We can see this engagement with geography from a more literature-centered *leishu* from the Tang, the *Yiwen leiju* 藝文類聚 (Classified Collection of Literary Classics), compiled in 624, which is more typical of a book of allusions: it connects the conception of the river's source to a larger literary corpus, through an extensive list of literary allusions. In it, the Yellow River is the first entry under the category of "river." It cites the *Mountain and Water Classic*

---

32 Although this issue is beyond the scope of the current paper, it is noteworthy that this bifurcation of place names has also occurred in the case of Liuqiu (流求 or 琉球). When it first appeared in Chinese sources in the Sui dynasty, it referred to Taiwan; later, it came to refer to the Ryukyu Islands, and the bifurcation of the name Liuqiu into a "Greater" and "Lesser" during the Ming dynasty reflected this shift in geographical referents.
33 Wang, *Spatial Imaginaries in mid-Tang China*, 7.

and names Mount Kunlun as its source (崑崙山, 河水出焉), but also lists two additional mountains – Mount Yangyu 陽紆 and Mount Lingmen 陵門 – as the river's source. Toward the end of the section in *Classified Collection of Literary Classics* and before the entry shifts to citations of literary-poetic allusions, it again cites the *Mountain and Water Classic* and mentions that below Mount Jishi, the river emerges from a stone gate (石門) and flows toward the southwest.[34]

Another *leishu* compiled by the mid-Tang poet Bai Juyi 白居易 (772–846), *Baishi liutie shilei ji* 白氏六帖事類集 (Bai's Collection of Categorized Matters in Six Tablets), is similarly focused on literary allusions. Chapter six includes the following entries under Yellow River (河): "The major [Yellow] River has its [ultimate] numinous source in Kunlun [Mountains]" (大河靈源出崑崙); "[Yu the Great] guided the River to Jishi [Mountain]" (導河積石); "After nine bends [the water] turns clear" (九曲一清).[35] During Bai Juyi's time, the Japanese Buddhist pilgrim Ennin, who in 840 was traveling in Yucheng 禹城 in Shangdong 山東 and arrived at a ferry point of the Yellow River, also noted the river's origin in the context of its overall layout. In his diary entry for the fourth month, eleventh day, he notes: "The river is about one *cho* and five *tan* wide and flows east. The Yellow River originates in the K'un-lun Mountains and has nine bends [九曲], six of which are in the land of the Tibetans and three in China."[36] Ennin's commentary about the river reflects at least in part a popular collective conception of its genesis as foreign, despite its cultural identity as a "Chinese" river.

By ordering topics in a top-down hierarchy, Tang-era *leishu* offers us glimpses into the perceived importance of topics, and by extension, the architecture of knowledge. For example, even though Mount Kunlun and Mount Jishi both have been identified as origins of the Yellow River, their placement within *leishu* categories show that they are conferred different ontological statuses. In the *Classified Collection of Literary Classics*, Mount Kunlun is the first entry under the category "mountains" (山), thereby taking up a position of primacy. In Bai Juyi's collection, Mount Kunlun is item number eight of nineteen, listed after the five marchmounts (五岳) and Mount Zhongnan 終南. By comparison, none of these Tang *leishu* have included Mount Jishi under the "mountains"

---

34 Dong Zhi'an, ed, *Tangdai si da leishu*, v.2, 822. This is echoed by an entry in the *Records of Encompassing Lands* (括地志), which adds that these are places once reached by King Mu (河水又出於陽紆、陵門之山者, 穆王之所至). Li Tai, *Kuo di zhi jijiao*, 1.39.

35 Dong Zhi'an, ed. *Tangdai si da leishu*, v.3, 1961.

36 (黃河源出昆侖山, 有九曲, 六曲在土蕃國, 三曲在大唐國) English translation from Reischauer, Edwin O. *Ennin's Diary: The Record of a Pilgrimage to China in Search of the Law*. (New York: Ronald Press Company, 1955), 205. I am grateful to Hannial Taubes for bringing this passage to my attention.

category. In short, these two mountains, both connected to the genesis of the Yellow River, are anything but equal. Mount Kunlun enjoys a mythopoetic allure, enhanced by its perception as *axis mundi* in early texts such as the *Mu tianzi zhuan* 穆天子傳 (Biography of the Son of Heaven Mu), in which the eponymous ruler is greeted by Queen Mother of the West at the storied Mount Kunlun. In other texts such as *Huainan zi* 淮南子 and *Bao pu zi* 抱朴子, Kunlun has also been connected to cosmography and forms of esoteric knowledge. This mythopeotic status of Mount Kunlun does not apply to Mount Jishi; this status of Kunlun explains at least in part its resilience in the long history of the evolving conception of the river's genesis.

3 Correlative hydrography: The Yellow River's celestial correspondences and underground flows

As we have seen, prior to the Tang, descriptions of the Yellow River's headwaters included subterranean water flows. The *Mountain and Water Classic* identifies a marsh (Youze 泑澤) as the place where the Yellow River's water "flows underneath."[37] In *Historical Records*, Sima Qian recorded that:

> West of Yutian [Khotan], all waters flow west to the Western Sea. On the east side of it the waters flow east into the salt lake. At the salt lake [water] moves underground, and on its south side emerges [as] the source of the [Yellow] River. [Yutian] has plenty of jade; the [Yellow] River flows into the Central Kingdom.
>
> 于實之西, 則水皆西流, 注西海; 其東水東流, 注鹽澤。鹽澤潛行地下, 其南則河源出焉。多玉石, 河注中國。[38]

The *Annotated Itineraries of Waterways* also includes commentary citing other early medieval sources that use *qianliu* 潛流 or *qianfa* 潛發 to describe the headwater.[39] Tang sources continue to take up this idea. As we have seen, descriptions in *Fundamentals of Learning* states that as soon as the river leaves

---

37 In the *Xishan jing* 西山經, Youze is described as "where the Yellow River's water flows underneath; its source gushes vigorously" (河水所潛也, 其源渾渾泡泡). Yuan Ke 袁珂, ed. *Shan hai jing jiaozhu* 山海經校注 [Annotated Mountain and Water Classic]. (Shanghai: Shanghai guji 1980), 40.
38 Sima Qian司馬遷, *Shiji* 史記 [Historian's Records] (Beijing: Zhonghua shuju, 1975), 123.3160.
39 Li Daoyuan. *Shuijing zhu jiaozheng*, 13.

Mount Kunlun, it "flows underground" (潛行地下); after it enters Lop Nor Lake, it is said to "flow underground again" before emanating from Mount Jishi.[40] This conception of the headwater divides its features into those that can be seen above ground (Kunlun, Lop Nor, Jishi) and those that are invisible (the two major river segments connecting these three points).

Not all the writers in the Tang subscribed to this idea, because subterranean flows could not be definitively verified. In the administrative history *Tong dian* 通典 (Comprehensive Statues), the historian Du You 杜佑 (735–812), for example, took stock of previous generations' written accounts of the river's source and criticized the idea of submerged flow, and in particular criticized *Annotated Itineraries of Waterways* for following unreliable sources which lacked empirical bases.[41] Despite Du You's categorical skepticism, the idea of a subterranean river flow held traction in the collective imagination, its popularity perhaps due to the fact that this conception also taps into a Daoist-inflected vision of the earth as full of voids and grottoes.

Tang informal writing – authored and circulated by the same collective of literati elite to which Du You belonged – elaborates on the premise in which a subterranean, unseen topography coexists with a visible, above-ground counterpart. Two examples of narratives that describe accidental glimpses of these subterranean worlds come from the ninth-century collection *Youyang zazu* 酉陽雜俎 (Mixed Morsels of Youyang) by Duan Chengshi 段成式 (ca. 803–863), which documents unusual and marvelous occurrences in the natural world and in the human realm. In an entry titled "Yongxing fang baixing" 永興坊百姓 (Commoners from the Yongxing Ward), a resident of the capital Chang'an, while digging a well, discovers what appears to be another neighborhood underneath the ground, complete with human voices and the sounds of chicken flocks. The narrative then recounts a similar occurrence from the Qin dynasty (221–206 BCE), and concludes with the musing that, "Thus we know that underneath the solid ground, there exist additional heavens and earths" (抑知厚地之下, 或別有天地也).[42]

Another anecdote in this collection elaborates on the belief that unbeknownst to most, extensive underground channels connect well water with rivers. It describes a well in the Changle 長樂 Ward of Chang'an, situated just south of the Daming Palace:

---

40 Dong Zhi'an, ed. *Tangdai si da leishu*, 3.1521b.
41 Du You 杜佑. *Tong Dian* (Wang Wenjin deng dian jiao) 通典 (王文錦等點校) [Comprehensive History of Institutions]. (Beijing: Zhonghua, 1988), *juan* 174.
42 Li Fang 李昉, ed. *Taiping guangji* 太平廣記 [Extensive Records for the Era of Supreme Peace]. (Beijing: Zhonghua shuju, 2003), 399.3208–9.

In the street in front of the Jinggong Temple, there had been a giant well commonly called the "Octagonal Well." In the early years of the Yuanhe, a princess passed the well in the summer. Since some commoners had just finished pulling up water, she ordered her servant-girl to fetch her some using a silver-edged bowl. [The servant] approached the well to fill it, but dropped the bowl into the well by accident. After a few months, the [same] bowl emerged in the Wei River.

景公寺前街中。舊有巨井。俗呼為八角井。唐元和初。有公主夏中過。見百姓方汲。令從婢以銀稜碗。就井承水。誤墜井。經月餘。碗出於渭河。[43]

Here, a precious vessel becomes a tracking device and renders visible the unseen hydrological connection between a residential well in Chang'an and the Wei River. This narrative joins a number of others about the wonders of wells and well water, and their capacity as unexpected portals into a larger body of water nearby. There were enough of these accounts such that in the 500-fascile Song-dynasty narrative compendium *Taiping guangji* 太平廣記 (Extensive Records for the Era of Supreme Peace), fascicle 399 is devoted to the category of "Water" (水), and consists of short prose pieces that are loosely bound by this theme, demonstrating that this idea was seen as plausible enough to be rendered in numerous variants in the larger corpus of informal writing from the Tang and early medieval China.[44]

If these examples merely suggest that subterranean geographies of rivers exist, other accounts make explicit that such unseen structures can be regulated as well. In one short account from the ninth century, collected in the *Taiping guangji* under the category heading of "Well" (井), the Tang chief minister Jia Dan 賈耽 (730–805) digs an octagonal well in Huatai 滑臺 in order to "quell the Yellow River" (以鎮黃河).[45] It takes up the notion that a river's behavior can be regulated not only from above-ground but also through its underground circulatory system: a strategically placed well relieves the Yellow River of excess water and prevents it from overflowing its banks.

Contemporary lore about the river that was more fantastical in nature also coexisted with inherited geographical knowledge of the Yellow River such as that described in *Fundamentals of Learning*. Such lore about the Yellow River even extended to the nature of its headwater itself. In the chapter titled "Wine

---

43 Li Fang, ed. *Taiping guangji*, 3207–3208. On the Zhao Jinggong Temple in Changle Ward in Chang'an, see Victor Cunrui Xiong, *Sui-Tang Chang'an: A Study in the Urban History of Medieval China* (Ann Arbor, MI: Center for Chinese Studies, University of Michigan, 2000), 306.

44 Li Fang, *Taiping guangji*, 3197–3210.

45 Ibid., 3207. Huatai 滑臺 is in present-day Henan; during the Tang it was in Huazhou 滑州 on the Yellow River. See Tan Qixiang 譚其驤, ed. *Zhongguo lishi ditu ji* 中國歷史地圖集 [Historical Atlas of China] (Shanghai: Ditu chubanshe, 1982), 5.44–45.

and Food" (酒食) in *Mixed Morsels of Youyang*, there is an entry about the role of this water in wine-making:

> The household of Jia Jiang of Wei was enormously wealthy. Jia was well educated and was fond of writing. He had a servant who was good at judging the quality of water. Jia often had him row a small punt into the Yellow River and use a bottlegourd to collect water from the river's source. The servant could get no more than seven or eight *sheng* in a day. Overnight, the color of the liquid would turn red, almost crimson [色如絳]. Jia used this water to make wine – he called the gourd "Kunlun goblet" [崑崙觴]. The bouquet and taste of this wine were out of this world, and once Jia presented thirty *hu* of this wine to Wei Zhuangdi.[46]

Here, although there is no mention of the topography of the Yellow River's source or how the servant might have reached it, the emphasis is placed on the otherworldly color and flavor of the water. The overnight transformation of the water into a crimson color (絳) hints at the celestial origins of the Yellow River, because, as noted in Bai Juyi's encyclopedia, the Milky Way is also interchangeably called the "Crimson River" (絳河).[47] The passage suggests that although the celestial connection of the Yellow River may not be immediately apparent, it reveals itself when given enough time. Thus in this late-Tang narrative, the source water also takes on a new role as a prized ingredient: the object of a kind of extreme gourmand connoisseurship.

4 Tang expeditions to the Yellow River's source

An important aspect of the process of knowledge formation regarding the river's source comes from eye-witness accounts from expeditions to the river's upper reaches. As previously mentioned, such accounts were recorded in Han histories[48] and continued in the Tang, after which Yuan and Qing-dynasty expeditions generated unprecedented details and focused observations.[49]

---

46 Carrie Reed, *A Tang Miscellany: An Introduction to Youyang zazu.* (New York: Peter Lang, 2003), 95–96.

47 See for example Bai Juyi's *leishu*. Dong Zhi'an, *Tangdai si da leishu*, v.3, 1961.

48 In Han historiography, Zhang Qian's observations were subject to debate as well. Sima Qian challenges the reliability of the Kunlun attribution as found in *Yu benji* 禹本紀 (Basic Annals of Yu), and notes that Zhang Qian did not verify the presence of Kunlun, and therefore concludes the appraisal with a sharp note of incredulity, that the "strange things" in the *Shanhai jing* are such that he "does not dare to speak of them." For a discussion and translation of this appraisal in the Biography of Dayuan (大宛列傳) by Sima Qian and also a similar opinion articulated by Ban Gu in the *Hanshu* 漢書, see Dorofeeva-Lichtmann, "Where is the Yellow River Source?" 72–3.

49 The Yuan expedition took place in 1280 and reported "Constellation Lake" as the definitive origin of the Yellow River. See a brief summary in Tian Shang, "Huanghe heyuan tantao," 339.

During the Tang, the Yellow River's headwater region lay outside of Chinese territory; it was first controlled by the Tuyuhun 吐谷渾 and later by the Tibetans. Tang historiography documents expeditions that, although not specifically aimed at finding the river's origin, briefly observed the Yellow River's headwaters. In the early Tang, one such expedition was headed by the military official Hou Junji 侯君集 (d. 643), who fought against Tuyuhun 吐谷渾 troops in 635. His biography in the dynastic histories records that his troops moved amidst snow-covered mountains, past the Constellation River (星宿川) and Cypress Lake (柏海), and he "looked out northward toward Mount Jishi and gazed at the source of the Yellow River,"[50] a place that, as one general in this campaign points out, "has never been reached since ancient times (古未有至者)."[51] Here, both Cypress Lake and Constellation River are mentioned as key stops en route to the river's source, but there are no details regarding any hydrological relationship to the river's source.

From textual citations of Tang-era maps that have since been lost, it seems that Constellation River in the Yellow River's source region appeared on administrative maps as *xingxiu hai* 星宿海 (Constellation Lake).[52] We see evidence of this on a Song-dynasty map of Tang administrative divisions, dated to 1100s and widely circulated in its time, and which was part of the atlas *Handy Geographical Maps throughout the Ages* (歷代地理指掌圖). This map of the Ten Circuits of the Tang Dynasty (唐十道圖) (Figure 2) shows *xingxiu hai* among a list of place names just outside the administrative borders of the Tang empire on its western edge.[53]

Later in the Tang dynasty, the Yellow River's source region changed hands and came under the control of the Tibetan empire. Under emperor Muzong 穆宗 (r. 820–824), Chinese delegates travelled to Tibet as part of a mission to sign a

50 Liu Xu 劉昫. *Jiu Tang shu* 舊唐書 [Old History of the Tang]. (Beijing: Zhonghua shuju, 1975), 69.2510. See also discussion in Li Faming 李發明. "也談唐代的 '柏海'与'河源' " [On "Cypress Lake" and "Yellow River's Source" during the Tang Dynasty]. Qinghai Normal University Journal, no. 4 (1984): 108–14.

51 Ouyang Xiu 歐陽修. *Xin Tang shu* 新唐書 [New History of the Tang]. (Beijing: Zhonghua shuju, 1975), 146.6225.

52 Sima Guang used one version of the Map of Ten Circuits of the Tang Dynasty (唐十道圖) and mentioned the name *xingxiu h*ai in connection with it. Li Faming, "On 'Cypress Lake' and 'Yellow River's Source' during the Tang Dynasty," 111.

53 The edition of *Handy Geographical Maps throughout the Ages* (歷代地理指掌圖) I refer to is a facsimile edition of the copy now held at the 東洋文庫 Toyo bunko. The atlas has been dated to the 1100s. Shui Anli 稅安禮. *Song ben lidai dili zhizhang tu* 宋本歷代地理指掌圖 [Song dynasty edition of "Handy geographical maps throughout the ages"]. (Shanghai: Shanghai guji, 1989), 62.

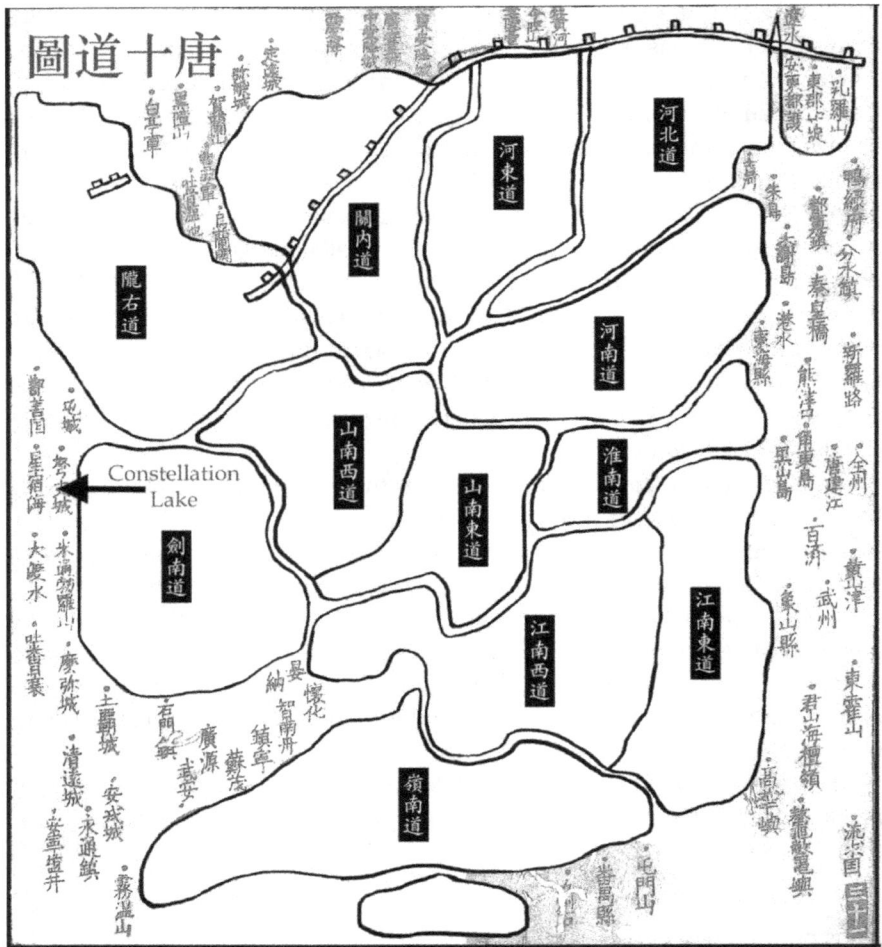

Figure 2: The earliest occurrence *xingxiu hai* 星宿海 (shown left of arrow) on extant maps, from a Song historical atlas showing the ten Tang administrative circuits (唐十道圖). Digital illustration by Tif Fan, based on Shui Anli 稅安禮. *Song ben lidai dili zhizhang tu* 宋本歷代地理指掌圖 [Song dynasty edition of "Handy geographical maps throughout the ages"]. (Shanghai: Shanghai guji, 1989), 62.

Sino-Tibetan treaty in 821, and arrived at the river's source region. In a set of observations undertaken by the Tang official Liu Yuanding 劉元鼎 as part of that diplomatic mission, the Yellow River's source is surveyed against a non-Chinese (Tibetan) landscape, and provided with more geographical detail:

[Liu] Yuanding crossed the Huang River [湟水], reached the Valley of Dragon Springs, and could look in the northwestern direction and see Shahu River. There, old fortifications left by Geshu Han were mostly still standing. The Huang River emerges from Meng Valley, and it merges with the [Yellow] River when it reaches Dragon Springs. As for the upper reaches of the [Yellow] River, two thousand *li* southwest of the Hongji Bridge [洪濟梁], the water is quite narrow.[54] During the spring it can be forded, and in the summer and autumn it can support boats. There are three mountain peaks three hundred *li* south of it, the middle peak stands taller than the others. It is called Purple Mountain, and faces the state of Greater Yangtong [大羊同國]. It is called Kunlun in antiquity. The Tibetans call it Mount Menmoli. It is five thousand *li* away from Chang'an in the east. The [Yellow] River originates from it, its stream flows clear downward, and with the confluence of some other rivers, it turns reddish in color, and, as it travels farther away, other waters join it and it becomes turbid. This is why everyone calls the territory of the western barbarians Hehuang. Heading northeast, the [Yellow] River's origin is nearly five hundred *li* from Moheyan at the desert's terminus. The desert is fifty *li* in width, and its northern edge is Shazhou. In the southwestern direction it gradually narrows as it enters [the area of] Tuyuhun, and this is why it is called "the desert's tail." Taking measure of this land, [one can see that] it is west of Jiannan [in China]. This is the broad extent of what [Liu] Yuanding saw.

元鼎踰湟水, 至龍泉谷, 西北望殺胡川, 哥舒翰故壁多在。湟水出蒙谷, 抵龍泉與河合。河之上流, 縣洪濟梁西南行二千里, 水益狹, 春可涉, 秋夏乃勝舟。其南三百里三山, 中高而四下, 曰紫山, 直大羊同國, 古所謂崑崙者也, 虜曰悶摩黎山, 東距長安五千里, 河源其間, 流澄緩下, 稍合眾流, 色赤, 行益遠, 它水并注則濁, 故世舉謂西戎地曰河湟。河源東北直莫賀延磧尾殆五百里, 磧廣五十里, 北自沙州, 西南入吐谷渾浸狹, 故號磧尾。隱測其地, 蓋劍南之西。元鼎所經見, 大略如此。[55]

This passage is preserved under the "Biography of the Tibetans" (*Tubo zhuan* 吐蕃傳) in the *New Tang Histories*. The mountain from which the Yellow River issues forth is associated with not one but three names: the Zishan (Purple Mountain), the ancient name of Kunlun, and the non-Chinese name of Menmoli Mountain.[56]

---

54 The Hongji Bridge is rendered as Hongji qiao 洪濟橋, in Tan Qixiang 譚其驤, ed. *Zhongguo lishi ditu ji* 中國歷史地圖集 [Historical Atlas of China] (Shanghai: Ditu chubanshe, 1982), vol. 5, 61–62.

55 Ouyang Xiu, *Xin Tang shu*, 216.6104. See also English translations of entries relating to Tibet in Tang dynastic histories, in Bushell, S. W. "The Early History of Tibet From Chinese Sources." *Journal of the Royal Asiatic Society* 12, no. 4 (1880): 435–541; 520. Liu Yuanding's account is also collected in *juan* 716 of the *Quan Tang wen* 全唐文 [Collected Tang Prose].

56 Based on the description of the three peaks and its approximate location, Menmoli can be associated with the Tibetan holy mountain Amyé Machen. Taubes, Hannibal. "'They Told us that Rivertown was the Ends of Heaven': The Upper Yellow River in the Chinese Literary-Cosmological Episteme, beginnings to 1750 CE," (Virtual conference) *Life Along the River: Interactions between Human Societies and Valley Environments in the Convergence Zone of the Inner Asian Highlands, 1600s–1950s.* July 22, 2021. Wu Jing'ao 吳景敖 associates Menmoli with the Bayan Har Mountains, whose name is Mongolian and which is situated to the west, but

These three names for the same mountain juxtaposes three frameworks of reference, and calls attention to the fact that geographical investigations such as tracing the Yellow River's source was steeped in a form of translation.[57] In comparison to the earlier case in which the Mount Jishi bifurcates into two names, here, the simultaneity of these frameworks reveals yet another strategy in the dynamic process of knowledge-formation in a polyglot context, in which insights added to Tang geographical knowledge, namely, the sighting in a foreign territory of the mountain with a transliterated Tibetan name, becomes aligned with an existing textural and cultural referent, that of "the ancient name of Kunlun." This set of observations differs from other Tang accounts of the river source in that its only reference to transmitted text is the naming of Kunlun, which by now has become a kind of moveable target.

In an article analyzing the *Mu Tianzi zhuan* 穆天子傳 [Biography of King Mu, Son of Heaven], Deborah Porter points out that within this text, Mount Kunlun – as well as other place names – functions as a cosmological rather than geographical referent.[58] Dorofeeva-Litchmann makes a similar argument about mentions of Kunlun in early Chinese texts such as the *Historical Records* and *History of the Han,* and points out: "attempts to determine which of the possible identifications of Kunlun and Jishi are the right ones, and where precisely they are found on the earth surface, does not seem to be a fruitful approach to these landmarks in the context of the 'true' location of the Yellow River source [. . .]."[59]

Returning to this ninth-century account by Liu Yuanding, the application of the name Kunlun to a mountain with two other names shows another moment of transition, as the "ancient name" of Kunlun is now deployed and *appended* as a cosmological referent in order to "domesticate" the geographical

---

does not give a reason for this association. Wu Jing'ao. *Xi chui shi di yan jiu* 西陲史地研究 [Research on the Historical Geography of the Western Frontiers]. (Shanghai: Zhonghua shuju, 1948), 12.

57 Here I am inspired by Patrick Manning's discussion of the process and the results of translation as an essential element of early modern knowledge making as applied to the natural world: "It was through the linguistic formulation in the mind of the translator that space, time, and cultural difference could be overcome to enable the steady development of widely dispersed funds of knowledge." Manning, Patrick, and Abigail Owen, eds. *Knowledge in Translation: Global Patterns of Scientific Exchange, 1000–1800 CE.* (Pittsburgh: University of Pittsburgh Press, 2018), 2–3.

58 Porter, Deborah. "The Literary Function of K'un-lun Mountain in the *Mu T'ien-tzu chuan*." *Early China* 18, no. 18 (1993): 73–106.

59 Dorofeeva-Lichtmann, "Where is the Yellow River Source?" 71.

referent of the mountain of Menmoli, as personally observed by a Chinese official while conducting diplomatic affairs. This is neither the first nor last time that Kunlun as a referent becomes the site for assimilating new geographical knowledge.

Understanding the changes in the representation of the Yellow River's fountainhead reveals the processes through which spatial imagination of a prominent geographical feature has evolved over centuries. Along with geographical treatises, textual references in the Tang – whether as part of an encyclopedic primer, literary collectanea, or informal prose narrative – grappled with the contradictory yet simultaneous references to the origin of the Yellow River inherited from previous eras, and combined contemporary notions of hydrological behavior, ideas of borders and sovereignty as well as religious and secular cosmographies to reach new conclusions. Tracing the changing beliefs of the Yellow River's provenance – as refracted in textual representation in this case, and later, in cartographic representation as well – makes a good case study for how such beliefs assimilated forms of geographical knowledge.

Bibliography

Bushell, S. W. "The Early History of Tibet From Chinese Sources." *Journal of the Royal Asiatic Society* 12, no. 4 (1880): 435–541.

Cen Zhongmian 岑仲勉. *Huanghe bianqian shi* 黄河變遷史 [A History of Changes for the Yellow River]. (Beijing: Renmin, 1957).

Dien, Albert E., *et al.*, eds. *Early Medieval Chinese Texts: A Bibliographical Guide.* (Berkeley, CA: Institute of East Asian Studies, 2015).

Dong Zhi'an 董治安, ed. *Tangdai si da leishu* 唐代四大類書. (Beijing: Qinghua daxue, 2003), vol. 3.

Dorofeeva-Lichtmann, Vera. "A History of a Spatial Relationship: Kunlun Mountain and the Yellow River Source from Chinese Cosmography through to Western Cartography," *Circumscribere [International Journal for the History of Science]* 11 (2012): 1–31.

——. "Where is the Yellow River Source? A Controversial Question in Early Chinese Historiography," *Oriens Extremus* 45 (2005): 68–90.

Du You 杜佑. *Tong Dian* (Wang Wenjin deng dian jiao) 通典 全五冊 (王文錦等點校) [Comprehensive History of Institutions]. (Beijing: Zhonghua shuju, 1988).

Greatrex, Roger. *The Bowu zhi: An Annotated Translation*. (Stockholm: Föreningen för Orientaliska Studier, 1987).

Ji Xianlin 季羨林, ed. *Da Tang xiyu ji jiaozhu* 大唐西域記校注. (Beijing: Zhonghua shuju, 1985).

Li Daoyuan 酈道元. *Shuijing zhu jiaozheng* 水經注校證 [Annotated Edition of the Annotated Itineraries of Waterways]. Edited by Chen Qiaoyi 陳橋驛. (Beijing: Zhonghua shuju, 2007).

Li Faming 李發明. "也談唐代的"柏海"與"河源" [On "Cypress Lake" and "Yellow River's Source" during the Tang Dynasty]. Qinghai Normal University Journal no. 4 (1984): 108–14.

Li Fang 李昉, ed. *Taiping guangji* 太平廣記 [Extensive Records for the Era of Supreme Peace]. 10 vols. (Beijing: Zhonghua shuju, 2003).

Li Tai 李泰. *Kuo di zhi jijiao* 括地志輯校 [Comprehensive Treatise of the Land]. Edited by He Cijun 賀次君. (Beijing: Zhonghua shuju, 1980).

Liu Xu 劉昫. *Jiu Tang shu* 舊唐書 [Old History of the Tang]. (Beijing: Zhonghua shuju, 1975).

Manning, Patrick, and Abigail Owen, eds. *Knowledge in Translation: Global Patterns of Scientific Exchange, 1000–1800 CE.* (Pittsburgh: University of Pittsburgh Press, 2018)

Moerman, D. Max. *The Japanese Buddhist World Map: Religious Vision and the Cartographic Imagination.* (Honolulu: University of Hawai'i Press, forthcoming).

Mostern, Ruth. "Mapping the Tracks of Yu: Yellow River Statecraft as Science and Technology, 1200–1600." In *Knowledge in Translation: Global Patterns of Scientific Exchange, 1000–1800 CE,* edited by Patrick Manning and Abigail Owen, 134–46. (Pittsburgh: University of Pittsburgh Press, 2018).

Ouyang Xiu 歐陽修. *Xin Tang shu* 新唐書 [New History of the Tang]. (Beijing: Zhonghua shuju, 1975).

Park, Hyunhee, "Information Synthesis and Space Creation: The Earliest Chinese Maps of Central Asia and the Silk Road, 1265–1270," *Journal of Asian History* 49, no. 1–2 (2015): 119–40.

Porter, Deborah. "The Literary Function of K'un-lun Mountain in the Mu T'ien-tzu chuan." *Early China* 18, no. 18 (1993): 73–106.

Qi Mingrong 祁明榮, ed. *Huanghe yuantou kaocha wenji* 黃河源頭考察文集 [Collected Essays on Surveys on the Yellow River's Origin]. (Xining: Qinghai Renmin, 1982).

Ray, Haraprasad, ed. *Chinese Sources of South Asian History in Translation: Data for Study of India-China Relations Through History.* (Kolkata: Asiatic Society, 2004), Vol. 2.

Reed, Carrie. *Chinese Chronicles of the Strange: The "Nuogao ji".* (New York: Peter Lang, 2001).

——. *A Tang Miscellany: An Introduction to Youyang zazu.* (New York: Peter Lang, 2003).

Reischauer, Edwin O. *Ennin's Diary: The Record of a Pilgrimage to China in Search of the Law.* New York: Ronald Press Company, 1955.

Shui Anli 稅安禮. *Song ben lidai dili zhizhang tu* 宋本歷代地理指掌圖 [Song-Dynasty Edition of "Handy geographical maps throughout the ages"]. (Shanghai: Shanghai guji, 1989).

Sima Qian 司馬遷. *Shiji* 史記 [Historian's Records]. (Beijing: Zhonghua shuju, 1975).

Strassberg, Richard E. *A Chinese Bestiary: Strange Creatures from the Guideways through Mountains and Seas = [Shan hai jing].* (Berkeley: University of California Press, 2018).

Tan Qixiang 譚其驤, ed. *Zhongguo lishi ditu ji* 中國歷史地圖集 [Historical Atlas of China]. (Shanghai: Ditu chubanshe, 1982), vol. 5.

Tian Shang 田尚. "Huanghe heyuan tantao" 黃河河源探討 [Discussion on the Source of the Yellow River]. *Dili xue bao* 地理學報 [Acta Geographica Sinica] 36, no. 3 (1981): 338–44.

Wang, Ao. *Spatial Imaginaries in Mid-Tang China: Geography, Cartography, and Literature.* (Amherst, New York: Cambria Press, 2018).

Wang Shiduo 汪士鐸. *Shuijing zhu tu* 水經注圖 [Maps for the Shuijing zhu]. Edited by Chen Qiaoyi 陳橋驛. (Jinan: Shandong Huabao, 2003), Vol. 2.

Wu Jing'ao 吳景敖. *Xi chui shi di yanjiu* 西陲史地研究 [Research on the Historical Geography of the Western Frontiers]. (Shanghai: Zhonghua shuju, 1948).

Xi Huidong 席會東. *Zhongguo gudai ditu wenhua shi* 中古代地圖文化史 [The Cultural History of Ancient Chinese Cartography]. (Beijing: Zhongguo ditu, 2013).

Xiong, Victor Cunrui. *Sui-Tang Chang'an: A Study in the Urban History of Medieval China.* (Ann Arbor, MI: Center for Chinese Studies, University of Michigan, 2000).

Yuan Ke 袁珂, ed. *Shan hai jing jiaozhu* 山海經校注 [Annotated Mountain and Water Classic]. (Shanghai: Shanghai guji, 1980).

Zhang, Ling. *The River, the Plain, and the State: An Environmental Drama in Northern Song China, 1048–1128*. (Cambridge: Cambridge University Press, 2016).

Zheng Xihuang 鄭錫煌. "Guanyu Fozu tongji zhong sanfu ditu zouyi" 關於《佛祖統記》中三幅 地圖芻議, in Cao Wanru *et al* eds., *Zhongguo gudai ditu ji (Zhanguo – Yuan)* 中國古代地 圖集 (戰國 – 元) (Beijing: Wenwu, 1990).

Zhipan 志磐. *Fozu tongji jiaozhu* 佛祖統紀校注 (Shanghai: Shanghai guji, 2012).

Daniel Patrick Morgan
Remarks on the Mathematics and Philosophy of Space-time in Early Imperial China

There are things you learn early in your academic training that stick with you, and that you hear repeated, but that you are no longer sure how you know – Truths, until otherwise proven, that even if unproven are difficult to unlearn. Two of the Truths that I picked up somewhere, and have heard repeated since, are that, first, Chinese thought is somehow unique in recognizing the interconnectedness of space and time, and that, second, Chinese astronomy is a "calendar science" dealing exclusively with the latter.[1] These Truths, it took me some time to realize, cannot both be *true* if for the simple reason that the one, *a priori*, excludes the other. I forgot how I had come to believe these things, and, to reassure myself that I had not made them up, I went back through the literature to familiarize myself with their genesis. Both go back to the nineteenth century, it turns out, and both have been problematized since before I learned to read, yet *both of them*, for whatever reason, flutter still like forgotten prayer flags generating merit in the wind.[2] The goal of this paper is to take them down.

What do I propose we say of Chinese thought as concerns space, time, cosmology, and the calendar if not this? Big picture, what I am proposing is very simple. First, I should like that we stop speaking about "the Chinese" and "Chinese thought" as if either were a single thing, let alone one informed exclusively by Marcel Granet's (1884–1940) *La pensée chinoise* of 1934.[3] If, as Martin Powers'

---

1 Both at once, Marc Kalinowski tells us for example that "Le système astronomique chinois n'était pas conçu dans l'espace mais dans le temps, sur la base du calendrier," then, three pages later, that "Dans sa *Pensée chinoise* (1934), Marcel Granet consacrait un chapitre aux conceptions de l'espace et du temps en Chine. Nul mieux que lui n'a mis en évidence l'indissociabilité de ces notions, leur interchangeabilité et leur dimension concrète" ("Astrologie calendaire et calcul de position dans la Chine ancienne: les mutations de l'hémérologie sexagésimale entre le IVe et le IIe siècles avant notre ère," *Extrême-orient, Extrême-occident* 18 [1996]: 71–113 [71, 74]). One should find this puzzling.
2 This paper began with a list compiled of statements similar to Kalinowski's, in Note 1, and reactions thereto spanning the eighteenth to the twenty-first century and organized by filiation. If I have singled out Kalinowski in the previous note it is for no other reason than that he attributes these truisms to a historical progenitor. It is the root rather than the branches, so to speak, that is the focus of this paper.
3 This is not to deny the value of Granet's pioneering study as concerns the metaphysics and metrosophy one finds in certain forms of divination and elite ritual, occult, political, and

chapter explores, a single artist could explore multiple and contradictory lines of sight within a single scene in the name of "naturalistic," "fact-based" representation of his immediate surroundings, we should assume no less his *civilization* when it comes to the abstractions of astronomical space and time. Second, in allowing for a plurality of *pensées*, I propose that one of the voices that sinologists should accommodate in a discussion of space, time, cosmology, and the calendar is that of the astronomer and of expert literature on these subjects. Based primarily on the peculiarities of the word *yuzhou* 宇宙 "space-time" for "cosmos" as it appears (no more than ten times) in early political and ethical philosophy, Derk Bodde asserts an "emphasis on space over time in Chinese thinking."[4] And maybe that's true *of early political and ethical philosophy,*[5] it is important to specify, but who would a *historian of mathematics* be fooling with a commensurate assertion about *politics and ethics* based on his particular corpus?

The interest in granting the astronomer a voice in a discussion of space and time is not simply *fairness*; it is that the expert voice, more often than not, has more interesting things to say, and that "the astronomer," more often than not, is but a role played by someone we otherwise know by a different label. More interesting than an outsider's musings about whether "Chinese thought" holds time over space or space over time, I hope to show, are the physics behind their interdependence, the plasticity with which they yield their forms, and the thought[s] of th[os]e Chinese who knew how to ply them to know the future, to move forwards and backwards in space and time, and to collapse the one into the other as effortlessly as a child might a string figure. Unlike mystics, our sources are only more than happy to share how they do this, and the goal of this chapter is to distil that literature into metaphors, images, stories, and explanations by which the non-

---

medical writing; it is rather to insist that what Granet is describing is not *unique* to China, *timeless*, nor *exclusive* of other "thought" therein. I am not the first to say this. For important critiques and alternatives, see Joseph Needham, *Science and Civilisation in China, vol.2: History of Scientific Thought* (Cambridge: Cambridge UP, 1956), esp. 288–9; John B. Henderson, *The Development and Decline of Chinese Cosmology* (New York: Columbia UP, 1984); A.C. Graham, *Yin-Yang and the Nature of Correlative Thinking* (Singapore: The Institute of East Asian Philosophies, National University of Singapore, 1986), esp. 8–11; Derk Bodde, *Chinese Thought, Society, and Science: The Intellectual and Social Background of Science and Technology in Pre-Modern China* (Honolulu: University of Hawaii Press, 1991).
4 *Chinese Thought, Society, and Science*, 119.
5 One notes that the counterpart in Bodde's East-versus-West binary – "whereas Westerners, in speaking of 'time and space', clearly give priority to the former" (ibid., 106) – is easily disproven via counting results on a Google search for "time and space" (137 million) versus "space and time" (140 million; checked October 9, 2020).

expert reader may visualise how the early Chinese astronomer experienced space and time from the big picture down to the fine grain.

Remembering how time works

The main problem with the opening propositions about space versus time, as any historian of astronomy would tell you, is that space *is* time when space is turning at a constant rate against a static point of reference. For short, *space is time when space is turning.*[6]

That, whether the reader is aware of it or not, is what is happening outside at this very moment: the sky is turning on its axis, east to west, carrying the sun from dawn to noon to dusk and back again in twenty-four hours just as reliably as the hour-hand of an analogue clock returns to twelve. The sun too is moving, albeit slower and in the opposite direction, charting its annual course through the ecliptic. In Cancer – where it was when I was born – it stands some twenty degrees north of the celestial equator, rising earlier, further north, and mounting higher in the sky over the course of a day; in Scorpio – where it was when one Vincent Leung was born – it has dropped just as far below the equator, rising later, towards the south, and culminating right where you can see it in your window. *All of these* – twelve o'clock, dawn and dusk, Cancer and Scorpio, summer and winter – *all of these* are *positions* (*wei* 位) as much as they are *times* (*shi* 時). Space is time when space is turning.

This simple fact is at the core of ancient correlative matrices of Yin and Yang, the five agents, and so on, and so too is at the core of modern discussions of "Chinese thought," but there is nothing particularly *Chinese* about it. The Chinese divided the "circumference of heaven" (*zhoutian* 周天) into $365\frac{1}{4}$, one *du* 度 – "span" – for each *day* of the solar year. The Mesopotamians divided *theirs* into 360 UŠ for much the same reason, approximating an "ideal year" to suit their sexagesimal numbers.[7] And so it was in Greece, in Rome, in India and in the caliphates

---

6 I offer this reductionist formula not because it is *true* from a *modern perspective* but because it is *helpful to think with* as reflective of a *pre-modern perspective* that it is the historian's duty to understand. In reality, it is not *space* that is turning on its axis but *the earth*, and both the earth's diurnal and annual motion experience minute fluctuations and secular change over time. For an introduction to the basics of astronomy through the perspective of ancient practices and ideas, see Christopher Cullen, *Heavenly Numbers: Astronomy and Authority in Early Imperial China* (Oxford: Oxford UP, 2017); James Evans, *The History and Practice of Ancient Astronomy* (New York: Oxford UP, 1998); Anthony F. Aveni, *Skywatchers of Ancient Mexico* (Austin: University of Texas Press, 1980).

7 See David Brown, "The Cuneiform Conception of Celestial Space and Time," *Cambridge Archaeological Journal* 10, no. 1 (2000): 103–22. On sexagesimal place value notation, see Georges

and empires in between that we, to this day, count sixty minutes to an hour, sixty seconds to a minute, and 360 degrees to a circle – because it is in sixties that the Mesopotamians counted, and because space is time when space is turning.

We use *hours*, of course, but so too did the Chinese, and what is an "hour" anyways except fifteen degrees of arc?[8] When the sun stands due south, on the median, at its highest point in the sky, that is what we call noon; an hour later – "post meridian" (P.M.) – it has moved fifteen degrees towards the west as measured in the plane of the celestial equator. In modern times, we call these "hour angles": an *angle* measured in *hours* that, if added to 12:00 P.M., gives *the time of day*.[9] In Greece, they called them χρόνοι ἰσημερινοί ("equatorial times") or simply χρόνοι ("times"); there were twenty-four and they named them in letters.[10] In China, they called them *jiashi* 加時 ("added times") or simply *chen* 辰 ("times"); there were twelve, or twenty-four, and they named them (primarily) in earthly branches (Figure 1).[11] Still today, *zhongwu* 中午 is noon, and it is time to eat *wufan* 午飯 (lit. "*wu$_n$* rice," thus "lunch"), but it is also the

---

Ifrah and David Bellos, *The Universal History of Numbers: From Prehistory to the Invention of the Computer* (New York: Wiley, 2000), esp. 23–46, 91–95, 121–161.

8 That 1h = 15° and 4m = 1° is a matter of reflex to astronomers, engineers, etc., used to working with these units. Consider Figure 1: we have a circle of, by definition, 360° that is divided into 24 hours: 360° ÷ 24 hours = 15°/hour, and 15° ÷ 60 minutes = 0.25°/minute.

9 See W.M. Smart, *Textbook on Spherical Astronomy*, ed. Robin M. Green (Cambridge: Cambridge UP, 1977), 25–32.

10 On χρόνοι "times' as measures of arc, see Gerald J. Toomer, *Ptolemy's Almagest*, 2d ed. (Princeton: Princeton UP, 1998), 23. On Greek alphabetic numbers, see Ifrah and Bellos, *The Universal History of Numbers*, 182–262.

11 As illustrated in Figure 1, to denote their places in their respective denary and duodenary cycles, I append Latin letters to the heavenly stems (*jia$_a$–gui$_j$*) and Greek letters to the earthly branches (*zi$_α$–hai$_μ$*), which when combined into the sexagenary cycle gives us *jiazi$_{aα}$–guihai$_{jμ}$*. One notes that while Granet speaks of these as "les nombres des séries dénaire et duodénaire" (op. cit., 129), the elements of these ordinal series are no more *numbers* than are "Sunday," "Monday," or "Tuesday." Where they appear in mathematical texts, they are usually "named off" (*ming* 命) rather than "counted" (*shu* 數), and they are certainly never added, subtracted, multiplied, or divided as is uniquely possible with what mathematical texts do identify as "numbers" (*shu*). Likewise, in the rare instances where the word *shu* appears in daybook (*rishu* 日書) hemerological manuscripts, one notes that it is usually to "count out" the days of the month ("day one" 一日, "day seven" 七日, etc.; Zhoujiatai M30 daybook, slips 132–151$_2$, 261–265) or, in the "Genshan" 艮山 hemerology, to count off circles on a diagram representing the "days (=stems?) and branches" 日及枳 of a thirty-day month starting from "new moon" 朔 (Shuihudi M11 daybook A, slips 47r$_3$–48r$_3$). For photos and transcriptions of these manuscripts, see *Guanju Qin-Han mu jiandu* 關沮秦漢墓簡牘, ed. Hubei sheng Jingzhou shi Zhouliang yuqiao yizhi bowuguan 湖北省荊州市周梁玉橋遺址博物館 (Beijing: Zhonghua shuju, 2001) and *Shuihudi Qin mu zhujian* 睡虎地秦墓竹簡, ed. Shuihudi Qin mu zhujian zhengli xiaozu 睡虎地秦墓竹簡整理小組

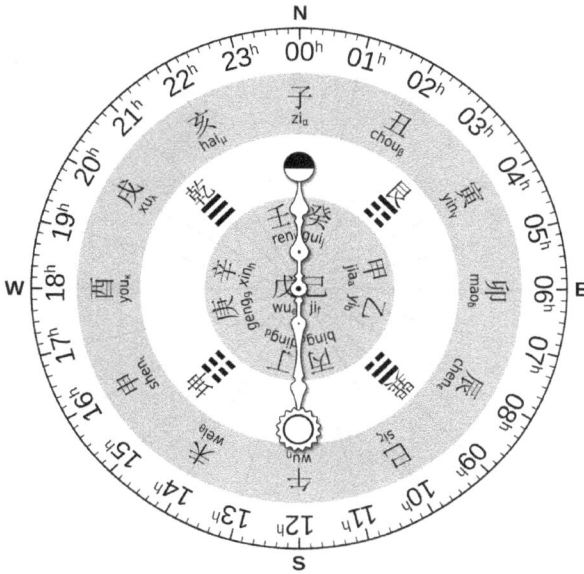

Figure 1: Early medieval twenty-four *chen* or *jiashi* typical of an armillary equatorial ring, as per Qu Anjing 曲安京. "Zhongguo gudai lifa zhong de jishi zhidu" 中國古代曆法中的計時制度. *Hanxue yanjiu* 漢學研究 12, no. 2 (1994): 157–72. The twenty-four *chen/jiashi* are an extension of the twelve "earthly-branch" (*dizhi* 地支) "double-hours," zi_α, $chou_\beta$, yin_γ, mao_δ . . . hai_μ, between which are inserted the eight non-medial "heavenly stems" (*tiangan* 天干), jia_a, yi_b, $bing_c$, $ding_d$, $geng_g$, xin_h, ren_i gui_j, and, in the "four corners" (*siwei* 四維), the *Book of Changes* trigrams Qian 乾 ☰, Kun 坤 ☷, Gen 艮 ☶, and Xun 巽 ☴. In later geomancy, or *fengshui*, this configuration is known as the "twenty-four mountains" (*ershisi shan* 二十四山). The clock hands represent the position of the sun and moon at noon (local apparent time), full moon day. Note that I have flipped this diagram upside-down so that the modern reader might feel more comfortable reading this with north/midnight at the top.

position of the sun (lit. "[sun] centered at wu_n"), opposite where it is at midnight (zi_α). Space is time when space is turning.

Sure, our units, coordinates, and usages are different, but *what we are counting is the same*, and *the way we do it is mathematically commensurable*.[12] The same

---

(Beijing: Wenwu chubanshe, 1990). I thank Donald Harper to alerting me to the latter example in a reader evaluation for another piece, received October 23, 2019.

12 There are, as always, interesting exceptions to such absolutist statements. The *du* and UŠ, for example, are not measures of *angle*, like the degree, but linear measures of perimeter. For some of the more interesting ramifications of this difference, see Huang Yi-long 黃一農, "Jixing yu gudu kao" 極星與古度考, *Tsing Hua Journal of Chinese Studies* 22, no. 2 (1992): 93–117.

goes for bees. Bees navigate by a combination of methods, one of which, for dead reckoning in the absence of salient landmarks, scientists call a "sun compass." In short, to get from a given location back to the hive, bees allocate familiar places with a *direction* and a *distance* home, the direction being relative to the sun. Distance, of course, they measure in time, and the same goes for direction, because while bees do not have rulers, they are installed with clocks.[13] The sky is always turning, and the same circadian clock by which they measure a distance flown they use to adjust the remembered vector in compensation for the sun's displacement. Because the sun is south at noon, because between south and north is east, and because bees are not afraid of a little astronomy, bees can always find their way right back home.

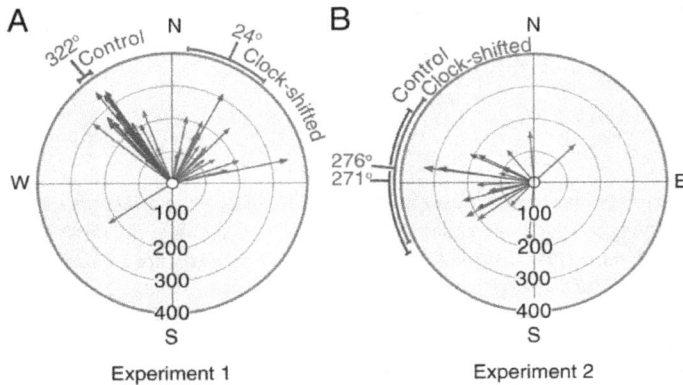

Experiment 1   Experiment 2

Figure 2: Initial vector flight components of captured and released bees from James F. Cheeseman et al., "Way-Finding in Displaced Clock-Shifted Bees Proves Bees Use a Cognitive Map," *Proceedings of the National Academy of Sciences* 111, no. 24 (2014): 8949–54 (p. 8951, Figure 3). Clock-shift = 6 hours, clock-shifted bees in red and control bees in blue. (*A*) Experiment 1: bees released in an open field; clock-shifted mean vector angle 24°, (95% CI 7°, 41°); control mean vector angle 322°, (95% CI 319°, 325°). (*B*) Experiment 2: bees released next to a familiar hedge; clock-shifted mean angle 276°, (95% CI 244°, 308°); control mean vector angle 271°, (95% CI 240°, 301°). Scale in meters.

They can, that is, unless you anaesthetize them for several hours so as to disable those clocks while the heavens go on turning. Then, as studies like Cheeseman et al. show, funny things begin to happen: they wake up, and they fly in the wrong direction, roughly as many degrees in error as the amount of time they

---

13 K. Tomioka and A. Matsumoto, "A Comparative View of Insect Circadian Clock Systems," *Cellular and Molecular Life Sciences* 67, no. 9 (2010): 1397–1406.

were unconscious (Figure 2). Space is time when space is turning, and "Chinese thought" is hardly unique for recognizing this as the foundation of our cosmos and the key to finding our way therein.

This is all no doubt somewhat mysterious to someone who's never studied these sorts of things, but it is nowhere near as mysterious as the idea that Chinese astronomy could somehow function independently of space. Saying this, as we were taught, is the equivalent of saying that this people could only (or, indeed, *could*) build one-dimensional clocks – an unmoving needle without a face. This might make for an excellent riddle or meditational aide, like the sound of one hand clapping, but bees know better, and so too should we. There is a reason behind this riddle, of course, but it is not one that has anything to do with physics or entomology.

Li: not your grandfather's calendar

The study of these things, which I just described, was called *li* 曆, and it was called that starting from at least the second century BCE.[14] It was called that when Buddhists brought *jyotiṣa* into the mix, the Nestorians *isṭrunumiia*, the Muslims *ilm al-nujuum*, and the Catholics, finally, *astronomia*. Each time, some Chinese expert took a look at this foreign thing and said, "I know that: that is *li*."[15] We have been less kind: *li* is the one among these that does not go back to the Greeks, and in as much as Greekness was a necessary condition for "science," "theory," "proof," and "abstraction" in nineteenth-century Europe, it was there decided

---

14 For a more nuanced explanation of the meaning of *li* 曆 than that offered here, see Jean-Claude Martzloff, *Le calendrier chinois: structure et calculs, 104 av. JC–1644* (Paris: Champion, 2009), esp. 367–72; Nathan Sivin, "Mathematical Astronomy and the Chinese Calendar," in *Calendars and Years II: Astronomy and Time in the Ancient and Medieval World*, ed. John M. Steele (Oxford: Oxbow Books, 2011), 39–51; Christopher Cullen, *The Foundations of Celestial Reckoning: Three Ancient Chinese Astronomical Systems* (New York: Routledge, 2017), esp. 7–25; Daniel P. Morgan, *Astral Sciences in Early Imperial China: Observation, Sagehood and the Individual* (Cambridge: Cambridge UP, 2017), chap. 1.
15 For recent studies on these various transmissions, see Bill Mak, "The Transmission of Buddhist Astral Science from India to East Asia: The Central Asian Connection," *Historia Scientiarum* 24, no. 2 (2015): 59–75; "Astral Science of the East Syriac Christians in China during the Late First Millennium AD," *Mediterranean Archaeology and Archaeometry* 16, no. 4 (2016): 87–92; Dror Weil, "Islamicated China: China's Participation in the Islamicate Book Culture during the Seventeenth and Eighteenth Centuries," *Intellectual History of the Islamicate World* 4, no. 1–2 (2016): 36–60; Catherine Jami, *The Emperor's New Mathematics: Western Learning and Imperial Authority during the Kangxi Reign (1662–1722)* (Oxford: Oxford UP, 2012). I thank Y. Isahaya for helping me sort out some of these actors' categories.

that *li* is nothing other (i.e. more) than the "practical," "concrete" art of "calendar-making."[16] This was decided, ironically, on a continent where the transmission of Arabic-language astronomy had, some centuries earlier, undermined and marginalized the indigenous tradition of computus on the self-same charge.[17] Regardless, this value judgement and the momentum of convention is the only reason we learn that *li* is "calendars" and that it is independent of space.

Li, however, are *not* calendars – not in any normal sense of the word – and anyone who doubts this is free to read one or to look for a single quote in early Chinese history to the effect of "Lunch tomorrow? Let me check my *li*."[18] *That thing* – the table of dates, and months, with holidays and the sort – *that thing* is called many things, and none of them is *li*: it is called *ri* 日 ("day/s"), *zhiri* 質日 ("duty day/s"?), and, yes, even *liri* 曆日 ("*li* day/s"; see Figure 3), but a *liri* is no more a *li* than a *matong* 馬桶 is a *ma* 馬.[19] To a Jean-Baptiste Biot (1774–1862), of course, a *matong* is precisely where *li* belongs:

---

16 Similar charges have been brought against the Mesopotamians, from which the Greeks learned much of their astronomy. For a critique of the discourse *Occident: theoretical: science:: Orient: practical: non-science* in this context, see Francesca Rochberg, *The Heavenly Writing: Divination, Horoscopy, and Astronomy in Mesopotamian Culture* (Cambridge: Cambridge UP, 2004), esp. 14–43.
17 See Charles Homer Haskins, *Studies in the History of Mediaeval Science* (Cambridge, MA: Harvard UP, 1924), chap. 5. I thank Philipp Nothaft for directing me to relevant sources on this topic (personal communication, March 6, 2017).
18 If you are curious to learn from first-hand experience about the nature of primary sources that self-identify as *li*, I suggest starting with the expertly annotated translations of the *Santong li* 三統曆 (*c*.5 CE), *Sifen li* 四分曆 (85 CE) and *Qianxiang li* 乾象曆 (*c*.206 CE) in Cullen, *Foundations of Celestial Reckoning* or that of the *Shoushi li* 授時曆 (1280 CE) in Nathan Sivin, *Granting the Seasons: The Chinese Astronomical Reform of 1280, with a Study of Its Many Dimensions and a Translation of Its Records* (New York: Springer, 2009).
19 On "calendars" in the sense of "a table showing the division of a given year into its months and days . . . " (*Oxford English Dictionary*), see Yoshimura Masayuki 吉村昌之, "Shutsudo kandoku shiryō ni mirareru rekihu no shūsei" 出土簡牘資料にみれる曆譜の集成, in *Henkyō shutsudo mokkan no kenkyū* 邊疆出土木簡の研究, ed. Tomiya Itaru 冨谷至 (Kyōto: Hōyū shoten, 2003), 459–516; Morgan, *Astral Sciences*, chap. 3. For a detailed look at how one produces a *liri* from a *li*, see Martzloff, *Le calendrier chinois*. Between the revision and the page setting of this chapter, the first bamboo manuscript unambiguously bearing the title *Li* 曆 was discovered in Hujia caochang 胡家草場 Tomb 12 (163 BCE). Distinct from the chronicles (titled *Suiji* 歲紀) and the daily calendar (titled *Rizhi* 日至) with which it was found, the manuscript *Li* comprises a table of lunations calculated a hundred years into the future. See Li Zhifang 李志芳 and Jiang Lujing 蔣魯敬, "Hubei jingzhou shi Hujia caochang Xihan mu M12 chutu jiandu gaishu" 湖北荊州市胡家草場西漢墓M12出土簡牘概述, *Kaogu* 考古 2020.2: 21–33; Hsu Ming-Chang 許名瑲, "Hujia caochang Han jian lijian tianxiang guankui" 胡家草場漢簡曆簡天象管窺, *Jianbo wang* 簡帛網, February 19, 2020, http://www.bsm.org.cn/show_article.php?id=3513.

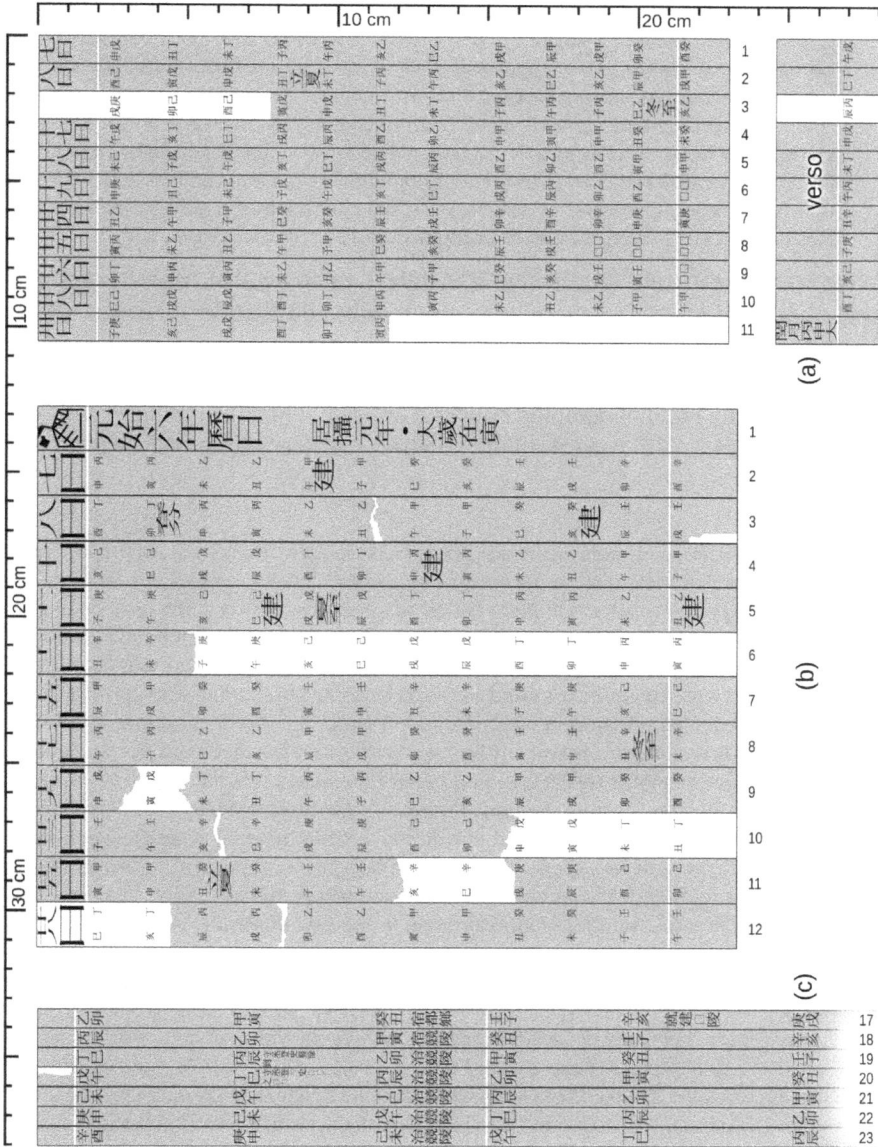

Figure 3: Wood bookmat *liri* 曆日-style day calendars. Right (a): Dunhuang 敦煌 T6b Shenjue year 3 (59 BCE) *liri*. Center (b): Jinguan 金關 T23 "Yuanshi liu nian liri" 元始六年曆日 (5 CE). Left (c): slips from the Zhoujiatai 周家臺 M30 Shihuang year 34 (213 BCE) *zhiri* 質日 for comparison. Note that the two *liri* are incomplete.

On s'est plu souvent à remarquer que les Chinois, dans leurs idées, dans leurs usages, leurs préjugés même, offrent un singulier et perpétuel contraste avec les peuples européens [. . .] Leur astronomie ne fait pas exception à cette règle. Elle n'a jamais constitué, chez eux, une **science spéculative**, apanage spécial d'un petit nombre d'esprits. Dans tous les siècles, elle a été une œuvre de gouvernement. Son principal office consiste à préparer chaque année, plusieurs mois à l'avance, le calendrier impérial. [. . .] Elle est chargée, en outre, de l'avertir personnellement des phénomènes extraordinaires qui arrivent dans le ciel, pour en tirer les présages, favorables ou défavorables, qui concernent son gouvernement. Aussi, mus par ces deux intérêts **purement pratiques**, a-t-on vu, de tout temps . . . [20]

What is at stake in translating *li* any differently is admitting that "Chinese thought" was capable of *science* or *spéculation* on its own, and that, in 1862, was a little much for "Western thought" to handle.[21] *All of this*, however, is a problem of observer's categories, and observer's categories are beside the point.

Li, befitting the bibliographic classification that it heads in the *Han shu* 漢書 "Yiwen zhi" 藝文志, is comprised of "numbers and procedures" (*shushu* 數術).[22]

---

20 *Etudes sur l'astronomie indienne et sur l'astronomie chinoise* (Paris: M. Lévy frères, 1862), 268; emphasis added. Note that, in the opening pages of his "Précis de l'histoire de l'astronomie chinoise," the only source that Biot cites as concerns this history is the *Rites of Zhou* as translated by his late son eleven years earlier. Coincidentally, his description of Chinese astronomy as constituting a "singulier et perpétuel contraste" to Europe, "dans tous les siècles," "de tout temps," etc., comes nearly word for word from the "Grand annaliste (*Ta-ssé*)" 大史 and "Officier chargé de préserver et d'éclaircir (*pao-tchang-chi*)" 保章氏 headings in Édouard Biot, *Le Tcheou-li, ou Rites des Tcheou, traduit pour la première fois du chinois par feu Édouard Biot*, ed. Jean-Baptiste Biot, 3 vols. (Paris: Imprimerie Nationale, 1851), vol. 2, 104–5, 113–14.

21 Note that the formula *Europe: astronomy: theoretical:: China: calendars: practical* is a historical construct introduced and popularized only in the last two hundred years. In *Observations mathématiques, astronomiques, geographiques, chronologiques et physiques* . . ., 3 vols. (Paris: Chez Rollin libraire, 1729–1732), for example, Jesuit astronomer Antoine Gaubil (1689–1759) instinctively translates the word *li* as *l'Aftronomie* or, in the case of specific procedure texts like the *Kaihuang li* 開皇曆 of 584 CE, *une Aftronomie*.

22 On the six-part bibliographic category "Shushu" 數術 and its historical evolution, see Marc Kalinowski, "Introduction générale," in *Divination et société dans la Chine médiévale: étude des manuscrits de Dunhuang de la Bibliothèque nationale de France et de la British Library*, ed. *idem* (Paris: Bibliothèque nationale de France, 2003), 7–33 (11–17). This actor's category has been appropriated by post-1980s scholars of excavated divinatory literature so as to place the study of subaltern, "superstitious" sources under the aegis of a sort of alternative history of science that at once lays claim to and excludes *li* and *suan* 算 mathematics. Whatever its peculiar relationship with math, this field does tend to recognize the "numbers and procedures" of *li* and *suan* as being the origin/inspiration of those *shushu* that deal neither with numbers or calculation; see Li Ling 李零, *Jianbo gushu yu xueshu yuanliu* 簡帛古書與學術源流, revised edn. (Beijing: Sanlian shudian, 2008), 403–4; Chao Fulin 晁福林, "Cong 'shushu' dao 'xueshu': shanggu jingshen wenming yanjin de yige xiansuo" 從「數術」到「學術」：上古精神文明演進的一個線索, *Gudai wenming* 古代文明 4, no. 4 (2010): 40–49 (p. 44).

A *li*, like the Han *Sifen li* 四分曆 (85 CE), more specifically, is a chain of numbers, tables and algorithms; it reads fortuitously like computer code,[23] and *translating it into computer code* is, fortuitously, one of the best ways to learn it.[24] This no doubt sounds very abstruse, so allow me to show you what this looks like.

The *Sifen li*, authored by *li* workers (*zhili* 治曆) Bian Xin 編訢 and Li Fan 李梵 and preserved in *Hou Han shu* 後漢書, *zhi* 3, opens with the following numbers (for the moment, don't worry yourself with "why?", just pretend you're watching a command-line process run):

當漢高皇帝受命四十有五歲[. . .]冬十有一月甲子夜半朔旦冬至, 日月閏積之數皆自此始[. . .]
In the forty-fifth year after Han Emperor Gao[zu] 高祖 (r. 206–196 BCE) received the mandate [. . .], in winter, month XI, day *jiazi*$_{aα}$ 甲子, at midnight, [at the coincidence of] new moon and winter solstice (00:00, December 25, 162 BCE) – all the numbers (*shu*) of solar and lunar intercalation and accumulation start from this point. . . .

又上兩元, 而月食五星之元, 並發端焉。[. . .]
Two origins (2 × 4,560 years) further up (00:00, December 25, 9282 BCE), and that is the origin for lunar eclipses and the five stars (planets), which all start from this point. [. . .]

元法 Origin divisor 4,560
紀法 Era divisor 1,520
紀月 Era months 18,800
蔀法 Obscuration divisor 76
蔀月 Obscuration months 940
章法 Rule divisor 19
章月 Rule months 235
周天 Circuits of heaven 1,461
日法 Day divisor 4
蔀日 Obscuration days 27,759
. . .
日餘 Day remainder 168
中法 Medial [*qi*] divisor 32
大周 Big circuits 343,335
. . .[25]

---

23 On thinking about the algorithms comprising *suan* procedure texts through the lens of computer language, see Karine Chemla, "Should They Read FORTRAN as If It Were English?," *Bulletin of Chinese Studies* 1, no. 2 (1987): 301–16.
24 Christopher Cullen, "Translating Ancient Chinese Astronomical Systems with EXCEL: How Not to Stew the Strawberries?," *Journal for the History of Astronomy* 36, no. 3 (2005): 336–8.
25 *Hou Han shu* (Zhonghua shuju edn., 1962; hereafter HHS), *zhi* 3, 3057–60. Note that here and what follows are my own translations and explanations, but that for more serious purposes one is advised to refer to those in Cullen, *Foundations of Celestial Reckoning*, chap. 3, whose numbering I have adopted.

The only datum the user need enter for things to begin is "the [number of years from] high origin to the year sought," which, for 2021, would be 2021 – –9,281 = 11,302 years.[26] Let's plug this into procedure 2:

Enter years from high origin: **11,302.**

推入蔀術曰:

[2.] Procedure for calculating [the sexagenary year number of] the obscuration entered:

以元法除去上元,

Eliminate (divide) the origin divisor (4,560) from the distance from (i.e., years passed since) high origin.[27]

$$11,302 \div 4,560 \rightarrow 2; \textbf{ rem. 2,182}$$

其餘以紀法除之, 所得數, 從天紀, 筭外則所入紀也。

With the remainder, eliminate (divide) it by the era divisor (1,520), and the number obtained, counting exclusively from "heaven origin," [leads you to] the era entered.[28]

$$2,182 \div 1,520 \rightarrow 1; \text{ rem. 662,}$$
i.e., filled 1 era, 662 years into era no. 2:
[1] heaven, **[2] earth,** [3] man.

不滿紀法者, 入紀年數也。

Any [remainder] that does not fill an era divisor (1,520) is the number of years entered into the [current] era.

Retrieve: **662 years** into the earth era.

以蔀法除之, 所得數, 從甲子蔀起, 筭外, 所入【蔀】歲名命之, [. . .]

Eliminate (divide) this by the obscuration divisor (76), and by the number obtained, counting exclusively from the obscuration $jiazi_{aa}$, name off the [the obscuration heads to find] the year name [of the obscuration] entered. [. . .][29]

---

26 There is no 0 BCE/CE, so for the sake of calculation 9282 BCE is –9281.

27 In the *Sifen li*, a **yuan** 元 is the coincidence of: (a) new moon, month XI, (b) winter solstice, (c) midnight, (d) day $jiazi_{aa}$, and (e) year $gengchen_{ge}$, where 1 "origin" = 4,560 years = 56,400 months = 1,665,540 days.

28 In the *Sifen li*, a **ji** 紀 is the coincidence of: (a) new moon, month XI, (b) winter solstice, (c) midnight, (d) day $jiazi_{aa}$, ~~and (e) year $gengchen_{ge}$~~, where 1 "era" = 1,520 years = 18,800 months = 555,180 days. Each "era," the sexagenary year of this coincidence shifts forward twenty places, from "the era of heaven," starting year $gengchen_{ge}$ 庚辰, to "the era of earth," starting year $gengzi_{ga}$ 庚子, to "the era of man," starting year $gengshen_{gi}$ 庚申, and back to the "era of heaven." Cullen, *Foundations of Celestial Reckoning*, 162–3, provides a look-up table omitted here.

29 In the *Sifen li*, a **bu** 蔀 is the coincidence of: (a) new moon, month XI, (b) winter solstice, (c) midnight, ~~(d) day $jiazi_{aa}$, and (e) year $gengchen_{ge}$~~, where 1 "obscuration" = 76 years = 940 months = 27,759 days. Each "obscuration," the sexagenary date of this coincidence shifts forward thirty-nine places from $jiazi_{aa}$. Ibid. provides a look-up table omitted here.

662 years ÷ 76 → 8; rem. 54,
i.e., filled 8 obs., 54 years into obs. 9:
[1] *jiazi*$_{aα}$, [2] *guimao*$_{jδ}$, . . . → [9] ***bingzi***$_{cα}$.

We now know that the last "obscuration head" (*bushou* 蔀首), 54 years prior, started with a coincidence of new moon, month XI and winter solstice at midnight, day *bingzi*$_{cα}$ 丙子 (January 7, 1968).[30] Now, to procedures 5 and 6 for 2021:[31]

推天正術:
[5.] Procedure for calculating astronomical month I:

置入蔀年減一,
Set out the years entered into the [current] obscuration and diminish (subtract) by 1.[32]

Retrieve: **54 years** into obs. no. 9, *bingzi*$_{cα}$,
54 − 1 → **53 ac. years**.

以章月乘之, 滿章法得一, 名為積月, 不滿為閏餘,
Mount (multiply) this by the rule months (235), and get 1 [for each time it] fills the rule divisor (19) – this is called the "months accumulated [into current obscuration]," and that which does not fill [the divisor] is the "intercalary remainder." [. . .][33]

53 ac. years × 235/19 → **655 ac. months**; rem. 10.

推天正朔日,
[6. Procedure for] calculating new moon day, astronomical month I:

置入蔀積月,
Set out the [integer number of] months accumulated since entry into [the current] obscuration.

---

30 Note that the true winter solstice fell on December 22, 1967, and the true new moon on December 2, 1967. The discrepancy in the *Sifen li*'s predictions here and in the following pages is due in part to a switch to the Gregorian calendar in my calculations past 1582 and, more importantly, to accumulated errors to be expected when using the *Sifen li* centuries beyond its intended lifespan. In 85 CE, the best of *li* were not expected to function beyond 300 years; see Morgan, *Astral Sciences*, 179–88.

31 Procedure 3 has to do with eclipses and can be skipped for our purposes here.

32 "Astronomical month I" = civil month XI = the month containing winter solstice, so for 2021 we need to count from the winter solstice of the year prior, 2020, thus the need to subtract 1.

33 In the *Sifen li*, a *zhang* 章 is the coincidence of: (a) new moon, month XI, (b) winter solstice, (c) midnight, (d) day *jiazi*$_{aα}$, and (e) year *gengchen*$_{ge}$, where 1 "rule" = 19 years = 235 months = 6,939¾ days. Each "rule," the hour of this coincidence shifts forward ¾ day. To convert from years to months, one multiplies by 235/19 (i.e. $12\frac{7}{19}$ months/year).

Retrieve: **655 ac. months**; rem. 10.

以蔀日乘之，滿蔀月得一，名為積日，不滿為小餘，

Mount (multiply) this by the obscuration days (27,759), and get 1 [for each time it] fills the obscuration months (940) – this is called the "days accumulated [into current obscuration]," and that which does not fill [the divisor] makes the "little remainder."[34]

655 ac. months × 27,759/940 → **19,342 ac. days**; rem. 665.

積日以六十除去之，其餘為大餘。以所入蔀名命之，筭盡之外，則前年天正十一月朔日也。[. . .]

With the accumulated days, remove [all] 60[s] by elimination (divide) therefrom – the remainder makes the "big remainder." [Counting down from this number], name off [the sexagenary days starting] from the name of [the sexagenary date heading] the obscuration entered, and that which lies after the counting rods are exhausted (i.e., counting exclusively) is the new moon day of astronomical month I – [civil] month XI – of the previous year. [. . .][35]

19,342 ac. days ÷ 60 → 322; **rem. 22**,
i.e., 22 days past sex. date at obs. head.

Retrieve sex. date at obs. head: ***bingzi*$_{c\alpha}$**.

Name off 22 sex. days from *bingzi*$_{c\alpha}$, exclusively:
[0] *bingzi*$_{c\alpha}$, [1] *dingchou*$_{d\beta}$, . . . → **[22]** *wuxu*$_{e\lambda}$.

For 2021, new moon, month XI, thus falls (665/940 day past midnight) on day *wuxu*$_{e\lambda}$ 戊戌 (December 21, 2020).[36] On to procedure 8 to find the winter solstice:

推二十四氣術曰：

[8.] Procedure for calculating the twenty-four *qi*:

置入蔀年減一，

Set out the [number of] years entered into the [current] obscuration and diminish (subtract) by 1.[37]

Retrieve: 54 years into obs. 9,
54 – 1 → **53 ac. years**.

以日餘乘之，滿中法得一，名曰大餘，不滿為小餘。大餘滿六十除去之，其餘以蔀名命之，筭盡之外，則前年冬至之日也。[. . .]

Mount (multiply) this by the day remainder (168), and get 1 [for each time it] fills the medial divisor (32) – this is called the "big remainder," and that which does not fill [the divisor] makes the "little remainder." With the big remainder, remove [all] full 60[s] by elimination (division) therefrom, and [counting down] from the remainder, name off the names of the [sexagenary days starting from] obscuration [head], and

---

34 As 1 "obscuration" = 76 years = 940 months = 27,759 days, to convert from months to days, one multiplies by 27,759/940 (i.e. $29\frac{499}{940} \approx 29.53085$ days/month).

35 HHS, *zhi* 3, 3062.

36 Note that the nearest new moon actually fell on December 15, 2020.

37 As to why one subtracts 1, see Note 32.

that which lies after the counting rods are exhausted (i.e., counting exclusively) is the day of the winter solstice of the previous year. [. . .][38]

53 ac. years × 168/32 → **278 ac. days**, rem. 8,
278 ÷ 60 → 4; **rem. 38**.

Retrieve sex date at obs. head: ***bingzi***$_{c\alpha}$.

Name off 38 sex. days from *bingzi*$_{c\alpha}$, exclusively:
[0] *bingzi*$_{c\alpha}$, [1] *dingchou*$_{d\beta}$, . . . → **[38]** ***jiayin***$_{ay}$.

For 2021, winter solstice thus falls (8/32 day past midnight) on day *jiayin*$_{ay}$ 甲寅 (January 6, 2021), sixteen days after new moon.[39] For subsequent new moons and *qi*, the elided text of procedures 5 and 6 instructs the user to cumulatively add $29\frac{499}{940}$ and $15\frac{7}{32}$ days, respectively, up to the end of said year. And at that, we have produced the luni-solar framework of a [*li/zhi*]*ri* calendar like those in Figure 3.[40]

How did this happen? Nathan Sivin long ago invited us to think of the numbers with which we have been operating as intricately connected gears. Describing the (different) values used by the *Santong li* 三統曆 (*c*.5 CE), he tells us that . . .

> We can look at this set of constants as a complex of circles turning upon each other (Figure [4]). The Epoch Cycle [元] simply specifies what motion of the integral system is needed to return all cycles simultaneously to their original orientations. In such a system, if we know the original orientation and the number of revolutions any one circle has passed through at a given moment, we can predict the orientation of any other circle. [. . .] an astronomical system [i.e. *li*] was meant to be like the gear train of a well-functioning machine, requiring no human intervention.[41]

---

38 HHS, *zhi* 3, 3063. In the *Sifen li*, 168/32 (= $5\frac{1}{4}$) is the number of days by which one solar year (= $365\frac{1}{4}$ days) exceeds six sexagenary cycles (= 360 days). As such, multiplying this by the years accumulated, from obscuration head gives us the days in the sexagenary cycle advanced therefrom.

39 Note that the winter solstice in question actually fell on December 21, 2020.

40 In the above presentation, I have elided matters of intercalation, otherwise treated in procedure 5 ("Procedure for calculating astronomical month I") and procedure 9 ("Calculating the position of the intercalary month" 推閏月所在).

41 "Cosmos and Computation in Early Chinese Mathematical Astronomy," *T'oung Pao* 2nd ser., 55, no. 1/3 (1969): 1–73 (13, 58). Note that the gear train metaphor goes back to Joseph Needham, who describes the various cycles surrounding the civil calendar and the *Santong li* as "cogwheels" (*Science and Civilisation in China, vol.3: Mathematics and the Sciences of the Heavens and the Earth* [Cambridge: Cambridge UP, 1959], 390–408). The metaphor persists; see for example Marc Kalinowski, "Fonctionnalité calendaire dans les cosmogonies anciennes de la Chine," *Études chinoises* XXIII (2004): 169–91 (88–9); Sun Xiaochun, "Chinese Calendar and Mathematical Astronomy," in *Handbook of Archaeoastronomy and Ethnoastronomy*, ed. C.L.N. Ruggles (New York: Springer, 2015), 2059–68 (2062).

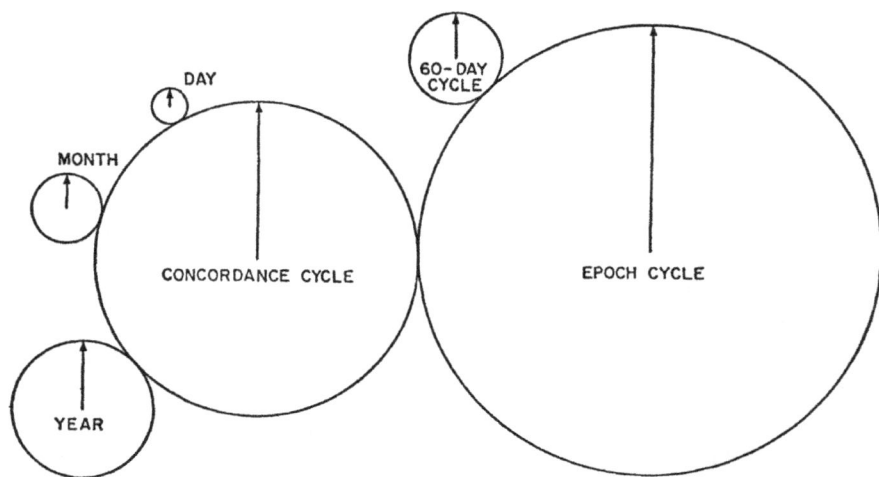

Figure 4: Sivin's gear train ("Cosmos and Computation," 13, Figure 1). Original caption: System of calendrical constants in the Triple Concordance treatise [*Santong li*]. In a scale model, circumference would be proportional to length of cycle. The rotating arrows all point upward at the same time only once every 4617 years.

It is an elegant metaphor, but it is one – contrary to Sivin's intentions – that subsequent scholars cite as evidence that "the history of astronomy in ancient China was largely a history of calendar making."[42] Think about it: what other kind of gear train could this be other than that you find in a clock? And is not a *clock*, like a "calendar," (just) for telling time?

One could bring in *astronomical clocks* like the Antikythera mechanism to buttress Sivin's metaphor, but instead I would like to propose another – that we *return*, to be more precise, to that with which contemporary actors conceived of what they were doing. Nothing is wrong with a little anachronism if it helps us grasp a difficult subject, but there are three points where the gear train metaphor falls short.

First, *li* are *not* written in computer code, nor is their operation nearly as "intervention"-less as either metaphor implies. *People* did these calculations, and they did them *by hand*. In the Eastern Han (25–220 CE) astronomical office – the Clerk's Office (*shiguan* 史官), office of the [Prefect] Grand Clerk (*taishi* [*ling*] 太史令) – this was the job of six "*li* workers" (*zhili*), like Bian Xin and Li Fan,

---

42 Sun Xiaochun, "Chinese Calendar and Mathematical Astronomy," 2059. Note that this precise equation dates back to Nakayama Shigeru: "The history of Chinese astronomy is, for the most part, the history of calendar-calculation" ("Characteristics of Chinese Calendrical Science," *Japanese Studies in the History of Science*, no. 4 [1965]: 124–31 [125]).

who were *daizhao* 待詔 "expectant appointees" specially appointed for their skills.[43] The Northern Dynasties (386–581 CE) and Sui (518–618 CE) furthermore saw the same office appoint erudites (*boshi* 博士) and students (*sheng* 生) to begin training their own talent in-house.[44] Why go to the trouble? Probably because *li*-calculation is anything but automatic. Converting between cardinal and ordinal numbers can be confusing, especially in a language that does not distinguish between them. Far more confusing, however, is a word like *chu* 除 "eliminate," which can refer to one of four mathematical operations (subtraction, division, *modulo*, or sequence subtraction). Get confused *just once* in this sort of text and the mistake propagates, leaving you a garbled mess for all your efforts.[45] Yes, *li* workers are "computers," but in an older sense of the word, and a *li* is a lot less like a machine or a computer program than it is a spell – a spell to be *performed* by a particular type of sorcerer.

Second, "origins," "eras," "obscurations," and "rules" are not just matters of *time*, like you might expect of clockwork, they are matters of *space-time*. The geartrain metaphor gets a little strained as we move, for example, to procedure 13:

推合朔所在度:
[13. Procedure for] calculating the position of syzygy in *du*:

置入蔀積月,
Set out the [integer number of] months accumulated [since] entry into the [current] obscuration.

Retrieve: **655 ac. months**; rem. 10.

---

43 On the role of the *daizhao* in the state astronomical office, see Lai Swee Fo 賴瑞和, "Tangdai de Hanlin daizhao he Sitiantai" 唐代的翰林待詔和司天臺, *Tang yanjiu* 唐研究 9 (2003): 315–42; Morgan, *Astral Sciences*, chap. 1.

44 On the Clerk's Office, see Thatcher Elliott Deane, "The Chinese Imperial Astronomical Bureau: Form and Function of the Ming Dynasty *Qintianjian* from 1365 to 1627" (Ph.D. diss., University of Washington, 1989); Chen Xiaozhong 陳曉中 and Zhang Shuli 張淑莉, *Zhongguo gudai tianwen jigou yu tianwen jiaoyu* 中國古代天文機構與天文教育 (Beijing: Zhongguo kexue jishu chubanshe, 2008).

45 This is precisely why Cullen, "Translating," proposes the use of spreadsheet software to perform these texts – they are too hard, time-consuming, and prone to cascading errors for the modern scholar to do by hand. On the problem of *chu*, see Karine Chemla, "Shedding Some Light on a Possible Origin of a Concept of Fractions in China: Division as a Link between the Newly Discovered Manuscripts and 'The Gnomon of the Zhou [Dynasty]'," *Sudhoffs Archiv* 97, no. 2 (2013): 174–98; "Observing Mathematical Practices as a Key to Mining Our Sources and Conducting Conceptual History: Division in Ancient China as a Case Study," in *Science after the Practice Turn in the Philosophy, History, and Social Studies of Science*, ed. Léna Soler et al. (New York: Routledge, 2014), 238–68; cf. Morgan, *Astral Sciences*, 127–31.

以蔀日乘之, 滿大周除去之, 其餘滿蔀月得一, 名為積度, 不盡為餘分。

Mount (multiply) this by obscuration days (27,759), remove full big circuits (343,335) by elimination (division) therefrom, and, with the remainder, get 1 [for each time it] fills the obscuration months (940) – this is called the "*du* accumulated [into current obscuration]," and that which is not exhausted makes the "remainder parts."

$$655 \text{ ac. months} \times 27{,}759 \rightarrow 18{,}182{,}145,$$
$$18{,}182{,}145 \div 343{,}335 \rightarrow 52; \text{ rem. } 328{,}725,$$
$$328{,}725 \div 940 \rightarrow \textbf{349; rem. 665.}$$

積度加斗二十一度, 加二百三十五分,

With the *du* accumulated, add Dipper$_{L08}$ 21 *du* and add 235 parts.[46]

$$349;665 + 21;235 \rightarrow \textbf{370;900,}$$
or Dipper$_{L08}$ 370 *du* and 900[/940] parts.

以宿次除之, 不滿宿, 則日月合朔所在星度也。

Sequentially eliminate (subtract) the [twenty-eight] lodges therefrom, and that which does not fill the [last] lodge is the star-*du* position of sun and moon at syzygy.[47]

$$370;900 - 8 \text{ (Ox}_{L09}) - 12 \text{ (Maid}_{L10}) \ldots - 11 \text{ (Basket}_{L07}) \rightarrow$$
$$\textbf{Ox}_{L09} \textbf{ 5 } \textit{du} \textbf{ and 665[/940] parts.}$$

What just happened? We started with a measure of *time*, we've plucked two "day" and "month" gears from the clockwork, looped them with a third, and suddenly we have *a position* in lodges and *du* (Figure 5). This isn't a calendar! This isn't how a gear train or a clock is supposed to work! And this starts, *after the calendar portion is done*, only thirteen of fifty-three procedures in!

Third, and far more importantly, none of our "*li* numbers" (*li shu* 曆數) bear measuring units.

Lü: water into wine

This last point may sound anti-climactic, but it is the most important of the three, because where similar lists of operable numbers without units are given in *suan* 算 mathematics, they are called *lü* 率, and there is a whole theoretical and philosophical apparatus surrounding them in early literature.[48] *Lü* is not a word that

---

46 In the *Sifen li*, **Dipper$_{L08}$** $21\frac{234}{940}$ *du* (= Dipper$_{L08}$ $21\frac{1}{4}$ *du*) is the right ascension – i.e. the *equatorial position* – of winter solstice, the zero-point of the solar year and celestial circuit.

47 HHS, *zhi* 3, 3063–4.

48 The treatment of *lü* in this and the following section draws extensively from Karine Chemla, "Mathematics, Nature and Cosmological Inquiry in Traditional China," in *Concepts of*

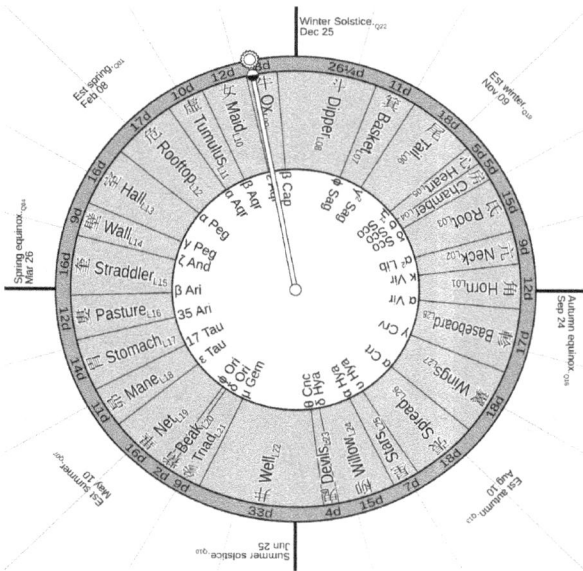

Figure 5: The twenty-eight equatorial lodges as per the *Sifen li* (85 CE). The sun and moon progress *counterclockwise* through the ring of lodges (L01–L28), and, unbeknownst to the *Sifen li*'s authors, the ring of lodges is effectively turning in the same direction vis-à-vis the twenty-four *qi* (the winter solstice$_{Q22}$, establishment of spring$_{Q01}$, spring equinox$_{Q04}$, etc.), albeit *very slowly*, in what we call the precession of the equinoxes. The letter *d* represents equatorial lodge-width, where one *du* 度 equals the displacement of the mean sun through the stars in one day, for an annual "circuit" of $365\frac{1}{4}$ *du* in $365\frac{1}{4}$ days. Due to their interrelation, *d* can be read either "*du*" or "days" and thought of in terms of time *or* space. As per our result for procedure 13, the sun and moon are represented here in conjunction – i.e. the point of "syzygy," at "new moon," where the two bodies fall on the same line in a given reference plane (here, the equator) – at "Ox$_{L09}$ 5 *du* and 665 parts," which is to say $5\frac{665}{940}$ *du* (equivalent to 5.61°, but as a measure of perimeter rather than angle) into Ox$_{L09}$ as counted from its 'guide star' (*juxing* 距星), β Capricorni. Note that the time/position of winter solstice and the other *qi* has since moved from where they are in this diagram, and that "Ox$_{L09}$ 5 *du* and 665 parts" is not a particularly accurate prediction for the right ascension of this particular syzygy (see Note 30).

Nature: A Chinese-European Cross-Cultural Perspective, ed. Günter Dux, Hans Ulrich Vogel, and Mark Elvin (Leiden: Brill, 2010), 255–84, and from discussions with her in person over the years of our work together. My principal contribution in what follows is simply the application of her insights in *suan* to *li*.

Figure 6: Visualizing *lü* 率, ancient and modern. Left: *Huilü* 匯率 "exchange rates," drawn after the real-world application *Huilü* 匯率 available on Android™ everywhere on Google Play. Right: the list of *lü* 率 under the heading "Norms for Grain Conversion" 粟米之法 at the opening of the *Jiuzhang suanshu*, chapter 2, as represented in the form the same sort smartphone app. On the left, the quantity entered is 91.150 TWD, and on the right it is 7 *dou* 8 *sheng* (= 78 *sheng*) of unhulled millet, as per the *Jiuzhang suanshu*, problem 2.16. The modern *lü* – a "rate" – comprises the juxtaposition of two quantities, the one of which is normally pegged at 1, and the other expressed as a decimal fraction (i.e. "1 USD: 30.485 TWD"). To find the equivalent of the starting value of 91.150 TWD in USD, one converts via the rule of three thus: $91.150TWD \times 1USD/30.485TWD = 2.9900USD$. The pre-modern *lü*, by contrast is a single integer value assigned to an element in a larger list (i.e. "unhulled millet *lü*: fifty" 粟率五十). To find the equivalent of the starting value of 78 *sheng* unhulled millet in fermented soy, one also converts via the rule of three – the " 'suppose you have' procedure" 今有術 – but one does so using the simpler integer values of the appropriate *lü*: $78 \times 63/50 = 98\frac{14}{50}$ *sheng* fermented soy.

translates, because it is not a mathematical construct that *exists* in other traditions, but rest assured that it is one that is nonetheless easy enough to grasp.

You know *lü*; you have seen them and you have used them in their modern form. You have seen them, namely, on reader boards and mobile applications like that in Figure 6: *huilü* 匯率 "exchange rates." You have used them in this form to go from one currency to another in your head – to calculate, as per Figure 6, that if a dollar gets you 30.48 TWD, 100 get you 304.85. Such a table is useful when changing money, but there are limits to what it can do. You can't (easily) go *backwards*, for example, or from euros to yen, but there's no one table by which you can convert *any two things* as simply as that, right? Wrong; and welcome to the world of *lü*.

Lü, in their *pre-modern form*, allowed exactly that, and to that end let us turn to the "classic" (*jing* 經) *Jiuzhang suanshu* 九章算術 (1 BCE/83 CE), which devotes one of its "nine chapters" to the topic.[49] Like the *Sifen li*, the chapter "Su mi" 粟米 (Unhulled and Hulled) begins with a table of unit-less numbers:[50]
After these numbers (*shu*) comes a procedure (*shu*):

粟率 **[Unhulled] millet *lü*** **50**
糲米 hulled grain 30
粺米 milled grain 27
鑿米 milled grain, fine 24
御米 milled grain, superior 21
小䵂 small oats 13½
大䵂 big oats 54
糲飯 hulled grain (cooked) 75
粺飯 milled grain (cooked) 54
鑿飯 milled grain, fine (cooked) 48
御飯 milled grain, superior (cooked) 42
菽荅麻麥 soy, adzuki, hemp or wheat 45
稻 Paddy rice 60
豉 **fermented soy** **63**
飧 diluted rice (cooked) 90
熟菽 soy (cooked) 130½
櫱 fermented grain 175

今有術曰: 以所有數乘所求率爲實。以所有率為法。實如法而一。

The "Suppose-you-have" procedure: Mount (multiply) the quantity of what you have by the *lü* of that which you seek to make dividend; take the *lü* of what you have as the divisor; and [divide] the dividend by the divisor.[51]

Using "Suppose-you-have" – i.e., the rule of three – with an appropriate list of *lü*, one can transform *any one thing* into *any other* in *whichever direction one desires*. Take for instance problem 2.16:

---

49 For a complete critical edition, translation, and study of the *Jiuzhang suanshu*, see Karine Chemla and Guo Shuchun, *Les neuf chapitres: le classique mathématique de la Chine ancienne et ses commentaires* (Paris: Dunod, 2004).
50 The following translation is modified from (hereafter "mod.") ibid., 222–3.
51 Tr. ibid., 222–5 (mod.).

今有粟七斗八升, 欲爲　 。問得幾何?

Suppose you have 7 *dou* 8 *sheng* (≈ 15.6 liters) of [unhulled] millet, and you desire to make it into fermented soy. How much do you get?

荅曰: 爲　 九斗八升二十五分升之七。

Answer: It makes 9 *dou* 8 *sheng* and 7/25 *sheng* (≈ 19.7 liters) of fermented soy.

術曰: 以粟求　, 六十三之, 五十而一。

The procedure: seeking fermented soy from [unhulled] millet, mount (multiply) by [the fermented soy *lü*] 63 and divide by [the millet *lü*] 50.[52]

> 7 *dou* 8 *sheng* = 78 *sheng*
> 78 *sheng* × 63 → 4914 *sheng*
> 4914 *sheng* ÷ 50 → **98 7/25 *sheng***

One can go backwards just as easily, of course, by flipping the *lü* in this ratio from 63/50 to 50/63, and either can be swapped with any other to get you something else.

This multiply–divide combo – "Suppose-you-have" – is precisely the same operation we see in *li* mathematical astronomy, and it is performed there using numbers that are identical in form, function and presentation to those in *suan*. It is probably safe to call these *lü*, particularly since that is what many of them call themselves: "circuit *lü*" 周率, "day *lü*" 日率, "coincidence *lü*" 會率, "discrepancy *lü*" 差率, "decrease–increase *lü*" 損益率, etc.[53] *Lü*, moreover, is exactly how contemporaries active in *suan* speak of these numbers in philosophizing upon the mathematics of *li* mathematical astronomy and *lü* 律 tono-metrology. Consider, for example, Li Chunfeng 李淳風 (602–70 CE). Li rose through the Tang (618–907 CE) Clerk's Office by merit of his talent in *tianwen* 天文 and *li* from an auxiliary appointment (*zhi* 直) in 627/629 CE to its directorship in 649 CE; in 656 CE, he also oversaw a project to commentate and canonize works like the *Jiuzhang suanshu* as part of the *Suanjing shishu* 算經十書 – the mathematical

---

52 Tr. ibid., 234–5 (mod.).
53 These examples are taken from the *li* translated in Cullen, *Foundations of Celestial Reckoning* (Cullen, unfortunately, translates *lü* throughout as "rate"). On *lü* in mathematical astronomy, see Morgan, *Astral Sciences*, 21–3; Daniel P. Morgan and Howard L. Goodman, "Numbers with Histories: Li Chunfeng on Harmonics and Astronomy," in *Monographs in Tang Official History: Perspectives from the Technical Treatises of the* History of Sui *(Sui Shu),* ed. Daniel P. Morgan and Damien Chaussende (Cham: Springer Nature Switzerland AG, 2019), 51–87 (76–8); Karine Chemla, "Conjunctions between the Sun and the Moon, and Pursuit Problems: Mathematical Reasoning in Chinese Writings on Astral Sciences," in *Mathematical Practices in Relation to Astral Sciences*, ed. Matthieu Husson et al. (forthcoming).

counterpart to the *Wujing zhengyi* 五經正義 of 653 CE.[54] Li knows his stuff, and this is how he presents the underpinnings of these pursuits in the *Sui shu* 隋書 "Lü-li zhi" 律曆志:

探賾索隱，鈎深致遠，莫不用焉。一、十、百、千、萬，所同由也。律、度、量、衡、歷、率，其別用也。故體有長短，檢之以度，則不失毫釐[. . .] 三光運行，紀以曆數，則不差晷刻。事物糅見，御之以率，則不乖其本。故幽隱之情，精微之變，可得而綜也。

In exploring the recondite and searching the hidden, in snaring what is deep and eliciting what is distant, [counting rods] can never be done without. Ones, tens, hundreds, thousands, and myriads derive alike from them, and pitches, lengths, capacities (≈ volumes), weights, *li* 曆, and *lü* 率 are [simply] their distinct applications. Thus it is that bodies can be long or short, but that if one examines them with a ruler, then one will not miss by [a single] hair; [. . .] that the three luminaries (i.e., the sun, moon, and planets) travel in revolutions, but that if one marks them with *li* numbers, then one will not err in gnomon and waterclock [timing]; and that matters and things can appear jumbled together, but that if one takes charge of them with *lü* 率, then one will not pervert their bases. Thus it is [– with counting rods –]that even dark and hidden natures (*qing* 情) and fine and subtle transformations (*bian* 變) can be fully grasped and synthesized.[55]

It is clear that these are the same *lü* 率 we see in *suan*, because Li Chunfeng next defines his terms via the chapters of the *Jiuzhang suanshu* in words borrowed from Liu Hui's 劉徽 263 CE commentary thereto:

夫所謂率者，有九流焉：一曰方田，以御田疇界域。二曰粟米，以御交質變易。[. . .]皆乘以散之，除以聚之，齊同以通之，今有以貫之。則算數之方，盡於斯矣。

Now, as for that which we refer to as "*lü*," there are nine [subjects] that flow from it: [chap.] 1, "Rectangular Field" 方田, for dealing with the boundaries and areas of cultivated fields; [chap.] 2, "Unhulled and Hulled" 粟米, for dealing with transformations (*bian* 變) and changes (*yi* 易) of the exchange of goods; [. . .] All of these [subjects/chapters] mount (multiply) to disaggregate them and simplify (divide) to assemble them; [they] homogenize and equalize to make them communicate and "Suppose-you-have" to link them together – and so it is that the methods of calculating numbers all come down to this (i.e., to *lü* 率).[56]>

---

54 See Howard L. Goodman, "The Life and Intellectual World of Li Chunfeng (602–670)," in *Monographs in Tang Official History*, 29–49.

55 *Sui shu* (Zhonghua shuju edn., 1973), 16.387. Note that Li Chunfeng is appropriating a parallel passage in *Han shu* 漢書 (Zhonghua shuju edn., 1962), 21a.956., and HHS, *zhi* 1, 2999, which he modifies to emphasize the centrality of *lü*.

56 *Sui shu*, 16.387, tr. Chemla, "Mathematics, Nature and Cosmological Inquiry," 278 (mod.). Li Chunfeng is citing Liu Hui's *Jiuzhang suanshu zhu* 九章算術注 as concerns the six-character chapter summaries and paraphrasing him in the conclusion: "Mount (multiply) to disaggregate them, simplify (divide) to assemble them, homogenize and equalize to make them communicate,

Going from a number of months to the position of the sun in *li*, as we did above, is a "transformation" (*bian*) that Li Chunfeng, for one, likens to that between millet and fermented soy in *suan* – a transformation mediated by *lü* and performed by "Suppose-you-have."[57] Yes, the mechanical metaphor is helpful for thinking about how "*li* numbers" (*li shu* 曆數) are *structured*, but a gear train can no better explain the procedures (*shu* 術) – the numbers' *use* – than it can the transformation of millet into soy, adzuki beans, or wheat. Luckily, we need not go searching for a better metaphor, because that with which our historical subjects have left us is rather fitting.

Of milfoil, counting rods, and transformation

When actors philosophize about such "transformations" in mathematics, as Karine Chemla has written about at length, they tend to turn to the *Book of Changes*.[58] This makes sense, and it makes sense on several levels.

Mythologically, both *li* and *suan* go back to the demiurge Fuxi's 伏羲 awakening to the incipient, civilizing order in heaven, earth, and the "myriad creatures" in between. The version of the story that *you* know, from the "Xici zhuan" 系辭傳, may end with the trigrams, but the version that mathematicians told went a little different. Here, for example, is Liu Hui on the origins of math:

> 昔在庖犧氏始畫八卦, 以通神明之德, 以類萬物之情, 作九九之術, 以合六爻之變。暨于黃帝神而化之, 引而伸之, 於是建曆紀, 協律呂, 用稽道原。

In the past, [Fu]xi first drew the eight trigrams to enter into communication (*tong* 通) with the virtue of the spirits-illuminant and to classify (*lei* 類) the inner tendencies of the

---

how could those not be the key-points of *suan* (computations/mathematics)?" 乘以散之, 約以聚之, 齊同以通之, 此其筭之綱紀乎 (tr. Chemla and Guo, *Les neuf chapitres*, 158–9 [mod.]).

57 On Li Chunfeng's treatment of *lü* 率 in the *Sui shu* "Lü-li zhi," see Chemla, "Mathematics, Nature and Cosmological Inquiry," 278–9; Morgan and Goodman, "Numbers with Histories," 76–8; Zhu Yiwen 朱一文, "Politics and Scholarship in Early-Tang China: Dynastic Legitimacy and Li Chunfeng's Technical Treatises on Harmonics and Calendrics," in *Monographs in Tang Official History*, 89–116.

58 Chemla, "What Is at Stake in Mathematical Proofs from Third Century China?," *Science in Context* 10, no. 2 (1997): 227–51; Chemla, "Philosophical Reflections in Chinese Ancient Mathematical Texts: Liu Hui's Reference to the *Yijing*," in *Current Perspectives in the History of Science in East Asia*, ed. Kim Yung Sik and Francesca Bray (Seoul: Seoul National UP, 1999), 89–100; Chemla, "Mathematics, Nature and Cosmological Inquiry."

myriad creatures; he [also] created the "nine-nine" procedure (i.e., the multiplication table) to accord with the transformations (*bian* 變) of the six lines (of the hexagrams). The Yellow Thearch, in his time, transformed (*hua* 化) them through spiritualization and expanded them through extension, thereupon establishing the rules of *li* and harmonizing the pitch-pipes (*lülü* 律呂), which [he] used to investigate the source of the *dao*.[59]

Going even further back, the *Zhoubi suanjing* 周髀算經 (1 BCE/178 CE) has the Duke of Zhou 周公 (r. 1042–1036 BCE) ask the following of Shang Gao 商高:

竊聞乎大夫善數也，請問古者包犧立周天曆度: 夫天不可階而升，地不可將尺寸而度，請問數從安出?

I have heard, sir, that you excel in numbers. May I ask how [Fu]xi laid out the *li du* of the circumference of heaven in ancient times? Heaven cannot be scaled like a staircase, and earth cannot be measured out with a footrule, [so I] would like to know where is it that these numbers come from.[60]

The answer, the Duke of Zhou learns, is that Fuxi derived them from the *lü* of "the circle and the square" 圓方, pertaining, respectively, to heaven and earth, and that "it was thus that Yu [the Great] was able to bring order to the subcelestial realm – this [triumph] was brought about by numbers" 故禹之所以治天下者，此數之所生也.[61]

Operationally, such *shushu* "numbers and procedures" literature does not speak of "calculating the corresponding number of" so much as *"making"* 為 *a* into *b*, the algorithm-based approach typical of *li* and *suan* being more a process of "transformation" ($\rightarrow$) than of equation (=).[62] With the *Sifen li*, we began with a single datum – a year, 2021 – which was transformed before our eyes into the date of the solstice (*jiayin*$_{ay}$), that of the new moon (*wuxu*$_{e\lambda}$), and the position of

---

59 Tr. Chemla and Guo, *Les neuf chapitres*, 127 (mod.). Note that, more typically, "it is said that Lishou 隸首 invented numbers" 云隸首作數 in conjunction with/service of the Yellow Emperor (*Sui shu*, 16.395).

60 *Zhoubi suanjing* (Sibu congkan 四部叢刊 edn.; rpt. Shangwu yinshuguan, 1919–36), 1. 1a–2a; tr. Christopher Cullen, *Astronomy and Mathematics in Ancient China: The Zhou Bi Suan Jing* (Cambridge: Cambridge UP, 1996), 174 (mod.).

61 *Zhoubi suanjing*, 1.4a; tr. Cullen, *Astronomy and Mathematics*, 174 (mod.). On the date and authenticity of the *Zhoubi*, see ibid., 138–56, and note that I have been able to narrow the respective dates of closure of the *Zhoubi* and *Jiuzhang suanshu* (above) via linguistic traits in Daniel P. Morgan "A Radical Proposition on the Origins of the Received Mathematical Classic the *Gnomon of Zhou (Zhoubi* 周髀)," in *Proceedings of the Second International Conference on the History of Mathematics and Astronomy, Northwest University, Xi'an, 2–8 December 2018*, ed. *idem* and Tang Quan 唐泉 (forthcoming). Elsewhere, the credit for *zuo* 作 "inventing" *li* often goes to a variety of figures surrounding the Five Thearchs, particularly Zhuanxu 顓頊.

62 Chemla, "Philosophical Reflections," 90.

the sun and moon at syzygy (Ox_{L09} 5 du and 665/940 *du*). More to the point, people of this time did not calculate as we do, let alone in the faux computer code offered above; they did so with counting rods (*suan* 筭), on a physical surface, using their own set of conventions. Within those conventions, the multiplication and division of the "Suppose-you-have" procedure present, in Chemla's words, "opposed but complementary operations" whose interplay vis-à-vis the object of change – the operand – is suggestive of the transformations of Yin and Yang.[63] Namely, on the calculating surface, "the digits of the number by which one multiplies all vanish" as they are carried into the product that they "mount" (*cheng* 乘); and so too is the product physically "eliminated" (*chu*) from the counting surface, step by step, in building the quotient (Figure 7).[64] In this sense, achilleomancy is not the only stick-based magic act in town.[65]

Terminologically, algorithms present a meditation upon "the capacity of realities to be transformed without being destroyed in the process,"[66] and philosophical commentators, like Liu Hui and Li Chunfeng, bring a similar vocabulary to bear upon the subject. Whether it be milfoil or counting rods, one speaks equally of "transformation" (*bian / hua*), "[ex]change" (*yi* 易), and "placing in communication" (*tong* 通). When speaking of mathematics, moreover, commentators tend to frame these transformations in parallel prose around Yin–Yang operational pairs: "homogenize" (*qi* 齊) and "equalize" (*tong* 同), "disaggregate" (*san* 散) and "assemble" (*ju* 聚), "gain" (*de* 得) and "loss" (*shi* 失), "advance" (*jin* 進) and "retreat" (*tui* 退).[67] We are, of course, talking about "advancing" place values,

---

63 "Mathematics, Nature and Cosmological Inquiry," 257.

64 Ibid., 261.

65 The ritual/symbolic parallel in physical support was not lost on contemporary actors. On *Changes* symbolism in philosophical treatments of counting rods, see Li Yan 李儼, "Suanchou zhidu kao" 算籌制度考, in *idem, Zhongsuan shi luncong* 中算史論叢 (Beijing: Kexue chubanshe, 1955), vol. 4, 1–8; Zhu Yiwen 朱一文, "Shu: suan yu shu – yi jiu shu zhi fangcheng weili" 數: 筭與術 – – 以九數之方程為例, *Hanxue yanjiu* 漢學研究 28, no. 4 (2010): 73–105. In this vein, it may prove interesting to compare the relevant liturgy for milfoil counting in, say, Zhu Xi's 朱熹 (1130–1200) *Zhouyi benyi* 周易本義, *j.* 14, with that for counting rods in mathematics (e.g. Karine Chemla, "Positions et changements en mathématiques à partir de textes chinois des dynasties Han à Song-Yuan. Quelques remarques," *Extrême-Orient, Extrême-Occident* 18, no. 18 [1996]: 115–47; "Mathematics, Nature and Cosmological Inquiry") and athletic score-keeping (e.g. Morgan, *Astral Sciences*, 163–74).

66 Chemla, "What Is at Stake," 243.

67 Ibid., 240–1; Chemla, "Mathematics, Nature and Cosmological Inquiry," 276–8. Compare these terms as they appear in the glossaries of Chemla and Guo, *Les neuf chapitres*, 897–1035, and Bent Nielsen, *A Companion to Yi Jing Numerology and Cosmology: Chinese Studies of Images and Numbers from Han (202 BCE–220 CE) to Song (960–1279 CE)* (London: RoutledgeCurzon, 2003).

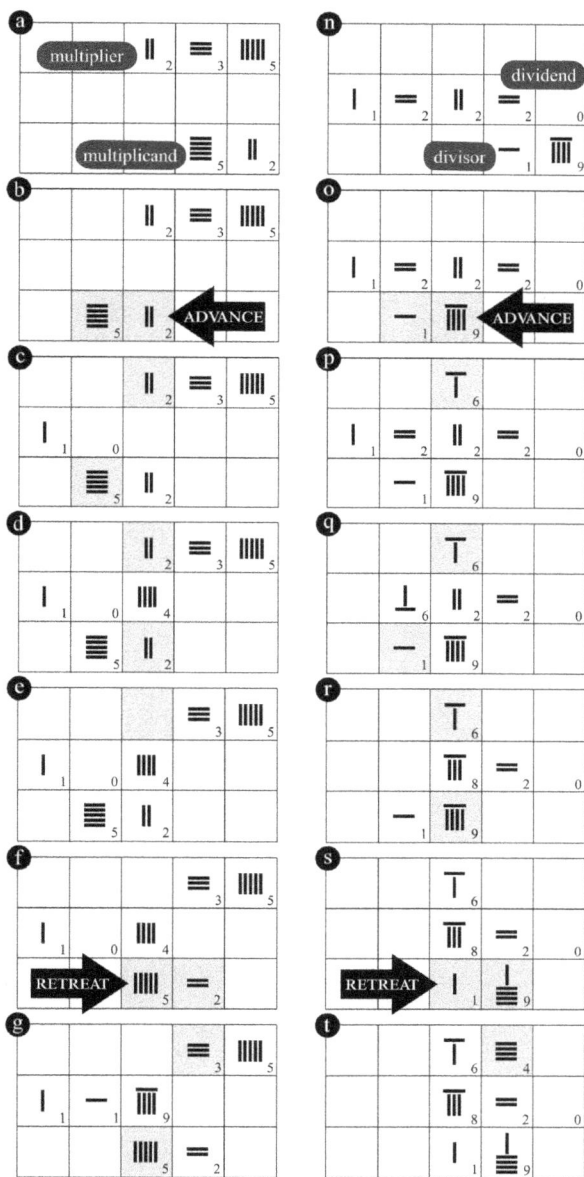

Figure 7: The "Suppose-you-have" procedure behind the *Sifen li*'s "[5.] Procedure for calculating astronomical month *l*" as performed with counting rods on a physical calculating surface for the year 2020, i.e. 52 × 235/19 (reconstruction after Chemla, "Mathematics, Nature and Cosmological Inquiry"). Note, on the left, how the multiplier in step *a* gradually disappears in "making" 為 the product in step *m*, on the right, how the dividend in step *n* likewise disappears but for the "little remainder" in "making" the quotient in step *z*, and, lastly, how the steps of multiplication and division, left and right, mirror one another at each step.

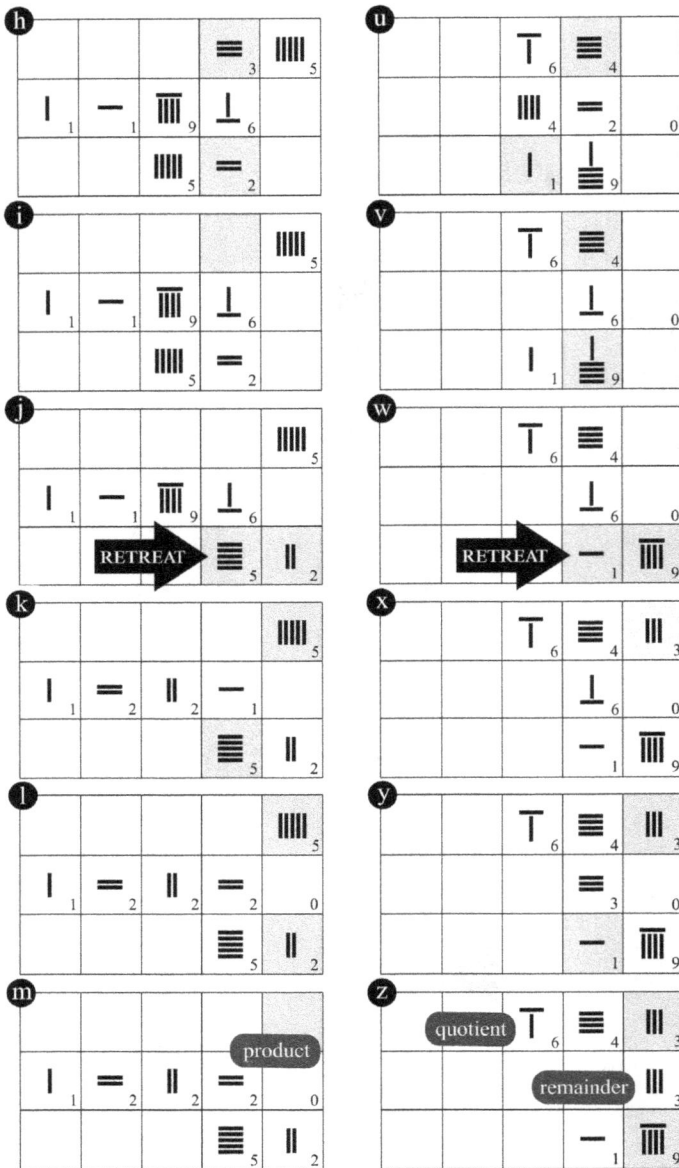

Figure 7 (continued)

"disaggregating" fractions, and "homogenizing" those with different denominators, but such is the magic that turns time to space and rice to beans.

Coming back to space, time, and their representation, therefore, we may think about *li* mathematical astronomy thus, from the perspective of the *Changes*. Time and space are the warp and woof of the self-same fabric – tug at one end, and the other comes mysteriously with.[68] This fabric is constant (*chang* 常), but only in so much as it is in constant flux – time is space when space is turning, but only *against a fixed background* and *at a constant rate*. Were you to stop that somehow, time and space would cease to be, because the two are only possible in concert, in opposition, and in flux – without the sun by day and stars by night, one couldn't tell north (zi_α) from south (wu_η), and without a fixed horizon by which to "clock" them, one couldn't tell midnight (zi_α) from noon (wu_η). Round and square, heaven and earth – space and time are *in communication* (*tong* 通), which means that you can *pass freely* (*tong* 通) from one to the other and back. You can, that is, if you know the trick, because long ago, before our day, "[Yao 堯] ordered Chong and Li to sever the *tong* of earth and heaven that there be no further descent and ascent [between]" 乃命重黎絕地天通，罔有降格.[69] By what sorcery, then, are we to tame the waters, conquer the world, achieve a destiny denied us by the gods, and move in and out of time and space?

You can do this with counting rods, and "if one takes charge of them with *lü* 率," Li Chunfeng promises, then "even dark and hidden natures and fine and subtle transformations can be fully grasped and synthesized" on the calculating surface. *Lü*, to reiterate, are unit-less integer numbers that, like time and space, Yin and Yang, bear meaning only in concert, in opposition and in flux – i.e., in proportional relationship to one another and in the act of "transformation." To insert a modern metaphor in place of another, *lü* are not so much cogs in a machine as they are a reader board of exchange rates that one (manually) consults when wanting to "change" (*yi*) a fistful of money, commodities, time, or space into something else – everything has a price, modern economics has taught us, and so too, in the ancient world, did everything have its *lü*. You cannot just "*make*" 為 water into wine, of course, but with a little imagination you might well "suppose you have," because in the sortilege on the calculating surface, at least, *the numbers* are physically transformed step by step via opposed but complementary operations until from "what you have" 所有 nothing is left but "what you seek" 所求.

---

68 In this vein, see David Pankenier, "Weaving Metaphors and Cosmo-Political Thought in Early China," *T'oung Pao* 2nd ser., 101, no. 1–3 (2015): 1–34.

69 *Shangshu zhushu* 尚書注疏 (*Chongkan Shisanjing zhushu* 重刊宋本十三經注疏 edn., 1815; rpt. Taibei: Yiwen yinshuguan, 1965), 19.297b; cf. Anne Birrell, *Chinese Mythology: An Introduction* (Baltimore: Johns Hopkins UP, 1993), 91–95.

Cosmos, empire, and colonialism

Echoing Jean-Baptiste Biot and later anthropologists of what would until the mid-twentieth century be unblushingly called "primitive" or "savage thought," Marcel Granet would argue that, as with astronomy, "Chinese thought" allowed no place for what we would call mathematics:

> L'idée de quantité ne joue autant dire aucun rôle dans les spéculations philosophiques des Chinois. Les Nombres, cependant, **intéressent passionnément** les Sages de l'ancienne Chine. Mais, – quelles qu'aient pu être les connaissances arithmétiques ou géométriques de certaines corporations (arpenteurs, charpentiers, architectes, charrons, musiciens . . .), – nul Sage n'a accepté de les utiliser, si ce n'est dans la mesure où, sans jamais contraindre à des opérations dont le résultat ne se pût commander, ce savoir facilitait des jeux numériques. [. . .] Un symbole numérique *commande* à tout un lot de réalités et d'emblèmes ; mais, à ce même mot, peuvent être attachés divers nombres, que l'on considère, *en l'espèce*, comme *équivalents*. À côté d'une valeur quantitative qui les distingue, mais **qu'on tend à négliger**, les Nombres possèdent une valeur symbolique **beaucoup plus intéressante**, car, n'offrant aucune résistance au génie opératoire, elle les laisse se prêter à une sorte d'alchimie. Les Nombres sont susceptibles de *mutations*. Ils le sont en raison de l'efficience multiple dont ils paraissent dotés et qui dérive de leur fonction principale ; ils servent et valent en tant que *Rubriques emblématiques*.[70]

---

[70] *La pensée chinoise* (Paris: La Renaissance du livre, 1934), 127–8; italics are original, bold is added to enforce the following point about the *négligance* of "uninteresting" sources. One sees an echo of Granet's interest in numbers as *emblèmes*, *symboles*, *aspects*, *ensembles*, and *groupements concrets* in E.B. Tylor's (1832–1917) "examination of the methods of numeration in use among the lower races": that, compared to "the philosopher" and "our advanced system of numeration," "the savage" counts in small numbers and concrete terms, and "the still-used Roman and Chinese numeration are indeed founded on savage picture-writing, while the abacus and the swan-pan [算盤], the one still a valuable school-instrument, and the other in full **practical use**, have their germ in the savage counting by groups of objects, as when South Sea Islanders count with coco-nut stalks, putting a little one aside every time they come to 10, [. . .] or when African negroes reckon with pebbles or nuts, and every time they come to 5 put them aside in a little heap" (*Primitive Culture: Researches into the Development of Mythology, Philosophy, Religion, Art, and Custom*, 2 vols. [London: John Murray, 1871], vol. 1, 219, 244–5). As to Granet's insistence on the exclusively "emblematic" (vs. quantitative) function of *les Nombres* as concerns time and space, one likewise hears an echo of Lévy-Bruhl (1857–1939): "These minds will not picture space as a uniform and immaterial quantum. On the contrary, to them it will appear burdened with qualities; its regions will have virtues peculiar to themselves; they will share in the mystic powers which are revealed therein. Space will not be so much imagined, as *felt*, and its various directions and positions will be qualitatively differentiated from one another. [. . .] To the primitive time is not, as it is to us, a kind of intellectualized intuition, an 'order of succession'. Still less is it a homogeneous quantity. It is felt as a quality, rather than represented" (*Primitive Mentality*, tr. Lilian A. Clare [London: George Allen & Unwin, 1923], 95, 124). On Granet's intellectual influences, see Miranda Brown, "Neither

Granet is wrong about *l'idée de quantité*, and he got there by conflating several things. He got there, first of all, by conflating what interests *les Chinois* and what interests Marcel Granet.[71] Of the eminent philosophers and classicists (*ru* 儒) of which you may have heard, here, for example, are a few from early and early imperial times that were involved in numbers in a quantitative sense: Mozi 墨子 (*c.*468–*c.*391 BCE), Sima Qian 司馬遷 (*c.*145–*c.*86 BCE), Yang Xiong 揚雄 (53 BCE–18 CE), Liu Xin 劉歆 (*c.*50 BCE–23 CE), Zheng Zhong 鄭眾 (d. 83 CE), Ban Zhao 班昭 (44/49–118/121 CE), Ma Rong 馬融 (79–166 CE), Zheng Xuan 鄭玄 (127–200 CE), Du Yu 杜預 (222–285 CE), Jia Gongyan 賈公彥 (*fl.* 637 CE), and Kong Yingda 孔穎達 (574–648 CE).[72]

He also got there by conflating imagery and substance, and in this he is not the first. Commentaries and introductions to mathematical works appeal to the *Changes* and its affiliated "cosmology/ies" as a *metaphor*, but magic numbers do indeed find their way into the *practice* of *li* mathematical astronomy. Indeed, when *li* emerges on the historical stage, it does so wrapped in the metrosophy of tono-metrics and the *Changes*. Liu Xin, whose *li* of *circa* 5 CE is the earliest to survive, cites the *Changes* throughout as the supposed origin of his *lü*,[73] and

---

'primitives' nor 'others,' but Somehow Not Quite Like 'us': The Fortunes of Psychic Unity and Essentialism in Chinese Studies," *Journal of the Economic and Social History of the Orient* 49, no. 2 (2006): 219–52.

71 I thank K. Chemla for revealing to me this pattern in Granet's writing: that his in use of the words *intérêt*, *intéressant*, and *intéresser*, Granet slips seamlessly between *nous ici* (us here) and *les chinois*, often justifying an exclusive focus on sources and themes fitting own *pensée*. For example, Granet often speaks about "the astronomer": "Concilier des classifications hétérogènes et les imbriquer – avec l'espoir que leurs chevauchements faciliteront les manipulations d'emblèmes et, par suite, la manipulation du réel, – tel est le métier, tel est l'idéal de l'astronome" (op. cit, 236). However, he cites nothing of the sort of sources featured in the present article beyond the *Tcheou pei* (*Zhoubi suanjing*), a strange, apocrypha-inspired work at the margins of *li* and *suan*. For similar criticism, see Needham, *Science and Civilisation in China*, vol. 2, p. 217.

72 On Mozi, see Graham, *Yin-Yang*, 8–11; *Later Mohist Logic, Ethics, and Science*, 2d ed. (Hong-Kong: Chinese UP, 2003). On the Han-era figures listed here, see Christopher Cullen, "People and Numbers in Early Imperial China: Locating 'mathematics' and 'mathematicians' in Chinese Space," in *Oxford Handbook of the History of Mathematics*, ed. Eleanor Robson and Jacqueline A. Stedall (Oxford: Oxford UP, 2009), 591–618. On the commentators, see Zhu Yiwen 朱一文, "Chutang de shuxue yu lixue: yi zhujia dui *Liji* 'Touhu' de zhushu wei li" 初唐的數學與禮學: 以諸家對『禮記·投壺』的注疏為例, *Zhongshan daxue xuebao (shehui kexue ban)* 中山大學學報(社會科學版) 57, no. 2 (2017): 160–68, and his earlier works cited therein.

73 On Liu Xin's historically-situated application of *Book of Changes* numerology to the synthesis of *lü* 律 tono-metrology and *li* mathematical astronomy as well as the limited historical shelf-life of said synthesis, see Morgan and Goodman, "Numbers with Histories" and the sources cited therein.

Liu Hong 劉洪 (fl. 167–206 CE), some two centuries later, would push this about as far as it could go. Here is Li Chunfeng on the latter:

> 其為之也，依易立數，遁行相號，潛處相求，名為乾象曆。又創制日行遲速，兼考月行，陰陽交錯於黃道表裏，日行黃道，於赤道宿度復有進退。方於前法，轉為精密矣。

> What [Liu Hong] did was establish numbers based on the *Changes* [such that] they called out to one another in hidden motion and sought each other out from secret parts – and [at this he] named it the *Qianxiang li* (after the hexagram Qian 乾 ䷀). Also, [he] created the solar/daily motion slow–fast while at once investigating lunar motion, [concluding that] Yin and Yang cross inside and outside the yellow road, and that the sun travels on the yellow road, experiencing advance and retreat in red-road lodge *du* – only with this was there a turn towards the fine and tight relative to prior methods.[74]

Compare this to Jia Kui's 賈逵 (30–101 CE) somewhat less enthusiastic appraisal of one Zhang Long 張隆:

> 永平中，詔書令故太史待詔張隆以四分法署弦、望、月食加時。隆言能用易九、六、七、八爻知月行多少。今案隆所署多失。臣使隆逆推前手所署，不應，或異日，不中天乃益遠，至十餘度。

> In [57/75 CE], there was an edict ordering Zhang Long, former expectant appointee to the Grand Clerk, to (predictively) note the added hour of [lunar phases] and eclipses according to the *Sifen* method. Long said that he was able to use the nine, six, seven and eight lines from the *Changes* to know the extent of lunar motion. [We] now know Long's [predictive] notes to have missed the mark in most cases. [I,] Your servant, made Long retrodict [added hours] noted by former hands, and they did not correspond, sometimes [even] falling on different days; he was even further off in failing to hit the mark in heaven, [erring a matter of] up to more than ten *du*.[75]

One of these men *no one* has heard of, the other was later enshrined at temple among those "renowned from the days of yore for calculating numbers" 自昔著名算數者, and you can probably guess which is which.[76] As it turns out, Liu Hong's numerology was only impressive in so far as it capped off "revolutionary" mathematical models for lunar anomaly (*chiji* 遲疾), latitude (*yinyang* 陰陽), eclipse "crossing" (*jiao* 交), and solar reduction to the equator (*jintui* 進退) – models thanks to which Liu Hong was winning predictive competitions against the living

---

74 *Jin shu* 晉書 (Zhonghua shuju edn., 1974), 17.498.

75 Cited in HHS, *zhi* 2, 3030. On the hexagram line numbers, see the entry "Da yan zhi shu 大衍之數" in Nielsen, *A Companion to* Yi Jing *Numerology*.

76 *Song shi* 宋史 (Zhonghua shuju edn., 1977), 105.2552. The correct answer is Liu Hong, who was posthumously promoted to Viscount of Mengyin 蒙陰子 and whose sacrificial icon was repainted according in King Wenxuan Temple 文宣王廟, Bianjing, in 1109; see Morgan, *Astral Sciences*, 177–78.

several decades after his death.[77] Liu Hong, moreover, was one of only two or three to actually bother; mostly, *li* men didn't dress up their *lü* as something else – as something, no less, that *didn't work.*[78]

Suan, for its part, is likewise devoid of similar contents: one does not perform a cubic root extraction with "fire," nor can one multiply or divide "metal," Yin, the hexagram Mingyi ䷣, or stems and branches.[79] There too, the question of "what one seeks" 所求 is not formulated in terms of the "bane" 凶 or "auspice" 吉 of human events, let alone colors or directions to "avoid" 避, but in the sort of 1–2–3 numbers of "what one has" 所有.[80] Where mathematicians *do* bring the vocabulary of the *Changes* into actual calculations, Chemla notes, it is "linked to the practice of proof in the context of exegesis, and, more precisely, to a specific function assigned to it: identifying the 'fundamental transformations' at play in all procedures."[81] It is deployed in establishing the correctness of an algorithm, in drawing parallels with others, and in unveiling the mathematical strategies, hidden operations and "reason"/"internal constitution" (*li* 理) behind the problems of the Classic. It is a heuristic framework, in other words, towards "a mathematical research on the rationality of change."[82]

And that's the thing about "numbers," and why *they* enjoyed a place among the "six arts" 六藝 of the gentleman and in the normal, imperial curriculum ever after: with numbers, "transformations" can be reliably reversed, repeated and explained, and with numbers, more importantly, there is *proof.* Proof is what a paperwork empire demands – proof of travel, proof of payment, proof of proficiency, and the list goes on – and there is a reason that that empire entrusted such things

---

77 On Liu Hong's technical innovations and posthumous victories in live-trial testing and debate, see ibid., 140–76, 199; Cullen, *Heavenly Numbers,* 325–92.

78 Martzloff, *Le calendrier chinois,* 38–44; Morgan and Goodman, "Numbers with Histories."

79 Excluding expressions like *jin* 金 "cash" and *zhi wuxing* 置五行 "set out five columns," the very words Yin–Yang, *wuxing,* "wood," "fire," etc., do not appear once in the base-text of the *Jiuzhang suanshu.* The one place where they do appear in the commentary, moreover, it is to explicitly deny them a place in such matters as calculating the volume of the sphere: "La théorie de Zhang Heng 張衡 (78–139 CE) veut naturellement s'accorder avec la théorie du pair et de l'impair, du *Yin* et du *Yang,* et ne prend pas en considération la precision" 衡說之自然, 欲恊其 陰陽奇耦之說, 而不顧疏密矣 (Chemla and Guo, *Les neuf chapitres,* 383). As to the *operability* of the heavenly stems and earthly branches, see Note 11.

80 "Bane," "auspice," "avoidance," etc., are problematics that come up in the other five subdivisions of the *Han shu* "Yiwen zhi" category "Shushu," notably the sort of "Five Agents" hemerology whose manuscript predecessors are studied in Donald Harper and Marc Kalinowski, eds., *Books of Fate and Popular Culture in Early China: The Daybook Manuscripts of the Warring States, Qin, and Han* (Leiden: Brill, 2017).

81 "Mathematics, Nature and Cosmological Inquiry," 280.

82 Ibid., 281.

as taxation, censuses, and market payments to *accountants*: because *quantities*, in this regard, are far more crucial to the work of sagecraft than are *Rubriques emblématiques*. And when it went about "observing the signs and granting the season" 觀象授時, so too is there a reason why the Empire appointed relevant experts to the task – why they recruited talent, why they hosted debates, why they ran competitive trials, and why Zhang Long, above, is introduced as a "former appointee." Time and space are commutable, and by numbers you can take command of them to literally see the future and to *prove* it, to all under heaven, all at once, in the minute the midday sun goes black.[83]

They may address different questions, but the "numbers and procedures" (*shushu*) of *li* and *suan* are by no means a lesser magic than the *Changes*. They are, let us recall, sister sciences revealed by the demiurge at the beginning of human time, and they are, in the *Documents*, the very first thing to which Yao 堯 and Shun 舜 attended upon the throne.[84] And where the *Han shu* "Lü-li zhi" opens on numbers citing a lost *Document* to the effect that "one must prioritize one's *suanming*" 先其算命[85] it is telling how Yan Shigu 顏師古 (581–645 CE) chooses to read this. Normally "fate divination," Yan, by virtue of its context, understands *suanming* to mean something altogether greater for the fate of man:

言王者統業, 先立算數以命百事也。

This means to say that, in consolidating his patrimony, he who is to be king must first establish the calculation of numbers so as to take command of the hundred affairs.[86]

---

83 On the subject of recruitment, debate, and testing in *li*, see Morgan, *Astral Sciences*, chaps. 1, 4; Cullen, *Heavenly Numbers*, chap. 7.

84 The "Yao dian" 堯典 chapter opens with Sage King Yao "ordering the Xi and He [brothers], in reverent accordance with prodigious heaven, to *li* and *xiang* the sun, moon and stars and respectfully grant the seasons of man" 乃命羲和, 欽若昊天, 歷象日月星辰, 敬授人時 (*Shangshu zhushu*, 2.21a). When Yao abdicates to Shun, furthermore, he does so by declaring that "the *li* numbers of heaven rest in thy person; ascend thou at last [to the throne] of the great sovereign" 天之歷數在汝躬, 汝終陟元后 (ibid., 4.55b; cf. *Analects* xx.1). Immediately following his ascension, lastly, Shun "attended to the Rotating Device and Jade Traverse (i.e., Beidou 北斗; UMa) so as to order the seven governors/government affairs" 在璿璣玉衡, 以齊七政 (*Shangshu zhushu*, 3.35b).

85 *Han shu*, 21a.956.

86 Ibid. (comm.). Cf. Archytas (428–347 bce) (B 3): "The invention of calculation put an end to discord and increased concord [. . .] A standard and a barrier to the unjust, it averts those who can calculate from injustice, persuading them that they would not be able to stay unexposed when they resort to calculation, and prevents those who cannot calculate from doing injustice by showing through calculation their deceit" (tr. Leonid Zhmud, *The Origin of the History of Science in Classical Antiquity*, tr. Alexander Chernoglazov [Berlin: de Gruyter, 2006], 71).

On that note – on the "mathematical mandate" – I want to end on a question concerning further Truths that we might want to rethink in Chinese studies: Why is it, for starters, that the *shushu* of *li* and *suan* have been systematically excluded from *shushu* studies? How is it also that that the *quantitative* study of space (*yu* 宇) and time (*zhou* 宙) is excluded from the discussion of "cosmology" (*yuzhou lun* 宇宙論)? Would not the story of "Chinese thought" be more *interesting* (let alone more *historically accurate*) if it were to include *all* of what the Chinese thought to do with numbers?

Bibliography

Aveni, Anthony F. *Skywatchers of Ancient Mexico*. Texas Pan American Series. Austin: University of Texas Press, 1980.

Biot, Édouard Constant. *Le Tcheou-li, ou Rites des Tcheou, traduit pour la première fois du chinois par feu Édouard Biot*. Edited by Jean-Baptiste Biot. 3 vols. Paris: Imprimerie Nationale, 1851.

Biot, Jean-Baptiste. *Etudes sur l'astronomie indienne et sur l'astronomie chinoise*. Paris: M. Lévy frères, 1862.

Birrell, Anne. *Chinese Mythology: An Introduction*. Baltimore: Johns Hopkins University Press, 1993.

Bodde, Derk. *Chinese Thought, Society, and Science: The Intellectual and Social Background of Science and Technology in Pre-Modern China*. Honolulu: University of Hawaii Press, 1991.

Brown, David. "The Cuneiform Conception of Celestial Space and Time." *Cambridge Archaeological Journal* 10, no. 1 (2000): 103–22.

Brown, Miranda. "Neither 'Primitives' nor 'Others,' but Somehow Not Quite like 'Us': The Fortunes of Psychic Unity and Essentialism in Chinese Studies." *Journal of the Economic and Social History of the Orient* 49, no. 2 (2006): 219–52.

Chao Fulin 晁福林. "Cong 'shushu' dao 'xueshu': shanggu jingshen wenming yanjin de yige xiansuo" 從「數術」到「學術」－－上古精神文明演進的一個線索. *Gudai wenming* 古代文明 4, no. 4 (2010): 40–49.

Cheeseman, James F., et al. "Way-Finding in Displaced Clock-Shifted Bees Proves Bees Use a Cognitive Map." *Proceedings of the National Academy of Sciences* 111, no. 24 (2014): 8949–54.

Chemla, Karine. "Conjunctions between the Sun and the Moon, and Pursuit Problems: Mathematical Reasoning in Chinese Writings on Astral Sciences." In *Mathematical Practices in Relation to Astral Sciences*, edited by Matthieu Husson, Karine Chemla, Agathe Keller, and John M. Steele, forthcoming.

Chemla, Karine. "Mathematics, Nature and Cosmological Inquiry in Traditional China." In *Concepts of Nature: A Chinese-European Cross-Cultural Perspective*, edited by Günter Dux, Hans Ulrich Vogel, and Mark Elvin, 255–84. Leiden: Brill, 2010.

Chemla, Karine. "Observing Mathematical Practices as a Key to Mining Our Sources and Conducting Conceptual History: Division in Ancient China as a Case Study." In *Science *after the Practice Turn in the Philosophy, History, and Social Studies of Science*, edited by Léna Soler, Sjoerd Zwart, Michael Lynch, and Vincent Israel-Jost, 238–68. New York: Routledge, 2014.

Chemla, Karine. "Philosophical Reflections in Chinese Ancient Mathematical Texts: Liu Hui's Reference to the *Yijing*." In *Current Perspectives in the History of Science in East Asia*, edited by Kim Yung Sik and Francesca Bray, 89–100. Seoul: Seoul National University Press, 1999.

Chemla, Karine. "Positions et changements en mathématiques à partir de textes chinois des dynasties Han à Song-Yuan. Quelques remarques." *Extrême-Orient, Extrême-Occident* 18, no. 18 (1996): 115–47.

Chemla, Karine. "Shedding Some Light on a Possible Origin of a Concept of Fractions in China: Division as a Link between the Newly Discovered Manuscripts and 'The Gnomon of the Zhou [Dynasty].'" *Sudhoffs Archiv* 97, no. 2 (2013): 174–98.

Chemla, Karine. "Should They Read FORTRAN as If It Were English?" *Bulletin of Chinese Studies* 1, no. 2 (1987): 301–16.

Chemla, Karine. "What Is at Stake in Mathematical Proofs from Third Century China?" *Science in Context* 10, no. 2 (1997): 227–51.

Chemla, Karine, and Guo Shuchun 郭書春. *Les neuf chapitres: le classique mathématique de la Chine ancienne et ses commentaires*. Paris: Dunod, 2004.

Chen Xiaozhong 陳曉中 and Zhang Shuli 張淑莉. *Zhongguo gudai tianwen jigou yu tianwen jiaoyu* 中國古代天文機構與天文教育. Beijing: Zhongguo kexue jishu chubanshe, 2008.

Cullen, Christopher. *Astronomy and Mathematics in Ancient China: The Zhou Bi Suan Jing*. Cambridge: Cambridge University Press, 1996.

Cullen, Christopher. *The Foundations of Celestial Reckoning: Three Ancient Chinese Astronomical Systems*. Scientific Writings from the Ancient and Medieval World. New York: Routledge, 2017.

Cullen, Christopher. *Heavenly Numbers: Astronomy and Authority in Early Imperial China*. Oxford: Oxford University Press, 2017.

Cullen, Christopher. "People and Numbers in Early Imperial China: Locating 'Mathematics' and 'Mathematicians' in Chinese Space." In *Oxford Handbook of the History of Mathematics*, edited by Eleanor Robson and Jacqueline A. Stedall, 591–618. Oxford: Oxford University Press, 2009.

Cullen, Christopher. "Translating Ancient Chinese Astronomical Systems with EXCEL: How Not to Stew the Strawberries?" *Journal for the History of Astronomy* 36, no. 3 (2005): 336–38.

Deane, Thatcher Elliott. "The Chinese Imperial Astronomical Bureau: Form and Function of the Ming Dynasty *Qintianjian* from 1365 to 1627." Ph.D. diss., University of Washington, 1989.

Evans, James. *The History and Practice of Ancient Astronomy*. New York: Oxford University Press, 1998.

Goodman, Howard L. "The Life and Intellectual World of Li Chunfeng (602–670)." In *Monographs in Tang Official History: Perspectives from the Technical Treatises of the History of Sui (Sui Shu)*, edited by Daniel Patrick Morgan and Damien Chaussende with the collaboration of Karine Chemla, 29–49. Cham: Springer Nature Switzerland AG, 2019.

Graham, A.C. *Later Mohist Logic, Ethics, and Science*. 2d ed. Hong Kong: Chinese University Press, 2003.

Graham, A.C. *Yin-Yang and the Nature of Correlative Thinking*. Singapore: The Institute of East Asian Philosophies, National University of Singapore, 1986.

Granet, Marcel. *La pensée chinoise*. Paris: La Renaissance du livre, 1934.

Guanju Qin-Han mu jiandu 關沮秦漢墓簡牘, ed. Hubei sheng Jingzhou shi Zhouliang yuqiao yizhi bowuguan 湖北省荊州市周梁玉橋遺址博物館. Beijing: Zhonghua shuju, 2001.

Han shu 漢書, Ban Gu 班固 et al., 111 CE, commentary by Yan Shigu 顏師古 (581–645 CE); punctuated critical edition, Beijing: Zhonghua shuju, 1962 (8 vols.).

Harper, Donald, and Marc Kalinowski, eds. *Books of Fate and Popular Culture in Early China: The Daybook Manuscripts of the Warring States, Qin, and Han*. Leiden: Brill, 2017.

Haskins, Charles Homer. *Studies in the History of Mediaeval Science*. Cambridge, MA: Harvard University Press, 1924.

Henderson, John B. *The Development and Decline of Chinese Cosmology*. New York: Columbia University Press, 1984.

Hou Han shu 後漢書 (HHS), Fan Ye 范曄 (398–445 CE) et al., commentary by Liu Zhao 劉昭 (sixth century CE) and Li Xian 李賢 (654–684 CE); punctuated critical edition, Beijing: Zhonghua shuju, 1965 (12 vols.).

Hsu Ming-Chang 許名瑲. "Hujia caochang Han jian lijian tianxiang guankui" 胡家草場漢簡曆簡天象管窺, *Jianbo wang* 簡帛網, February 19, 2020, http://www.bsm.org.cn/show_article.php?id=3513

Huang Yi-long 黃一農. "Jixing yu gudu kao" 極星與古度考. *Tsing Hua Journal of Chinese Studies* 22, no. 2 (1992): 93–117.

Ifrah, Georges, and David Bellos. *The Universal History of Numbers: From Prehistory to the Invention of the Computer*. New York: Wiley, 2000.

Jami, Catherine. *The Emperor's New Mathematics: Western Learning and Imperial Authority during the Kangxi Reign (1662–1722)*. Oxford: Oxford University Press, 2012.

Jin shu 晉書, Fang Xuanling 房玄齡 et al., 648 CE; punctuated critical edition, Beijing: Zhonghua shuju, 1974 (10 vols.).

Kalinowski, Marc. "Astrologie calendaire et calcul de position dans la Chine ancienne: les mutations de l'hémérologie sexagésimale entre le IVe et le IIe siècles avant notre ère." *Extrême-orient, Extrême-occident* 18 (1996): 71–113.

Kalinowski, Marc, ed. *Divination et société dans la Chine médiévale: étude des manuscrits de Dunhuang de la Bibliothèque nationale de France et de la British Library*. Paris: Bibliothèque nationale de France, 2003.

Kalinowski, Marc. "Fonctionnalité calendaire dans les cosmogonies anciennes de la Chine." *Études chinoises* XXIII (2004): 169–91.

Lai Swee Fo 賴瑞和. "Tangdai de Hanlin daizhao he Sitiantai" 唐代的翰林待詔和司天臺. *Tang yanjiu* 唐研究 9 (2003): 315–42.

Lévy-Bruhl, Lucien. *Primitive Mentality*. Translated by Lilian A. Clare. London: George Allen & Unwin, 1923.

Li Ling 李零. *Jianbo gushu yu xueshu yuanliu* 簡帛古書與學術源流. Revised edition. Beijing: Sanlian shudian, 2008.

Li Yan 李儼. "Suanchou zhidu kao" 算籌制度考. In *Zhongsuan shi luncong* 中算史論叢, by Li Yan 李儼, 1–8, Rpt. from 1929. Beijing: Kexue chubanshe, 1955.

Li Zhifang 李志芳 and Jiang Lujing 蔣魯敬. "Hubei jingzhou shi Hujia caochang Xihan mu M12 chutu jiandu gaishu" 湖北荊州市胡家草場西漢墓 M12 出土簡牘概述, *Kaogu* 考古 2020.2: 21–33.

Mak, Bill M. "Astral Science of the East Syriac Christians in China during the Late First Millennium AD." *Mediterranean Archaeology and Archaeometry* 16, no. 4 (2016): 87–92.

Mak, Bill M. "The Transmission of Buddhist Astral Science from India to East Asia: The Central Asian Connection." *Historia Scientiarum* 24, no. 2 (2015): 59–75.

Martzloff, Jean-Claude. *Le calendrier chinois: structure et calculs, 104 av. JC–1644: indétermination céleste et réforme permanente: la construction chinoise officielle du temps quotidien discret à partir d'un temps mathématique caché, linéaire et continu.* Paris: Champion, 2009.

Morgan, Daniel Patrick. *Astral Sciences in Early Imperial China: Observation, Sagehood and the Individual.* Cambridge: Cambridge University Press, 2017.

Morgan, Daniel Patrick. "A Radical Proposition on the Origins of the Received Mathematical Classic the *Gnomon of Zhou (Zhoubi* 周髀)." In *Proceedings of the Second International Conference on the History of Mathematics and Astronomy, Northwest University, Xi'an, 2–8* December 2018, ed. Daniel Patrick Morgan and Tang Quan 唐泉 (forthcoming).

Morgan, Daniel Patrick, and Howard L. Goodman. "Numbers with Histories: Li Chunfeng on Harmonics and Astronomy." In *Monographs in Tang Official History: Perspectives from the Technical Treatises of the* History of Sui *(Sui Shu),* edited by Daniel Patrick Morgan and Damien Chaussende with the collaboration of Karine Chemla, 51–87. Cham: Springer Nature Switzerland AG, 2019.

Nakayama 中山茂 Shigeru. "Characteristics of Chinese Calendrical Science." *Japanese Studies in the History of Science*, no. 4 (1965): 124–31.

Needham, Joseph. *Science and Civilisation in China, Vol. 2: History of Scientific Thought.* Cambridge: Cambridge University Press, 1956.

Needham, Joseph. *Science and Civilisation in China, Vol. 3: Mathematics and the Sciences of the Heavens and the Earth.* Cambridge: Cambridge University Press, 1959.

Nielsen, Bent. *A Companion to Yi Jing Numerology and Cosmology: Chinese Studies of Images and Numbers from Han (202 BCE – 220 CE) to Song (960–1279 CE).* London: RoutledgeCurzon, 2003.

Pankenier, David W. "Weaving Metaphors and Cosmo-Political Thought in Early China." *T'oung Pao* 101, no. 1–3 (2015): 1–34.

Qu Anjing 曲安京. "Zhongguo gudai lifa zhong de jishi zhidu" 中國古代曆法中的計時制度. *Hanxue yanjiu* 漢學研究 12, no. 2 (1994): 157–72.

Rochberg, Francesca. *The Heavenly Writing: Divination, Horoscopy, and Astronomy in Mesopotamian Culture.* Cambridge: Cambridge University Press, 2004.

Shangshu zhushu 尚書正義, pre-Qin (< 221 BCE), commentary by Kong Anguo 孔安國, subcommentary by Kong Yingda 孔穎達 (574–648 CE), 653 CE; edition Shisanjing zhushu 重刊宋本十三經注疏, 1815; reprint Taibei: Yiwen yinshuguan, 1965.

Shuihudi Qin mu zhujian 睡虎地秦墓竹簡, ed. Shuihudi Qin mu zhujian zhengli xiaozu 睡虎地秦墓竹簡整理小組. Beijing: Wenwu chubanshe, 1990.

Sivin, Nathan. "Cosmos and Computation in Early Chinese Mathematical Astronomy." *T'oung Pao* 2d ser., 55, no. 1/3 (1969): 1–73.

Sivin, Nathan. *Granting the Seasons: The Chinese Astronomical Reform of 1280, with a Study of Its Many Dimensions and a Translation of Its Records.* New York: Springer, 2009.

Sivin, Nathan. "Mathematical Astronomy and the Chinese Calendar." In *Calendars and Years II: Astronomy and Time in the Ancient and Medieval World*, edited by John M. Steele, 39–51. Oxford: Oxbow Books, 2011.

Smart, W.M. *Textbook on Spherical Astronomy.* Edited by Robin M. Green. Cambridge: Cambridge University Press, 1977.

Song shi 宋史, Tuotuo 脱脱 (1314–1355) et al.; punctuated critical edition, Beijing: Zhonghua shuju, 1977 (40 vols.).

Souciet, Étienne. *Observations mathématiques, astronomiques, geographiques, chronologiques et physiques: tirées des anciens livres chinois, ou faites nouvellement aux Indes et à la Chine & ailleurs, par les Peres de la Compagnie de JESUS*. 3 vols. Paris: Chez Rollin libraire, 1729–1732.

Sui shu 隋書. Wei Zheng 魏徵 (580–643 ce), Linghu Defen 令狐德棻 (582–666 ce), et al., 656 CE; punctuated critical edition, Beijing: Zhonghua shuju, 1973 (3 vols.).

Sun Xiaochun 孫小淳. "Chinese Calendar and Mathematical Astronomy." In *Handbook of Archaeoastronomy and Ethnoastronomy*, edited by C.L.N. Ruggles, 2059–68. New York: Springer, 2015.

Tomioka Kenji 富岡憲治, and Matsumoto Akira 松本顯. "A Comparative View of Insect Circadian Clock Systems." *Cellular and Molecular Life Sciences* 67, no. 9 (2010): 1397–1406.

Toomer, Gerald J. *Ptolemy's Almagest*. 2d ed. Princeton: Princeton University Press, 1998.

Tylor, Edward B. *Primitive Culture: Researches into the Development of Mythology, Philosophy, Religion, Art, and Custom*. 2 vols. London: John Murray, 1871.

Weil, Dror. "Islamicated China: China's Participation in the Islamicate Book Culture during the Seventeenth and Eighteenth Centuries." *Intellectual History of the Islamicate World* 4, no. 1–2 (2016): 36–60.

Yoshimura Masayuki 吉村昌之. "Shutsudo kandoku shiryō ni mirareru rekihu no shūsei" 出土簡牘資料にみれる暦譜の集成. In *Henkyō shutsudo mokkan no kenkyū* 邊疆出土木簡の研究, edited by Tomiya Itaru 冨谷至, 459–516. Kyōto: Hōyū shoten, 2003.

Zhmud, Leonid. *The Origin of the History of Science in Classical Antiquity*. Translated by Alexander Chernoglazov. Berlin: de Gruyter, 2006.

Zhoubi suanjing 周髀算經, anon., 1 bce/178 ce, commentary by Zhao Shuang 趙爽 (fl. 314 ce), subcommentary by Zhen Luan 甄鸞 (fl. 535–570 ce) and Li Chunfeng 李淳風 (602–670 ce) et al.; edition Sibu congkan 四部叢刊, Shanghai: Shangwu yinshuguan, 1919–1936.

Zhu Yiwen 朱一文. "Chutang de shuxue yu lixue: yi zhujia dui *Liji* 'Touhu' de zhushu wei li" 初唐的數學與禮學: 以諸家對『禮記·投壺』的注疏為例. *Zhongshan daxue xuebao (shehui kexue ban)* 中山大學學報(社會科學版) 57, no. 2 (2017): 160–68.

Zhu Yiwen 朱一文. "Politics and Scholarship in Early-Tang China: Dynastic Legitimacy and Li Chunfeng's Technical Treatises on Harmonics and Calendrics." In *Monographs in Tang Official History: Perspectives from the Technical Treatises of the* History of Sui *(Sui Shu)*, edited by Daniel Patrick Morgan and Damien Chaussende with the collaboration of Karine Chemla, 89–116. Cham: Springer Nature Switzerland AG, 2019.

Zhu Yiwen 朱一文. "Shu: suan yu shu – yi jiu shu zhi fangcheng weili" 數: 筭與術 – – 以九數之方程為例. *Hanxue yanjiu* 漢學研究 28, no. 4 (2010): 73–105.

Garret Pagenstecher Olberding
Diplomacy as Transgression in Early China

The transgressive potential of the diplomat

At base, diplomacy is driven by the aim for a non-militaristic negotiation of frequently competing interests, a negotiation that ideally should reinforce the definition of each party's sovereign realm and palliate any conflict between them. But this negotiation is also, by the very act of transacting across political and cultural boundaries, a kind of transgression, and thus a danger to the integrity of the state polity, for in diplomacy, the interests of the state can not only be unsuccessfully negotiated but intentionally undermined, just as, in military campaigns, the interests of the state can be subverted, and betrayed, by false, or careless, action, or even intentional inaction, as is so often depicted in the early Chinese narrative histories.[1] Indeed, the very reason for Sima Qian's brutal castration is his support of a general, Li Ling, who "treasonously" capitulated to the Xiongnu after a failed engagement.[2] As von Clausewitz's by now clichéed equation so aptly insinuates, military and diplomatic engagement are aspirationally congruent: War is the continuation of politics "by other means."[3]

---

[1] Anne McClintock analogously asserts that sailors and explorers, as members of the liminal condition also were "dangerous": "There on the margins between known and unknown, the male conquistadors, explorers and sailors became creatures of transition and threshold . . . the dangers represented by liminal people are managed by rituals that separate the marginal ones from their old status, segregating them for a time and then publicly declaring their entry into their new status. Colonial discourse repeatedly rehearses this pattern – dangerous marginality, segregation, reintegration." Anne McClintock, *Imperial Leather: Race, Gender and Sexuality in the Colonial Contest* (New York: Routledge, 1995), 24–25.

[2] For the most detailed *Shiji* accounts of the Li Ling failure, see *SJ* 110.2918 and *SJ* 109. 2877–78. For lengthier accounts, one must peruse the *Hanshu*. See *HS* 54.2451–2457 and 62.2730.

[3] Carl von Clausewitz, *On War* (New York: Penguin Books, 1982), 119: "We see therefore, that War is not merely a political act, but also a real political instrument, a continuation of political commerce, a carrying out of the same by other means. All beyond this which is strictly peculiar to War relates merely to the peculiar nature of the means which it uses." This congruence is evident in various ministerial addresses and debates represented as part of the Warring States and Han eras. For my close, detailed analysis of these addresses and debates, see Garret Olberding, *Dubious Facts: The Evidence of Early Chinese Historiography* (Albany, New York: SUNY Press, 2012), chapters six and eight.

For diplomatic interface, transgression resides not only in the possibility of betrayal and rearrangement or distortion of alliances, and thus state action, but also in the actual rhetorical reframing of one's diplomatic mission or of the representation of the current state of affairs.[4] I argue that understanding the transgressive activity of the diplomat requires a nuanced understanding of a ritualized conceptualization of early Chinese diplomacy, which we can acquire through the examination of formal restrictions on ambassadorial exchange, obligations to and from guests, and the idea of the "alien" or "monstrous." To gain greater depth in these examinations, I hazard that an analogous diplomatic transgression of boundaries is that pursued by the *wu* 巫, "spirit mediums" (employed by the state as "invocators," *zhu* 祝) who act as diplomatic intermediaries between the physical and supernatural, their sacrifices cognate with monarchial tribute, their prayers with diplomatic pleadings.[5] Using an invocator was to conduct diplomacy with the spirits. Indeed, rulers very clearly relied on assistance from the spiritual realms for not only maintenance of their realms, but also their expansion.[6] According to Michael Puett, in the Shang, the ritual of the

---

4 As expressed by the figure of Confucius in the *Zhuangzi*, the conveying of messages between rival sovereign parties is very difficult and dangerous: "Whenever we are dealing with neighbours we have to rub along with each other on a basis of trust; but with people more distant we have to show our good faith in words, and the words must have some messenger. To pass on the words of parties both of whom are pleased or both of whom are angry with each other is the most difficult thing in the world. In the one case there are sure to be a lot of exaggerated compliments, in the other a lot of exaggerated abuse. Every sort of exaggeration is irresponsible, and if language is irresponsible trust in it fails, and the consequence of that is that the messenger is a doomed man. Therefore the book of rules says: 'If you report the straightforward facts and omit the exaggerated language, you will be safe enough.'" 凡交近則必相靡以信, 遠則必忠之以言, 言必或傳之。夫傳兩喜兩怒之言, 天下之難者也。夫兩喜必多溢美之言, 兩怒必多溢惡之言。凡溢之類妄, 妄則其信之也莫, 莫則傳言者殃。故法言曰：『傳其常情, 無傳其溢言, 則幾乎全。』 (*Zhuangzi*, "Renjian shi" 人間世 ("Worldly business among men"; *Chuang-Tzŭ: The Inner Chapters*, trans. A. C. Graham (Indianapolis, Indiana: Hackett Publishing Company, 2001), 70; *Zhuangzi zhushu* 庄子注疏 (Beijing: Zhonghua shuju, 2011), 86–87. *Analects* 14.25 also has Confucius ostensibly ruing the impolitic critique by an envoy of his lord.
5 One could say that among the most famous of Christian quotations is the request by Jesus of Nazareth who asks, in the position of the diplomat, for the monarch God not to punish those who are mistreating God's missionary representative, himself, Jesus: "Forgive them, Father, for they know not what they do." Luke 23:34. One could go even further to suggest that Jesus's performance of healing miracles is as one who transgresses the divide between the human and spirit world and that his actions are seen, in some way, as transgressions of the natural order, as its deformation, and thus, dangerous to it.
6 As the First Emperor of Qin stated in an edict: "Insignificant person that I am, I have called up troops to punish violence and rebellion. Thanks to the help of the ancestral spirits, these six kings have all acknowledged their guilt and the world is in profound order." 「寡人以眇眇之身, 興兵誅

"guest" (*bin* 賓), in use for the "entertainment" of spiritual powers, was to both maintain a hierarchy and to bring alien deities, such as Di, into the ancestral pantheon.[7] The spirits "descend" (*jiang* 降) into the world and involve themselves in its affairs through a spirit medium, a vertical journey that the monarch or his representatives replicate through ascent on natural or constructed elevations.[8] But these deities, Puett maintains, could not be depended upon for any assistance and in point of fact, at least in the Shang, "the assumption seemed to be that spirits were capricious and quite possibly malicious."[9] Whether the relationship between the spirit and human worlds was later ever fully harmonized, there was necessarily a rift, and potential conflict, between the two, requiring the diplomatic intervention of spiritual mediators, however unreliable their own allegiances were. In view of this, we may ask, as Linda Feng does in her essay above, how does the religious organization of space impact its secular organization and, furthermore, what does any transgression of religiously sanctified boundaries effect?

The profession of the diplomat or envoy – either within the human world, or, I hypothesize, analogously as priests or spirit mediums toward the spirit world – involved manifold tasks that could conceivably, and very easily, compromise the sovereignty of and very concretely the territorial extent governed by the monarch. Succeeding is a partial list of the envoy's commonly sanctioned activities: Pass messages; obtain information directly and indirectly, as the sovereign's official informant; act as the monarch's representative in ritual, political, and military fora; and, most invidiously, speak on the monarch's behalf. It is not clear what plenipotentiary powers the envoys of the sovereign were afforded; one would suspect it would depend on the envoy's politico-military status and the task at hand. Regardless, in their activities, they could covertly exceed their prerogatives, impinging on or brazenly usurping the monarch's prerogative. Whatever their official charge, their powers abroad were, somewhat similar to the generals acting as the monarch's representatives on the battlefield, potentially destabilizing, bringing "disorder" (*luan* 亂).[10] Most

---

暴亂, 賴宗妙之靈, 六王咸服其辜, 天下大定。」 *SJ* 6.236; Sima Qian, *Records of the Grand Historian: Qin Dynasty,* trans. Burton Watson (New York: Columbia University Press, 1993), 42.

7 Michael J. Puett, *To Become a God: Cosmology, Sacrifice, and Self-Divinization in Early China* (Cambridge, Massachusetts: Harvard Asia Center Publications, 2002), 52.

8 Mark E. Lewis, *The Construction of Space in Early China* (Albany, New York: SUNY Press, 2006), 300.

9 Puett, *To Become a God: Cosmology, Sacrifice, and Self-Divinization in Early China*, 53.

10 "I, Your servant, have heard that when the high ancient kings dispatched generals, they kneeled and pushed the axle [to the generals' carts], saying, 'Within the city gates, I, the solitary person, make regulations, outside the city gates the generals make regulations. The

flagrantly, they would upend the monarch's sovereignty, intentionally eroding or abrogating his position in their negotiations with other powers. Such opportunities for misdeeds were certainly a reason for the monarch to secure "*immutable mobiles*" such as visual representations of distant areas, "representations which can be detached from the place (or object) which they represent," by which the monarch could, in Bruno Latour's phrase, "act at a distance."[11]

But indirect undermining was more the rule: Envoys could have supposed "enemies" of the monarch dispatched, when these "enemies" were really those of the envoy or his associates; could make self-serving political and economic pacts; could embezzle, and thereby betray the economic order, or miscarry politico-legal justice, for instance by punishing without warrant. Even more frequent was their habit to distort messages to and from the monarch or to collude with the enemy in their presenting of sensitive information, as Jing Ke 荊軻 was to do in presenting what was taken to be a strategically valuable map of Yan 燕 territory to the first Qin emperor. It is furthermore plausible that, with the interaction with the spirits perceived as having manifest effect on the affairs of the human world, that the envoy, in his capacity as representative in ritual sacrifices,[12] could attempt to "negotiate" with the spirits against the interests of the sovereign.

---

degrees of merit, orders of honor, and material rewards to be awarded to members of the army are all determined abroad. Only when you return do you present them.' This is not an empty saying." 臣聞上古王者遣將也, 跪而推轂, 曰:『閫以內寡人制之, 閫以外將軍制之; 軍功爵賞, 皆決於外, 歸而奏之.』此非空言也。See *HS* 50.2314; Olberding, *Dubious Facts: The Evidence of Early Chinese Historiography*, 64.

11 Ola Söderström, "Paper Cities: Visual Thinking in Urban Planning," *Ecumene* 3, no. 3 (1996), 253.

12 See, e.g., in *HHS* 3.14, "使使者祠唐堯於成陽靈臺" or *HHS* 3.144, "遣使者祠太上皇於萬年, 以中牢祠蕭何、霍光。" David Schaberg, in an essay, associated the position of the envoy, or *shi* 使, with that of the *shi* 史, the professional ancestor of which conceivably was the spiritual medium or "shaman" (*wu* 巫). He notes that none of the typical terms for "envoy" – *shi* 使, *shizhe* 使者, or *xingren* 行人 – appeared "as such" in sources portraying the Western Zhou, whether the bronze inscriptions or received texts. In the *Zuozhuan*, Schaberg states, the most common duties of the *shi* 史 were "the duties relating to sacrifices, especially to natural spirits or in response to natural disasters. The *shi* 史 are responsible for identifying and responding appropriately to unknown spirits and for conducting sacrifices at such sites as the Luo river . . . Perhaps due to this responsibility for sacrifices to natural powers, they also serve frequently as interpreters of divinations (usually by milfoil), omens, and dreams and more generally as prophets of good and ill fortune." See David Schaberg, "Functionary Speech: On the Work of *Shi* 使 and *Shi* 史." In *Facing the Monarch: Modes of Advice in the Early Chinese Court*, edited by Garret Olberding (Cambridge, Massachusetts: Harvard Asia Center Publications, 2013), esp. 21, 23, and 27–28.

In short, like a passage in the *Hanshi waizhuan* 韓詩外傳 asserts, envoys were the pivots of the state's survival, the crux of any gain or loss.[13] It should therefore not be surprising that a classicist Warring States text devoted to expounding on proper governance, the *Xunzi* 荀子, dedicates a lengthy passage to the prescribed and proscribed behavior of official representatives. The official representative is not to deviate from his charge, not "to add or subtract." He is to have no inclination but to serve his lord properly. These officials must be trustworthy enough to be "employed in far away places to make clear [the lord's] intentions and resolve uncertainties."[14] While they cannot abrogate the responsibilities associated with polite, formal interaction, they also must defend the state, and the monarch, against insults, to maintain its, and his, claims to sovereignty. Deference was to be shown to the monarch's representative, as would be shown to the monarch himself.[15] Without such reliable representatives, the state, according to the *Xunzi*, will fall.[16] But this faithful rhetorical

---

13 "Thus those advisors and assistants who serve as envoys, they are the crux of survival or demise, the essential point of gain or loss. This must not be ignored!" 故輔弼左右所任使者、有存亡之機, 得失之要也, 可無慎乎! See Han Ying 韓嬰, *Hanshi waizhuan jishi* 韓詩外傳集釋 (Beijing: Zhong hua shu ju, 2009), j. 5, zhang 18, 186.

14 Xunzi, "The Way to Be a Lord" 君道; *Xunzi: The Complete Text*, trans. Eric L. Hutton (Princeton, New Jersey: Princeton University Press, 2014), 131–132; Wang Xianqian 王先謙, ed., *Xunzi jijie* 荀子集解 (Beijing: Zhonghua shuju, 1997a), 244–245.

15 "When a message from the ruler comes (to a minister), the latter should go out and bow (to the bearer), in acknowledgment of the honour of it. When the messenger is about to return, (the other) must bow to him (again), and escort him to the gate. If (a minister) send a message to his ruler, he must wear his court robes when he communicates it to the bearer; and on his return, he must descend from the hall, to receive (the ruler's) commands." 君言至, 則主人出拜君言之辱; 使者歸, 則必拜送于門外。若使人於君所, 則必朝服而命之; 使者反, 則必下堂而受命。*Liji*, "Quli" A 曲禮上, *Li Chi: Book of Rites,* trans. James Legge (New York: Oxford University Press, 1885), 86. In this aspect, the early Chinese envoy was akin to a medieval European *nuncius*: "Dealing with a *nuncius* was, for legal and practical purposes, the same as dealing with the principal . . . How complete the identification was between *nuncius* and principal can be further gauged from the fact that a *nuncius* could receive and make oaths that ought to be performed in the presence of the principal. It was also clear that the status of the *nuncius* was reflected in the immunity from harm which he was expected to be given. All diplomatic messengers from the earliest times had been accorded some kind of security for their persons, usually on religious grounds, and the special status of ambassadors was clearly understood. In the case of *nuncii*, there was a special sense that harming a *nuncius* was the same as harming his principal, as there was that a *nuncius* should be received with the ceremony that would be due to his principal." Keith Hamilton, and Richard Langhorne, *The Practice of Diplomacy: Its Evolution, Theory and Administration* (New York: Routledge, 1995), 24–25.

16 "And so, the ruler of men must have people who will suffice for being employed in far away places to make clear his intentions and resolve uncertainties, and only then are they

adherence to monarch's prerogative was irregular. As David Schaberg acknowledges, representatives frequently spoke irreverently and impoliticly.[17] If advisers could be acidly condescending toward their rulers while at court, as envoys, they could easily be so. Even more dangerously, their transmission of the ruler's intentions, and relevant information, was also suspect.

This is likely a significant reason for the widespread regulatory controls pertaining to the preservation and recording of diplomatic missives, and their carriers, detailed in both received and excavated sources. Information in general was insecure and comparatively difficult to verify in the ancient world;[18] this would be ever more the case when the information could be used to personal advantage. Jidong Yang has observed in the Xuanquan manuscripts that foreign envoys were under strict supervision, at all times accompanied by a Chinese official and required to carry a passport:

> The original passport had to be carried by the foreign envoys at all times when traveling within the Han empire. On arriving at a postal station or a local government mansion, the envoy would show the travel document to the officials in charge in order to receive accommodation; the officials offering the service would furthermore make a copy of the passport for their own records.[19]

These diplomatic precautions are easily comprehensible for, as Yang mentions, most designated envoys (*shizhe* 使者) from Central Asia acted as merchants who rarely moved far beyond the empire's perimeter, interacting and socializing with the officials of these border areas. These interactions were monitored carefully, with the duration of the stay, the departing direction and time of

---

acceptable. Their demonstrations and persuasions must suffice to dissolve worries. Their wisdom and deliberations must suffice to resolve uncertainties. Their swiftness and decisiveness must suffice to ward off disasters. They must not circumvent protocols or act confrontationally toward other lords, but nevertheless their response to derogatory treatment and their defense against troubles must suffice to uphold the state's altars of soil and grain." 故人主必將有足使喻志決疑於遠方者，然後可。其辯說足以解煩，其知慮足以決疑，其齊斷足以距難，不還秩，不反君，然而應薄扞患，足以持社稷。*Xunzi*, "The Way to Be a Lord" 君道; *Xunzi: The Complete Text*, trans. Eric L. Hutton (Princeton, New Jersey: Princeton University Press, 2014), 131; Wang Xianqian 王先謙, ed. *Xunzi jijie* 荀子集解 (Beijing: Zhonghua shuju, 1997a), 244–245.

17 David Schaberg, "Playing At Critique: Indirect Remonstrance and the Formation of *Shi* Identity," in *Text and Ritual in Early China*, ed. Martin Kern (Seattle, Washington: University of Washington Press, 2005).

18 Olberding, *Dubious Facts: The Evidence of Early Chinese Historiography*, 61.

19 Jidong Yang, "Transportation, Boarding, Lodging and Trade Along the Early Silk Road: A Preliminary Study of the Xuanquan Manuscripts," *Journal of the American Oriental Society* 135, no. 3 (2015), 428.

departure, and the number of meals offered recorded,[20] conceivably to inhibit collusion between border officials and foreign powers, just as the fastidious recording of each article of mail passing through the Xuanquan station[21] probably also in part aimed to do. Envoys were to act as spies for their lords,[22] but, as mentioned above, they also acted as informants for the lord's rivals.

The envoy's moving into a non-state space, without the protections, such as they were, of state protocols and laws, was in itself dangerous. Indeed, a passage in the *Liji* advises rulers be cautioned about leaving the state with the admonishing query, "Why are you leaving the altars of the spirits of the land and grain?" suggesting not only a danger to the state but also to the ruler himself.[23] To be exiled, to be sent abroad without state protections was for this reason a punishment, for it could very readily mean death or serious injury. Non-state territory was *defined* by this very lack of administrative oversight, and was a place where societal cast-offs, where the socially "dead" could be sent.[24] This area of the unknown and unprotected was the place of the symbolically monstrous and the effaced. Indeed, as Martin Kern has noted, the sovereign space was measured by "the terminal points to which all crime is relegated." According to Han commentators of the "Canon of Shun" (*Shundian* 舜典) in the *Canon of Yao* 堯典, the "four criminals" and "their places of exile or execution were associated with the barbarian areas of the four directions: Dark Province in the north, Exalted Mountain in the south, Threefold Precipice in the West, and Feathered Mountain

---

20 Yang, "Transportation, Boarding, Lodging and Trade Along the Early Silk Road: A Preliminary Study of the Xuanquan Manuscripts," 428–429.

21 Yang, "Transportation, Boarding, Lodging and Trade Along the Early Silk Road: A Preliminary Study of the Xuanquan Manuscripts," 426.

22 "Upon arriving at Jinyang, [Liu Bang, the future Han emperor] heard that Han Xin together with the Xiongnu wished to attack the Han armies. Liu Bang was very angry and sent an envoy to the Xiongnu. The Xiongnu hid their strong soldiers and fat cows and horses, only revealing the old and weak and the young herd animals. The envoy came ten times and always said the Xiongnu could be attacked." 至晉陽, 聞信與匈奴欲共擊漢, 上大怒, 使人使匈奴。匈奴匿其壯士肥牛馬, 但見老弱及羸畜。使者十輩來, 皆言匈奴可擊。*SJ* 99.2718.

23 *Liji*, "Quli" B 曲禮下: "When the ruler of a state (is proposing to) leave the state, they should (try to) stop him, saying, 'Why are you leaving the altars of the spirits of the land and grain?'" 國君去其國, 止之曰:「奈何去社稷也!」*Li Chi: Book of Rites*, 107; *Liji jijie* 禮記集解 (Beijing: Zhong hua shu ju, 2010a), 125.

24 According to Danielle Allen, casting out the dead from the city, from the acculturated center, was practiced very literally by the ancient Greeks. A return to civilized space, to the city, was a return to the world of the living. See Danielle Allen, *The World of Prometheus: The Politics of Punishing in Democratic Athens* (Princeton, New Jersey: Princeton University Press, 2000), 207.

in the East."[25] For those not being punished, being sent into the wilds, as Shun himself was by Yao,[26] was a perilous trial, of one's person and one's loyalties.

Ritual obligations involved in travel abroad

Oddly enough, comparatively little has been written on the general form of premodern diplomacy, whether in China or even in Europe, apart from broader concerns of foreign relations. At base, diplomacy assumes a secure source of political power that can actually be represented, for which negotiations can be made and agreements secured. If there is no secure source of power, if power is too fragmentary, diplomats naturally have no one stable subject or entity to represent. Between diplomatically symmetrical entities, that is, between those polities that are treated as of reciprocally recognizable structure, diplomats are treated as representational metonyms of their supporting polities; between asymmetrical entities, the "superior" polity condescends to demand for tribute or obeisance but will not offer corresponding duties to the "inferior." Thus when the Han opposed the Xiongnu polity organized under the *shanyu*, they engaged in high-level diplomatic exchanges and negotiations, with both sides treating the diplomatic representatives according to protocols. According to the *Shiji*, the Xiongnu's protocols for interacting with diplomats depended on the diplomat's status. Early idealizing literature such as the *Zhouli*, *Yili*, and *Liji* preserves ritualized protocols for diplomatic interface but whether any approximation of such was properly and fully applied to foreign, non-Chinese adversaries cannot be certain. As will be discussed later, if the debate of 51 BCE about the status of a Xiongnu *shanyu* in relation to the Han aristocrats is any indication, full application was probably the exception. What *is* clear, from the Zhangjiashan legal texts, is that there were strict regulations about who could travel abroad, and with what objects they could travel. Metal tools, for instance, were tightly regulated, presumably because of the danger of their being transformed into weaponry. Even coffins were inspected for illegal items, though

---

25 Martin Kern, "Language and the Ideology of Kingship in the 'Canon of Yao'," in *Ideology of Power and Power of Ideology in Early China*, ed. Yuri Pines, Paul R. Goldin, and Martin Kern (Leiden: Brill, 2015), 140.
26 Kern, "Language and the Ideology of Kingship in the 'Canon of Yao'," 135.

this was ruled improper.[27] When there were disagreements, each side would hold the other's emissaries hostage.[28]

Ritual obligations impinged heavily on travel abroad for those with official status. When travel was not properly sanctioned, the itinerant could face severe consequences, a loss of title, or worse, a loss of identity, becoming essentially stateless. As Wang Haicheng notes, travelers were expected to pass forts located at "strategic points such as ferries and mountain passes."[29] The Han ordinances on fords and passes discovered at Zhangjiashan detail punishments for commoners who cross frontiers without permission, including tattooing, building walls for men, pounding grain for women, and amputation of the left foot.[30] For county officials, fines were assessed.

Especially for representatives of the sovereign state, such as diplomats, crossing boundaries without permission was in effect the nullifying of one's position, one's subjecthood.[31] In the *Zuozhuan*, for instance, were a nobleman to flee, "as long as he had not crossed the border, the ruler could stop him and request his return, and presumably his status would be unaffected."[32] Were a nobleman to flee his home state, the news would be formally passed to other regional rulers:

> In any case of a nobleman of the regional lords departing, it was reported to the regional lords, saying, "The lineage head, So-and-so of Such-and-such a clan, has failed to keep watch over the ancestral temple. We dare report it." (Zuǒ, Xuān 10, 706).[33] 凡諸侯之大夫違, 告於諸侯曰: 「某氏之守臣某, 失守宗廟. 敢告。」

Crossing a state boundary without proper sanction, Newell Ann van Auken has noted, was equal to the "abandonment of state altars, that is, with abdication

---

27 Osamu Oba, "The Ordinance on Fords and Passes Excavated From Han Tomb #247, Zhangjiashan," *Asia Major* 14, no. 2 (2001), 124.

28 *SJ* 110.2911.

29 Haicheng Wang, *Writing and the Ancient State: Early China in Comparative Perspective* (New York: Cambridge University Press, 2014), 204.

30 In Wang, *Writing and the Ancient State: Early China in Comparative Perspective*, 207. See also Oba, "The Ordinance on Fords and Passes Excavated From Han Tomb #247, Zhangjiashan," 122–3.

31 In a reversal of this power, as Paul J. Kosmin details, in the Seleucid empire, borders could also be the point at which one's status was augmented; for instance, from prince into king. See Paul J. Kosmin, *The Land of the Elephant Kings: Space, Territory, and Ideology in the Seleucid Empire* (Cambridge, Massachusetts: Harvard University Press, 2014), 131–134.

32 Newell Ann Van Auken, "What If Zhào Dùn Had Fled? Border Crossing and Flight Into Exile in Early China," Journal of the American Oriental Society 139, no. 3 (2019), 581.

33 Van Auken, "What If Zhào Dùn Had Fled? Border Crossing and Flight Into Exile in Early China", 581.

of religious responsibilities as head of state."[34] Indeed, according to a passage in the *Zuozhuan*, ritual invocators were not permitted to cross a frontier borderland (*jing* 竟), "if the domain's altars do not move."[35] Van Auken observes that "Similar language was used in reference to nobility, but instead of abandoning the state altars, a nobleman was said to have 'failed to keep watch over the ancestral temple' 失守宗廟."[36] Those eastern Zhou officials or aristocrats who left their states without sanction relinquished their noble status by leaving the state, becoming a threat – or just officially "dead" – to the state.[37] As van Auken suggests, this transgression was not simply one toward the living but also toward the spiritual world.[38]

Van Auken has also mentioned that in the *Zuozhuan*, before any official interstate travel a ruler had to give sanction (*ming* 命), with specific religious ceremonies held and reports (*gao* 告) rendered to the ancestors, presumably in the temple, before departure.[39] This requirement, van Auken observes, is reflected in the "Pin li" 聘禮 ("Rites for Peer Visitation") section of the *Yili* 儀禮 (*Book of*

---

34 Van Auken, "What If Zhào Dùn Had Fled? Border Crossing and Flight Into Exile in Early China", 580.

35 "The rules for officials stipulate that an invocator does not cross the border if the domain's altars do not move. When the ruler travels with the army, he performs a purification sacrifice at the altar of earth, and he anoints the drums with blood; the invocators accompany him to attend to their duties, and in this way the group crosses the borders." 社稷不動, 祝不出竟, 官之制也。君以軍行, 被社、釁鼓, 祝奉以從, 於是乎出竟。 See *Zuo Tradition (Zuozhuan): Commentary on the Spring and Autumn Annals*, trans. Stephen Durrant, Wai-yee Li, and David Schaberg (Seattle, Washington: University of Washington Press, 2016c), Ding 4.1b, 1746–1747; Yang Bojun 楊伯峻, ed. *Chunqiu Zuozhuan zhu* 春秋左傳注 (Beijing: Zhonghua shuju, 1981d), 1535.

36 Van Auken, "What If Zhào Dùn Had Fled? Border Crossing and Flight Into Exile in Early China", 580; Zuǒ, Xuān 10, 706. Yuri Pines notes a similar tension in his study of Qin almanacs, in the making of offerings before travel, with the area beyond state boundary walls becoming a dangerous space: "A special exorcist ritual had to be performed upon leaving the state, similar to the ritual performed upon leaving one's native settlement." Yuri Pines, "The Question of Interpretation: Qin History in Light of New Epigraphic Sources," *Early China* 29 (2004), 41.

37 Van Auken, "What If Zhào Dùn Had Fled? Border Crossing and Flight Into Exile in Early China", 583.

38 Van Auken, "What If Zhào Dùn Had Fled? Border Crossing and Flight Into Exile in Early China", 584.

39 These religious ceremonies announcing the departure of a potentially politically destabilizing force, the diplomat, are somewhat similar to those held by military officials before embarking on a campaign or engaging in battle: "[A]ccording to a passage in the *Zuo zhuan* 左傳, the army commander received his orders in the ancestral temple (*miao* 廟)." See Albert Galvany, "Signs, Clues, and Traces: Anticipation in Ancient Chinese Political and Military Texts," *Early China* (2015), 4.

Ceremony and Rites),[40] as well as in the "Zengzi wen" 曾子問 ("The Inquiries of Zengzi") section of the *Liji* 禮記 (*Record of Rites*). For my analysis, the passage in the *Liji* bears particular notice. It speaks of the regional lord, when setting out to pay court to the son of Heaven or another regional ruler, making reports to not only his father's shrine but to the altars of grain and soil and to the spirits of mountains and rivers.[41] Ritual activities furthermore surrounded arrivals in another state as well as returns to one's home state.[42]

If we can adopt the official travels abroad of those who were deemed *shi* 使 – commonly translated as "emissary" or "diplomat" – in the early histories as being somewhat representative of diplomatic engagement, we can get a sense of the range of the duties of early Chinese diplomats. David Schaberg provides the following list:

> Besides their ritually scheduled visits and occasional trips for wedding preparations, funerals, and the recognition of newly acceding rulers, there were also journeys to meetings (*hui* 會), whether for covenants or for joint military action. Battlefield confrontations with enemies also brought states together and required sensitive communication through intermediaries. Prisoners taken in battle and hostages – sometimes envoys detained in the course of their missions – were yet another part of the web, as were noble brides and the retinues accompanying them to their new home.[43]

---

40 *Yili zhushu* 儀禮注疏 (Beijing: Beijing daxue chubanshe, 1999), 356–375.

41 Van Auken, "What If Zhào Dùn Had Fled? Border Crossing and Flight Into Exile in Early China", 579; *Liji*, "Zengzi wen" 曾子問: "Confucius said, 'When princes of states are about to go to the (court of the) son of Heaven, they must announce (their departure) before (the shrine of) their grandfather, and lay their offerings in that of their father. They then put on the court cap, and go forth to hold their own court. (At this) they charge [the liturgist or invocator] and the recorder to announce (their departure) to the (spirits of the) land and grain, in the ancestral temple, and at the (altars of the) [mountains] and rivers." (孔子曰: 「諸侯適天子, 必告于祖, 奠于禰, 冕而出視朝。命祝、史告於社稷、宗廟、山川. . .」 *Liji jijie* 禮記集解 (Beijing: Zhong hua shu ju, 2010b), 510–511) When state princes visit one another, they too are obliged to inform (and presumably ask permission of) the spirits, both at home before they leave, through an invocator, and while enroute, to the spirits of the hills and rivers they pass: "[T]hey charge the [liturgist or invocator] and the recorder to announce (their departure) at the five shrines in the ancestral temple, and at the altars of the hills and rivers which they will pass." (命祝、史告于五廟、所過山川。 *Liji jijie* 禮記集解, 511.) In both of the above instances, travelers are also to present sacrifices to the spirits of the roads. For the above translations, see *Li Chi: Book of Rites*, 314–315.

42 Van Auken, "What If Zhào Dùn Had Fled? Border Crossing and Flight Into Exile in Early China", 579. As she mentions, "for a description of the rites involved when a *pìn* mission crossed the border into another state, see Yí lǐ 儀禮, "Pìn lǐ" 聘禮, *SSJZS*, 19.9ab (230); trans. Steele, 193–195." Van Auken, "What If Zhào Dùn Had Fled? Border Crossing and Flight Into Exile in Early China", 579n36.

43 Schaberg, "Functionary Speech: On the Work of *Shi* 使 and *Shi* 史," 32.

Schaberg also acknowledges the connection between the religious and non-religious duties of the *shi* 使, captured in their cognate relationship to the *shi* 史 (commonly translated as "scribe"), but he phrases this connection in terms of a mastery of "specialized speech" and their exercising "some discretion in determining the appropriate speech to use on specific occasions."[44] There is a further cognate association: that of acting as intermediaries across boundaries, whether secular or sacred, with the leadership of other states, or the spiritual powers, particularly, as Schaberg notes, natural spirits, that have a hand in matters of state.[45] These transactional interfaces across boundaries, political and spiritual, were within the purview of the envoy.

The ritual status of the guest

The envoy being received, his status and treatment was that due to a "guest," *bin* 賓 or *binke* 賓客.[46] Thus the ceremonial protocols due the guest give a sense to what was ceremonially due an envoy while abroad. With the offices they undertook religiously sanctified, the diplomat himself was sacralized. As Hugo Grotius (1583–1615) states in "On the Right of Legation" relating to Roman norms, "Pomponius says: 'If any one has struck the ambassador of an enemy, it is thought that a crime has been committed against the law of nations, because ambassadors are considered sacred.' Tacitus calls this right which we are treating 'the right of enemies and sanctity of embassy and divine law of nations.'"[47] Like the spirit medium, who interceded on behalf of others with the spiritual powers, or military generals paying tribute at the altar before starting battle,[48] the diplomat's secular office was to pay tribute and intercede on behalf of others with earthly powers. The attention directed to the conduct between host and guest in the *Liji* suggests their relationship is almost as significant as the mourning rites, or any number of other basic social relationships, such as between father and son, or husband and wife. In the twilight of one's life, release from duties to

---

44 Schaberg, "Functionary Speech: On the Work of *Shi* 使 and *Shi* 史," 39.

45 Schaberg, "Functionary Speech: On the Work of *Shi* 使 and *Shi* 史," 27–28, 30.

46 This equation is sometimes explicitly rendered, as in this passage from the *Shiji*: 諸侯賓客 使者相望於道. *SJ* 85.2513.

47 G. R. Berridge, ed. *Diplomatic Classics: Selected Texts From Commynes to Vattel* (New York: Palgrave Macmillan, 2004), 107.

48 Tamara Chin draws this analogy between the general and the diplomat. Tamara Chin, *Savage Exchange: Han Imperialism, Chinese Literary Style, and the Economic Imagination* (Cambridge, Massachusetts: Harvard University Asia Center, 2014), 173.

guests comes late, at seventy, with only mourning responsibilities left to endure, according to the "Royal Regulations" (*Wangzhi* 王制). All other duties requiring any physical exertion had by then been abrogated.

For the *Liji*, embedded within the duties between hosts and guests were the norms of *yi* 義, often translated thickly as "righteousness," but which more conservatively could be simply and broadly translated as "social propriety," the moral attitude that shapes proper social interaction, especially in formal contexts. Duties between foreign guests of noble peerage and their hosts were articulated in the "Pin yi" 聘義 chapter, this chapter title mostly explicitly rendered as "social propriety with regard to visiting dignitaries of noble peerage." But non-peerage foreign visitors were also treated as "guests," as numerous texts, such as the *Bamboo Annals* (*Zhushu jinian* 竹書紀年) reveal. In the *Bamboo Annals*, many foreign tribes "come to court as guests," *lai bin* 來賓.

We may find further insight into the character of "guests" by the territories prescribed to them. The duties prescribed for those whose territory, and thus political association, is described as being in the "guest realm" *binfu* 賓服, are distinct from those in more associationally distant realms, such as the *yaofu* 要服 or the *huangfu* 荒服. The *binfu* is the second distant from the central monarchial *dianfu* 甸服, following after the *houfu* 侯服, the realm of the aristocrats or lords. The *binfu* is substituted in two early texts, the *Shangshu*'s "Levies of Yu" (*Yugong* 禹貢) and the *Shiji*'s "Annals of the Xia" (*Xia benji* 夏本紀), replaced by the *suifu* 綏服, the "Security" or "Pacification" Realm. In the *Xunzi*, the *Guoyu* 國語, and the *Shiji*'s "Annals of the Zhou" (*Zhou benji* 周本紀), the *binfu* is the third realm from the center. Each of these realms is denoted by their relation to the central court, in what manner their "submission" (*fu* 服) can be characterized.

"Guests" are those who are submissive, are associationally considered somewhat reliable but who are at the liminal edge of the perimeters of loyalty. As the *Shangshu* states about its Security/Pacification Realm, its denizens were enjoined to cultivate the "virtues" (*de* 德) or prepare military defenses[49] – two activities meant to protect against internal disloyalty and external incursions. Beyond the "guest" realm lies the realms regularly associated with non-Chinese tribes whose loyalties were unreliable, suspect. According to the *Xunzi*, the

---

49 五百里綏服: 三百里揆文教, 二百里奮武衛。 (Xueqin 李學勤 Li, ed. *Shangshu Zhengyi* 尚書正義 (Beijing: Beijing daxue chubanshe, 1999), "Yu gong" 禹貢, 168–169) Kong Yingda's (574–648 CE) commentary interprets the activities of those in this zone to be aimed at pacifying and keeping at bay those hostile elements in the adjacent "Guard" zone: 要服去京已遠, 王者以文教要束使服.

Man 蠻 and Yi 夷, southern tribespeople collectively,[50] lay in the fourth *yao* 要 realm (the "Guard" realm, not infrequently the zone of somewhat allied non-Chinese); the Rong 戎 and Di 狄, northern tribespeople, in the last, distant *huangfu* 荒服, the realm of the "wilds."[51] It was in the *huangfu* in which the Xiongnu would later be located in the *Shiji* chapter devoted to them, the "Account of the Xiongnu," *Xiongnu zhuan* 匈奴傳.

The symbolism of these realms naturally does not exclude the extension of the term "guest" to those visiting from beyond any "guest" realm. And yet the treatment of guests most certainly depended on their politico-cultural associations. Guests who were perceived to be from within accepted cultural groups were handled – or at least were *expected* to be handled – differently from those who weren't. Arguably the status distinctions across peers or apparent supporters and sympathizers in their treatment as guests remained in some manner even between those considered foes – in other words, status distinctions were more important than loyalty. Evidence for this is vividly present in the debate of 51 BCE surrounding the ritual obligations, including the awarding of gifts and bestowing of a title, to the visiting Xiongnu *shanyu*. The status of those who felt themselves internal and integral to the sovereign realm of Han was impugned, threatened by the inclusion and elevation of the *shanyu*. In the 51 BCE debate, two high-level officials, Imperial Counselor Huang Ba 黃霸 and Chancellor Yu Dingguo 于定國 contended that because of his cultural exteriority, the political standing of the *shanyu* needed to be below that of the Liu family kings, a position they justified using the above realm divisions. Arguing the adverse, Xiao Wangzhi 蕭望之 nevertheless situates his contention to place the *shanyu* in a position superior to the Liu kings in the very ritualized exteriority Huang Ba and Yu Dingguo utilized to demote him.[52]

---

50 Erica Brindley notes that the the southern Yue were employed historiographically as foils of the Chinese self, "but instead of being a lesser or odious 'other' (aka 'barbarian'), they often served in varying roles as an exaggerated reflection of the self or instantiation of human existence at the remote corners of both the world and individual psyche. Especially in contexts that do not provide a strong articulation of the notion of Hua-xia cultures and polities, the Yue other appears to be a foil used to critique or shed light on the nature of the localized self." The Yue were associated with "the extremity of common ideals." Erica Brindley, *Ancient China and the Yue* (New York: Cambridge University Press, 2015), 121–122.

51 This outermost region within this "wild" zone was that to which convicts were to be sent. One might hazard that the locating of particular tribespeople in the zones may reveal how much of an issue their associated area might be at the time of that particular text's composition.

52 *HS* 78.3282. For a discussion of this debate, see Luke Habberstad, "How and Why Do We Praise the Emperor? Debating and Depicting a Late Western Han Court Audience," *Journal of the Economic and Social History of the Orient* 60, no. 5 (2017).

According to protocol manuals such as the *Zhouli* (*The Rites of Zhou*), guests, such as envoys, were to receive strictly ritualized treatment, but they also were intimately connected with other ritual activities in the texts. In the *Liji*, for instance, the rendering of sacrifices (*jisi* 祭祀) and the receiving of guests (*binke* 賓客) are frequently paired. Powerful and potentially destablizing social relationships, such as host and guest, father and son, husband and wife, or the spiritual relationship between the living and dead, which itself mirrored social relationships, were treasured and monitored because of their potential to enhance or damage socio-political structures. The lack of due deference could signal or effect drastic changes impacting the welfare of the state. Without ritualized social interactions between host and guest, and prescriptions on the guest's speech and behavior, restrictions imposed both by the host and the official delegating the guest abroad, envoys would free themselves uninhibitedly from codes that preserved the privileges and responsibilities of group membership. Andrea Nightingale quotes an observation by C. A. Morgan about ancient Greek official trips abroad to religious festivals: "For the individual as citizen of a state, going 'beyond the bounds' was a dangerous move, since community boundaries mark the extent of the security and status conferred by group membership. Yet for the individual, it allowed the freedom to act in whatever way he might deem to be in his own interest." As Nightingale quotes further in a footnote, "the sanctuaries and institutionalized cults within [community boundaries] served (to some extent) to 'limit the actions of individuals to those acceptable to the city'."[53] Intrinsically, the guest was also an intruder, the bringer of the "monstrous" foreign unknown, dangerous outside, even when integrated into known norms.

Of course, in early China, ritual prescriptions for behavior toward guests was not limited to the Chinese, nor were the concerns about envoys' pernicious influence. According to the *Shiji*, the Xiongnu had protocols for managing the potential manipulations and conniving of arriving Chinese diplomats. They were keenly aware of the kinds of speech to expect from different types and statuses of Chinese guests – palace eunuchs versus classicists, young strivers versus seasoned elders.[54] One can presume that concerns about visiting envoys

---

53 From Andrea Wilson Nightingale, "The Philosopher at the Festival: Plato's Transformation of Traditional *Theōria*," in *Pilgrimage in Graeo-Roman and Early Christian Antiquity: Seeing the Gods*, ed. Ján Elsner, and Ian Rutherford (New York: Oxford University Press, 2005), 161, quoting Catherine A. Morgan, "The Origins of Pan-Hellenism," in *Greek Sanctuaries: New Approaches*, ed. Nanno Marinatos and Robin Hägg (London: Routledge, 1993), 31.
54 In Enno Giele's (modified) translation: "It is a Hsiung-nu habit that, when they receive a Han envoy and he is not a palace eunuch, but a Confucian scholar, they assume that he wants

and the need to keep any nefarious influence in check governed such Xiongnu protocol responses as deeply as they governed Chinese ones.

The duties to one's guests, and the guests' acknowledgement of and respect for these duties are all symbols of soft sovereign power, of the power to regulate action and attitude across the various lines of power – economic, political, and otherwise. The diplomatic jostling between sovereign entities – encapsulated in letters between the Han emperor and the *shanyu* – reveals unadulteratedly how the powers of state, and their territorial boundaries, required careful, intricate negotiation. In contrast to the negotiations of diplomat-persuaders whose allegiances to the state are ever dim and uncertain, in the negotiations between heads of state, in the persons of the state *themselves*, we can lay bare the possible transgressions of diplomatic boundaries, and thus the boundaries of state power itself. In these direct interactions, traded insults, sarcasm, borrowed marks of tradition, and purposeful omissions themselves are the actual diminution of the other's sovereignty. A potent instance of this is found in the diplomatic exchanges between Emperor Wen and the Xiongnu *shanyu*.

According to the *Records*, in 179 BCE, the first year of the reign of Emperor Wen of Han, the Xiongnu and the Han attempt to reclaim a peaceable, diplomatic relationship. Two years earlier, in 181 BCE, a Xiongnu king, the Worthy King of the Right, invaded and occupied the region south of the Yellow River, marauded and robbed non-Chinese people (*Manyi*) at the Bao Barrier 葆塞, murdering and kidnapping them. Thereupon Emperor Wen issued an edict to the Chancellor Guan Ying 灌嬰 to send out 85,000 units of chariots and cavalry to travel to the Gaonu 高奴 district and attack the Worthy King of the Right. The Worthy King of the Right fled beyond a military barrier. Because of revolts elsewhere, these attacks were broken off. The next year, the *shanyu* sent the Han emperor a letter, which is followed by a response by the emperor craftily excerpting from the *shanyu*'s missive. The underlined passages are those quoted by the Han emperor in his later reply:

> The great Xiongnu *shanyu*, established by Heaven, respectfully inquires whether the August Thearch is free from worry. In past the August Thearch spoke of the matter of peaceful negotiations (*heqin*), promoting the notions of the [agreement] document. [In this we are in] friendly accord. The Han frontier officials invaded the area of and insulted the Worthy King of the Right. The Worthy King of the Right, not requesting

---

to [persuade] and [skew] his [distinctions]; when he is a youth, they assume he wants to [make his words] sting and [skew the substance of what he is saying]." 匈奴俗, 見漢使非中貴人, 其儒先, 以為欲說, 折其辯; 其少年, 以為欲刺, 折其氣。 *SJ* 110.2913; Ssu-ma Ch'ien, "Xiongnu," in *The Grand Scribe's Records*, ed. William H. Nienhauser Jr. (Indianapolis, Indiana: Indiana University Press, 2011), 294–295.

[permission], listened to the plans of [the Xiongnu general] Yilu Hounanzhi, among others, to repulse the Han officials, abrogate the agreement of the two leaders (i.e., the Han emperor and Xiongnu shanyu), and cool the close relationship between older and younger brother. The August Thearch's chastising letters [related to this issue] repeatedly arrived, and [We] dispatched envoys to deliver letters in reply, but they did not return, nor did Han envoys come. If because of this the Han is not in harmony [with Us], other neighboring states will not support [the Han]. Now, though [Your] petty officials are the reason for our agreement being ruined, [We] have punished the Worthy King of the Right and dispatched him to the west to request [territory from] the Yuezhi and to attack them. Having Heavenly fortune, good officials and infantry, and strong horses, [the Worthy King of the Right] used [Our] barbarians to crush the Yuezhi tribes, completely cutting them down, killing or subjugating them. He subdued the Loulan, Wusun, Hujie, and their bordering twenty-six states, all of whom became Xiongnu. [Because of his success,] all of the bow-drawing common people have now joined together into one household. With the northern regions being subdued, [We] wish to allow the troops to rest, to release the officers and infantry and pasture the horses, to have done with the earlier matter [involving the King of the Right] and return to our old agreement, in order to give peace to the common people on the frontier and to accord with the [state of] earliest antiquity, to allow the young to reach their maturity and the elderly to live peacefully in their domiciles, generation upon generation tranquil and happy. Not having received the August Thearch's envisioned intentions, [We] are sending Palace Attendant Xiyu Qian to present a letter requesting [a response], offering one camel, two cavalry horses, and two outfitted chariots. If the August Thearch does not desire the Xiongnu to approach the barriers, He should immediately issue an edict commanding the officials and common people to reside more distantly [from the barriers]. After the envoy has arrived [to deliver this message], immediately dispatch him [with a reply]."

「天所立匈奴大單于敬問皇帝無恙 。前時皇帝言和親事, 稱書意, 合歡。漢邊吏侵侮右賢王,右賢王不請, 聽後義盧侯難氏等計, 與漢吏相距, 絕二主之約, 離兄弟之親。皇帝讓書再至, 發使以書報, 不來, 漢使不至, 漢以其故不和, 鄰國不附。今以小吏之敗約故, 罰右賢王, 使之西求月氏擊之。以天之福, 吏卒良, 馬彊力, 以夷滅月氏, 盡斬殺降下之。定樓蘭、烏孫、呼揭及其旁二十六國, 皆以為匈奴。諸引弓之民, 并為一家。北州已定, 願寢兵休士卒養馬, 除前事, 復故約, 以安邊民, 以應始古, 使少者得成其長, 老者安其處, 世世平樂。未得皇帝之志也, 故使郎中系雩淺奉書請, 獻橐他一匹, 騎馬二匹, 駕二駟。皇帝即不欲匈奴近塞, 則且詔吏民遠舍。使者至, 即遣之。」 [55]

The Han emperor's excerpts underscore a perception of Xiongnu self-interested disingenuousness in their confrontation with the Yuezhi. The emperor's letter also removes references to traditional Chinese religio-moral standards, whether to "Heaven" or to "ancient" precedents, to any "accord with the origins of antiquity" (應始古). Indeed, as if to stress how little Chinese religio-moral norms pertain to their interaction, no mention is made to Heaven in Emperor Wen's letter at all, an absence made all the more pregnant when placed in comparison

---

55 *SJ* 110.2896.

to the manifold references to "Heaven" in communications to Chinese peers. When the early precedents of the sage rulers are referred to, it is done so patronizingly, in approving the *shanyu*'s appreciation of their wisdom. In his summary judgment, the Han emperor caustically, sarcastically indicts the *shanyu* for any abrogation of peaceful, "brotherly" relations:

> The Han and the Xiongnu agreed to be as brothers; thus we have been very generous to the *shanyu*. Yet those who have repudiated the agreement and abandoned the close relation of brothers have frequently been among the Xiongnu. If the matter of the Worthy King of the Right occurred before the imperial amnesty, the *shanyu* should not condemn him too strongly. Were the *shanyu* to want to promote the [agreement] document's notions, he would openly instruct his many officials [to do so], directing [everyone] not to go back on the agreement, to faithfully [adhere to it], to respectfully [act] in accord with the *shanyu*'s [agreement] document. My envoy states that the *shanyu* himself led attacks against states [hostile to the Han] and was successful, and is deeply pained by military affairs [and thus would be reluctant to take them up against the Han].

> 漢與匈奴約為兄弟, 所以遺單于甚厚。倍約離兄弟之親者, 常在匈奴。然右賢王事已在赦前, 單于勿深誅。單于若稱書意, 明告諸吏, 使無負約, 有信, 敬如單于書。使者言單于自將伐國有功, 甚苦兵事。[56]

At the end of his missive, Emperor Wen lists various gifts his intermediaries are to present to the *shanyu*, in accord with the "meaning" of the station of the *zhongdafu* 中大夫, to which, in the emperor's eyes, the *shanyu* belongs. Thus the list of gifts themselves are symbolic insults, gifts for a station far below that of a formidable leader.

This exchange distorts, makes mockery of a more respectful diplomacy. Within the exchange there is little mutual feeling or understanding, the alienated distance expressed pointedly through the ease in which negotiations were abrogated, with only the pretense of ritual civility on display. Indeed, the emperor's ignoring the *shanyu*'s (possibly sarcastic) use of traditional religio-moral references in his response clearly denies the assertion of any ritual connection, whether genuine or not, by the *shanyu*. The disingenuously offered list of gifts, a common feature in ritualized negotiations, similarly signaled such a denial. The assertion or denial of ritual norms is a sign for or against the acceptance of diplomatic parity. For the Xiongnu side, when Han diplomats did not accede to Xiongnu diplomatic norms, such as tattooing his face with ink (the tattooing of the face in the Chinese realm being the mark of a criminal and thus starkly transgressive), the envoy would not be allowed to enter the Xiongnu yurts and treated

---

[56] *SJ* 110.2897.

with diplomatic parity.[57] Each side attempts, through barbed remarks and gestures, to reduce the other's claims to sovereign action and status, to treat the other as foreign, unworthy of ritual propriety. On the Chinese side, this informs the sense of the wilds, the areas of the strange and the monstrous.

The alien

Among the earliest passages about the perils of venturing into the wilds, the world beyond civilized space, is that in the *Zuozhuan* about the casting of depictions of various beings into the nine bronze tripods:

> In the past, just when Xia possessed virtue, men from afar depicted various creatures, and the nine superintendents submitted metal, so that cauldrons were cast with images of various creatures. The hundred things[58] were therewith completely set forth, and the people thus knew the spirits and the evil things. That was why when the people entered rivers, marshes, mountains, and forests, they would not meet what could harm them, and the sprites of the hills [i.e., trees and rocks][59] and waters could not get at them. Thus, they were able to harmonize with those above and below them and to receive Heaven's blessings.[60]

> 昔夏之方有德也, 遠方圖物, 貢金九牧, 鑄鼎象物, 百物而為之備, 使民知神姦, 故民入川澤山林, 不逢不若, 螭魅罔兩, 莫能逢之, 用能協于上下, 以承天休。

The attribution to the Xia fits with the common flood narratives regarding Yu's labors to distinguish the human from the animal world.[61] In these diagrammatic

---

57 *SJ* 50.2913.

58 Robert F. Campany notes that the traditional interpretation of the "many things," propounded by the likes of Du Yu 杜預 (222–284) and Wang Chong 王充 (27–100), is that they are strange. (Robert Campany, *Strange Writing: Anomaly Accounts in Early Medieval China* (Albany, New York: SUNY Press, 1996), 103n3) Certainly this accords with several references to this passage in the *Lüshi chunqiu* 呂氏春秋, such as those in the "Xianshi lan pian" 先識覽篇 and the "Shiwei pian" 適威篇. *Lüshi Chunqiu jishi* 呂氏春秋集釋 (Beijing: Zhong hua shu ju, 2011), 398, 532; *Annals of Lü Buwei*, trans. Jeffrey Riegel and John Knoblock (Stanford, California: Stanford University Press, 2000), 376, 496.

59 Harper, "A Chinese Demonography," HJAS 1985, 481. *Wangliang* is a tree and rock sprite.

60 *Zuo Tradition (Zuozhuan): Commentary on the Spring and Autumn Annals,* trans. Stephen Durrant, Wai-yee Li, and David Schaberg (Seattle, Washington: University of Washington Press, 2016a), 600–603; Yang Bojun 楊伯峻, ed. *Chunqiu Zuozhuan zhu* 春秋左傳注 (Beijing: Zhonghua shuju, 1981b), Xuan 3, 669–671.

61 Yu is explicitly named as their creator in the *Shuowen*'s entry for the character, *ding* 鼎: 昔禹收九牧之金, 鑄鼎荊山之下, 入山林川澤者, 螭魅蝄蜽, 莫能逢之, 以協承天休。(Xu Shen 許慎, *Shuowen jiezi zhu* 說文解字注 (Shanghai: Shanghai guji chubanshe, 1988), 319a.) For

definitions, Yu's labels not only distinguish but also demonize, casting the world of the spirits, of sprites and other "evil things" as perils to be avoided. Concomitantly, the bronze cauldrons themselves, as avatars of the civilized world, stand stalwartly and stolidly against the unknown multifariousness of the natural world – the world in which monsters roam untrammeled – as patriarchal, monarchial protectors of the basis of sovereign power, the common people. Robert F. Campany argues that the many strange, "evil" things are represented on the cauldrons "to neutralize their danger, allowing safe passage for 'civilizers' from the center and thus securing Heaven's favor for the people of these liminal zones."[62] From the identifying and locating of strange beings we can see where boundaries are uncertain: "the presence of monsters not only marks boundaries, but also indicates where lines or demarcation are problematic, with weird hybrid bodies the signs of a breech or a crossing, or of some other uncommon connection between worlds."[63]

Clearly, as evident in the designs of Shang and Zhou bronzes, which often include depictions of natural and "strange" beings, there is a connection to and concern with the natural world, a connection that perhaps suggests a concern with managing or controling its powers. However, nowhere in early Chinese texts mentioning the nine bronze tripods is there any insinuation that the common people are wanting or needing broad, apotropaic protection from central powers in defense against the natural world, that they are frightened of or imperiled by it, and covetous of their leaders' protection. Just as likely, the dangers are fabricated, or the fictions reinforced, to dissuade commoners from straying too far from the civilized, settled areas, and their economic duties to these areas. This connection between natural forces and the strange is also demonstrated in sacrifices and portents. In the *Liji* essay, "The Method of Sacrifices," natural places – mountains, forests, streams, valleys, hills, and mounds – at which one might perform sacrifices, would manifest their powers in the production of climatic events, such as clouds, wind and rain, but also in the appearance of "strange things," *guaiwu* 怪物. Only to those natural powers within their realms were the many lords to perform sacrifices.[64]

Lewis's observations about these labors, see Mark Edward Lewis, *The Flood Myths of Early China* (Albany, New York: SUNY Press, 2006), 71.

62 Campany, *Strange Writing: Anomaly Accounts in Early Medieval China*, 104.

63 Karin Myhre, "Monsters Lift the Veil: Chinese Animal Hybrids and Processes of Transformation," in *The Ashgate Research Companion to Monsters and the Monstrous*, ed. Asa Simon Mittman and Peter Dendle (Burlington, Vermont: Ashgate, 2012), 222.

64 *Liji jijie* 禮記集解 (Beijing: Zhong hua shu ju, 2010c), 1194–1196.

The *Zuozhuan* passage I just cited spatializes the notion of *de*, identifying it with the area of sanctioned sovereign control. By passing beyond the frontiers, into the wilds, the traveller, or exile, was penetrating into the fearsome unknown, into the "disordered" (*luan* 亂) "wilds" (*ye* 野). The wilds are where the monarch attempts to broaden his influence, through sacrifices and enforced cultural integration.[65] Those areas that are defined as wild are those that to some extent remain imperfectly attached or integrated. The farther away from the "central" regions, the more unpredictable, uncertain, and unstable. This sentiment is captured most picturesquely and frighteningly in those texts portraying mysterious, monstrous phenomena, including spiritual phenomena. Until the spirits themselves were included ritually by official processes into the central order, they remained dangerous and malevolent toward that order.

The most conspicuous example texts of monstrosities would be those detailing the strange and unnatural, whether the *Shanhaijing* 山海經 or chapters from a large number of other books, such as the *Lunheng* 論衡, *Fengsu tongyi* 風俗通義, or *Baopuzi* 抱朴子, among others.[66] But there also exist any number of passages from a host of texts – historical, philosophical and literary – that speak of animalia in terms that suggest the references are actually, or associationally, to "bestial" human cultures, the most widely referenced being the analogizing of Qin with predatory animals.[67] Conversion into or being affected by "bestial," uncivilized peoples was to be converted into the unrecognizable, the monstrous, the fearsome. Such was the risk for the envoys and other representatives of the state, military or not, who passed over into the "beyond," the distant wilds, just as would possession or being affected by unknown or unintegrated

---

65 For a recent analysis of the integration of southern non-Chinese peoples in the early Han dynasty, see Alexis Lycas, "Représenter l'espace dans les textes du haut moyen âge chinois: Géographie politique, humaine et culturelle de la région du Jingzhou," diss., École Pratique des Hautes Études, 2015).

66 For a sampling list of texts on anomalous occurrences, see Campany, *Strange Writing: Anomaly Accounts in Early Medieval China*, 32–99.

67 Karin Myhre observes this associational phenomenon in her discussion of the generations of commentaries attempting to identify the referent of *yu* 蜮: "The identification of the word *yu* as a place, a people, a creature, *and* a food recalls images of the shifting and illusionistic *taotie* as well as presaging critical thinking about 'others': those beings definitively distinct which simultaneously express most perfectly the essential nature or values of the group from which they are circumscribed." Myhre, "Monsters Lift the Veil: Chinese Animal Hybrids and Processes of Transformation", 223. Similar associational identification were made between humans and animals in Warring States and Han writings, "according to natural criteria such as geography, climate, and biotype." Roel Sterckx, *The Animal and the Daemon in Early China* (Albany, New York: SUNY Press, 2002), 93.

spirits. Being possessed or simply affected by the beyond, as both spirit mediums and earthly diplomats were, was to become, in a sense, strange and monstrous. Possession by external powers was not just a loss of the representative but was the possibility of bringing the infection of chaos, both literally and figuratively, into the state.

Across cultures, the wild power of nature, of feral creation, and the monstrous are intimately intertwined. The roots of misogyny, particularly of the male fear of female fecundity and thus her sexual attractions, pass through much of world literature. As with other wildnesses – disease, foreign cultures – the female symbolizes a savagery that can contaminate and destroy the order prepared and cultivated by patriarchies. According to C. R. Whittaker, in relation to ancient Greece and Rome, "The boundary was a magico-religious line between the sacred and the profane, between the outside and the inside, and it was often signalled by sexual landmarks, such as the phallus, Hermes or Priapus. Such symbols possessed power to mediate the act of crossing the threshold, but also to penetrate or pierce the feminized, often dangerous unknown."[68] Many Greek monstrosities – harpies, gorgons, medusas – are either described as female or have aspects that are symbolically associated with female physicality. For instance, according to D. Felton, in early Mediterranean societies, serpents are associated with chthonic forces, Greek harpies ooze fluids in ways that suggest menstruation, and medusas have serpentine hair and lower bodies, and freeze their male combatants by their (gendered) gaze.[69] But it is also the case that Greek monsters are often representing or are located in wild areas, not infrequently near mountains and rivers.[70] Similarly, in early China, as Mark Lewis points out, mountains were the "homes and the topographic equivalents for the hybrid creatures who blended elements of the human and the unearthly, and who moved as omens and messengers between the world of spirits and that of men."[71] It is no coincidence that the taming of waters and appropriation of the products and

---

68 Whittaker, *Rome and Its Frontiers: The Dynamics of Empire*, 127.

69 In a footnote, C. R. Whittaker refers to A. McClintock's list of how many gendered boundary phenomena there are: sirens, mermaids, female ship figure-heads, et cetera. See Whittaker, *Rome and Its Frontiers: The Dynamics of Empire*, 140n50. McClintock states: " . . . the feminizing of terra incognita was, from the outset, a strategy of violent containment." McClintock, *Imperial Leather: Race, Gender and Sexuality in the Colonial Contest*, 24.

70 D. Felton, "Rejecting and Embracing the Monstrous in Ancient Greece and Rome," in *The Ashgate Research Companion to Monsters and the Monstrous*, ed. Asa Simon Mittman and Peter Dendle (Burlington, Vermont: Ashgate, 2012), 105.

71 Mark E. Lewis, "The *Feng* and *Shan* Sacrifices of Emperor Wu of Han," in *State and Court Ritual in China*, ed. Joseph P. McDermott (New York: Cambridge University Press, 1999), 56.

spiritual powers of mountains is a repeated theme in the civilizing of the world by sages, whether Moses, Jesus of Nazareth (whose walking on water and pacifying winds and waters demonstrates his control over these natural powers), or the Chinese sage-king Yu 禹.

The conquering or subjection of wild forces, in pre-history or history, in nature, female forces, or "bestial" peoples, is represented as a triumph of civilization. Indeed, as Mark Lewis observes, the very founders of civilization "appear as progenitors of the most distant peoples . . . and as actors at the remote periphery."[72] One of the four reasons Lewis cites for the sages' appearance as such is their aim to separate humans from animals. In primordial time, humans lived in common with animals, physically and morally intertwined. The Chinese sages "created the tools and introduced the moral and ritual practices that rescued people from their animal condition and created distinctions where none had existed before."[73] Non-Chinese peoples, from the enforced central perspective, can be defined by their closer association with animality, with the wearing of animal skins, furs, and feathers, with their animal morals and practices, and their animistic religions.

To reiterate, occasionally when early texts speak of animals, it is not certain whether they are literally speaking about non-human animals, or more figuratively about those peoples who are perceived as being animalistic or bestial.[74] In the three instances in which the term, *qinshou* 禽獸, appears in the *Zuozhuan*, it is employed analogously, for the "bestial" non-Chinese people who are not sufficiently civilized. In the first instance, in the chapter for Duke Xiang's 襄公 third year, the Rong are simply defined as "animals," or, more precisely,

---

72 Lewis, *The Flood Myths of Early China*, 70.

73 Lewis, *The Flood Myths of Early China*, 71.

74 Indeed, Mark Lewis mentions, "As noted in Roel Sterckx's discussion of the early Chinese discourse on animals, local custom and animal character formed a single complex tied to their places of origin. The extreme form of this discourse was accounts of barbarians in distant lands who took on the attributes of the animals with whom they lived." Lewis, *Construction of Space in Early China*, 235. Sterckx writes, "Numerous sources portray barbarians who shared the habitats of the exotic bestiaries in the periphery of the Chinese cultural epicenter as having the inner disposition of animals. The bodily function and behavioral features of foreign tribes and exogenous peoples were said to have undesirable animal associations. Their temperaments and desires were equated with those of animals." Sterckx, *The Animal and the Daemon in Early China*, 159. Additional support for the identification of the barbarian Other with animals can be found in Roderick Campbell's *Violence, Kinship, and the Early Chinese State*, when he argues that the word *qiang* 羌 in Shang sacrificial inscriptions instantiates "a process of 'pseudo speciation' rendering captives available for ancestral consumption along with cattle, sheep, pigs and dogs." See Roderick Campbell, *Violence, Kinship and the Early Chinese State* (New York: Cambridge University Press, 2018), 206–210.

animals of feather and fur (*Rong qinshou ye* 戎禽獸也). The second and third, in the entries for Duke Xiang's twenty-first and twenty-eighth year, insults various people by comparing them to animals, the speakers declaring that they would eat them and sleep on their skins.[75] One might argue this is only analogy, but in other texts, the analogy seems to suggest that there are peoples who are in the same class as animals, so far removed from what is civilized that they can be categorized simply as animals of "feather and fur." Indeed, the defining feature of most animals in texts such as the *Mencius* and the *Xunzi* is their lack of civilizing, ritual habits.

If this is broadly the case, then the distinction is not only of species but of civilized versus non-civilized, of those close, integrated, settled peoples who are under the influence of Chinese ritual culture and those distant, non-Chinese peoples who are not. This distinction is the definitional constant both in classicist, "Confucian" literature and in Daoist literature. To have a heart of a beast is just identifiable with not having the requisite ritual and social habits to be considered fully "human." But beasts can be redeemed and educated, as Roel Sterckx explains.[76] Are we to believe that this education was meant literally, or simply, for animals, or also, and more especially, for those who are analogous with animals, those who are not sufficiently enculturated? I would suggest that the insufficiently civilized peoples are perhaps the truer referent of these attempts at enculturation, and thus of the "civilizing," normalizing aspirations of the Chinese court, pursued through their diplomatic representatives.

Conclusion

The above observations and analyses highlight the dangers to the sovereignty of the state of the adventures of the diplomat beyond the bounds of the state, bounds whose ritual force is symbolic of devotion to its cultural norms and political structures. In his very occupation, the diplomat is in the exceptional position to ignore and even undermine such norms and structures, whether through nefarious revelation and rhetorical reframing, or simply inept representation. The more stark the ritual divide, the more unable the parties to see each other as peers, the more "monstrous" the opposing side can appear to be, and the more perilous to one's state of contact. The "Chinese," however defined, were not alone in their

---

75 Xiang 21: 「臣為隸新，然二子者，譬於禽獸，臣食其肉而寢處其皮矣。」 Xiang 28: 盧蒲嫳曰：「譬之如禽獸，吾寢處之矣。」 Yang Bojun 楊伯峻, ed. *Chunqiu Zuozhuan zhu* 春秋左傳注 (Beijing: Zhonghua shuju, 1981c), 1063–1064, 1146.
76 Sterckx, *The Animal and the Daemon in Early China*, 137–147.

diplomatic and sovereign vulnerabilities; their non-Chinese counterparts felt them as well.

It is in the diplomat's transgressive negotiations that one can view the liminal aspect of state sovereignty and the dangers in the very contact with the foreign. Thus through analysis of diplomatic exchanges, we can perceive yet another definitional and also very much spatialized aspect of the parameters of political sovereignty, an aspect that can affect immediately the maintenance of past and establishment of additional areas of sovereignty. These diplomatic exchanges are not just with terrestrial others but with spiritual powers. Diplomacy's transgressive aspect inheres an uncertain effect, the uncertainty of a multiplicity of outcomes. It is a discourse that involves intimately not only possible future action but ritualized systems of knowledge and their negotiations, producing movements of territorialization and de-territorialization, with realities being not "a matter of the absolute eyewitness, but a matter of the future."[77]

Bibliography

Allen, Danielle. *The World of Prometheus: The Politics of Punishing in Democratic Athens*. Princeton, New Jersey: Princeton University Press, 2000.
Annals of Lü Buwei. Translated by Jeffrey Riegel, and John Knoblock. Stanford, California: Stanford University Press, 2000.
Berridge, G. R., ed. *Diplomatic Classics: Selected Texts from Commynes to Vattel*. New York: Palgrave Macmillan, 2004.
Brindley, Erica. *Ancient China and the Yue*. New York: Cambridge University Press, 2015.
Campany, Robert. *Strange Writing: Anomaly Accounts in Early Medieval China*. Albany, New York: SUNY Press, 1996.
Ch'ien, Ssu-ma. "Xiongnu," In *The Grand Scribe's Records*, edited by William H. Nienhauser Jr., 237–303. Indianapolis, Indiana: Indiana University Press, 2011.
Chin, Tamara. *Savage Exchange: Han Imperialism, Chinese Literary Style, and the Economic Imagination*. Cambridge, Massachusetts: Harvard University Asia Center, 2014.
Chuang-Tzŭ: The Inner Chapters. Translated by A. C. Graham. Indianapolis, Indiana: Hackett Publishing Company, 2001.
Felton, D. "Rejecting and Embracing the Monstrous in Ancient Greece and Rome." In *The Ashgate Research Companion to Monsters and the Monstrous*, edited by Asa Simon Mittman and Peter Dendle, 103–31. Burlington, Vermont: Ashgate, 2012.
Galvany, Albert. "Signs, Clues, and Traces: Anticipation in Ancient Chinese Political and Military Texts." *Early China* (2015): 1–43.
Guanzi Jiaozhu 管子校注. Beijing: Zhong hua shu ju, 2004b.

---

77 Jean-François Lyotard, *The Differend: Phrases in Dispute*, 53.

Habberstad, Luke. "How and Why Do We Praise the Emperor? Debating and Depicting a Late Western Han Court Audience." *Journal of the Economic and Social History of the Orient* 60, no. 5 (2017): 683–714.

Hamilton, Keith, and Richard Langhorne. *The Practice of Diplomacy: Its Evolution, Theory and Administration*. New York: Routledge, 1995.

Han Ying 韓嬰. *Hanshi Waizhuan Jishi* 韓詩外傳集釋. Beijing: Zhong hua shu ju, 2009.

Kern, Martin. "Language and the Ideology of Kingship in the 'Canon of Yao'." In *Ideology of Power and Power of Ideology in Early China*, edited by Yuri Pines, Paul R. Goldin, and Martin Kern, 118–50. Leiden: Brill, 2015.

Kosmin, Paul J. *The Land of the Elephant Kings: Space, Territory, and Ideology in the Seleucid Empire*. Cambridge, Massachusetts: Harvard University Press, 2014.

Lewis, Mark E. *The Construction of Space in Early China*. Albany, New York: SUNY Press, 2006.

Lewis, Mark E. "The *Feng* and *Shan* Sacrifices of Emperor Wu of Han." In *State and Court Ritual in China*, edited by Joseph P. McDermott, 50–80. New York: Cambridge University Press, 1999.

Lewis, Mark Edward. *The Flood Myths of Early China*. Albany, New York: SUNY Press, 2006.

Li Chi: Book of Rites. Translated by James Legge. New York: Oxford University Press, 1885.

Liji jijie 禮記集解. Beijing: Zhonghua shuju, 2010a.

Liji jijie 禮記集解. Beijing: Zhonghua shuju, 2010b.

Liji jijie 禮記集解. Beijing: Zhonghua shuju, 2010c.

Li, Xueqin 李學勤, ed. *Shangshu zhengyi* 尚書正義 Beijing: Beijing daxue chubanshe, 1999.

Lüshi Chunqiu jishi 呂氏春秋集釋. Beijing: Zhong hua shu ju, 2011.

Lycas, Alexis. "Réprésenter l'espace dans les textes du haut moyen âge chinois: Géographie politique, humaine et culturelle de la région du Jingzhou," diss., École Pratique des Hautes Études, 2015.

Lyotard, Jean-François. *The Differend: Phrases in Dispute*. Minneapolis: University of Minnesota Press, 1988.

McClintock, Anne. *Imperial Leather: Race, Gender and Sexuality in the Colonial Contest*. New York: Routledge, 1995.

Morgan, Catherine A. "The Origins of Pan-Hellenism," In *Greek Sanctuaries: New Approaches*, edited by Nanno Marinatos, and Robin Hägg, 18–44. London: Routledge, 1993.

Myhre, Karin. "Monsters Lift the Veil: Chinese Animal Hybrids and Processes of Transformation." In *The Ashgate Research Companion to Monsters and the Monstrous*, edited by Asa Simon Mittman and Peter Dendle, 217–36. Burlington, Vermont: Ashgate, 2012.

Nightingale, Andrea Wilson. "The Philosopher At the Festival: Plato's Transformation of Traditional *Theōria*." In *Pilgrimage in Graeo-Roman and Early Christian Antiquity: Seeing the Gods*, edited by Ján Elsner, and Ian Rutherford, 151–80. New York: Oxford University Press, 2005.

Oba, Osamu. "The Ordinance on Fords and Passes Excavated From Han Tomb #247, Zhangjiashan." *Asia Major* 14, no. 2 (2001): 119–41.

Olberding, Garret. *Dubious Facts: The Evidence of Early Chinese Historiography*. Albany, New York: SUNY Press, 2012.

Pines, Yuri. "The Question of Interpretation: Qin History in Light of New Epigraphic Sources." *Early China* 29 (2004): 1–44.

Puett, Michael J. *To Become a God: Cosmology, Sacrifice, and Self-Divinization in Early China*. Cambridge, Massachusetts: Harvard Asia Center Publications, 2002.

Schaberg, David. "Playing At Critique: Indirect Remonstrance and the Formation of Shi Identity." In *Text and Ritual in Early China*, edited by Martin Kern, 194–225. Seattle, Washington: University of Washington Press, 2005.

Schaberg, David. "Functionary Speech: On the Work of Shi 使 and Shi 史." In *Facing the Monarch: Modes of Advice in the Early Chinese Court*, edited by Garret Olberding, 19–41. Cambridge, Massachusetts: Harvard Asia Center Publications, 2013.

Sima Qian. *Records of the Grand Historian: Qin Dynasty*. Translated by Burton Watson. New York: Columbia University Press, 1993.

Söderström, Ola. "Paper Cities: Visual Thinking in Urban Planning." *Ecumene* 3, no. 3 (1996): 249–81.

Sterckx, Roel. *The Animal and the Daemon in Early China*. Albany, New York: SUNY Press, 2002.

Van Auken, Newell Ann. "What If Zhào Dùn Had Fled? Border Crossing and Flight into Exile in Early China." *Journal of the American Oriental Society* 139, no. 3 (2019): 569–90.

von Clausewitz, Carl. *On War*. New York: Penguin Books, 1982.

Wang, Haicheng. *Writing and the Ancient State: Early China in Comparative Perspective*. New York: Cambridge University Press, 2014.

Wang Xianqian 王先謙, ed. *Xunzi jijie* 荀子集解. Beijing: Zhonghua shuju, 1997a.

Whittaker, C. R. *Rome and Its Frontiers: The Dynamics of Empire*. New York: Routledge, 2004.

Xu Shen 許慎. *Shuowen jiezi zhu* 說文解字注. Shanghai: Shanghai guji chubanshe, 1988.

Xunzi: The Complete Text. Translated by Eric L. Hutton. Princeton, New Jersey: Princeton University Press, 2014.

Yang Bojun 楊伯峻, ed. *Chunqiu Zuozhuan zhu* 春秋左傳注. Beijing: Zhonghua shuju, 1981b.

Yang Bojun 楊伯峻, ed. *Chunqiu Zuozhuan zhu* 春秋左傳注. Beijing: Zhonghua shuju, 1981c.

Yang Bojun 楊伯峻, ed. *Chunqiu Zuozhuan zhu* 春秋左傳注. Beijing: Zhonghua shuju, 1981d.

Yang, Jidong. "Transportation, Boarding, Lodging and Trade Along the Early Silk Road: A Preliminary Study of the Xuanquan Manuscripts." *Journal of the American Oriental Society* 135, no. 3 (2015): 421–32.

Yili Zhushu 儀禮注疏. Beijing: Beijing daxue chubanshe, 1999.

Zhuangzi zhushu 庄子注疏. Beijing: Zhonghua shuju, 2011.

Zuo Tradition (Zuozhuan): Commentary on the Spring and Autumn Annals. Translated by Stephen Durrant, Wai-yee Li, and David Schaberg. Seattle, Washington: University of Washington Press, 2016a.

Zuo Tradition (Zuozhuan): Commentary on the Spring and Autumn Annals. Translated by Stephen Durrant, Wai-yee Li, and David Schaberg. Seattle, Washington: University of Washington Press, 2016b.

Index

Note: Page numbers in italics indicate illustrations.

Academy of Scholarly Worthies (Jixiandian shuyuan) 集賢殿書院 33, 39–40, 49
achilleomancy 174
Allen, Danielle 195n24
Anavatapta Lake 阿那婆答多池 128
Anping tomb mural *104*, 106–107, 110–120
Antikythera mechanism 164
Aquinas, Thomas 15
armillary equatorial ring *153*
astronomical clocks 164
astronomy 149, 155–158
axonometric perspective 103, 114–120, *119*

Bachhofer, Ludwig 12
Bai Juyi 白居易 (772–846 CE) 11, 15–16, 136, 140
Ban Gu 班固 (32–92 CE) 82–83, 126n9, 140n48
Ban Zhao 班昭 (44/49–118/121 CE) 179
Barnhart, Richard 18
bees *154*, 154–155
Bian Xin 編訢 159–160
Biot, Édouard 158
Biot, Jean-Baptiste 156–158, 178
Bodde, Derk 150
Bohr, Niels 103n1
Bol, Peter 11
Born, Max 103n1
Brindley, Erica 202n50
Bryson, Norman 12
Buddhism 136, 155
– Chan 63
– founders of 132
– geography of 127–129
Bulling, Anneliese 116

"calendar science," 149. *See also li*
calligraphers 29–33, 38
Campany, Robert F. 207n58, 208
Canon of Yao 堯典 195–196
Canterbury Cathedral 12
cartography 103–107, 118, 192

– landscapes and 105–106, 109–110
– townscapes and *104*, 106–107, 110–113, 116–120, *119*
Cen Zhongmian 岑仲勉 130n20
Chavannes, Édouard 56n2
Cheeseman, James F. *154*, 154–155
Chemla Karine 172, 174
Chen Qiaoyi 陳橋驛 56n2
Chen Yixing 陳夷行 (d. 843 CE) 49
Cheng Xiuji 程修己 (804–863 CE) 30, 46–51, *48*
Chin, Tamara 200n48
"Chinese perspective." *See* axonometric perspective
chorography 105–106, 119–120
Chuci 楚辭 (*Chu Lyrics*) 77–98
– poetics of displacement in 85–90
– politics of space and 91–98
Chuci zhangju 楚辭章句 (*Chapter and Verse Commentary to the Lyrics of Chu*) 78–83
Chuxue ji 初學記 (*Fundamentals of Learning*) 129–131, 133, 137–140
ci-honors 36, 41, 49
Città Dipinta fresco 118–120, *119*
Clausewitz, Carl von 189
"cognitive maps," 107
Confucius 190n4, 199n41
Constellation Lake 星宿海 124, *142*
Coswell, James 115–116
Cullen, Christopher 159n25

Da Tang xiyu ji 大唐西域記 (*Record of the Western Regions*) 128–129
diplomats 189–207, 212–213
– messages to 193n15
– misdeeds of 191–192
– rituals of 190–192
– *Shiji* on 203–204
– travel obligations of 196–200
– *Xunzi* on 193–194
Dong You 董卣 (1031–1095 CE) 19

Dong Yuan 董源 (934–962 CE) 25–26, *25, 26*
Dorofeeva-Lictmann, Vera 126, 144
Du Fu 杜甫 (712–770 CE) 16–17, 19, 23,
   25, 26
Du You 杜佑 (735–812 CE) 138
Du Yu 杜預 (222–285 CE) 179, 207n58
Du Zeng 杜曾 (d. 319 CE) 73
Duan Chengshi 段成式 (ca. 803–863 CE)
   125, 127

emic/etic perspectives 105, 107, 120
Ennin (Buddhist pilgrim) 136
Epoch Cycle 163, *164*
Euclidian optics 115
eunuchs 37–38, 203
exchange rates *168*, 168–169
exegesis 57

Fangmatan tomb 放馬灘 110
Fanyangcheng townscape 116
Farish, William 117–118
Faxian 法顯 (ca. 340–421 CE) 128
Feng, Linda Rui 123–145
fengshui *153*
Fenton, D. 210
Five Sacred Peaks (*wu yue*) 五嶽 60–62
flood narratives 207–208
Foguo ji 佛國記 (Records of the Buddhist
   Kingdoms by Faxian) 128
Foong Ping 29–52
Foucault, Michel 104, 108, 120
Fozu tongji 佛祖統紀 (General Records of the
   Founders of Buddhism) 132, *134*

Ganges River 128
Geographic Information System (GIS) 120
geometry 117–118
Gou Yanguang 苟延光 64
Graham, Elspeth 107
Granet, Marcel 149, 178–179
Grotius, Hugo 200
Gu Kaizhi 顧愷之 (344–406 CE) 17–18
guaiwu 怪物 (strange things) 208
Guan Ying 灌嬰 (d. 176 BCE) 70, 204
Guangwudi 光武帝, Han Emperor
   (r. 25–57 CE) 68
"guest" rituals (*bin* 賓) 190–191, 200–207

Han Andi 漢安帝 (r. 94–125 CE) 79
Han Wudi 漢武帝 (r. 141–87 BCE) 82
Han Yu 韓愈 (768–824 CE) 15
Hanlin Academy (Hanlinyuan) 翰林院 31–32,
   34–35, 38–39
Hanlin *daizhao* 翰林待詔 (Expectant
   Official of the Hanlin) 31–32, 34,
   49, 165
– as inner court title 37
– during Tang dynasty 36, 45
– titles of 40–44, *42*
Hanlin Institute of Academicians (Hanlin
   xueshiyuan) 翰林學士院 37
Hanlin Painting Academy 38–39
Hanshi waizhuan 韓詩外傳 193
Hanshu 漢書 (History of the Han) 126,
   140n48, 158
Harley, J. B. 108
Harrist, Robert 18
Hawkes, David 90
Heisenberg, Werner 103–104, 107
Helinge'er tomb 116
Homer 58
Hsu-Tang, H. M. Agnes 103–120
Hu Fen 胡奮 (d. 288 CE) 73
Huan Xuan 桓玄 (369–404 CE) 65–66
Huang Ba 黃霸 202
Huang Jubao 黃居寶 32
Huang Jucai 黃居寀 (933–ca. 993 CE) 32,
   41–43, 51
Huang Quan 黃筌 (903?–965 CE) 31–32,
   41–44, 51
Huang Tingjian 黃庭堅 (1045–1105 CE) 17
Huang Xiufu 黃休復 (b. ca. 954–959 CE)
   40–44
Huanghe 黃河. *See* Yellow River
Huayang guo zhi 華陽國志
   (Monograph of the regions south
   of Mt. Hua) 57
huazhi 畫直 (illustrators on painting duty)
   33, 49
Huhehaotetatu excavations 114

Ianniciello, Celeste 103
"imageability," 106, 107
Indus River 128
Islam 155–156

Jacob, Christian 105, 111
Jesus of Nazareth 190n5, 211
Jia Dan 賈耽 (730–805 CE) 139
Jia Gongyan 賈公彥 (fl. 637 CE) 179
Jia Kui 賈逵 (30–101 CE) 180
Jing Cuo 景瑳 80
Jing Hao 荊浩 (c. 855–915 CE) 18
Jing Ke 荊軻 108–109, 192
jinwu 金吾 (supernatural bird) 69n60
Jixiandian 集賢殿 (Institute of the
    Assembled Wise) 37

Kalinowski, Marc 149n1
Kern, Martin 195–196
khoros (place) 105–106
Knapp, Ronald 112
Kong Yingda 孔穎達 (574–648 CE)
    179, 201n49
Korea 132
Korzybski, Alfred 106–107
Kosmin, Paul J. 197n31
Kuo di zhi (Comprehensive Treatise of the
    Land) 括地志 127–128

Lambert, Johann Heinrich 117
landscape maps 105–106, 109–110
landscape poetry (shanshui shi) 山水詩 85
la Rocca, Eugenio 119–120
Latour, Bruno 192
Leung, Vincent S. 77–98, 151
Lewis, Mark 210, 211
Li Ang 14–15
Li Bai 李白 (701–762 CE) 130
Li Chunfeng 李淳風 (602–70 CE) 170–171,
    174, 177, 180
Li Daoyuan 酈道元 (d. 527 CE) 55–74,
    130–131
Li Fan 李梵 159–160
Li Gonglin 李公麟 (1049–1106 CE) 18–20
Li Tai 李泰 (618–652 CE) 127–128
Li Wencai 李文才 (10th century) 41–43, 51
Li Yanshou 李延壽 (618–676 CE) 55n1
li 曆 150, 155–166, 170–173
Liji (Record of Rites) 禮記 193n15, 195–196,
    199–201, 203
– on sacrifices 208
linear perspective 115. See also perspective

Liu An 劉安 (179–122 BCE) 125
Liu Bei 劉備 (161–223 CE) 70
Liu Biao 劉表 (142–208 CE) 73
Liu Hong 劉洪 (fl. 167–206 CE) 180–181
Liu Hui 劉徽 (fl. 3rd century CE) 171–174
Liu Qi 劉琦 (d. 209 CE) 73
Liu Qin 劉秦 (fl. 8th century) 34–36, 39,
    40, 51
Liu Xiang 劉向 (79–8 BCE) 82
Liu Xin 劉歆 (46 BCE–23 CE) 82, 179–180
Liu Yi 劉毅 (d. 412 CE) 65–66
Liu Yuanding 劉元鼎 142–143, 144
Liu Zongyuan 柳宗元 (773–819 CE) 15, 17
Lop Nor Lake. See Puchang Lake
Lu Su 魯肅 (Lu Zijing 魯子敬) (172–217 CE)
    70, 70n62
Lü Yao 呂嶤 (fl. 9th century CE) 30, 44–45,
    50–51
lü 率 166–173, 167, 168, 177
luan 亂 (disorder) 191–192
Luoyang Qielan ji 洛陽伽藍記 (Record of the
    Monasteries of Luoyang) 57
Lycas, Alexis 55–74, 127
Lynch, Kevin 107

Ma Rong 馬融 (79–166 CE) 179
Maier, Charles 77
Manning, Patrick 144n57
Mao Zedong 毛澤東 13
"mathematical mandate," 183
Mawangdui 馬王堆 tomb 110, 120
McClintock, Anne 189n1
megaliths 63–65
Mencius 孟子 212
Meng Chang 孟昶 (b. 919, r. 934–65 CE) 31
Meng Zhixiang 孟知祥 (879–934, r. 934 CE)
    Emperor, 32, 43
"mental map," 107, 111, 118
meritocracy 14–16
merit titles 37–38, 43
Mi Fu 米芾 (1051–1107 CE) 25–26
milfoil divination 172, 174, 192n12
mingshi 名實 theory 15
monoliths 73
Morgan, C. A. 203
Morgan, Daniel Patrick 149–183
Mostern, Ruth 124n4

Mote, Frederick 113
Mount Guiqi 規期山 130, 131
Mount Jishi 積石山 124–125, 128–131,
    133–138
Mount Kunlun 崑崙山 124, 128, 130–131,
    136–138, 144–145
– as *axis mundi* 125, 137
– Liu Yuanding on 143
– Sima Qian on 126n9
Mount Langya 琅邪山 93
Mount Lingmen 陵門山 136
Mount Tu 塗山 67
Mount Wu 巫山 63
Mount Yangyu 陽紆山 136
Mount Zhifu 之罘山 92
Mount Zhongnan 終南山 136
Mozi 墨子 179
Murck, Alfreda 16–17, 23
Mu Tianzi zhuan 穆天子傳 (Biography of the
    Son of Heaven Mu) 137, 144
Muzong, Emperor 穆宗 (r. 820–824 CE)
    141–142
Myhre, Karin 209n67

Needham, Joseph 115
nei gongfeng 內供奉 (emperor's
    attendants) 34–35
Nestorianism 155
Nightingale, Andrea 203
Ningcheng townscape 116–117
non-Euclidian geometry 117

Olberding, Garret Pagenstecher 1–9,
    189–213

painters
– career paths of 50–51
– court titles of 29–33, 38–43, *42*
– temporary appointments of 36
perspective
– axonometric (parallel) 103, 114–120
– bird's-eye 106, 115, 117, 118
– emic/etic 105, 107, 120
– "isometrical," 117–118
– linear 115
– pictorial 117
pinax (map) 110

Pines, Yuri 198
Porter, Deborah 144
Powers, Martin J. 11–27
prestige titles 37–38
Puchang (or Lop Nor) Lake 蒲昌海 124, 130,
    131, 133, 134, 138
Puett, Michael 190–191

Qiao Daofu 譙道福 62
Qiao Zhongchang 喬仲常 (fl. early 12th
    century) 20–26, 20–27
Qu Yuan 屈原 (fl. 4th–3rd centuries BCE) 69,
    80–83, 87
quantum physics 103

Ruan Weide 阮惟德 (fl. 10th century CE)
    41–43, 51
Ruan Zhihui 阮知誨 (fl. 10th century CE)
    41–43, 51

Santong li 三統曆 163–164, *164*
Schaberg, David 192n12, 194, 199–200
Schneider, Bernard 115
shaman 192n12
Shang Gao 商高 173
Shangshu 尚書 (Book of Documents) 91, 94,
    125, 201
Shanhai jing 山海經 (Mountain and Water
    Classic) 57, 125, 130, 137
shanyu 單于 (Xiongnu leader) 196, 202–207
Shen Kuo 沈括 (1031–1099 CE) 19
shenhui 神會 (imaginative encounter) 19
Shenzong, Emperor 宋神宗
    (r. 1067–1085 CE) 24
Shiji 史記 (Records of the
    Historian) 108–109, 126, 203–204
shishu 侍書 (Attendant Calligrapher) 33
shizhe 使者 (envoy) 192n12, 194–195, 199
Shundian 舜典 (Canon of Shun) 195–196
Shui Anli 稅安禮 *142*
Shuijing 水經 (Itineraries of Waterways) 56
Shuijing zhu 水經注 (Annotated Itineraries
    of Waterways) 55–74, 126–128,
    130–131, 137
Shuijing zhu tu 水經注圖 (Maps for the
    Annotated Itineraries of Waterways) 132
shuzhi 書直 (writers on clerical duty) 33

Sifen li 四分曆 159, 160nn27–33, *167*, 169, 173–174, *175–176*,
siheyuan 四合院 (residential quadrangle) *104*, 111, 112
Sima Qian 司馬遷 (c. 145–c. 86 BCE) 108–109, 140n48, 179, 189
– on Yellow River's origin 126, 137
Sima Xiangru 司馬相如 (179–117 BCE) 94
sinecures 31
Sivin, Nathan 163–164, *164*
Skinner, William 113–114
Song Yu 宋玉 (fl. early third century BCE) 80
space-time 149–155
Stea, David 107
Stein, Rolf 56n2
Steinhardt, Nancy S. 113, 117
stelae 71–74, 93
– calligraphy of 33–34
Sterckx, Roel 211n71, 212
Su Shi 蘇軾 (1037–1101 CE) *20–26*, 20–27
sumptuary laws 32
Sun Hao 孫皓 (242–284 CE) 69–70
Sun Quan 孫權 (182–252 CE) 69, 70
"sun compass," 154

Tacitus 200
Taiping guangji 太平廣記 (Extensive Records for the Era of Supreme Peace) 139
Tang Suzong, Emperor 唐肅宗 (r. 756–62 CE) 35
Tang Xizong, Emperor 唐僖宗 (r. 873–88 CE) 41, 45, 50
Tang Xuanzong, Emperor 唐玄宗 (r. 712–56 CE) 34, 35
Tao Baolian 陶葆廉 (1862–1938 CE) 125n5
Tao Yuanming 陶淵明 (317–420 CE) 17, 19
Taoism, messianic 63
tattoos 197, 206
Thompson, Lydia 115
tianzhen 天真 (natural and authentic) 26
Tibet 141–143
titles 37–38, 41–43, *42*
Tong dian 通典 (Comprehensive Statutes) 138
topography 105, 110
Toulouse-Lautrec, Henri de 13
towers *104*, 113

townscape
– of Anping tomb *104*, 106–107, 110–113, 116–120
– of *Città Dipinta* fresco 118–120, *119*
– of Fanyangcheng 116–117
– of Ningcheng 116–117
Trajan's Bath fresco 118–120, *119*
tujing 圖經 (map-guide) 124
Tylor, E. B. 178n70

van Auken, Newell Ann 197–199

Wang Anshi 王安石 (1021–1086 CE) 24
Wang Ao 135
Wang Chong 王充 (27–100 CE) 207n58
Wang Dun 王敦 (266–324 CE) 73
Wang Fan 王蕃 (228–266 CE) 69–70
Wang Fuzhi 王夫之 (1619–1692 CE) 24
Wang Haicheng 197
Wang Mang, Emperor 王莽 (45 BCE–23 CE) 68–69
Wang Shiduo 汪士鐸 (1802–1889 CE) 132
Wang Wei 王維 (699–759 CE) 19
Wang Yan, Emperor 王衍 (r. 918–25 CE) 43
Wang Yi 王廙 (276–322 CE) 73, 78–84
Wang Zixiang 王子香 69
"wayfinding," 107
Wei Shou 魏收 (506–572 CE) 55n1
Wei River 110
Wen Fong 117
Wen of Han, Emperor 漢文帝 (r. 180–157 BCE) 204
Whittaker, C. R. 210
Wölfflin, Heinrich 12
Woodward, David 108
Wright, Frank Lloyd 107
Wu, Han Emperor 漢武帝 (r. 141–87 BCE) 68, 126
Wu Hung 115
Wu Liang shrine 115
Wu Zetian 武則天 (r. 690–705 CE) 14
wu 巫 (spirit medium) 190–191, 192n12, 200
Wuchang ji 武昌記 (Record of Wuchang) 69

Xiao Baoyin 蕭寶寅 (487–530 CE) 55n1
Xiao Wangzhi 蕭望之 202
Xiaowu, Emperor 孝武 (r. 453–464 CE) 65

Xie Lingyun 謝靈運 (385–443 CE) 85

xingxiu chuan 星宿川 (Constellation River) 124

xingxiu hai 星宿海 (Constellation Lake) 124, *142*

Xiongnu 匈奴 195n22, 196, 202–207

Xu Yinong 114

Xuanzang 玄奘 (602–664 CE) 128–129, 132, 133

Xunzi 荀子 193–194, 201–202, 212

Yan Shigu 顏師古 (581–645 CE) 182

Yan Zhitui 顏之推 (531–591 CE) 67

Yang Jidong 194–195

Yang Shoujing 56n2

Yang Xiong 楊雄 (53 BCE–18 CE) 82, 179

yanhua 巖畫 (petroglyphs) 64–65

Yellow River 109, 123–145

yi 義 (social propriety) 201

Yili 儀禮 (Book of Ceremony and Rites) 196, 198–199

Yinan tomb 115

Ying Shao 應劭 (140–206 CE) 69

yin privilege 32, 47

Yin-Yang 174–175

Yiwen leiju 藝文類聚 135–136

Youyang zazu 酉陽雜俎 (*Mixed Morsels of Youyang*) 8, 125, 138, 140

Yu the Great 禹 67, 71, 173, 207–208, 211
– Basic Annals of 禹本紀 126n9, 127–128, 140n48
– Tributes of 禹貢 91, 94, 125, 201

– Yellow River and 61–62, 136

Yu Dingguo 于定國 202

Yuan Shansong 袁山松 63–64

Yuanhe junxian tuzhi 元和郡縣圖志 (Records and Illustrations of the Prefectures and Counties of the Yuanhe Era) 131n23, 133–134

Yuan shen qi 援神契 (Documents Adducing Spirits) 129

Zhang Long 張隆 180, 182

Zhang Qian 張騫 (d. 114 BCE) 126, 140n48

Zhang Zhao 張昭 (156–236 CE) 70

Zhao Qi 趙岐 (108–201 CE) 72

Zhen Dexiu 真德秀 (1178–1235 CE) 24

Zheng Xuan 鄭玄 (127–200 CE) 179

Zheng Zhong 鄭眾 (d. 83 CE) 179

Zhou Changshan 114

Zhou Fang 周昉 (ca. 730–800 CE) 46, 47, 73

Zhoubi suanjing 周髀算經 173

Zhouli 周禮 (*Rites of Zhou*) 196

Zhu Jingxuan 朱景玄 (fl. ca. 806–840 CE) 46, 49

Zhu Maichen 朱買臣 (fl. 120–110 BCE) 82

Zhu Qian 竹虔 (fl. 9th century CE) 30, 44–45, 50–51

zhu 祝 (invocators) 190–191, 198n35

Zhuge Liang 諸葛亮 (181–234 CE) 70

Zhushu jinian (*Bamboo Annals*) 竹書紀年 201

ziran 自然 (naturalistic) 26

Zuozhuan 左傳 197–198, 207–209, 211–212

www.ingramcontent.com/pod-product-compliance
Lightning Source LLC
Chambersburg PA
CBHW020531270326
41927CB00006B/524